Renaissance Readings
of the
Corpus Aristotelicum

RENÆSSANCESTUDIER
Edited by FORUM FOR RENÆSSANCESTUDIER, University of Copenhagen
ISSN 0902 9907

1 *Litteratur og lærdom* – Dansk-svenske nylatindage 1985
Redigeret af Marianne Alenius og Peter Zeeberg.
1987. 161 p. ISBN 87 7289 0185

2 *Renæssancen – Dansk, europæisk, globalt*
Artikelsamling redigeret af Minna Skafte Jensen og Marianne Pade.
1988. 193 p., ill. ISBN 87 7289 0533

3 *Tro, håb & forfængelighed*
Af Hanne Honnens de Lichtenberg.
1991. Out of print. ISBN 87 7289

4 *La Corte di Ferrara / The Court of Ferrara 1441-1598*
Eds.: Marianne Pade, Lene Waage Petersen og Daniela Quarta.
1990. 367 p. ISBN 87 7289 0509

5 *Latin og nationalsprog i Norden efter reformationen*
Redigeret af Marianne Alenius, Birger Bergh, Ivan Boserup, Minna Skafte
Jensen og Karsten Friis-Jensen.
1991. 328 p. ISBN 87 7289 9907

6 *Om menneskets værdighed*
Af Pico della Mirandola, oversat af Jørgen Juul Nielsen.
1996. 2. printing, 88 p. ISBN 87 7289 0649

7 *Tycho Brahes Urania Titani – et digt om Sofie Brahe*
Udgivet med indledning, latinsk originaltekst, kommentar og kildesamling
af Peter Zeeberg.
1994. 327 p. ISBN 87 7289 2781

8 *Poesi og politik – Lejlighedsdigtningen ved enevældens indførelse 1660*
Af Sebastian Olden-Jørgensen. Mit deutscher Zusammenfassung.
1996. 207 p. ISBN 87 7289 3710

9 *Renaissance Readings of the Corpus Aristotelicum*
Papers from the Conference in Copenhagen 1998
Edited by Marianne Pade
2001. 261 p. ISBN 87 7289 5853

MUSEUM TUSCULANUM PRESS
UNIVERSITY OF COPENHAGEN

Renaissance Readings of the *Corpus Aristotelicum*

Proceedings of the conference held in
Copenhagen 23-25 April 1998,
edited by
Marianne Pade

MUSEUM TUSCULANUM PRESS
UNIVERSITY OF COPENHAGEN
2001

Renaissance Readings of the Corpus Aristotelicum
Edited by Marianne Pade

© Museum Tusculanum Press and the authors 2001
Cover design by Pernille Kleinert
English revision by John Blundell
Composition by Ole Klitgaard, set in Garamond
Printed in Denmark by Narayana Press
ISBN 87 7289 585 3

Renæssancestudier vol. 9
ISSN 0902-9907

Published with the support of
The Danish Research Council for the Humanities

Museum Tusculanum Press
University of Copenhagen
Njalsgade 92
DK-2300 Copenhagen S
www.mtp.dk

Contents

Preface 7

Gert Sørensen
The Reception of the Political Aristotle in the Late Middle Ages
(from Brunetto Latini to Dante Alighieri).
Hypotheses and Suggestions 9

David A. Lines
Ethics as Philology: A Developing Approach to Aristotle's
Nicomachean Ethics in Florentine Humanism 27

Marianne Marcussen
Aristotle and Perspective in the Early Italian Renaissance 43

John Monfasani
Greek and Latin Learning in Theodore Gaza's *Antirrheticon* 61

Eckhard Kessler
Metaphysics or Empirical Science? The two Faces of Aristotelian
Natural Philosophy in the Sixteenth Century 79

Heikki Mikkeli
The Aristotelian Classification of Knowledge in the Early
Sixteenth Century 103

Cesare Vasoli
Giovan Francesco Pico e i presupposti della sua critica ad Aristotele 129

Olaf Pluta
The Transformations of Alexander of Aphrodisias'
Interpretation of Aristotle's Theory of the Soul 147

CONTENTS

Peter WAGNER
Renaissance Readings of the Corpus Aristotelicum –
not Among the Herbalists 167

Kristian JENSEN
Description, Division, Definition – Cæsalpinus and the study
of plants as an independent discipline 185

Sten EBBESEN
Caspar Bartholin 207

Antonis FYRIGOS
Joannes Cottunios di Verria e il neoaristotelismo padovano 225

Bo LINDBERG
Political Aristotelianism in the Seventeenth Century 241

INDEX
of names and passages in Aristotle's works 255

Preface

This volume contains the proceedings of the conference "The New Aristotle: Renaissance readings of the *Corpus Aristotelicum*", Copenhagen 23-25 April 1998. The conference was a part of the international research network on "Renaissance: the origins of modernity" and organized by the Forum for Renaissance Studies, University of Copenhagen, in collaboration with prof. Eckhard Keßler, Institut für Geistesgeschichte des Humanismus, Munich. The network as well as the publication of the proceedings have been supported by the Danish Research Council for the Humanities. The articles are printed in an approximately chronological subject order.

Marianne Pade
Copenhagen, November 2000.

THE RECEPTION OF THE POLITICAL ARISTOTLE IN THE LATE MIDDLE AGES

(FROM BRUNETTO LATINI TO DANTE ALIGHIERI).
HYPOTHESES AND SUGGESTIONS

by Gert Sørensen

Problem and method
A twentieth-century definition of politics runs like this: "Politics are the kind of activity which concerns the seizing, the organization, the distribution and the exercising of power within the limits of a State or the relations between States".[1] In many respects, this typical post-Machiavellian idea, well known from modern political science, converts politics to purely technical questions of how to seize and consolidate power. In doing so the theory of politics runs a great risk of cutting the links with ethics and ethical discussions of the means and purposes of politics. This possible outcome may lead us to analyse the components of our political concepts with reference to their historical genesis. In this way, we liberate ourselves from the modern one-eyed versions, which we are so used to that we have generally accepted the reduction of politics to cynical games of power. Following the track back to the Aristotelian origins, we will soon encounter concepts of politics concerning on the one hand good government and civic participation and on the other the possible deviations from these.

With Christianity this pagan concept of politics almost disappeared from the vocabularies of intellectuals, as they turned their minds from *civitas terrena* to *civitas Dei*. In the first centuries of the second millennium, however, after the magic year 1000, the relations between political and theological thinking were changing[2] as a result of economic growth and the

---
[1] G. Pasquino, "Politica", *Alla ricerca della politica. Voci per un dizionario*, a cura di A. d'Orsi, Torino 1995, 266.
[2] M.S. Sapegno, "Il trattato politico e utopico", *Letteratura italiana*, 3.2, a cura di A. Asor Rosa, Torino 1984, 951.

increasing urbanization of Europe, in particular of France and Northern and Central Italy. It is in this context of socio-economic and intellectual awakening that the revival of Aristotle has to be analysed.[3] It was a period that had not yet invented its own scientific languages, but to which Aristotle offered a whole encyclopedia of knowledge not quite in conformity with the dominant Christian culture but ready to be 'recycled'. Curtius stated that these centuries saw "the inroads of the 'new' Aristotle".[4] And Vasoli argued that the increasing spread of the writings on logics, metaphysics, physics and in particular ethics and politics challenged the philosophical and theological culture of the time with an entirely "new theoretical perspective" on the natural character of the political institutions. These were no longer to be seen only as remedies for a corrupt and sinful mankind but first and foremost as instruments to fulfil man's basic needs of material and purely intellectual improvement.[5] In 1270 the papal authorities forbade this new Aristotelianism, declaring it false teaching too much influenced by Arab philosophers like Averroës. They critized, among other things, the assertion that the world is eternal and not created; that the first man never existed; that body and soul are unified; that man's will is determined to do what is good and right and thus able to avoid what is bad and wrong.[6] Nevertheless, this was also the period of the complete Latin editions of Aristotle's works on *Ethics* and on *Politics* (respectively translated ca. 1240 by Robert Grosseteste and ca. 1260 by William of Moerbeke, both from the Greek).

The Church did not succeed in removing Aristotle from the programmes of the emerging intellectual centres, in particular the university of Paris, and it was forced to look for other solutions. It is a common view that this new and revised Aristotle furthered the development of scholastic theories. Thomas Aquinas succeeded in incorporating the Greek philosopher into

---

[3] F. van Steenberghen, *Aristotle in the West. The Origins of Latin Aristotelianism*, Louvain 1970, 59.
[4] E.R. Curtius, *European Literature and the Latin Middle Ages*, (German edition 1948) New York and Evanston 1963, 55.
[5] C. Vasoli, "Il carattere 'naturale' dello Stato", *Aristotelismo politico e ragion di Stato*. Atti del convegno internazionale di Torino 11-13 febbraio 1993, a cura di A. Enzo Baldini, Firenze 1995, 58.
[6] F. van Steenberghen, *Thomas Aquinas and Radical Aristotelianism*, Ann Arbor, Mich. 1980, 1-28.

dominant theological thought,⁷ and this incorporation was fully accepted after his death. As a result the heterogeneous and controversial elements of Aristotelianism were isolated, although Thomism too met temporary resistance with the ban imposed in 1277 by Étienne Tempier, Bishop of Paris. If we leave Aristotle to one-sided Thomistic interpretation, we forego other possible readings which correspond better to larger and more complex contexts of experiences and expectations of the period, and which might enable us to take into account the existence of extremely unconventional forms of knowledge, based on a heterodox and even radical Aristotle.

Charles B. Schmitt has pointed out that the reception of Aristotle is well-known down to about 1300. He does not, however, agree with those who emphasize the break between the Middle Ages and the Renaissance and think that, as far as Aristotle is concerned, there is nothing relevant to search for after that time.⁸ Following Garin's and Kristeller's pioneerings works, he rejects the idea of a purely medieval and scholastic Aristotle.⁹ Consequently, Schmitt puts forward another and more promising and farsighted thesis connecting the 'recycling' of the Aristotelian tradition with the emergence of the modern world.¹⁰ Thus the new Aristotle initiated

---

⁷ H.V. Jaffa, *Thomism and Aristotelianism. A Study of the Commentary by Thomas Aquinas on the Nicomachean Ethics*, Chicago 1952, 5-6.

⁸ Ch.B. Schmitt, *A Critical Survey and Bibliography of Studies on Renaissance Aristotelianism 1958-1969*, Padova 1971, 52. The author classifies his work as "intellectual history" (27).

⁹ E. Garin, "Le traduzioni umanistiche di Aristotele nel secolo XV", *Atti e memorie dell'Accademia fiorentina di scienze morali "La Colombaria"*, N.S. 2 (1947-50), 55-104. P.O. Kristeller, *Studies in Renaissance Thought and Letters*, Rome 1956, 337-53.

¹⁰ Schmitt 1971, 117. Hankins has suggested that through the Renaissance translation by Leonardo Bruni, Aristotle's political works may have gained in linguistic perfection what they lost in incisiveness, cf. J. Hankins, "Translation Practice in the Renaissance: the Case of Leonardo Bruni", *Etudes classiques. IV. Rencontres Scientifiques de Luxembourg 1992.3.* Actes du colloque "Méthodologie de la traduction: de l'Antiquité à la Renaissance", édités par Ch. M. Ternes, Centre Universitaire Luxembourg 1994, 154-75. Rackham perhaps goes too far in his eagerness to modernize the new Aristotle, when in his introduction to the Loeb edition of Aristotle, *The Nicomachean Ethics* (translation and introduction by H. Rackham), London-Cambridge (Mass.) (1926) 1968, XXVIII, he proclaims the work to be "a touchstone for that modern idea of the gentleman, which supplies or used to supply an important part of the English race with its working religion".

a crisis in the religious and institutional hegemony of the Church rather than supported it.[11]

Although it is clear that this aspect of his work cannot be isolated from other aspects, this paper focuses on the political Aristotle and in particular the impact he had on Dante Alighieri, author of the somewhat overshadowed work on the universal monarchy (*Monarchia*),[12] and also on Brunetto Latini, Dante's teacher and author of the encyclopedia *Tresor*. Methodological inspiration has been drawn from what is called the "New History of Political Thought", a trend which alludes to the school of Quentin Skinner and their work on political discourses in early modern Europe.[13] Following Wittgenstein and Austin, they look upon texts as linguistic acts performed in certain historical contexts, and which within these historically defined settings absorb, transform and produce concepts and meanings. Another important idea comes from political science.[14] The concept of hegemony has proved to be very helpful in our attempt to understand textual acts as ongoing articulations or disarticulations of broader settings of cultural and social power. Obviously this does not become less evident with the increasing antagonism between the Church, the Empire, the Kingdom of France and the dynamic urban civilization of the thirteenth and early fourteenth centuries.

The general rewriting of Aristotle within this frame of often unpredictable historical happenings can be analysed in six modalities: 1) translation; 2) imitation (the well-known practice of copying without naming the source); 3) commentaries; 4) quotations; 5) manipulation; 6) selection of important examples in compendiums.[15] A more detailed approach will confirm that Brunetto Latini and Dante both made use of this many-layered intellectual practice, and that Latini did so to an even

---

[11] Van Steenberghen 1970, 60.

[12] P.G. Ricci, *Introduzione* to Dante, *Monarchia*, Milano 1964, 126, stresses that the title is *Monarchia* and not, as tradition maintains, *De Monarchia*.

[13] Q. Skinner, *The Foundations of Modern Political Thought*, 2 voll. Cambridge 1979-80. A. d'Orsi, *Guida alla storia del pensiero politico*, Firenze 1995, 210-22.

[14] A. Gramsci, *Quaderni del carcere*, Torino 1975. M. Foucault, *L'archéologie du savoir*, Paris 1969. E. Laclau & C. Mouffe, *Hegemony and Socialist Strategy*, London 1985.

[15] B. Godorecci, *After Machiavelli. "Re-writing" and the "Hermeneutic Attitude"*, West Lafayette 1993, 34-35. For the connection between translation and commenting, cf. E. Jacobsen, "Translation a Traditional Craft", *Classica et Mediaevalia*. Dissertationes VI, Copenhagen 1958.

greater extent, appropriating almost all six modalities and so revealing a lesser degree of 'originality' as compared with his pupil. The choice of modalities and of specific reinterpretative strategies very largely determines whether the text confirms or challenges the frames of context, and to what extent.

Brunetto Latini (1220/25-93) and civic Humanism
According to many commentators[16] the author of the *Tresor*[17] was Dante's teacher, whom the grateful pupil honoured in the fifteenth canto of the *Inferno* by condemning him to suffer among the sodomites. Nevertheless, the Brunetto figure is represented with great dignity and pride. His last recommendation to Dante still reveals warm feelings ("sieti raccomandato il mio Tesoro nel qual io vivo ancora"), which Dante repays by classifying Brunetto among "quelli che vince, non colui che perde" (119-24). So Brunetto may be a counter-ideal to all those who are harshly described in the next canto XVI – also on sodomites – as "la gente nova e' subiti guadagni orgoglio e dismisura han generata" (73-74), that is those who had corrupted the city of Florence with the wealth they had acquired too easily.[18]

In real life, however, Brunetto Latini must have been a respected intellectual, well-known as a scholar and politician. In 1260, returning from a mission to Alfonso X of Castile, he, as a Guelf, was forced to seek refuge after the defeat of the Guelf party by the Ghibellines at Montaperti. Brunetto was exiled to France, just in the period in which radical Aristotelianism was beginning to penetrate the intellectual life of Paris.[19] He is supposed to have attended lectures at the university there.[20]

---

[16] Pietro di Dante (Dante's son), *Commentarium* (Biblioteca Laurenziana, cod. Ashb. 841, f. 64 v.); Jacopo della Lana, *Commedia di Dante degli Alighieri col commento* (ed. L. Scarabelli), Bologna 1866-67, 280: "Il qual ser Brunetto fu un tempo maestro di Dante", cf. Ch. T. Davis, "Brunetto Latini and Dante", *Studi medievali* VIII.1.1967, 440n.; Th. Sundby, *Brunetto Latinis levnet og skrifter*, Copenhagen 1869 (*Della vita e delle opere di Brunetto Latini*, trans. by R. Renier, Firenze 1884).
[17] Brunetto Latini, *Li livres dou tresor* (édition critique par Francis J. Carmody), Berkeley and Los Angeles 1948.
[18] Davis 1967, 446.
[19] Steenberghen 1970, 198.
[20] Carmody, *Introduction* to Brunetto Latini, XXVII.

Six years later, after the battle at Benevento (1266) in which the Ghibelline Emperor Manfredi,[21] the illegitimate son of Frederick II, was killed, Latini returned to his native city and soon became a leading member of the Florentine government. In 1282 the city-republic got a new constitution with the birth of the *priorato*. Each *priore* was recruited exclusively from guilds of craftsmen and merchants in an attempt to prevent the nobles from gaining any access to power. The priors held office for a period of 2 months. Latini himself was a prior from 15th August to 15th October 1287. The constitution of '82 was only the first step. It was followed by a number of constitutional and institutional innovations, which changed the relations of power and decision-making between *il Popolo* and *i Magnati* and culminated in 1293-95 with the *Ordinamenti della Giustizia*. More than a century later, in his *Laudatio Florentinae Urbis*, probably written in 1403-04, Leonardo Bruni, the later Florentine chancellor, praises this republican tradition after Florence had shown its superiority in the war against the tyrant of Milan, Giangaleazzo Visconti.

Giovanni Villani, in his Chronicles, portrayed Brunetto Latini as the "maestro" who taught the Florentines to speak well and to govern their republic by the rules of politics ("secondo la politica"),[22] thereby underlining the connection between politics and constitutionally organized urban life. Latini wrote his principal work *Li livres dou Tresor* during his exile and in French, "por çou que la parleure est plus delitable et plus commune a tous langages".[23] An Italian translation was made soon after.[24] It was an encyclopedia, an all-embracing reflection on "des choses naturaus, et des divines, et des humaines",[25] and structured in three books. Book one deals with theology, universal history, geography and the physical world, the second book with ethics, and the third with rhetoric and politics. Of the numerous sources Aristotle, *Ethics* ('recycled' in book II), Cicero, *De Inventione* (in the first parts of book III) and Giovanni da Viterbo, *De Regimine Civitatum* (in the second and last part of book III)

---

[21] Brunetto Latini, 80; Manfredi's Empire is called "tyrannie".
[22] G. Villani, *Croniche* VIII.10, Trieste 1857, 174
[23] Brunetto Latini, 18.
[24] Normally attributed to Bono Giamboni (1240-1292), later published as *Il Tesoro*, (Venezia 1528) Venezia 1839. This attribution has been questioned, cf. Sapegno 1984, 953n.
[25] Brunetto Latini, 18.

are the most outstanding in the field of "human things" which takes up most of the work.

This account of the contents makes it clear that there is little of a religious nature in *le Tresor*. Indeed, Carmody suggests[26] that even the contemporary monks who copied Latini's books were worried by the scarcity of proper religious themes, although these are not completely lacking. So several manuscripts, one of which dates from the period just before the crucial year 1270, have been interpolated to bring them more into line with dominant teaching. I would suggest the Aristotelian connection is one main reason for these somewhat secular priorities in Latini's work. His rewriting of Aristotle on "human things" can be analysed on two levels. First, he applied almost all modalities of rewriting to the *Nicomachean Ethics* or better the so-called *Compendium Alexandrinum*,[27] on which he relied heavily in book II. He probably had no knowledge of Aristotle's work on politics, which was translated ca. 1260 too late to be integrated in his ongoing project.[28] Raw materials for the last part of book III on politics were provided by Giovanni da Viterbo's *De Regimine Civitatum*.[29] This does not make any difference, however, because Aristotle already gives the key to the following book on *Politics* in the last chapters of his *Ethics*. It was not only that the *Nicomachean Ethics* was translated into Latin before the *Politics*. This order of dealing with the themes also strictly followed the logical relation which Aristotle himself saw between the two books; and this fact brings us to the second level of the Aristotelian connection. Thus the structural organization of the *Treasure* books, at least in the last two parts, mirrors the gradual expansion of rational thinking on "human things", proceeding from ethics (book II) to politics (last part of book III, after the chapters on rhetoric), which is

---

[26] Carmody, *Introduction* to Brunetto Latini, XXXIII.

[27] *Compendium Alexandrinum* (a cura di C. Marchesi, *L'Etica Nicomachea nella tradizione latina medievale*), Messina 1904.

[28] Carmody, *Introduction* to Brunetto Latini, XXVIII, XXVI. Rubinstein suggests that Aristotle's *Politics*, in the translation by Moerbeke, cannot be traced back any earlier than the political works of Thomas Aquinas, cf. N. Rubinstein, "The History of the Word 'politicus' in Early-modern Europe", *The Languages of Political Theory in Early-modern Europe*, ed. by A. Pagden, Cambridge 1987, 42.

[29] Giovanni da Viterbo, *Liber de regimine civitatum*,1240? a cura di G. Salvemini, in *Scripta anecdota Glossatorum* (Biblioteca Iuridica Medii Aevi), Bologna 1901. For the present purpose it is not neccessary to give a more detailed analysis of the importance of Giovanni da Viterbo.

described as "la plus haute science et dou plus noble mestier ki soit entre les homes, car ele nos ensegne governer les estranges gens d'un regne et d'une vile, un peuple et une comune en tens de pes et de guerre, selonc raison et selonc justice".[30]

At the beginning of the last chapter (X 9) of the *Ethics* Aristotle asks "If then we have sufficiently discussed in their outlines the subjects of Happiness and of Virtue in its various forms, and also Friendship and Pleasure, may we assume that the investigation we proposed is now complete? Perhaps however, as we maintain, in the practical sciences the end is not to attain a theoretic knowledge of the various subjects, but rather to carry out our theories in action. If so, to know what virtue is is not enough; we must endeavour to possess and to practise it, or in some other manner actually ourselves to become good".[31]

How, then, do we ourselves ensure that virtue is not only a theoretical object but is also used and becomes real? Aristotle relies upon the idea of man being motivated by nature for the good. But even for him nature was not enough; confronted with the possibility of moral deviation, he feels the need to introduce constraining rules and laws so as better to persuade, especially the younger generations, to do what is right. Consequently, in the same last chapter of his *Ethics* he briefly outlines the next step, moving on to the laws, the objects of politics: "As then the question of legislation has been left uninvestigated by previous thinkers, it will perhaps be well if we consider it for ourselves, together with the whole question of the constitution of the State, in order to complete as far as possible our philosophy of human affairs".[32]

These remarkable final words of the *Nicomachean Ethics* look forward to the beginning of his next book on the constitutions, with its more exalted status. The opening lines of the *Politics* are as follows: "Every state is as we see a sort of partnership, and every partnership is formed with a view to some good (since all the actions of all mankind are done with a view to what they think to be good). It is therefore evident that, while all partnerships aim at some good, the partnership that is the most supreme of

---

[30] Brunetto Latini, 21.
[31] Aristotle, *The Nicomachean Ethics*, X.9, 629.
[32] Aristotle, *The Nicomachean Ethics*, X.9, 643. Brunetto Latini, 391: "politique, c'est a dire des governemens des cités, ki est la plus noble et la plus haute science et li plus nobles offices ki soit en tiere, selonc ce que Aristotles prueve en son livre".

all and includes all the others does so most of all, and aims at the most supreme of all goods; and this is the partnership entitled the state, the political association".[33]

Regarding these two books, Brunetto Latini certainly keeps very close to the philosophical programme of Aristotle, while supplementing it from Cicero and Giovanni da Viterbo. And I find it worth noting that Latini did not proceed from ethics to theology or from *civitas terrena* to *civitas Dei*, as might have been expected, given that Christianity was the dominant culture and was regarded as the best remedy for human insufficiencies. Latini prefered secular or even pagan learning on the subject of how to govern the city. To him a city was "uns assamblemens de gens a abiter en un lieu et vivre a une loi". A city, then, implies a territory, a population and a government with a constitution.[34] What Latini had in mind was explicitly the Italian city-republics, which he considered second to no other forms of government because they elected their leaders and had regard to the welfare of their citizens. Compared to Italian republicanism, the French monarchy, which he knew from his exile, was in his eyes corrupted by the practice of buying and selling public offices. He therefore proposes two opposite forms of government: "Et cil sont en .ii. manieres; uns ki sont en France et es autres païs, ki sont sozmis a la signorie des rois et des autres princes perpetueus, ki vendent les provostés et les baillent a ciaus ki plus l'achatent (poi gardent sa bonté ne le proufit des borgois); l'autre est en Ytaile, que li citain et li borgois et li communité des viles eslisent lor poesté et lor signour tel comme il quident qu'il soit plus proufitables au commun preu de la vile et de tous lor subtés".[35]

In the very first chapter of his Encyclopedia Brunetto Latini points out the superiority of the Italian way ("selonc les us as ytaliens"[36]), outlining the whole idea of his work as a kind of manifesto for the republican city-life. Aristotle (or in places Giovanni da Viterbo and the civic hero Cicero) was made to serve this purpose. Latini even went so far as to misquote the

---

[33] Aristotle, *Politics*, translation and introduction by H. Rackham, London-Cambridge, Mass. (1932) 1977, 1252a.

[34] Brunetto Latini, 391. M.H. Hansen, *Polis and the City-State. An Ancient Concept and its Modern Equivalent* (Acts of the Copenhagen Polis Centre Vol. 5), Copenhagen 1998, 36-40, argues that territory, population and government constitute the three basic elements of a state.

[35] Brunetto Latini, 392.

[36] *Ibid*. 17.

Ethics to achieve intellectual consistency in his project. An example may illustrate how Latini manipulates the Greek philosopher in order to present him as a spokesman for genuine city-republicanism. In book VIII of his *Ethics* Aristotle discusses the three well-known forms of government, aristocracy, monarchy, timocracy, and their deviant forms. Latini reads this passage as if Aristotle preferred the timocracy to the others: "la tierce est des communes, laquele est la trés millour entre ces autres". Aristotle meant quite the opposite.[37]

Dante Alighieri and universal monarchy

Dante's political career followed very closely the institutional and constitutional development of Florence until the crises in the years immediately after 1300. From November 1295 until April 1296 he was a member of the *Consiglio speciale del Capitano del Popolo*, then he was elected to the *Consiglio dei Cento* for the rest of the year 1296. Dante was sent on diplomatic missions to Pope Bonifacius VIII, whose interference in internal Florentine affairs he strongly opposed. He was then appointed *priore* for the two-month period from 15th June to 14th August 1300. As a supporter of the White party he was forced into a lifelong exile in 1302.[38]

These unhappy experiences clearly motivated Dante's increasing lack of confidence in the genuine city-republicanism of Florence and other Italian communes, and hastened the development of his political thought. In a much later letter to his wicked ("scelestissimi") countrymen, his diagnosis was quite clear: "Ytalia misera, sola, privatis arbitriis derelicta omnique publico moderamine destituta".[39] And: "Vos autem divina iura et humana

---

[37] *Ibid.* 211. Aristotle, *Ethics*, VIII.10, 489; Sundby, 153; N. Rubinstein, "Le dottrine politiche nel Rinascimento", *Il Rinascimento. Interpretazioni e problemi*, a Eugenio Garin nel suo settantesimo compleanno, a cura degli editori Laterza, Bari 1983, 189-90; quotes the *Compendium Alexandrinum* (LXXIII) of Aristotle's *Ethics*: "principatus civiles tres sunt ... Et omnium optimus est regum principatus" (there are three types of government..., of which monarchy is the best).

[38] F. Mazzoni, *Teoresi e prassi in Dante politico*, introduction to Dante Alighieri, *Monarchia. Epistole politiche*, Torino 1966, XII-XVII. V. Russo, "La *Monarchia* di Dante (tra utopia e progetto), *Letture classiensi*, 7, 1979, 59-60.

[39] Dante, *Epistola* VI (31.3.1311), in Dante, *Monarchia. Epistole politiche* (a cura di F. Mazzoni), Torino 1966, 224 (Poor Italy, alone, abandoned to the will of private individuals and without any public government [English translation by the author]). Cf. Dante, *Purg.* VI, 76-78: "Ahi serva Italia, di dolore ostello,/nave sanza nocchiere in gran tempesta,/ non donna di provincie, ma bordello".

transgredientes, quos dira cupiditatis ingluvies paratos in omne nefas illexit ... An ignorantes, amentes et discoli, publica iura cum sola temporis terminatione finiri, et nullius prescriptionis calculo fore obnoxia?"[40] From these quotations it is plain that the Florentine crisis was Italy's as well. This obliged Dante to refine his political thinking by introducing much more comprehensive and universal concepts. By focusing on monarchy Dante broke with his teacher Brunetto Latini's city-republicanism, as in his opinion this political system had come to an end.

The dating of the *Monarchia*[41] has been discussed for a long time without any final conclusions. Witte has suggested the year 1300, Nardi 1308, while Ricci and others have proposed 1317 or even later. Vinay, however, and most other scholars agree with Boccaccio, who in his *Trattatello* dated the work to the period when Henry VII invaded Italy in order to be crowned as the new Emperor, that is between 1311 and 1313.[42] The period was rather chaotic. Pope Clemente V and the Holy See had moved to Avignon. Hence Henry VII had to be crowned by a substitute. Soon after this the Emperor died (1313) and was succeeded by Louis of Bavaria. Clemente V died in 1314; his successor was another French pope, Giovanni XXII, who did not acknowledge Louis as the new Emperor but entrusted Italy to the Frenchman Robert d'Anjou. The politics of the Church towards the Empire were still dictated by the papal bull *Unam Sanctam* (1302) of the hardliner Bonifacius VIII.

This impasse raised political questions about government, legitimacy, peace and justice, which Dante expressed very clearly in the famous letter to Henry VII (1311) entitled "Cesaris et Augusti successor" or "sol noster"

---

[40] *Ibid.* 226 (You, who violate the rights of God and of man, are made willing malefactors, enticed by the horrible greed of avarice ... Are you not aware, you insane and perverse people, that public right comes to an end only with the end of time and will not be subject to the slightest exception? [English translation by the author]).

[41] Dante, *Monarchia*, Testo, introduzione, traduzione e commento a cura di G. Vinay, Firenze 1950.

[42] F. Mazzoni, 1966, LXI-LXIII, suggests 1314; A.-M. Chiavacci-Leonardi, "La 'Monarchia' di Dante alla luce della 'Commedia'", *Studi medievali*, 18, 1977, 747-49; Boccaccio, *Trattatello*, in *Idem, Opere in versi. Corbaccio. Trattatello in laude di Dante. Prose latine. Epistole*, a cura di P.G. Ricci, Milano-Napoli 1965, 637: "Similmente questo egregio auttore nella venuta di Arrigo VII imperadore fece un libro in latina prosa, il cui titolo è *Monarchia*".

or "Dei minister".⁴³ Dante reproaches Henry for staying too long in Northern Italy and forgetting to uphold his authority ("gloriosa potestas") in Dante's own Tuscany.⁴⁴ The very tone of the letter reveals the impact of historical events on Dante's political language, as he turns away from Latini's dichotomy between republicanism and (French) monarchy towards a dichotomy between Church and Empire involving what we might call universal republicanism. This new dichotomy is characterized by the same conflicts between "iura publica" and "arbitria privata"⁴⁵ but on a different scale. The next question is to what extent Aristotle serves as a vehicle for Dante's new political orientations.

Almost every page of the *Monarchia* quotes, directly or indirectly, from the writings of Aristotle, of which the works on ethics and politics were known to Dante probably through the commentaries of Thomas Aquinas.⁴⁶ Others are quoted, among them the Arab philosopher Averroës. But nobody else is quoted so extensively as Aristotle who is generally called "the philosopher" ("phylosophus"), a title which Dante expects his readers to recognize.⁴⁷ As the highest ranking of the ancient philosophers, Aristotle provided a paradigm of ideas which Dante could use in the treatment of his main theme.

In spite of Aristotle's dominant position, it is misleading and anachronistic to make Dante a secular or even pagan thinker. Dante thought within the religious hegemony of his time and was very much influenced by the great Thomas Aquinas. Like Dante, Thomas Aquinas also regarded the monarchy as the best form of government, although this identity of views did not mean that Dante agreed with him in everything. In fact, several scholars have emphasized Dante's eclecticism and his making a breach between *humana civilitas* and *christianitas*, *ratio* and *fides* within the

---

⁴³ Dante, *Epistola VII* (17.4.1311), in Dante, *Monarchia. Epistole politiche*, a cura di F. Mazzoni, Torino 1966, 242. The well-known greyhound (*il Veltro*), introduced in canto I of the *Inferno* and destined to kill the Roman she-wolf (the Pope), probably stands for the Emperor, cf. F. Mazzoni, 1966, XXXIII, and A. Solmi, *Il pensiero politico di Dante*, Firenze 1922, 82-91.

⁴⁴ *Ibid.* 245. Many of the political reflections of the *Monarchia* can also be found in Dante, *Convivio* IV, cf. B. Nardi, *Dal "Convivio" alla "Commedia"*, Roma, 1960, 37-151.

⁴⁵ Cf. notes 39 & 40.

⁴⁶ Vinay, Introduction to Dante, *Mon.* 1950, VII.

⁴⁷ Cf. Dante, *Inf.* IV, 131; Aristotle is "'l maestro di color che sanno". *Ibid. Conv.* IV.8.15: "magister sapientium". *Ibid.*, *Inf.* IV, 144; Averroës is the one who "'l gran comento feo".

dominant religious and hierarchic dualism. He works in the more open field of investigation offered by an Aristotelian paradigm which contains elements both of the radical Arab version of Aristotle's philosophy and of Thomism. The idea of metaphysical happiness (*felicitas* or *beatitudo*) was never abandoned in his mental universe. Dante, however, did not reduce "human things" to merely temporary affairs; in fact, he even believed that they had a rationality of their own.[48]

The increasing resistance to Dante's ideas became evident when Louis of Bavaria went to Italy in 1327 to be crowned in Rome. The Pope, Giovanni XXII, denied the Emperor his right. As a countermove – this is the story that Boccaccio tells us – Louis promoted Pietro della Corvara to be the new Pope with authority to crown the Emperor. To strengthen his position he referred to the main thesis of the *Monarchia*, so making the work even more dangerous to the Church. Giovanni XXII's reaction was severe and immediate, when Cardinal Bertrando del Poggetto arranged a public burning of the book.[49]

The *Monarchia* is composed of three books. Each of them presents an important argument, of which the last was the most controversial:

1. An [monarchia] ad bene esse mundi necessaria sit;
2. An Romanus populus de iure Monarche officium sibi adsciverit;
3. An auctoritas Monarche dependeat a Deo inmediate vel ab aliquo Dei ministro seu vicario.[50]

Dante opens with a metaphysical statement. Man, he says, is driven towards the truth (*veritas*) by a higher nature (*natura superior*[51]), which has provided him with intellectual powers (*virtus intellectiva*) to be realized through speculative thought or concrete action. For Dante, the realization of the intellectual powers is the purpose of man both as an individual and as a collective subject. This is the *principium inquisitionis directivum*, the

---

[48] Russo 1979, 64-66; Mazzoni 1966, LXXXIX-XCII.

[49] Boccaccio, *Trattatello*, 1965, 638-39. Russo 1979, 56. G. Vernani, *De reprobatione Monarchie composite a Dante* (written between 1327 and 1334).

[50] Dante, *Mon.* (I.2), 1950, 10 (First we must raise and discuss the question whether temporal monarchy is necessary for the well being of the world; second, whether the Roman people assumed the function of monarch by right; and third, whether the authority of the monarch is derived from God directly or from another, God's minister or vicar. Cf. Dante, *Monarchia* [translated with a commentary by R. Kay], Toronto 1998, 7)

[51] *Ibid.* (I.1), 2. It has been suggested that 'the higher nature' is God; in his comment Vinay prefers to see the term as an "espressione generica".

guiding principle of his investigation, for which he was probably indebted to the radical Aristotelian Averroës, whose comments on Aristotle's *De Anima* he mentions on one occasion.[52] Without being a radical Aristotelian himself he uses the Arab philosopher for his own purposes. In approaching his specific field of investigation, he first distinguishes between things beyond our reach that we can only reflect on but not transform or manipulate (the world of divine things), and those that we can reflect on and also transform and manipulate, that is, the world of *humana civilitas*. So Dante does not abandon the idea of man's two ends (*fines*): on the one hand the felicity (*beatitudo*) of this life (*paradisus terrestris*) and on the other the felicity of eternal life (*paradisus celestis*).[53] He simply attributes a greater importance to civil life than was customary.

Secondly, man's transformation of the world of things has two dimensions. Man acts consciously, aims at something (*agere*); this differs from doing things mechanically (*facere*). This last transformation of things to *factibilia* refers to trade and manufacture. The first and in this context more important category of acts transforms things to *agibilia*, which are regulated by political skill (*politica prudentia*).[54] With this further distinction, Dante defines his specific field of investigation, that is the political act, the source of every well-organized form of government (*fons atque principium rectarum politiarum*)[55] from the level of the family up to those of the city and the monarchy. Each of these institutions aims at *utilitas publica* or *pax universalis*. Politics or *politica prudentia* unifies within orthodox the specific world of *agibilia* what the Church and more theological thought would like to separate, that is intellect and act, constitution and welfare (*politia* and *felicitas*).

Like Aristotle in the last chapter of the *Nicomachean Ethics*, Dante also relies upon the idea that man is driven towards the truth. But he too is well aware of the need for external guidance, especially among the younger generations. A single will (*voluntas una*)[56] is necessary, that of the supreme ruler and law-maker. His supremacy does not mean, however, that those

---

[52] *Ibid.* (I.3-4), 18-26; Mazzoni 1966, LXIX; Nardi 1960, 88-89; *Idem.* "Filosofia e teologia ai tempi di Dante", in Nardi, *Saggi e note di critica dantesca*, Milano-Napoli, 1966, 59.
[53] *Ibid.* (III.16), 280-82.
[54] *Ibid.* (I.3), 26.
[55] *Ibid.* (I.2), 12.
[56] *Ibid.* (I.16), 98.

who have to obey the law do so for his benefit. On the contrary, it is he who makes the law for their benefit.[57] The laws form the basis of the government. The political act, therefore, is also an act of law-making. Dante defines "ius" on which society is based as a "realis et personalis hominis ad hominem proportio, que servata hominum servat societatem, et corrupta corrumpit".[58] This was the legacy of the Roman Empire (the issue discussed in the second book), which in Dante's analysis was an Empire not of violence but of legality.

Now some brief remarks on the third book, undoubtedly the most controversial part of *Monarchia*, where the thesis is that monarchy is a form of government directly dependent on God without the mediation of the Church. Dante does not try to hide the fact that he wants to provoke and embarrass those who hold the opposite. He criticizes the Church for its assertion that the Empire was directly dependent on it, an assertion which it tried to legitimate by referring to the Holy Bible and tradition. *Genesis* tells us that God created two great lights (*duo magna luminaria*), the sun and the moon. Hence the official syllogism:

A. Luna recipit lucem a sole qui est regimen spirituale
B. Regimen temporale est luna
C. Ergo regimen temporale recipit auctoritatem a regimine spirituali[59]

The moon gets its light from the sun, that is, the moon is an allegory of the Empire and the sun of the Church; therefore the Empire depends on the Church. According to Dante this argument proves nothing. It is false and lacks logic (*ratio*). If it is merely a question of ignorance, Dante says that he will not hesitate to forgive the Church. Otherwise one has to act against the Church as one would against tyrants who look to their own interests rather than those of the community (*communis utilitas*).

---

[57] *Ibid.* (I.12), 78.

[58] *Ibid.* (II.5), 130 (Law is a real and personal relationship between two people, which serves human society when it is observed and destroys it when broken. Cf. English translation, 123); H. Kelsen, *La teoria dello Stato in Dante* (German edition, 1905), Bologna 1974, 54; L. Chiappelli, "Dante in rapporto alle fonti del diritto", *Archivio Storico Italiano*, n. 249, 1908, 25.

[59] *Ibid.* (III.4), 222 (The moon receives light from the sun, which is the spiritual directive power; the temporal directive power is the moon; therefore, the temporal directive power receives authority from the spiritual directive power. Cf. English translation, 231).

Therefore Dante rejects the idea of the moon and the sun as allegories of two different forms of government, the first of which is subordinated to the second. In categorical terms the two forms of government, the Empire and the Church, are *accidentia*, which presuppose the existence of a *subjectus*, that is man, in relation to whom they realize certain temporal and spiritual ends, as being products of human action (*agere*). The problem is – and this is quite a convincing objection – that the moon and the sun (in other words the Empire and the Church) were created on the fourth day, while man was created on the sixth. Thus the *accidentia* were created before the *subjectus*, which is nonsense.[60]

Another example of Dante's reasoning about the idea of the Church's supremacy over the Empire is related to the legend that Constantine the Great assigned Rome to Pope Silvester (by the *Donatio Constantini*) for having healed his leprosy. Dante did not doubt the genuineness of the document as Lorenzo Valla was to doubt it in the fifteenth century. He doubted only the legal validity of the following syllogism:[61]

A. Ea que sunt Ecclesie nemo de iure habere potest nisi ab Ecclesia
B. Romanum regimen est Ecclesie
C. Ergo ipsum nemo de iure habere potest nisi ab Ecclesia[62]

In accordance with his belief in legality as the only basis of human society Dante replies that the Church has no legal right to Rome, because the Emperor, for his part, is not in a legal position to grant it. The argument runs like this: the Empire is built on legal norms (*iurisdictio*) which define the function of the Emperor. From a legal point of view the Empire was not an instrument in the hands of the Emperor. He was the servant of the Empire. Hence, the Emperor was not allowed to dispose of the Empire as if it were part of his personal belongings.[63] When the Church pleads for its

---

[60] *Ibid.* (III.4), 210-22.

[61] Dante, *Inf.* (XIX, 115-17): "Ahi, Costantin, di quanto mal fu matre,/non la tua conversion, ma quella dote/che da te prese il primo ricco patre!".

[62] Dante, *Mon.* (III.10), 248 (No one can rightfully have those things that are the Church's except from the Church [.....]; Roman directive power is the Church's: therefore, no one is able to have it rightly except from the Church. Cf. English translation, 265).

[63] *Ibid.* (III.10), 250-52. Neither was the Church in a position to receive it, as Dante argued with reference to the Bible, *Matth.* (X.9); Kelsen 1974, 130; B. Nardi, *Nel mondo di Dante*, Rome, 1944, 109-59.

legal right to the Empire Dante does not accept these claims, since "usurpatio iuris non facit ius".[64]

Epilogue
Dante's attempts to mark out for himself an autonomous area of investigation within the religious hegemony of his time provoked severe reactions from the Church, which banned *Monarchia* for more than three centuries (1554-1881). To conclude our discussion on Aristotle and his long after-life, one might say that the modernity of the 'new' Aristotle is not directly due to the works of the ancient philosopher themselves. More decisive for this status are 1) the 'recycling' of Aristotle made by outstanding figures like Brunetto Latini and Dante Alighieri, the first of which related to the city-republics and the second to the conflicts between the Pope and the Emperor; and 2) the way of integrating the political works of the Greek philosopher as challenges to the hegemony of dominant religious culture, now submitted to theoretical contradictions and a greater complexity of broader intellectual stratifications.

One would agree with the Italian political scientist Umberto Cerroni, who has recently stated that after the defeat of Dante the political thinkers of Italy suffered an important setback in the development of political thought, and so missed the opportunity for the kind of state-building achieved elsewhere, in France under Philip the Beautiful and in England under Edward I.[65]

---

[64] *Ibid.* (III.10), 256 (usurpation of a right does not make a right. Cf. English translation, 277).
[65] U. Cerroni, *L'identità civile degli italiani*, Lecce 1997, 84, 172.

ETHICS AS PHILOLOGY:
A DEVELOPING APPROACH TO ARISTOTLE'S
Nicomachean Ethics IN FLORENTINE HUMANISM[*]

by David A. Lines

Renaissance readings of Aristotle tend to be studied through one of two genres: commentaries or translations. Ironically, it is the less studied genre – translations – that is often said to represent the humanists' main contribution to the study of Aristotle. Thus, one might expect this paper to concentrate on the new and influential Renaissance translations of Aristotle's *Nicomachean Ethics* by well known fifteenth-century figures such as Leonardo Bruni and John Argyropoulos. This angle offers rich possibilities: despite the studies by Garin, Hankins, and other scholars, many aspects of these translations remain unknown, such as their relationship to the older translations, the rapidity with which they spread, and their popularity as a base for new commentaries.[1] This paper, nonetheless, concentrates on the humanist *commentary* tradition on the *Ethics*,

---

[*] The writing of this article was made possible through financial support from the Netherlands Organization for Scientific Research (NWO), grant 200-22-295. I thank my colleagues at Nijmegen's center for Medieval and Renaissance Natural Philosophy for their insights into the Aristotelian commentary tradition.

[1] See E. Garin, "Le traduzioni umanistiche di Aristotele nel secolo XV", *Atti e memorie dell'Accademia fiorentina di scienze morali 'La Colombaria'*, 16 (1947-50), 55-104; Ch.B Schmitt, "Aristotle's *Ethics* in the Sixteenth Century: Some Preliminary Considerations", in *Ethik im Humanismus*, eds. W. Rüegg and D. Wuttke (Beiträge zur Humanismusforschung, V), Boppard 1979, 87-112 (especially 87-103), rpt. in Ch.B. Schmitt, *The Aristotelian Tradition and Renaissance Universities*, London 1984. On Bruni's translation, see most recently J. Hankins, "Translation Practice in the Renaissance: The Case of Leonardo Bruni", in *Méthodologie de la traduction: de l'antiquité à la Renaissance*, Actes du Colloque, Rencontres Scientifiques de Luxembourg, ed. Charles Marie Ternes, Luxembourg 1994, 154-175 and idem, *Repertorium Brunianum. A Guide to the Writings of Leonardo Bruni*, I (Fonti per la Storia d'Italia, Subsidia, IV), Rome 1997. On Argyropoulos, see at least L. Frati, "Le traduzioni aristoteliche di G. Argiropulo e un'antica legatura Medicea", *La bibliofilia*, 19 (1917), 1-25 (especially 3-8); Garin, "Le traduzioni", 82-87; Ch.B Schmitt, *Problemi dell'aristotelismo rinascimentale*, Naples 1985, 107-112.

partly because it is better known[2] and partly because it well illustrates that the humanist contribution was not only formal or aesthetic. This paper will argue that the Florentine humanists' increasingly philological approach to the *Ethics* between the end of the fifteenth and the beginning of the sixteenth centuries led to a novel use of Aristotle's text, breaking the long-standing understanding of ethics as a *scientia practica*. The commentaries by Niccolò Tignosi, Donato Acciaiuoli, and Pier Vettori are especially indicative of this development. I begin with the latest commentary, by Pier Vettori, because it exemplifies the full application of philological methodology to the *Ethics*. In fact, Vettori's *Commentarii in X libros De moribus ad Nicomachum*, published in Florence in 1584, is known to scholars as one of the greatest sixteenth-century achievements in classical philology.[3]

When Vettori (1499-1585) published his commentary, he was very near the end of his life, which he had spent in the study and teaching of Greek and Latin. A former pupil of Francesco Cattaneo Diacceto, he was almost forty years old in 1538, when he was appointed by Cosimo I to teach Latin at the university in Florence. In 1543 Vettori also became professor of Greek language and literature and continued his teaching until 1583.[4]

---

[2] The most useful surveys of Renaissance *Ethics* commentaries are: R.A. Gauthier, "Introduction", in R.A. Gauthier and J.Y. Jolif, *L'Éthique à Nicomaque: Introduction, traduction, et commentaire*, 2 vols., 2nd ed., Louvain-Paris 1970, especially I, 138ff; J. Kraye, "Moral Philosophy", in *The Cambridge history of Renaissance philosophy*, ed. Ch.B. Schmitt with Q. Skinner, E. Keßler, and J. Kraye, Cambridge 1988, 303-386; eadem, "Renaissance Commentaries on the *Nicomachean Ethics*", in *Vocabulary of Teaching and Research between Late Middle Ages and Renaissance*, ed. O. Weijers (Etudes sur le vocabulaire intellectuel du moyen âge, VIII), Turnhout 1995, 96-117. Also see D.A. Lines, *Teaching Virtue in Renaissance Italy: Latin Commentaries on Aristotle's* Nicomachean Ethics, Ph.D. dissertation (Harvard University 1997), chs. 4-5.

[3] See R. Pfeiffer, *History of classical scholarship*, Oxford 1976, 135-136.

[4] For the literature see Ch.H. Lohr, *Latin Aristotle Commentaries, II: Renaissance Authors*, Florence 1988, 482-83. Vettori appears on the rolls of the Pisan *studio* (for teachings in Florence) only until 1581-82 (Morale e lingua greca, fl. 300), but for the next few years the teachers in Florence are not listed. See Archivio di Stato di Pisa (ASPi), Università , II° versamento, G.77, ff. 198r-200r, modern pagination. For the teachings and payments of Italian university professors during this period, see my *Teachers of Arts and Medicine in the Italian Universities ca. 1350-1630* (electronic database; first release 2000/01) which includes bibliographical references.

In his commentary, Vettori gave snippets of the Greek text of the *Ethics* that he had already published in 1547,[5] but he also provided his own Latin translation and then several lines of explanation for each passage under consideration (see fig. 1). Typically, Vettori's interpretative procedure is first to paraphrase Aristotle's text, often referring to specific Greek words and discussing their usage in classical Greek. Next he places Aristotle's points into a broader context, sometimes by referring to discussions of similar topics in the *Eudemian Ethics* and *Magna Moralia* or by other classical authors such as Cicero. As Jill Kraye has pointed out, Vettori's explanations also examine stylistic features in the text, solve variant readings, refer to historical examples, and quote classical poets.[6] He also writes, as one might expect of such a humanist, in a highly polished classical style.

Vettori's acuteness and philological skill have been widely recognized. However, two points about his commentary are especially noteworthy for our purposes here. The first is that Vettori's concern with Aristotle's *text* is joined with a comparative disinterest in its philosophical *problems*. For example, at the end of Book I, Aristotle discusses the various parts of the soul, in order to prepare his discussion of the acquisition of virtue in Book II. This passage represented a *locus classicus* for Aristotle's commentators, who in Italy as elsewhere discussed the differences between this partition of the soul and that found in the *De anima* and debated – *inter alia* – about the role of the will in producing virtuous actions. In his treatment of this last chapter of Book I, Vettori does note very briefly that Aristotle's account of the soul here is one of which he did not approve in the *De anima*, but he does not attempt in any way to reconcile the two views or to determine which one is correct. Vettori is equally unwilling to debate whether or not the inferior appetite that somehow partakes of reason should be identified with the will. He simply states that it is common knowledge (*notum est*) that the will, anger, and concupiscence reside in this particular part of the soul.[7] He then goes on with his textual observations.

---

[5] Kraye, "Renaissance Commentaries", 114.
[6] Kraye, "Renaissance Commentaries", 114-115.
[7] Vettori, p. 68. Vettori's reference to Aristotle's different partition of the soul in the *De anima* is on p. 65. Vettori treats this last chapter of Book I on pp. 62-70.

Φαίνεται δὲ καὶ ἄλογον, διττόν· τὸ μὲν γὰρ φυτικὸν, οὐδαμῶς κοινωνεῖ λόγῳ· τὸ δ' ἐπιθυμητικόν, καὶ ὅλως ὀρεκτικόν, μετέχει πως, ᾗ κατήκοόν ἐστιν αὐτοῦ, καὶ πειθαρχικόν, οὕτω δὲ καὶ τοῦ πατρὸς, καὶ τῶν φίλων φαμὲν ἔχειν λόγον, καὶ οὐχ ὥσπερ τῶν μαθηματικῶν.

Perspicitur igitur, & quod spoliatum ratione est duplex esse: quod enim proprium est eorum, quae gignuntur è terra; nullo modo communicat ratione, id autem in quo vigent cupiditates, demumq́ appetitiones, aliquo modo particeps est; ea parte qua non alienum est ab ea audienda: ipsíq́ obtemperandum: sic igitur dicimus & patris, & amicorum rationem habere, & non quemadmodum rerum mathematicarum.

PERSPICI iam inquit ex ijs, quae modo dicta sunt, animi partem, vacuam a ratione, non vnius generis esse, sed duplicem: ipsius enim genus quoddam est, quod funditus expers est rationis, illud inquam, quod φυτικὸν appellatur, quia quae gignuntur è terra, herbae inquam, frutices, atque arbores participes ipsius sunt, quare viuere dicuntur: alterum genus est, in quo cupiditates vigent: demumque quod est fomes appetitionum omnium, nam ὀρεκτικὸν genus esse; continereque in se & voluntatem, & iram, & cupiditatem notum est: hoc igitur aliquo modo particeps est rationis, quem modum, qui sit, indicat: auscultare enim ipsum inquit rationem, & obtemperare illi, cum libet: neque enim semper in potestate eius est; cum autem ipsum pati se persuaderi de eo pronuntiasset, vel potius habere ipsum rationem, & ἔχειν, vt loquuntur Graeci; hocque non vno modo dicatur, significat quomodo accipi hoc velit; aitque se hoc sensu edidisse, quomodo mos est dicere, quempiam rationem habere patris, & amicorum, idest sequi, ac probare consilia ipsorum; inducereque in animum ita facere, & non quomodo, mos est loquendi de rebus mathematicis, theorematis alicuius nos rationem habere; idest nosse, quomodo ipsum demonstrari possit: nec deesse argumentum, quo id comprobetur, ac verum esse intelligatur.

Fig. 1. Pier Vettori, *Commentarii in X libros De moribus ad Nicomachum* (Florence, 1584).

Vettori's reluctance to treat philosophical issues philosophically is perhaps one of the reasons why he refers so rarely to other commentators' interpretations of specific passages, unless to clarify the meaning of a particular practice referred to by Aristotle, or of a particular term.[8] Vettori's explicit avoidance of *multae et difficiles quaestiones* in his commentary also seems to confirm his main interest in clarifying and illustrating Aristotle's *verba* rather than addressing its philosophical problems. It is noteworthy that, although Vettori praises the *doctissimae elucubrationes* of St. Thomas' commentary,[9] the distance between the two works is as great as that between commentaries on philosophical and literary texts.

In addition to representing the *fullest* philological treatment of the *Ethics* in the sixteenth century, Vettori's commentary is also the *earliest* such treatment of Aristotle's work. It may seem surprising or even implausible that one has to wait until 1584 to find a philological commentary on the *Ethics*. After all, Leonardo Bruni had finished his retranslation of the *Ethics* already by 1417,[10] and the fifteenth century had seen other skillful translations of the work by able Hellenists such as Giannozzo Manetti and John Argyropoulos.[11] Yet, the studies by Rotondò, Bianchi, and Kraye[12]

---

[8] Vettori, for example, complains on p. 64 that other commentators did not understand Aristotle's reference to a specialist in healing the eyes on 1102b19-20. On the same page he generically praises some past commentators for having explained what Aristotle meant by *exoterikoi logoi* (*exoterici sermones,* an expression that had caused much difficulty for medieval interpreters); however, Vettori does not explain the expression.

[9] After pointing out that Aristotle considered inappropriate to ethics an overly subtle approach, Vettori maintains that several interpreters went against Aristotle's wishes by inserting numerous and difficult questions, which besides being obscure contribute little or nothing to training in ethics and in fact disturb more than they help. He praises instead the example of St. Thomas, who inserted few or no such questions in his own exposition: "Utilis autem valde, vel potius necessaria fuit haec praeceptio: cum multi in hoc labantur ac peccent, ut fortasse etiam non nulli fecerunt eorum, qui studio ac labore suo declarare hos libros voluerunt; inseruerunt enim huc multas et difficiles quaestiones, quae ut obscurae sunt, ita etiam saepe aliquando nihil, aut parum faciunt ad hanc de moribus disciplinam, potiusque perturbant, quam iuvent. ... Argumento huius rei esse potest, quod D. Thomas sapientissimus vir, nullas, aut paucas admodum huiuscemodi in suas doctissimas elucubrationes in hos libros inseruit" (7, spelling normalized).

[10] See Hankins, "Translation Practice", with bibliography.

[11] See Garin, "Le traduzioni umanistiche", passim.

[12] A. Rotondò, "Nicolò Tignosi da Foligno (Polemiche aristoteliche di un maestro di Ficino)", *Rinascimento,* 9 (1958), 217-255, especially his statement: "una filologia sul testo di Aristotele ... nel '400 in fondo non ci fu e ci fu soltanto tardi, con Pietro Vettori" (255); L. Bianchi, "Un commento 'umanistico' ad Aristotele: L'*Expositio super libros Ethicorum*

31

have shown that no commentary before that of Vettori really treats the *Ethics* philologically. Donato Acciaiuoli's commentary (first redacted in 1463–64)[13] can no longer be considered[14] the first application of philological methodology to the *Ethics*. And, although the commentary by the Frenchman Jacques Lefèvre d'Étaples[15] was important for delivering philosophy from countless *quaestiones* and *dubia*, it too did not go very far in the direction of philological analysis.[16] Denys Lambin may seem to be a better candidate, but his philological annotations on the *Ethics*, published in 1558, were not part of a commentary.[17]

What were the reasons for this late application of philology to the *Ethics*? Why is it that the *Ethics* was tackled long after other works in classical Greek? Many factors could be mentioned, including the immaturity of philology before Poliziano; here, however, I would like to emphasize two points: the changing institutional context of the *Ethics* in the university of Florence and the new understanding and use of the *Ethics* itself. As will become clear, these factors also played a role in Vettori's relative avoidance of philosophical argument in his commentary.

Vettori's treatment of the *Ethics* as a work of literature is doubtless connected with a change in the teaching of the *Ethics* at the university of Florence–Pisa. Traditionally the *Ethics* had been considered a work of moral philosophy, and as a branch of philosophy it had often been taught, in Italy, by natural philosophers. Not surprisingly, then, teaching appointments were often made to *philosophia naturalis et moralis*. During the fifteenth century, Florence saw a gradual weakening of this connection between ethics and natural philosophy: beginning with Andrea di Piero da Milano in 1422–23, it was not uncommon for ethics to be taught by

---

di Donato Acciaiuoli", *Rinascimento*, II s., 30 (1990), 29-55; Kraye, "Renaissance Commentaries".

[13] Donatus Acciaiolus, *Expositio super libros Ethicorum*, Florence 1478. See especially the autograph in Florence, BNC, Naz. II.I.104 (XV), 206ff.

[14] As had been suggested by E. Garin, *Medioevo e Rinascimento. Studi e ricerche*, 2nd ed., Rome, 1987, 240-44; idem, *La cultura filosofica del Rinascimento italiano. Ricerche e documenti*, Florence 1961; rpt. Milan, 1994, 102-106; Schmitt, *Problemi*, 42; and even Kraye, "Moral Philosophy", 328.

[15] Jacobus Faber Stapulensis, *Commentarii in X librorum moralium Aristotelis tres conversiones...*, Paris 1497.

[16] Kraye, "Renaissance Commentaries", 104.

[17] On Dionysius Lambinus, *In libros De moribus ad Nicomachum annotationes*, Basel 1558, see Kraye, "Renaissance Commentaries", 111.

teachers of rhetoric. Still, the connection with rhetoric was not at all stable during the fifteenth century: the teaching of ethics was assigned almost alternately to rhetoricians and to natural philosophers. One has only to recall names such as Simone Venturini, Guglielmo Becchi, Johannes Argyropoulos, Oliviero Senese, Calcondila, and Poliziano to appreciate the very different backgrounds of ethics teachers in fifteenth-century Florence.[18] The situation during the beginning years of the sixteenth century, until the temporary closure of the Florentine–Pisan *studio* in 1525, has barely been studied. However, in each of the nine years for which the teaching of moral philosophy is recorded, ethics is combined with one or another branch of philosophy.[19] The great change came in 1543, when the *studio* reopened. In that year, in Florence, Pier Vettori was charged with the teaching of ethics in addition to that of Latin and Greek;[20] a similar change occurred in Pisa in 1556, when Ciriaco Strozzi's appointment to Greek became "Philosophia moralis graeca et alia."[21] It is hard, of course, to know whether the folding of ethics into the course on Greek and Latin merely symbolized or instead encouraged the treatment of this text as a work of literature. However, Vettori's approach seems to be well in line with the new classification of this work in Florence–Pisa.

---

[18] See D.A. Lines, "The Importance of Being Good: Moral Philosophy in the Italian Universities, 1300-1600," *Rinascimento*, II s., 36 (1996), 139-93 (especially 169-71). On Florence's encouragement of both scholastic and humanistic studies, especially during the first half of the Quattrocento, see C. Vasoli, "L'insegnamento filosofico: uno studio tra scienza e 'humanae litterae' ", in *Storia dell'Ateneo fiorentino. Contributi di studio*, 2 vols., Florence 1984, I, 147-99.

[19] Specifically, Franciscus Zenobii de Diacceto was to teach either *philosophia ordinaria* or *ethica* in 1502-03 (A.F. Verde, *Lo studio fiorentino, 1473-1503*, 5 vols., Florence 1973-1994, II, 218-19); in 1503-1504, he was to teach moral and Platonic philosophy (Florence, Bib. Moreniana, ms. Bigazzi 109, f. 1r-2v). Raphael Donati de Franceschis taught logic and moral philosophy in 1509-11 (ms. Bigazzi 109, ff. 20v, 23r-24v); from 1518 to 1523 he taught moral philosophy along with *philosophia extraordinaria* (Archivio di Stato di Firenze, Studio fiorentino e pisano, n. 8, ff. 133v-134r, 136r-v, 138v and 98r).

[20] Lohr, *Renaissance Authors*, 482. But the university rolls do not list him as teaching "Morale e greca" until 1578-79 (ASPi, Università, II° versamento, G.77, ff. 188r-190r, new pag.).

[21] ASPi, Università, II° versamento, G.77, f. 144r (new pag.); cf. D. Barsanti, "I docenti e le cattedre dal 1543 al 1737," in *Storia dell'Università di Pisa*, 2 vols., Pisa 1993, II, 505-65 at 565.

This change in classification was apparently accompanied by a change in the audience of the *Ethics*.[22] For, whereas during the fifteenth century the *Ethics* was almost always a feast-day subject in Florence, with Vettori and Strozzi it gained the status of a regular and "ordinary" course.[23] This change had several consequences; from a strictly methodological viewpoint, it meant that teachers could expect their audience to have a particular preparation (in this case, knowledge of Latin and Greek); they were not addressing a general audience of interested persons whose level of preparation might be highly variable. However, whereas this change made it easier for teachers like Vettori to indulge in their philological analyses and still be followed by their students, it apparently led to no hightened expectation of the students' preparation in philosophy.[24]

The late application of philology to the *Ethics* is connected, not only with Florence's institutional context, but also with a changed understanding of this work as a promoter of virtue. As Georg Wieland has shown,[25] ethics had become a philosophical discipline in the thirteenth century, thanks especially to the efforts of Albert the Great and Thomas Aquinas. However, the philosophical treatment of the *Ethics* did not mean that the emphasis was on theoretical knowledge; rather, countless commentators insisted that the goal of such a study was well-ordered action. An understanding of what virtue is, how it is acquired and exercised, and how it helps us to flourish, should move us toward becoming good. In Wieland's view, fifteenth-century Italian humanists did not like to consider ethics as a philosophical discipline, and tried instead to connect it with their own *Bildungs-programm*, stressing the humanities as more proper studies

---

[22] For a fuller examination of this phenomenon, see my "*Faciliter edoceri*: Niccolò Tignosi and the Audience of Aristotle's *Ethics* in Fifteenth-Century Florence", *Studi medievali*, III S., 40.1 (June 1999): 139-68.

[23] On the distinction between "ordinary" and "extraordinary" courses in the medieval universities see especially O. Weijers, *Terminologie des universités au XIIIe siècle* (Lessico Intellettuale Europeo, 39), Rome 1987, 306-15. Weijer's descriptions, however, are not necessarily valid for the Renaissance period.

[24] Lines, "The Importance of Being Good", 152-53.

[25] G. Wieland, *Ethica – scientia practica: Die Anfänge der philosophischen Ethik im 13. Jahrhundert*, Habilitationsschrift for the Dept. of Philosophy, Rheinische Friedrich-Wilhelms-Universität, Bonn (Beiträge zur Geschichte der Philosophie und Theologie des Mittelalters, New series, XXI), Münster 1982, 4-5. For a different view, see Anthony Celano, "The End of Practical Wisdom: Ethics as Science in the Thirteenth Century," *Journal of the History of Philosophy*, 33.2 (April 1995), 225-243.

and exalting the combination of wisdom and eloquence. They too, however, thought of ethics as having practical aims and studied it avidly.

It seems to me that this view, so helpful for the medieval interpreters of the *Ethics*, should instead be slightly revised when it comes to the Italian humanists, at least to those in Florence. For, while it is certainly true that the humanists studied the *Ethics* avidly, it is not so clear that fifteenth-century humanists did not consider it a branch of philosophy;[26] on the other hand, whereas this philosophical view of the *Ethics* did not hinder its practical use in the fifteenth century, sixteenth-century humanists such as Pier Vettori do not really seem to have emphasized its practical aspects, in spite of paying lip-service to this feature in their verbose prefaces and dedications. For fifteenth-century Florence, the humanistically oriented commentaries on the *Ethics* by Niccolò Tignosi and Donato Acciaiuoli are especially relevant here, so I now turn to their handling of the *Ethics*.

Niccolò Tignosi (1402–1474) is best known as a physician and teacher of medicine in Florence and Pisa.[27] He produced a commentary on the *Ethics* sometime before 1464 (perhaps as early as 1458), when he was still active in Florence.[28] Tignosi's commentary is one of the first Florentine

---

[26] See, for example, Alamanno Rinuccini's thoughts on education, outlined and summarized by Verde, *Lo studio fiorentino*, IV.1, 77-84.

[27] The most important studies are L. Thorndike, "Some Unpublished Renaisance Moralists and Philosophers of the Second Half of the Fifteenth Century", *Romanic Review*, 18 (1927), 114-33; *idem, Science and Thought in the Fifteenth Century*, New York 1929, 161-79; Rotondò, "Nicolò Tignosi"; M. Sensi, "Niccolò Tignosi da Foligno: l'opera ed il pensiero", *Annali della Facoltà di Lettere e Filosofia, Università degli Studi di Perugia*, 9 (1971-72), 359-495; I. Barale Henneman, *Aspekte der aristotelischen Tradition in der Kultur der Toskana des XV. Jahrhunderts. Der philosophische Unterricht an der Universität Pisa von 1473-1502*, Pisa 1974, 33-111; *Convegno di studi maceratesi, 17: Francesco Filelfo nel quinto centenario della morte. Tolentino, 1981*, Padua 1986; and A. Field, *The Origins of the Platonic Academy of Florence*, Princeton 1988, 138-58.

[28] *Commenta in Ethicorum libros*. The work, never printed, survives in four manuscripts known to us: Florence, BNC, Gino Capponi, 314 (now missing Books V and X); Florence, B. Laur. Plut. LXXVI, 48 and 49; and Perugia, BCom. Augustea, L, 79. These manuscripts, first listed in Henneman, *Aspekte*, are briefly described in Field, *Origins,* 140-41, note 44. Ch.H. Lohr, "Medieval Latin Aristotle Commentaries. Authors Narcissus-Richardus," *Traditio*, 28 (1972), 306 overlooks the Perugian manuscript. The dating of Tignosi's commentary is not agreed upon. Based on internal evidence, Field places it between 1458 and 1461 (*Origins*, 141). Kraye instead dates it between 1461 and 1464 ("Renaissance Commentaries," 101). The commentary could also have been written considerably earlier, should Tignosi have inserted the references to contemporary events only later. The *terminus ante quem* is provided by Tignosi's defense treatise.

interpretations to cover all ten books of the *Ethics* and to base itself upon Bruni's translation; it also explains Aristotle's text fairly directly, does not often name other commentaries (although it does interact with them), and makes only moderate use of *quaestiones*. Tignosi's commentary is also meant for the followers of the *studia humanitatis* (as appears from the *Opusculum* in which he defended his commentary). All of these are characteristics it shares with the contemporary commentary by the Augustinian Hermit Guglielmo Becchi.[29] However, in many ways Tignosi uses techniques that are quite different from those of Becchi; for example, his work is not a paraphrase such as Becchi's, but a commentary in the proper sense; it differs from Becchi's and from other models available to Tignosi by almost completely neglecting the *divisio textus*; by introducing syllogisms to explain Aristotle's arguments only rarely, and even then not formally; by his occasional use of the original Greek rather than of Latinized Greek forms; by his abundant use of historical examples, taken from the classics but also from contemporary events; and by his references to (and quotations from) classical poets and poetry.

A nearly contemporaneous and much better known commentary is that by Donato Acciaiuoli.[30] Acciaiuoli's commentary was first printed in 1478 and is closely related to the lectures on the *Ethics* given by the Byzantine John Argyropoulos in Florence, starting in February 1457.[31] Like Tignosi's commentary, it too is based on a new translation (but by Argyropoulos), covers all ten books, is meant for a humanistic audience, may be described as a literal commentary, and names other commentators only rarely, although it too makes great use of them. Like Tignosi's, but more deftly and frequently, it too refers to the original Greek. Also like Tignosi's, it is not written in Ciceronian Latin and solves various *dubia* and questions.[32]

---

[29] Guillelmus Becchius Florentinus, O.E.S.A., *Commentum super X libris Ethicorum*, in Florence, BLaur., Aed. 153 (A.D. 1456), ff. 128. Cf. Ch.H. Lohr, "Medieval Latin Aristotle Commentaries. Authors G-I," *Traditio*, 24 (1968), 195.

[30] The main discussions of Acciaiuoli's *Expositio super libros Ethicorum* are by Garin in *Medioevo e Rinascimento,* 199-267; Field, *Origins*, ch. 8; and Bianchi, "Un commento"; also see Kraye, "Renaissance Commentaries", 99-101.

[31] See the prolusion in Florence, Bib. Riccardiana 120 (XV), ff. 1-36.

[32] Several of these characteristics are pointed out in Bianchi, "Un commento". Bianchi notes the persistence of philosophical questions in Acciaiuoli's commentary even though they are not introduced in the traditional scholastic manner.

Indeed, this last feature points to a common interest on the part of both commentators: to explore and solve philosophical problems. An example is the last chapter of Book I, the same passage on which Vettori commented so unphilosophically. Tignosi devotes several questions to the various parts of the soul and to the location of moral virtues; after distinguishing five parts within the soul, Tignosi centers his attention on the last three elements. He views the sensitive appetite as subservient to the rational appetite, which is in turn subservient to reason; he identifies the rational appetite with the will and describes this as the place in which moral virtues really reside (f. 28ra–va). Tignosi explains that the intellective or rational appetite inclines one toward what the intellect has judged to be good or otherwise. Acciaiuoli likewise discusses the philosophical issues of this passage in some detail (ff. 36v–39r). He describes at length the parts of the soul and especially points out that the *appetitus sensitivus* or *concupiscens* is only rational *per partecipationem* and not *per essentiam*. He presents the contrasting views by Plato and Scotus on the *potentiae animae* (f. 37r–v); he stops to comment that the division of the soul shows that man is intermediate between the separate substances and the brutes (f. 39r). He responds to possible objections against Aristotle's arguments, clarifies the meaning of enigmatic phrases (e.g. *externi sermones*), inserts *notabilia*. The attention is fully on the philosophical issues and on the articulation of Aristotle's arguments. There really can be no question that both Tignosi and Acciaiuoli consider ethics to be a part of philosophy and treat Aristotle's text philosophically.

This does not mean, however, that they see Aristotle's text as a mere intellectual playground, much as is done in philosophy classes today. Rather, their application of rhetorical techniques to their exposition points in the opposite direction. Tignosi, for example, does not make much use of syllogisms or of the *divisio textus*; instead, he enlivens his prose by the use of historical examples and quotations from poetry – a practice which he later had to defend.[33] The defense itself is noteworthy: Tignosi justifies his use of poetry and historical examples by appealing to the example of Plato, Aristotle, and other philosophers, who referred to these kinds of matters in their own works. He is explicit about his intention to follow in their

---

[33] The full title of Tignosi's defense treatise, often just referred to as *Opusculum*, is *Nicolai Fulginatis ad Cosmam Medicem in illos qui mea in Aristotelis commentaria criminantur opusculum*. The treatise is edited in Sensi, "Niccolò Tignosi", whose edition I follow. For a fuller examination of the treatise, see my "*Faciliter edoceri*".

steps.[34] Thus, Tignosi's technique is in part explained by the humanists' oft-repeated desire to imitate the style of the ancients. To my knowledge, this was the first time in Florence that such a desire was applied to the exposition of Aristotle's *Ethics*. Second, although Tignosi did not dare say so explicitly, one suspects that poetry and examples from history were to provide Aristotle's text with the persuasive and edifying power whose absence Petrarch had lamented a century earlier in his *De sui ipsius et multorum ignorantia*. Admittedly, this point is hard to prove, but Tignosi's strategy seems to have had the same purpose as that adopted years later by Lefèvre d'Étaples: to encourage even the amateurish first-comer toward an immediate exercise of virtue. Thus, Tignosi's work was practical in a double sense: it both explained the principles of ethics and actively encouraged the reader to practice them.

Acciaiuoli's commentary does not quote the poets or cite historical examples as does Tignosi's, but this does not necessarily indicate that there is not, in Acciaiuoli's commentary, a close relationship between rhetoric and moral philosophy. Acciaiuoli simply chooses different strategies from those of Tignosi: for example, the work includes apostrophes to Aristotle and makes heavy use of syllogisms to outline Aristotle's arguments. Both of these techniques had been features of Eustratius' commentary and were part of the Byzantine rhetorical tradition. Furthermore, Acciaiuoli does, now and then, cite classical authors (especially Cicero). If Acciaiuoli did not follow Tignosi in his use of the poets and historians, he had many reasons to do so – from the pressure of tradition to a desire to present his readers with the very words of the great Byzantine teacher. Certainly it could be said that Acciaiuoli's rhetorical techniques – including the very detailed and sometimes annoying division of the text into chapters, sections, and subsections – served the purpose of enhancing clarity, which was also one of the goals of Tignosi's commentary. In the end, though, one must concede that Acciaiuoli's commentary contains none of the strategies that both enlivened Tignosi's prose and gave it a function of immediate edification for the reader. Nor does Acciaiuoli seem very anxious to discuss practical issues of education that are directly connected with the teaching and acquisition of virtue. Thus, while Acciaiuoli's commentary certainly retains the potential of being ultimately practical by first providing a theory of ethics, it also represents a step backward when compared with the

---

[34] "Ego vero secuturus istorum vestigia, puto" (Sensi, "Niccolò Tignosi," 479).

immediately practical intent of Tignosi's work. In any case, what is important is that, while applying rhetorical (but not philological) techniques to their explanation of the text, both Tignosi and Acciaiuoli wish to deal with the *Ethics* as ethics: as a branch of philosophy whose principles must be understood and then practiced. There is, in their approach, none of Poliziano's desire to treat philosophical texts as a *grammaticus,* or of Vettori's emphasis on the philological aspects of the work. It would seem that, as philology matured in the hands of these two great Florentine scholars, some aspects of the texts themselves had to be sacrificed: Aristotle's *Ethics* lost its character as a practical guide to virtue under the searching scalpel of the philologist looking for things other than philosophy or exhortations to virtue.

We might conclude that, in their approach to the *Ethics,* Florentine humanist commentaries underwent an evolution. The works by Tignosi and Acciaiuoli both apply rhetorical techniques, but remain firmly centered on the philosophical issues in the *Ethics.* Thus, both can rightly claim to combine wisdom and eloquence according to the model of fifteenth-century humanism. Although to a different degree, both works also still treat ethics as a practical science. Already, however, it is possible to detect some developments that would have long-term effects. For example, Acciaiuoli's commentary has a philosophical agenda (the reconciliation of Plato and Aristotle)[35] that is quite absent in Tignosi's work and that in fact shocked Tignosi. Many later commentaries engaged in their own particular kinds of reconciliations or tried to prove particular philosophical (or even theological) points.[36] A further development concerns the issue of style: for, whereas Tignosi did not consider stylistic elegance necessary in a commentary,[37] Acciaiuoli obviously did; his commentary may not be written in Ciceronian Latin, but it is surely far more polished than Tignosi's. For Vettori, stylistic considerations were of such importance that

---

[35] On this aspect of Acciaiuoli's commentary see especially Field, *Origins,* 209-21.

[36] See especially Kraye, "Moral philosophy", 319-25 and 342-48 on the Renaissance attempts to reconcile classical and Christian ethics. On the reconciliation of Plato and Aristotle in Florence and especially in Padua in the sixteenth century, see A. Poppi, "Il problema della filosofia morale nella scuola padovana del Rinascimento: Platonismo e Aristotelismo nella definizione del metodo dell'Etica", in *Platon et Aristote à la Renaissance* (De Pétrarque à Descartes, XXXII), Paris 1976, 103-46, rpt. in A. Poppi, *L'etica del Rinascimento tra Platone e Aristotele,* Naples 1997, 11-87.

[37] Sensi, "Niccolò Tignosi", 470-71.

he dismissed Acciaiuoli's style as "barbarous".[38] The link between Acciaiuoli and Vettori is surely Lefèvre d'Étaples, who wrote his commentary in Ciceronian Latin and gave ever less attention to philosophical problems.[39] However that may be, this growing concentration on stylistic issues may be taken as an indication of what increasingly captivated the Florentine humanists as they approached the *Ethics*.

To say this is, of course, to challenge the orthodoxy that the humanists – whether viewed as rhetoricians or as philosophers – had a methodology that can easily be isolated and that retained similar emphases during the fifteenth and sixteenth centuries. An examination of humanist *Ethics* commentaries both within and outside of Florence will readily show both assumptions to be questionable. Sometimes the emphasis of a commentary is on philosophical issues (as in Tignosi and Acciaiuoli); at other times it centers on philological points (as in Vettori); and sometimes the two emphases are combined (as in Muret's teaching in Rome). Some commentaries are written in classicizing style, but others not. Every commentary depends on its own special blend of Greek and Latin commentaries. Some commentaries are intent on promoting a specific theological or philosophical viewpoint; others leave these considerations aside altogether. Some commentaries refer constantly to the Greek text, whereas others do not; the choice of Latin translation is also highly variable.[40] As we have seen, the *Ethics* is not even, in the same way, a promoter of virtue for its various interpreters.

We are already familiar with the concept of multiple Aristotelianisms in the Renaissance.[41] We also know that, already in the fifteenth century, there were serious divergences of opinion – even among the humanists – as to the relationship between philosophy on the one hand and rhetoric or philology on the other.[42] From here it seems but a small step to admit that humanist

---

[38] See Vettori's letter from around 1546 in L. Cesarini Martinelli, "Contributo all'epistolario di Pier Vettori (Lettere a don Vincenzio Borghini, 1546-1565)", *Rinascimento*, II s., 19 (1979), 189-227 at 199.

[39] See Kraye, "Renaissance Commentaries", 104-06.

[40] For a survey of different approaches to the *Ethics* in the Renaissance, see Kraye, "Renaissance Commentaries". Also see my forthcoming *Moral Education in Renaissance Italy: Aristotle's* Ethics *and the Universities*.

[41] See Ch.B. Schmitt, *Aristotle and the Renaissance*, Cambridge, Mass. 1983.

[42] See most recently Jill Kraye's excellent article, "Philologists and Philosophers," in *The Cambridge companion to Renaissance humanism*, ed. J. Kraye, Cambridge 1996, 142-60.

approaches to Aristotle may have changed over time. If the idea of applying philology to the *Ethics* was barely practiced in fifteenth-century Florence, it would no longer be so in the sixteenth century. But this is no reason for isolating, say, Vettori's approach as the truly humanistic one, while giving only half-humanistic status to the approaches by Tignosi or Acciaiuoli.[43] To be sure, in the end the largely grammatical and philological concerns of humanists like Poliziano would win the upper hand in Florence; but in the case of the *Ethics,* this development occurred only at the cost of divorcing the fifteenth-century humanistic union of wisdom and eloquence and of revising the long-standing treatment of Aristotle's *Ethics* as a practical science. These were changes that could occur only through an evolution within humanist Aristotelianism in Florence.

The fact that humanist understandings and treatments of the *Ethics* were multifarious and underwent a development does not, however, necessarily mean that they had nothing in common. In particular, two general features are noteworthy. First, there is a common ideal, based on a more or less common audience. For example, Tignosi's commentary displays an unusual concern with making Aristotle's text as clear as possible to non-specialists in Aristotelian philosophy. Of course, he does not direct his exposition to those who are not even willing to *attempt* an understanding of the text, but he does concentrate on explaining it to the non-initiate.[44] The style in which Acciaiuoli's commentary is written, as well as its explanation of fairly elementary concepts, shows a similar preoccupation. As we have seen, Vettori's commentary is also directed to those without much background in philosophy. The level of preparation of the humanists' audience is significant. Explanations of Aristotle's text (at least in the case of the *Ethics*) had to be adapted to their needs, interests, and background. In contrast with the scholastics, whose technical vocabulary was forbidding to outsiders, the ideal was to make Aristotle's text accessible to the professional and the newcomer alike. Thus, whereas the text may have been interpreted and approached in many different (and even contradictory) ways, the ideal and audience did provide something in common – whether or not the ideal was actually fulfilled or the audience satisfied.

---

[43] Kraye, for example ("Renaissance Commentaries", 101-02), describes Tignosi's approach to the *Ethics* as "creeping humanism" given his continued use of several traditional expository techniques. But assigning commentaries different levels of humanism raises more problems than it solves.

[44] See my "*Faciliter edoceri*".

A second common feature of humanist commentaries on the *Ethics* is the application of rhetorical techniques to the exposition of the text. As we have seen in the cases of Tignosi and Acciaiuoli, one need not expect the *same* techniques to be used, nor should one confuse rhetorical techniques with philological discussions. Again, an interpreter need not be a professional rhetorician in order to apply such techniques. Still, the ideal of clarity and the needs of the audience seem to have encouraged the use of rhetorical strategies; although the use of these strategies to stimulate virtue seems not to have survived in sixteenth-century *Ethics* commentaries, their encouragement of a close encounter with Aristotle's text did. In this connection, it is worth noting a deliberation of Florence's Ufficiali dello Studio in 1499: teachers of ordinary philosophy were reminded to teach the commentaries on Aristotle's works only after having taught the text itself.[45] One may well think of this as an effect of humanist methodology on the teaching of Aristotle in the university.

Admittedly, there is some fuzziness to these characteristics of humanist Aristotelianism: ideals, audiences, and rhetorical techniques do not translate into universally recognizeable features that allow one to immediately label a commentary as "humanistic" or not. Still, if humanist Aristotelianism is to be a useful concept for historical discussions, a fuzzy view that takes into account variations in time and place may be preferable to forcing humanist discussions into a single mould and arguing as to which treatment of Aristotle best conforms to this ideal type. True incarnations are hard to come by; human history has experienced only One.

---

[45] The text, dated 25-X-1499 and taken from Archivio di Stato di Firenze, Ufficiali dello Studio, 6, f. 57r-v is published in Verde, *Lo studio fiorentino*, IV, 1339.

ARISTOTLE AND PERSPECTIVE IN THE EARLY ITALIAN RENAISSANCE

by Marianne Marcussen

In art history we constantly reconsider a problem which has never been fully solved, namely how perspective came into being in the first quarter of the fifteenth century. In this paper I want to suggest that the works of Aristotle, and especially the distinction he draws between pure and applied mathematics, might have helped to pave the way for the invention of perspective and the manner in which it was put into pictorial practice.

From documentary evidence we know that it was an artist who invented perspective, the architect Filippo Brunelleschi (1377-1444), and not a philosopher, a mathematician, a natural philosopher, or a specialist in the science of optics. But the invention must have taken both advanced mathematical and other intellectual and technical abilities to make it work in a pictorial and artistic context. Using a term current in Italian Renaissance studies, we could call the inventor of perspective a humanist, meaning an interdisciplinary specialist, drawing on knowledge from many different fields, presumably without any uneasy feeling of trespassing into foreign disciplines.

In the *Dictionary of the History of Ideas,* under the heading of "Infinity", the mathematician Salomon Bochner writes:

> The standard perspective of the visual arts, which was created in the sixteenth century, features a "vanishing point." This is a concrete specific point ... in an underlying geometry ... Mathematics since then, and especially in the nineteenth century, has introduced various mathematical constructs with infinitely distant points in them ... There were no such tangible developments before the Renaissance.[1]

In all the literature on perspective it is hard to find a more precise statement, albeit unsupported in the article by references from art history. But this is a perceptive and attentive mathematician, who realises that there is more to the problem than meets the eye. And with whatever premises we try to explain the advent of perspective, there is one thing we must

---

[1] *Dictionary of the History of Ideas*, vol. II, New York 1973, 604-617, at p. 612.

necessarily underline: its uniqueness. Whatever is there before in the artistic representation of space, is different.

But Salomon Bochner's statement does not deal with the development of perspective as art historians would do, namely with reference to the dating problem and the problem of the construction of space in itself. He focusses on a more specific part of the perspective problem in the mathematical sciences, as it appeared in the development of projective geometry in the sixteenth and seventeenth centuries. To go further with this distinction, it obviously makes no sense to look for the origins of the construction and its mathematical implications in style analysis or in the history of style as traditionally understood. The necessary conceptual framework is one which present-day researchers have gradually come to find more relevant than it appeared earlier.[2]

Here I focus on the impact of Aristotle. The ancient philosopher – or, as he was called in the Middle Ages, the Philosopher – has been almost absent from the literature on the development of perspective, except in the famous article of Erwin Panofsky, *Perspective als symbolische Form*, dating from 1927.[3] So can Aristotle play a part in the solution of a pictorial problem?

In the first written account of perspective, Leon Battista Alberti's *De Pictura* of 1435, we read: "... no one will deny that things which are not visible do not concern the painter, for he strives to represent only the things that are seen."[4] This phrase is logically puzzling, since art works often depict a non-visible reality, for example God, angels, monsters etc. Therefore, when we interpret pictures and identify objects in them, we are often reasoning about the iconography of mental images, images in our imagination, and images we can recall, a process described in Aristotle's *De Memoria et Reminiscentia*, to which I shall return.

Alberti's phrase, in my opinion, acquires a deeper meaning if we consider the passage in *De Sensu* where Aristotle says:

---

[2] For example Hubert Damisch, *The Origin of Perspective*, Cambridge, Mass. 1994, (orig. in French, *Origines de la Perspective*, Paris 1987); James Elkins, *The Poetics of Perspective*, Ithaca, London, 1994 and J.V. Field, *The Invention of Infinity*, Oxford 1997.

[3] Erwin Panofsky, "Perspektive als symbolische Form", *Vorträge der Bibliothek Warburg 1924-25*, Leipzig, Berlin 1927, 258-330, (English translation, *Perspective as Symbolic Form*, New York 1991).

[4] Leon Battista Alberti, *On Painting and On Sculpture. The Latin texts of De Pictura and De Statua*, edited with translation and introduction by Cecil Grayson, London, Bath 1972, 37.

> A difficulty might arise as to whether, if every body is susceptible of infinite division, the attributes *perceived* are also so susceptible, . . . (And he concludes:) But its parts must be perceptible, for they *cannot* consist of mathematical abstractions (my italics).[5]

Since the quotation is from *De Sensu* this argument relates to visual perception rather than mathematics. The distinction he draws is one which he worked out in the *Physics,* and concerns the difference between pure and applied mathematics. In Aristotle's own words:

> . . . we have next to consider how the mathematician differs from the physicist . . . for natural bodies have surfaces and occupy spaces, have lengths and present points, all which are subjects of *mathematical* study (my italics).[6]

The distinction Aristotle is making therefore sets pure mathematics apart from physics, in the sense that the investigation of mathematical problems and the manipulation of volumes, lines and points are "in separation from the motions of the bodies".[7] As far as motion is concerned, his sharp distinction did not survive the fourteenth century. It had to be rephrased to meet new scientific developments in natural philosophy. Keith Devlin points out that "the key to the development of a mathematical treatment of motion and change was to find a way to handle infinity".[8] But besides that, it seems that this quest either had an effect on painting or, as Salomon Bochner hinted, actually began in the world of art.

In relation to perspective we could argue (Fig. 1a and b) that the vanishing lines (the orthogonals) meeting in a vanishing point, Vp, represent infinitely/ indefinitely long lines, e.g. l. In perspective the orthogonals can be divided by transversals, e.g. t, indefinitely, before meeting at the vanishing point. Therefore lines of a *finite length*, namely from the groundline, Gl, to the vanishing point, Vp, represent a sample of infinitely/indefinitely long lines being divided indefinitely.

But since painting deals with visualization, it is essential to consider perception. In relation to optics (the science of vision) and perception Aristotle says in the *Physics* that "the geometer deals with physical lines, but

---

[5] Aristotle, *On the Soul, Parva Naturalia, On Breath*. English translation by W.S. Hett, London, Cambridge Mass. 1925, 255.

[6] Aristotle, *The Physics* with an English translation by Philip H. Wicksteed and Francis M. Cornford, London, Cambridge Mass. 1929, 193b, p. 119.

[7] *Ibid.*

[8] Keith Devlin, *Mathematics. The Science of Patterns*, New York 1994, 76.

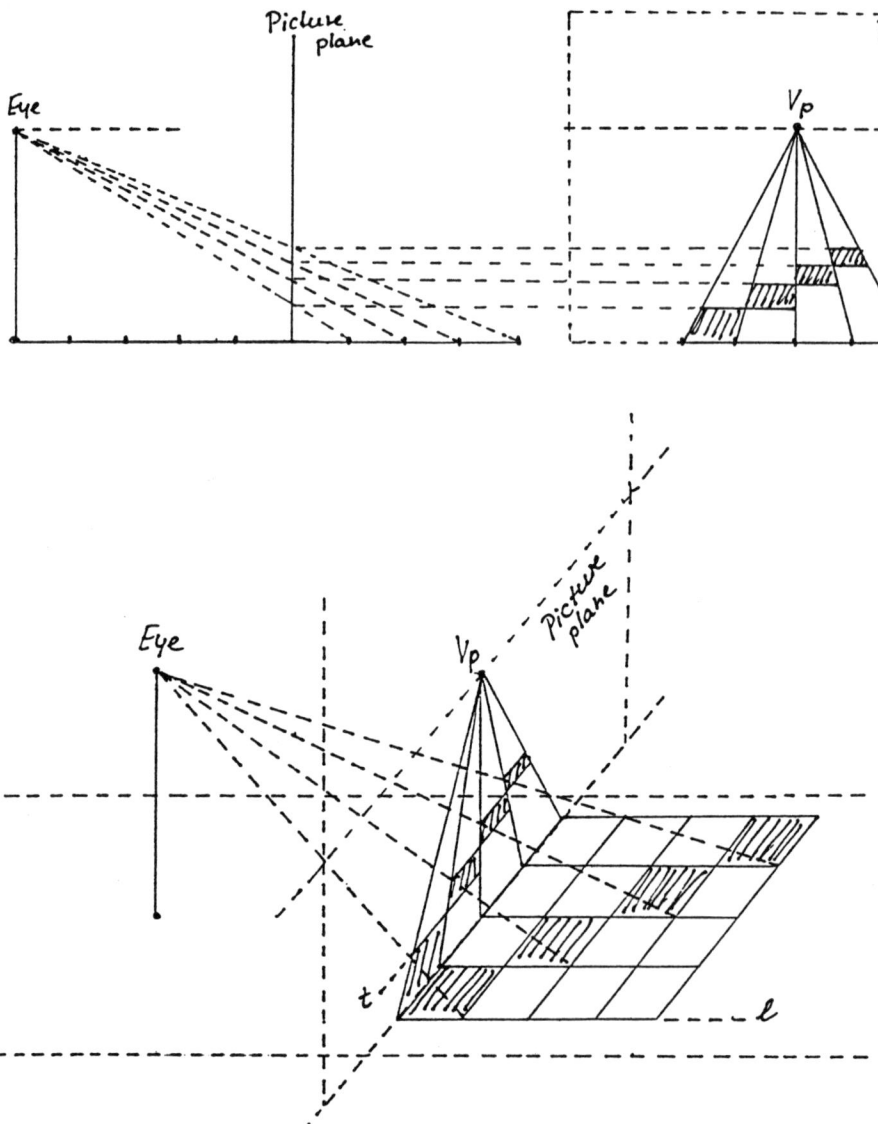

Fig. 1a-b. The most common interpretation of Leone Battista Alberti's description of the perspective construction from *De Pictura* (fig. 1a). None of the early manuscripts are illustrated. The drawing of the foreshortened chequerboard "floor" must be thought of as transparent, in Alberti's words as a "window" (fig. 1b).

not *qua* physical, whereas optics deals with mathematical lines, but *qua* physical not *qua* mathematical."[9] This distinction may, I think, have been of importance for the development of perspective, as paving the way for a fresh study of the difference between natural and pictorial perception. This study helped to coordinate those optical, mathematical and other concepts which were necessary for the perspective construction.

In the first place we could argue that perspective is applied mathematics – in this case applied geometry – which is also the tool for describing things seen or perceived in geometrical optics. And the way in which the two sciences are handled in Alberti's treatise is necessarily an application of mathematics, because painting has to do with a visualization of the mathematical concepts of point, line, plane and volume. Presumably it is for this reason that Alberti, already in the midst of definitions which have been investigated by mathematicians since Antiquity, writes a few lines later that "a point is a sign which one might say is not divisible into parts". And he continues: "I call a sign anything which exists on a surface so that it is *visible to the eye*" (my italics).[10]

Alberti's two statements might sound like a contradiction, but he seems to follow Aristotle's reasoning in *De Sensu*. And it was maybe this idea that Piero della Francesca developed and explained in his *De prospectiva pingendi* (mid or late fifteenth century). He says that a point is visible, and so small that it can (accurately) be perceived by the eye, "tanto picholina quanto è posibile ad ochio comprendere".[11] Alberti's and Piero's views may therefore be inspired by Aristotle's *De Sensu*, where we also learn that:

> It is of course clear that every sensible object is a magnitude, and that no sensible object is indivisible ... But the interval over which it can be seen is limited ... But there is an extreme point of the interval at which it is not seen, and a first point at which it is seen. This point must necessarily be indivisible, the point beyond which it is impossible to see anything, and within which one must be able to see it.[12]

Therefore the vanishing point Vp in fig. 1 can represent a point or the limit when things become visible or invisible. This does not violate mathematical ideas, since we are involved here not in pure mathematics but in a discourse

---

[9] Aristotle, *The Physics, op. cit.*, 194a, p. 121.
[10] Leon Batista Alberti, *op. cit.*, 37.
[11] Piero della Francesca, *De prospectiva pingendi*, a c. di G. Nicco Fasola, Firenze 1974, 65.
[12] Aristotle, *On the Soul, op. cit.* 277.

on vision and/ or visual perception. Therefore both Alberti and Piero uphold – so far – the Aristotelian distinction between pure and applied mathematics. And the distinction is present, perhaps often as a tacit presupposition, in medieval treatises on vision, including late perspectivists such as John Pecham (ca. 1235 – 1292), Domenico de Clivaxo (mid-fourteenth century) and Blasius de Parma (ca. 1345 – 1416),[13] even if the definitions of the point and the line and the concepts of volume, change, continuity and infinity are necessary to both pure and applied mathematics.

If we focus on the definition of the point and the line, then we might compare Aristotle's statement in *De Sensu*, where a point may be either invisible or visible, with the description of the visual ray and the eye(point) in Euclid's *Optics*.

If we look at three different translations, the interpretation of Euclid's definition seems to vary: "Let it be assumed . . . that the rectilinear rays proceeding from the eye diverge indefinitely . . ."; "Let it be assumed that lines drawn directly from the eye pass through a space of great extent . . . "; and "The ray issues from the eye in straight lines while producing straight paths of infinite multitude".[14]

Translation is always extremely difficult, and the tacit presuppositions of a given age are quite understandably incorporated in a text so as to make it comprehensible. The second translation may be the most cautious, since in the first the word "diverge" implies an endlessly expanding visual angle (the visual angle is explained in the next sentences of Euclid's text), and the word "indefinitely" as well as the word "infinite" in the third suggests infinity, a notion which may not be intended by Euclid? The concept of

---

[13] The late perspectivists are following Witelo, see Graziella Federici Vescovini, *Studi sulla prospettiva medievale*, Torino 1965, 22. Perspective means the construction in pictorial representation, perspectivists are the scientists who described the function and perception of vision. In the Renaissance we find the distinction between "perspectiva naturalis", meaning optics, and "perspectiva picturalis", meaning (pictorial) perspective.

[14] David C. Lindberg, *Theories of Vision from Al-Kindi to Kepler*, Chicago 1976, 12; Harry Edwin Burton, "The Optics of Euclid", *Journal of the Optical Society of America*, 15, 5 (May 1945), 357; Elaheh Kheirandish, *The Arabic Version of Euclid's* Optics, I-II, ed. and translated with historical introduction (Sources in the History of Mathematics and Physical Sciences, 16), New York 1999, I, 2; Wilbur R. Knorr has discussed the translation problem in relation to Euclid's *Elements*, in "The Wrong Text of Euclid: On Heiberg's Text and its Alternatives", *Centaurus*, 38 (1996), 208-276. Lindberg may also be taking the commentaries of Theon on Euclid's *Optics* into consideration.

infinity and the indefinite is discussed particularly in Aristotle's *Physics*,[15] and we might ask if Aristotle's distinction between pure and applied mathematics underlies Euclid's writings, since he turns from pure mathematics in the *Elements* and the *Data* to applied mathematics in the *Optics* and *Catoptrics*. In any case the treatment of the visual ray and eye(point) in the *Optics* and later optical treatises seems to have been so relevant for the explanation of vision and/or visual perception that the distinction is upheld, even during the invention of perspective in the fifteenth century, when, as will be shown presently, the inventor/s of perspective must have twisted, rephrased or softened it to meet the new demands of pictorial art.

The distinction between pure and applied mathematics is under pressure in the fourteenth century, basically as a result of the discussions of infinity in mathematics, natural philosophy and logic. One of the most sensible and inventive – scientists of the whole century, Nicolas Oresme (ca. 1325-1382), neatly balances the Philosopher's arguments on this problem and those of his fourteenth-century supporters and opponents.[16] When considering the definition of the point, he seems to find Euclid's definition from the *Elements*, "a point is that which has no part", unsatisfactory,[17] and he rephrases it as follows: "a point is that which has no part, but has position in a continuum" (Marshall Clagett's interpretation).[18] Oresme's use of the notion of position may have been inspired by Euclid's *Data*.[19]

---

[15] As far as the concept of infinity, continuity and position is concerned I have relied on John J. Cleary, *Aristotle and Mathematics. Aporetic Method in Cosmology and Methaphysics*, Leiden, New York, Köln 1995 (Philosophia Antiqua. A Series of Studies on Ancient Philosophy, vol. 67).

[16] I have relied here on: *Infinity and Continuity in Ancient and Medieval Thought*, ed. Norman Kretzmann, Ithaca, London 1982, (esp. articles by Norman Kretzmann, "Continuity, Contrariety, Contradiction and Change", 270-296, and Paul Vincent Spade, "Quasi-Aristotelianism", 297-307).

[17] Euclid, *The Thirteen Books of The Elements*, English translation and commentary by Thomas Heath (1. ed. 1908), repr. Dover Publications 1956, Book I, 155.

[18] Marshall Clagett, *Studies in Medieval Physics and Mathematics*, London 1979, 219 and 221 (esp. article on "The Use of Points in Medieval Natural Philosophy and most particularly in the *Questiones de spera* of Nicole Oresme", 215-221).

[19] I regard Euclid as a likelier source than Aristotle here, because Oresme is searching for a mathematical description of motion. For the Aristotelian definition of position see John J. Cleary, *op. cit.*, 144-45.

Oresme needed the concept of position, since he was working on the description of motion and wanted to describe it with the aid of pure mathematics. Likewise, several decades later, the inventor of perspective needed to determine the position of the eyepoint in order to make the mathematical construction of space work. For his own purposes Oresme had to soften the Aristotelian distinction. His argument sounds a new note, when he says:

> Every measurable thing except numbers is imagined in the manner of continuous quantity. Therefore, for the mensuration of such a thing, it is necessary that points, lines, and surfaces, or their properties, be imagined. For in them (i.e. the geometrical entities) as the Philosopher has it, measure or ratio is initially found . . . Although indivisible points or lines are non-existent, still it is necessary to feign them mathematically for the measures of things and for the understanding of their ratios.[20]

Oresme not only describes motion by means of pure mathematics but also visualises motion in his configuration doctrine. In his arguments for this he refers to visual models, for example triangles, taken from the science of optics, especially Witelo's *Perspectiua* of ca. 1270, but uses them in a different way.[21] That is, rather than describing vision with the help of geometry based on comparison or the notion of equal or unequal visual angles, as Euclid and the later perspectivists had done in their optical treatises, he describes motion by combining the visual models with the rules from Euclid's *Elements* on proportionalities.

In much the same way it was necessary in perspective to combine the definition of the visual angle, symbolized as a triangle, with the rules of proportionalities. Of this there is ample proof in Alberti's treatise *De pictura*.[22] And it was not difficult to associate motion with perspective, since points in given objects (existing or not) had to be "moved" along lines (represented by visual rays) on to the picture plane from positions behind it. Therefore it was necessary to bridge a conceptual gap between scientific

---

[20] *Nicole Oresme and the Medieval Geometry of Qualities and Motions. A treatise on the uniformity and difformity of intensities known as Tractatus de configurationibus qualitatum et motuum*. Edited with an introduction, English translation and commentary by Marshall Clagett, Madison 1968, 165; Marshall Clagett, 1979, 221 and Norman Kretzmann, *op. cit.* (esp. article of Calvin G. Normore, "Walter Burley on Continuity", 258-269).

[21] *Nicole Oresme and the Medieval Geometry*, 51.

[22] Leon Battista Alberti, *op. cit.*, 51ff, 59.

and pictorial traditions, before a visual model could make sense as a theoretical description both of motion and of visual representation in painting.

In optics we are in the realm of applied mathematics, and the visual rays, which Euclid believes to emanate from the eye, extend only as far as we can see. Likewise Aristotle pointed out that we cannot see infinitely long distances, though he did not hold that rays emanate from the eye. Moreover, we cannot see or perceive infinitely small quantities, for example on a given line segment. As soon as we turn our attention to such an approach to the infinity problem, we have moved into pure mathematics.

When Euclid and later scientists describe the act of seeing, the basic notions are the eyepoint and the visual angle. Euclid uses the notion of relation between the sizes of two or more visual angles, but, like later perspectivists, he does not convert those relations to proportionalities between line segments representing distances to the things seen. This kind of gauging (trigonometry) finds a mathematical form in Ptolemy's *Almagest*. But Ptolemy, who also held that rays emanate from the eye, did not apply this to the description of vision in his *Optics*.[23] Nevertheless, he regarded the distance to the objects seen as an important parameter in vision. In the later middle ages John Pecham also focussed on distance in visual perception, but did not apply the rules of proportionalities from Euclid's *Elements* to the description of vision. This idea became important, however, for the invention of perspective.

Euclid proves in his *Optics* that we do *not* gauge the size of two equal parallel quantities in the visual field in proportion to their distances from the eye (see fig. 2).[24] Euclid and later perspectivists use the notion of relations: greater than, less than, higher or lower than, to describe our judging of sizes, distances, and positions in the visual field – thereby relating vision to the position of the eye, defined as the vertex of the visual cone. This approach to optics did not change until Kepler, but that is another – and very well known – story, mentioned here only to recall the way in which vision was explained in optics in the early Renaissance. Therefore perspective is basically a different concept, a fact which supports

---

[23] A. Mark Smith, *Ptolemy's Theory of Visual Perception: An English Translation of the Optics*, Philadelphia 1996, 21ff (Transactions of the American Philosophical Society, New ser. vol. 86, no. 2).

[24] Burton, *op. cit.* 358 and Kheirandish, *op. cit.* I, 26.

Salomon Bochner's statement given at the beginning of this article. In relation to vision or perception, Euclid's geometrical proof makes sense even today, since it has not been proved that we do perceive sizes in the visual field in mathematical proportion to the distances from the eye. In consequence perspective cannot be regarded as identical to visual perception.

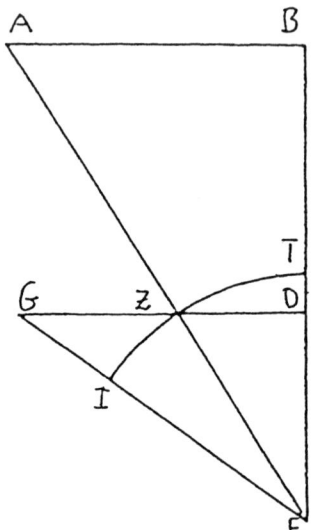

Fig. 2.
The diagram which in most editions accompanies Euclid's proof that we do not experience (equal) magnitudes (AB and GD) in the visual field in proportion to their distances (EB and ED) from the eye (E). Euclid holds that we measure magnitudes (AB and DG) in the visual field by the visual angles (AEB and DEG). Euclid concludes: since the ratio GD/ZD=BE/ED (GD=AB) is *larger* than the ratio between the angles EIT (spanning magnitude DG) to EZT (spanning magnitude AB), we do not experience the magnitudes in proportion to their distances from the eye.

The relevance to this discussion of position in the mathematical sense is not easily explained, but one may refer to Euclid's definition in the *Data*, where a point is said to be in position when it is determined by the intersection of two lines in position.[25] The position of the eye is in fact represented in the *Optics* as the intersection of any two legs of a visual angle; the angle is represented as the section of a cone having the eye at its vertex. If we refer to the definitions of the *Data*, a point is said to be given in position if it always occupies the same place. The eye-point given in

---

[25] *The Data of Euclid*. Translated from the text of Menge by George L. McDowell and Merle A. Sololik with introduction by Richard Delahide Ferrier, Baltimore 1993, prop. 25.

position, as described in Euclid's *Optics*, is certainly a point which occupies the same place; otherwise the visual perception of a thing within the visual angle would change as the position of the eye changes. This eventually becomes a basic notion in perspective.

As far as perspective is concerned, the notion of position of the eye point might also be derived from the *Optics* of Ptolemy, where it is much more elaborately described than in Euclid. Important for perspective is the priority given to the central visual ray:

> And since (each) visual ray terminates at its own unique point, what is seen by the central ray – i.e., the one that lies upon the axis (of the visual cone) – should be seen more clearly than what is viewed to the side (of the visual axis) by lateral rays... among objects whose appearance depends upon the quality of (radiative) effects, those that lie directly in front of, and at *right angles* to the rays are seen more clearly than those that do not (my italics).[26]

Ptolemy's definition is mirrored both in the medieval treatises on optics and in Alberti's definition of extrinsic rays, median rays and the central ray: "We call the centric ray the one which alone strikes the quantity in such a way that *the adjacent angles on all sides are equal*" (my italics).[27] If we apply this to perspective, what Alberti describes here is a frontal perspective, in which the position of the eye is at right angles to the groundplane, the picture plane and the object(s) depicted. Whether there are in fact any objects "out there" seems to be irrelevant (see the position of the eye in fig. 1).

As yet the gap has not been bridged between the pure mathematics of the *Elements* and *Data* and the "relational" geometry in the *Optics* and *Catoptrics* and later perspectivists. We can now look at this problem as it concerns perspective.

In Alberti's description proportionality is tied to the definition of perspective as a section of the visual pyramid (cone) represented by a triangle.[28] Moreover, he gives no mathematical explanation of his method, even though this is absolutely necessary for the construction of perspective. It is Piero who gives the proof, the first to do so, as far as I am aware; and we must infer that Brunelleschi – if his paintings really did use perspective in the geometrical sense – must have reflected on this problem and found

---

[26] A. Mark Smith, *op. cit.*, II 20 and II 19, 76-77.
[27] Leon Battista Alberti, *op. cit.*, 43, supposedly to mean a quantity in frontal position.
[28] Leon Battista Alberti, *op. cit.*, 49.

a way to span the gap between pure and applied mathematics. Here again Aristotle may have provided the inspiration. In *De Memoria*, which has many references to painting, he says:

> Let it be granted that one possesses a faculty by which to distinguish lesser and greater time; it is natural to suppose that we can distinguish these as we distinguish magnitudes... How then, when the mind thinks of bigger things, will it differ in thinking of them from when it thinks of smaller things? For all things inside are smaller, and in a sense *proportionate* to those outside. Perhaps, then, just as we suppose that there is something in man corresponding to figures, we may assume that there is something similarly corresponding in distances (my italics).[29]

To elucidate the gap between pure and applied mathematics in the two fields of depiction and motion, a comment is necessary on the relation between the concepts of dimension and depiction. In optics, even if most explanations of vision, perception and the judging of sizes and distances in the visual field are demonstrated by two-dimensional figures, vision operates in a three-dimensional ambience, and three-dimensional perceptions and judgments are the result. Oresme's visual model of motion represents motion in two dimensions. It has been shown, however, that he develops the idea that the mathematical model can be extended to represent three dimensions. Marshall Clagett says concerning Oresme's configuration doctrine:

> Finally we ought to suggest that our author (*sic!*) ... ignores (if indeed he knew of) Oresme's suggestion that the configuration doctrine might be extended to three dimensions to represent a surface quality. (*in Oresme's words*): Now reverting to the subject at hand, just as the quality of a point is imagined as a line, and the quality of a line by a surface, so the quality of a surface is imagined as a body whose base is the surface informed with the quality.[30]

Oresme develops this idea in his *Tractatus de configurationibus qualitatum et motuum*, where he has many references to Aristotle as well as to the perspectivists of the thirteenth century, especially Witelo.[31] Therefore we

---

[29] Aristotle, *On the Soul, op. cit.*, 321.
[30] Marshall Clagett, 1979, "The Pre-Galilean Configuration Doctrine: 'The Good Treatise on Uniform and Difform Surface'", IV, 5; *Nicole Oresme and the Medieval Geometry*, 175-77.
[31] *Nicole Oresme and the Medieval Geometry*, 51, 238-40.

can at least argue that science in the later middle ages focuses on visual model-making and the way in which the models can be combined with propositions from pure mathematics.

The same kind of reasoning seems to take place in the visual arts, where the construction of space is "lifted out" of the painting surface to be developed in abstracto, in two dimensions represented as two planes at right angles to each other, before the picture, representing three-dimensional space, is actually painted. This is shown in fig. 1.

Piero della Francesca gives the mathematical proof of the construction of perspective when he demonstrates the foreshortening of a square (fig. 3).[32] Here he shows how to bridge the gap between applied mathematics (a proposition from Euclid's *Optics*: "... and those (things) seen within equal angles appear to be of the same size"[33]), and pure mathematics (propositions on proportionalities from the *Elements*, VI, 2 and 4). See fig. 3: the eyepoint, A, is set in position in relation to a picture plane, BF. From the eyepoint each of the depicted sides of the square is *perceived* as being of the same size (according to Euclid's *Optics*); and then it is proved with the help of the *Elements* that since proportionality exists between the size of the foreshortened side EH, and the side furthest away, CG, this proportion relates to the position of the eyepoint and the picture plane. Moreover the foreshortening EH of CG will appear to be of the *same size*, on the same horizontal level in the picture plane, no matter where the eye is situated in the picture plane.[34] This proof could, I suppose, only have been arrived at if the picture plane was conceived of as a plane in terms of pure mathematics.

It seems, therefore, that there is a similarity in the treatment of pure and applied mathematics in the cases of Oresme's configuration doctrine and of the construction of perspective, and that Aristotle never ceased to be influential. The logicians of the Merton School, the scientists investigating the concept of the point, the line, space and the void, the concept of proportionality and its application to different physical situations achieved their breakthroughs in the period leading up to the fifteenth century.

---

[32] *De prospectiva pingendi*, tav. IV, fig. XIII.

[33] *De prospectiva pingendi*, tav. IV, fig. XIII and p. 76.

[34] *De prospectiva pingendi*, tav. IV, fig. XIII and p. 76.

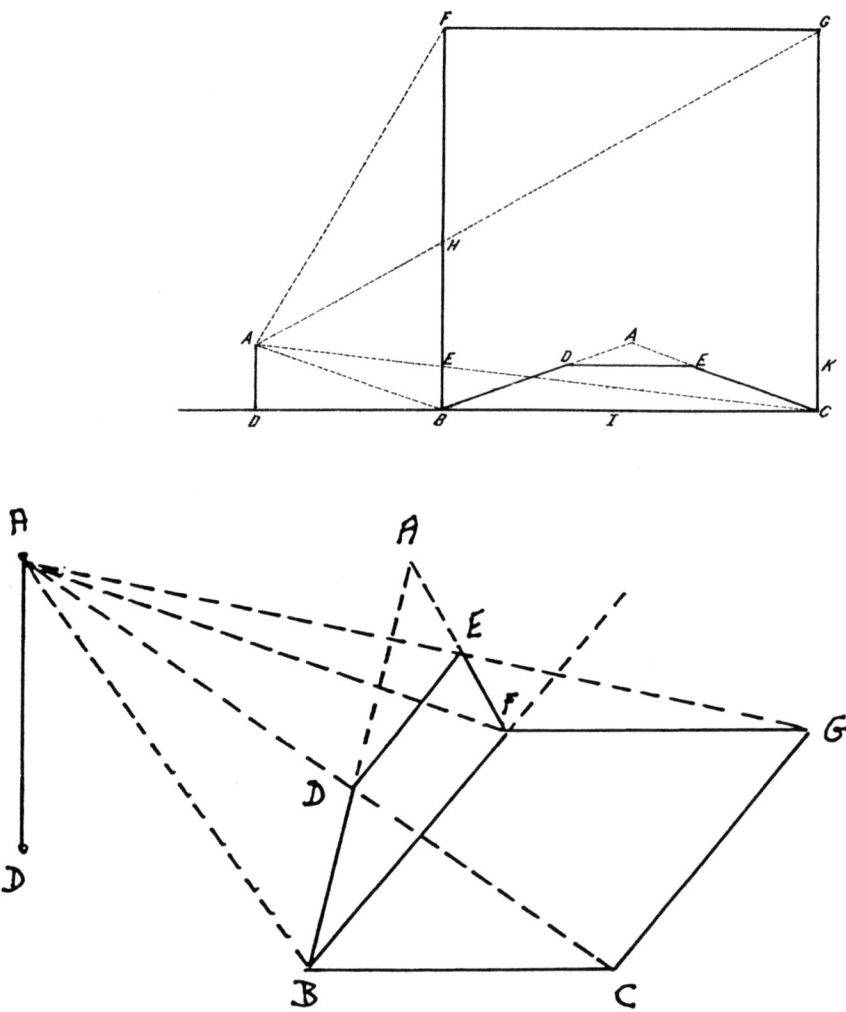

Fig. 3. Piero della Francesca's diagram XIII from *De prospectiva pingendi*. A represents the eye, AD the eyeheight, BCFG the square to be foreshortened, BCDE the foreshortened square. DE=EH (se below fig. 4), accompanied with a drawing in "3D", to show what Piero´s diagram represents as pictorial space.

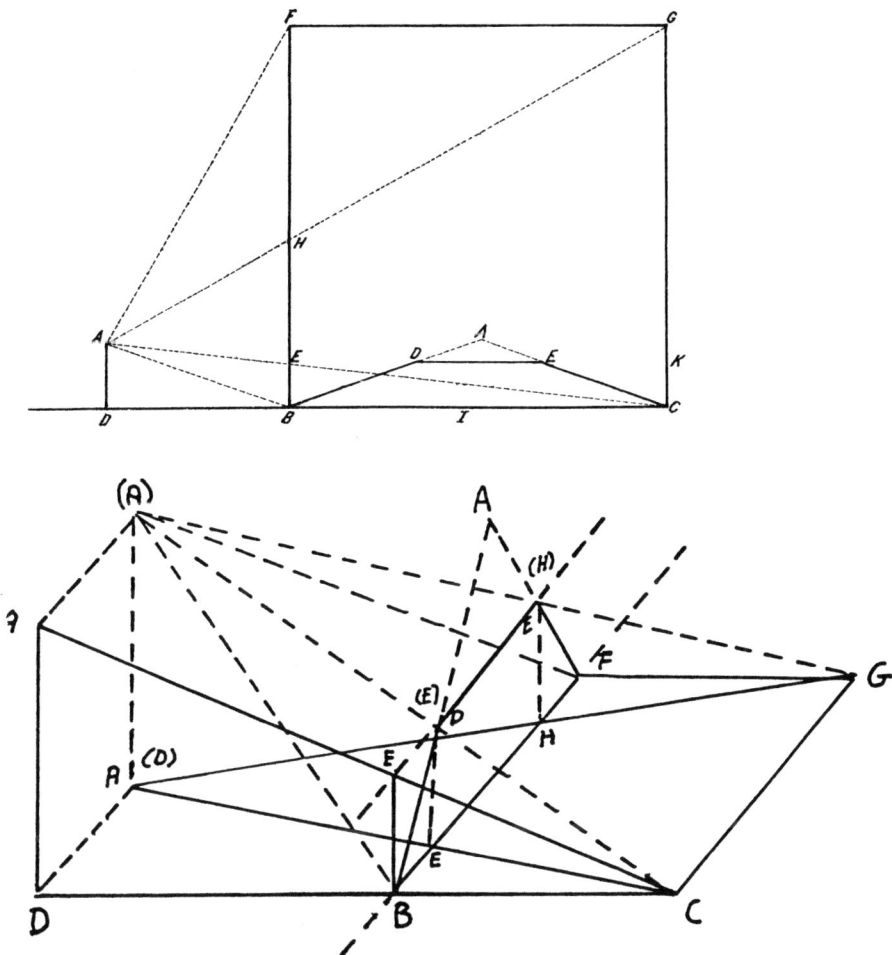

Fig. 4a- b. Piero's diagram XIII from *De prospectiva pingendi* compared to a "3D" drawing to give an idea – visually – of the proof Piero gives of the correctness of the foreshortening of the square. First Piero explains that BC will look alike to BE, (see Piero's diagram) since they are both "seen" under angle BAC (BF is representing the picture plane); CG will look alike to EH, since they are both "seen" under angle CAG; and FG will look alike to FH, since they are both "seen" under angle FAG.

Triangle DAC in Piero's diagram (4a) is identical to triangle DAC in the "3D" drawing (4b) and must be "seen" vertical (at right angles to the ground plane). Triangle CAG in Piero's diagram is identical to triangle C(D)/AG in the "3D" drawing and must be "seen" horizontal (lying in the groundplane). AD =(A)A/(D) and BE=ED/(E)=EH/(H). Since A/(D)C (see "3D" drawing) is common to triangle, A/(D)DC, (A)A/(D)C and A(D)CG, sides are in proportion, as a consequence of the fixed position of the eye A in relation to the picture plane. Therefore EH in Piero's diagram will be the same as DE in the foreshortened square. See "3"D drawing where EH=D/(E)E(H).

We have, however, no documentary evidence that Brunelleschi read Oresme, Swineshead, Burley or Heytesbury. On the other hand, some of the Italians certainly did, for example Casali;[35] and nobody would maintain that inspiration can have come only from Oresme.

As far as the concept of dimension is concerned, I should point out that Oresme imagines there to be a fourth dimension in a mathematical sense, though he does not elaborate the idea further. As far as depiction goes, perspective was called into question in consequence of the discussion of dimension in nineteenth-century mathematics.[36] So we can argue that in pure mathematics there lie embedded theories of depiction, which, when interpreted and applied, make sense as a depiction of space – or spatial illusion – in art. There has been no attempt here to arrive at a general theory of how to overcome the many "transformational" problems between art and the sciences. If we compare geometry and art works, we can see that no paintings are simply representations of a mathematical construction as such. Art works usually convey more to the observer than a diagram, since they involve visual or pictorial illusion. To study those problems it is necessary to take account of the artist's application of mathematics to works of art. Therefore we need to focus on the conceptual or philosophical aspects of the problems involved.

On the other hand a theoretical comment on the concept of explanation is necessary at this point. Supposing that Brunelleschi did in fact read a tract of Oresme's, we cannot conclude that he either liked it or made use of it. Equally, if he did not read anything by Oresme, we cannot rule out the possibility that he could have learnt about his ideas from someone else. As for the concept of the picture plane, the art of painting itself could have provided it. What I am sure was new was the detaching of the picture plane both conceptually and practically from the picture surface, and the contemplation of it as a mathematical plane having theoretical extension in relation to an eyepoint in a given position. It seems to me *a fortiori* that Brunelleschi must have reflected on the conceptual framework first. Without an extensive discussion of the relationship between depiction in

---

[35] *Nicole Oresme, and the Medieval geometry*, 66-71; Marianne Marcussen, "Space in Artistic Representation and Geometry", and "Perspective to Abstraction", *Pre-prints*, (Artikler om Rum og Farve), Institute for Art History and Theatre Research, University of Copenhagen, 1996, 1-16 and 231-254.

[36] Linda Dalrymple Henderson, *The Fourth Dimension and Non-Euclidian Geometry in Modern Art*, Princeton 1983, Marianne Marcussen 1996, 231-254.

art and the visual model-making for example of the natural philosophers, I would suggest that the gap could not have been bridged at all.

To conclude: When one starts to investigate the reasons for a change in the rendering of space in the visual arts, it is impossible to regard this change as one which took place entirely within the world of art. The concepts involved belong to a range of subjects of which I am sure the artists were well aware, at least those who participated in this development. But I do not think that the artists read all of mathematics, physics, philosophy, logic or optics. In some ingenious way they selected from ongoing discourses the ideas and concepts they found relevant to their art.

The introduction of perspective was a fundamental change for the whole world of art. It came into being, in my opinion, as one of the consequences of the fact that visual models became increasingly relevant for the natural sciences in the late fourteenth century.

GREEK AND LATIN LEARNING IN THEODORE GAZA'S *Antirrheticon*

by John Monfasani

Theodore Gaza's *Antirrheticon*[1] (in English, *Refutation*) was a product of the fifteenth-century Plato-Aristotle controversy. Yet, it itself had essentially nothing to do with the issues of the controversy. Furthermore, although it was written in Greek by a Greek to a Greek, it was provoked by a Latin text, had at its core a question of Latinity, and is only understandable with a knowledge of medieval Latin philosophy. Finally, though it is a work of philosophy, its most interesting aspects are psychological and historical. It has a lot to tell us about Theodore Gaza, Cardinal Bessarion, and John Argyropoulos.

The editor of the *Antirrheticon*, Ludwig Mohler, was right to say that this work had been misunderstood by some earlier commentators.[2] Unfortunately, Mohler himself did not understand it very well. He thought it was Gaza's most important Aristotelian work. He thought Gaza corrected with great philosophical depth and detail John Argyropoulos' mistranslation of a passage of Bessarion's *In Calumniatorem Platonis*.[3] This

---

* This article is not the talk I gave at the conference, but rather an expansion upon one of the topics I treated in the talk.
[1] Edited in Ludwig Mohler, *Kardinal Bessarion als Theologe, Humanist und Staatsmann*, 3 vols, Paderborn 1923–1942 (reprint, Aalen 1967), 3: 204–235.
[2] L. Stein, "Der Humanist Theodor Gaza als Philosoph. Nach handschriftlichen Quellen dargestellt. I. Leben und philosophische Schriften", *Archiv für Geschichte der Philosophie*, 2 (1889), 426–458, clearly had not read the work; he said (451) that it was a refutation of Pletho related to the issue of whether Nature deliberates. A. Gercke, *Theodoros Gazes*, Greifswald 1903, 38, said that it concerned the defense of Plato. But A. Gaspary, "Zur Chronologie des Streites der Griechen über Plato und Aristoteles im 15. Jahrhundert", *Archiv für Geschichte der Philosophie*, 3 (1890), 51–53, got it right as far as he went, showing that Gaza was answering Arygropoulos's criticism of a passage in Bessarion's *In Calumniatorem Platonis*. Gaspary wisely voiced no opinion on the details and quality of the *Antirrheticon*, which he had not read.
[3] Mohler, 3: 204–05: "Gazes ging in seinem *Antirrheticon*, das wohl als die bedeutendste Schrift dieses Aristotelikers zu erachten ist, in tiefgründiger Untersuchung auf die aufgeworfene Frage ein." Cf. *ibid.*, 1: 397: "Gazes schrieb jetzt sein *Antirrhetikon*, eine

is exactly what Gaza claimed to have done. But anyone who reads the work without preconceptions will recognize that the *Antirrheticon* is not a serious contribution to philosophy, but rather an exercise in rank sophistry as Gaza tried to justify a minor, but nonetheless embarrassingly ignorant error by his patron Cardinal Bessarion, which Argyropoulos had rightly corrected.

Why Argyropoulos picked a quarrel with Cardinal Bessarion in the first place is difficult to explain. Both Bessarion[4] and Gaza[5] remark upon the great length of the letter[6] Argyropoulos sent to correct the cardinal. As we shall see, in the letter Argyropoulos also offered his opinions on matters of zoology and psychology apparently in connection with the Plato-Aristotle controversy. So perhaps Bessarion had given him an opening by addressing a series of questions to him. Whatever the occasion, Argyropoulos went into an excruciatingly complicated refutation of what was really a simple error, as if he were rubbing the cardinal's nose in the matter. No wonder Bessarion felt insulted. Given Bessarion's status as the preeminent patron of Greek émigrés in the Latin West and the possibility that Bessarion might become pope, Argyropoulos' action would certainly seem to have been rash. Furthermore, the letter of criticism contradicts, at least in tone, the fulsome praise Argyropoulos heaped upon the cardinal's *In Calumniatorem Platonis*, in a letter of 27 October 1469.[7]

What we know is this. The printers Sweynheym and Pannartz published Bessarion's *In Calumniatorem Platonis* in Rome about August 1469.[8] Bessarion then sent out copies to friends and potential supporters. One recipient was Argyropoulos. Argyropoulos thanked Bessarion with the letter of 27 October 1469. He opened the letter by mentioning the pain he had suffered at the recent death of two of his sons. Then he launched into

---

trockene, aber eingehende Untersuchung, mit der er die Frage in aristotelischem Sinne entschied. Im ganzen ist diese neue Schrift eine Vereinigung von Einzeluntersuchungen, die als solche den Aristotelismus der Renaissance charakterisieren."

[4] *Ibid.* 3: 545.18–19 (recte 545.1–7): "τοσοῦτον λόγων πλῆθος ἀντέθηκας, οὐδέν, ὡς οἶμαι, δέον."

[5] *Ibid.* 3: 231.39–232.1: "τοιοῦτος ὁ λόγος τοῦ ἐναντίου, ὄγκον μὲν ἔχων πολύν, ἀπόδειξιν δὲ οὐδεμίαν."

[6] That Argyropoulos cast his critique in the form of a letter is clear from what Gaza says, as Mohler, 3: 204 notes; see *ibid.*, 3: 225.13: "ἐν ἄλλοις τῷ ἡμετέρῳ ἐπιστέλλων αὐθέντῃ."

[7] Edited in Mohler, 3: 601–02.

[8] See J. Monfasani, *George of Trebizond: A Biography and a Study of His Rhetoric and Logic*, Leiden 1976, 219.

a panegyric of Bessarion's intellectual brilliance, stylistical elegance, and erudition in defending Plato against the *foedissimus calumniator* (the unnamed George Trapezuntius). This is exactly the sort of letter one would have expected from Argyropoulos or from any Greek émigré who, unlike Trapezuntius, had hopes of benefiting from Bessarion's patronage. There were also other reasons for Argyropoulos to flatter the cardinal. One was that he himself admired Plato and agreed with Bessarion's Neoplatonic concordistic understanding of the relationship between Plato and Aristotle. He said as much in his letter of 27 October 1469.[9] In his lectures on Aristotle in Florence, Argyropoulos had many opportunities to criticize Plato, but, as far as I can tell, he consistently praised Plato and strove to explain away Aristotle's criticisms.[10] Another Greek émigré, Michael Apostolis, even wrote Argyropoulos two letters in which he assumed that Argyropoulos shared his enthusiasm for the neopagan, Neoplatonist philosopher and former teacher of Bessarion, George Gemistus Pletho.[11] If we take seriously a reference in Bessarion's covering letter to the *Antirrheticon*,[12] Argyropoulos and Bessarion also seem to have been friends for a very long time, perhaps as far back as Constantinople in the 1420s or 1430s. So why risk antagonizing Bessarion so late in life?

It does no good to suppose that Argyropoulos suddenly got uppity when his old teacher at Padua, Francesco della Rovere, became Pope Sixtus IV on 9 July 1471. True, by October 1471 Argyropoulos had already taken up residence in Rome under Sixtus IV's patronage.[13] But being in Rome, he would have had no need to write a long letter to Bessarion. Moreover, in

---

[9] Mohler, 3: 602.4–8: "Neque enim posthac huiusmodi ineptiis seduci poterunt [sc., Latini] et ea quibus ab Aristotele carpi Plato videretur ita ut capienda sunt accipient, et Platonem insuper talem fuisse qualis natura, moribus, scientia fuit, si auctoritati doctorum hominum credere, si rationibus obtemperare voluerint, existimabunt."

[10] The evidence will be contained in my forthcoming study of the Plato-Aristotle controversy; but see J. Monfasani, "The Averroism of John Argyropoulos and His *Quaestio utrum intellectus humanus sit perpetuus*", *I Tatti Studies: Essays in the Renaissance*, 5 (1993), 157-208, at 173.

[11] Edited in George Gemistus Pletho,, *Traité des Lois*, ed. C. Alexandre; tr. A. Pellissier, Paris 1858 (reprint Amsterdam 1966), 372–75.

[12] Mohler, 3: 546.4–5: ". . . οὐδὲν τῆς ἀρχαίας περὶ σὲ διαθέσεως ἠμείψαμεν." It is conceivable that they met only in Italy. Bessarion took up permanent residence in Italy in 1440; we can place Argyropoulos in Padua from 1441 to 1444, after which time he returned to Constantinople; after the fall of Constantinople he had returned to Italy by 1454.

[13] G. Cammelli, *I dotti bizantini e le origini dell'Umanesimo. II. Giovanni Argiropulo*, Florence 1941, 135–36.

the early spring of the next year Bessarion did Argyropoulos a good turn by recommending his son Isaac to Duke Galeazzo Maria Sforza of Milan.[14] In two letters of 1473, after Bessarion had died, Gaza referred in friendly fashion to Argyropoulos, who was with him in Rome.[15] So whatever unpleasantness had taken place between Argyropoulos on one side and Bessarion and Gaza on the other probably occurred well before Argyropoulos came to Rome in October 1471.

My guess is that Argyropoulos wrote his critique of Bessarion in late 1469, not long after his letter of 27 October 1469. The latter was a public letter, meant to express Argyropoulos' solidarity with Bessarion in the Plato-Aristotle controversy. That is why he wrote it in Latin. The former was a private communication, meant to correct a minor slip in his friend's book. That is why he wrote it in Greek. However, Agryropoulos made his correction in too professorial a manner, lecturing the cardinal at length on what he, Argyropoulos, understood to be the implications of the cardinal's error. What was no less bad form, Argyropoulos apparently talked about or showed his criticism to others.[16] Bessarion took umbrage. Argyropoulos may have been slightly older than Bessarion;[17] uniquely for Greeks of his generation, he had earned a degree in arts from the University of Padua in 1444;[18] in the decade before the fall of Constantinople he had become a distinguished teacher amongst the Greeks;[19] he had reestablished himself in the Latin West as an acclaimed professor of philosopher at the University of Florence;[20] and he was now also making a name for himself as a

---

[14] In a letter of 3 April 1472, edited in Mohler, 3: 563–64.

[15] T. Gaza, *Epistolae*, ed. Pietro A. M. Leone, Naples 1990, 81.15 (18 June 1473) and 90.128 (28 Oct. 1473); and *idem*, *Epistole*, ed. E. Pinto, Naples 1975, 88.15 and 111.15.

[16] Mohler, 3: 546.9–10: "... μαλισθ᾽ ὅτι καὶ μετὰ πάντας τοὺς ἄλλους ἡμῖν ἐκοινώσω, δέον πρὸ πάντων ἡμῖν, εἰ ἀπ᾽ εὐνοίας, ὡς φής, ἐγεγόνει."

[17] I believe that Agyropoulos was born about 1405 (see Monfasani, "Averroism of John Argyropoulos", 158–61) and Bessarion about 1408 (see J. Monfasani, "Platina, Capranica, and Perotti: Bessarion's Latin Eulogists and His Date of Birth', in *Bartolomeo Sacchi Il Platina (Piadena 1421–Roma 1481): Atti del convegno internazionale di studi per il V centenario (Cremona, 14–15 novembre 1981)*, ed. P. Medioli Masotti, Padua 1986 [reprinted in J. Monfasani, *Byzantine Scholars in Renaissance Italy: Cardinal Bessarion and Other Emigrés*, Aldershot 1995], 119–23).

[18] Cammelli, 14–27; Monfasani, "Averroism of John Argyropoulos", 161–62.

[19] Cammelli, 29–42; Monfasani, "Averroism of John Argyropoulos", 162.

[20] Cammelli, 85–129; Monfasani, "Averroism of John Argyropoulos"; and A. Field, *The Origins of the Platonic Academy of Florence*, Princeton 1988, 53–126.

translator of Aristotle.[21] It would not be implausible to suspect that he wanted to prove something to Bessarion about his superior capacity in philosophy. The cardinal disdained to respond. Instead he had Gaza write a refutation to put Argyropoulos back in his place. Agyropoulos had said that he wrote in good will.[22] In the covering letter which accompanied Gaza's refutation, Bessarion told Argyropoulos that he, Bessarion, now expected Argyropoulos to accept this correction with the same good will and without any anger.[23] I would think that Argyropoulos subsequently issued a suitably humble acknowledgement in order to get back into the cardinal's good graces.

*

What provoked Argyropoulos into writing his critique was a passage at the start of Bessarion's *In Calumniatorem Platonis*. Bessarion explained that there had recently come into his hands a comparison of Plato and Aristotle, i. e., Trapezuntius' *Comparatio Philosophorum Platonis et Aristotelis*, though Bessarion does not name the author. He began to read the comparison, Bessarion says, in the hope of seeing what it had to say about standard issues in such a comparison. One of these issues was, as Bessarion put it in his original 1458 Greek text:[24] [to ask] "if some forms[25] are separable or completely inseparable, and if separable, whether self-subsistent or resident in simple concepts."[26] Bessarion was paraphrasing a famous passage at the start of Porphyry's *Isagoge*, where Porphyry declines to answer the question because it goes to a level deeper than what is fitting for an introductory text.[27] Bessarion acknowledged his borrowing. When Argyropoulos criticized the logical form of Bessarion's question (see *infra*),

---

[21] Cammelli, 116–17, 183–84; and E. Garin, "Traduzioni umanistiche di Aristotele nel secolo XV", *Atti dell'Accademia Fiorentina di scienze morali "La Colombaria"*, 8 (1950), 55–104, at 82–86.

[22] See note 16 above.

[23] Mohler, 3: 546.12–16.

[24] On the date see Monfasani 1976, 162–170.

[25] The Greek could mean "species," but I am following Bessarion's later Latin translation here; see Appendix 1, item 4.

[26] See Appendix 1, item 3.

[27] *Ibid.*, item 1.

Bessarion responded that his rough-and-ready formulation was the only alternative to a literal quotation of Porphyry.[28]

But what threw everything into confusion is what Bessarion did next. In the Latin translation he himself made of the *In Calumniatorem Platonis* and circulated among friends in the mid-1460s,[29] he cast the question as: "whether some forms are separated or utterly unseparated, and if separated, whether they self-subsist or are located in the second concepts of the soul."[30] Bessarion's great mistake was to translate as *secunda concepta* in Latin what he and Porphyry called *psilai epinoiai* in Greek. Some humanists, including Lorenzo Valla, a favorite of Bessarion's, scorned Boethius, but in fact Boethius did a much better job here than did the cardinal. In his translation of Porphyry, he rendered *psilai epinoiai* as *sola nudaque intellecta*.[31] While no great stylist, Bessarion had excellent control of Latin. So it is very improbable that he thought that the Latin adjective *secundus* was a fair translation of the Greek *psilos*. It is possible that trying to be too clever by half he thought he was accurately rendering the compound *epi-noia* by using two words in Latin.[32] But most probably he deliberately meant the common term *secundae intentiones* or *secunda intellecta* of medieval Latin philosophy. The substitution of *concepta* for *intentiones/intellecta* was his attempt at more elegant Latin.[33]

---

[28] Mohler, 3: 545.17–18 (recte 545.6–7): "ἄλλως γὰρ ἂν ἐνῆν τὰ Πορφυρίου πρὸς ἔπος ἐκθέσθαι γνώριμα καὶ παισὶν ὄντα."

[29] For the date see J. Monfasani, "Il Perotti e la controversia tra platonici ed aristotelici", *Res Publica Litterarum*, 4 (1981), 195–213 (reprinted in *idem* 1995), at 197–98; and *idem*, "Bessarion Latinus", *Rinascimento*, ser. 2, 28 (1981), 165–209 (reprinted in *idem* 1995), at 172.

[30] See Appendix 1, item 4.

[31] *Ibid.*, item 2. It is possible that in writing "in solis nudisque intellectibus" Boethius intended the ablative plural of *intellectus* rather than of *intellectum*; but given the later Latin tradition, I have opted for the latter.

[32] The revised Liddell-Scott *Greek-English Lexicon* gives as second and third meanings of *epinoia* "afterthought, second thought" (Sophocles) and "reflection on experience, retrospection" (Plotinus), but neither correspond to what medieval Latins meant by *secunda intentio*.

[33] For comparative purposes it is worth noting that Bessarion's contemporary, George Scholarius, turned *secundae intentiones* as δεύτεραι ἐπίνοιαι in his translation of Radulphus Brito; see S. Ebbesen and J. Pinborg, "Gennadios and Western Scholasticism: Radulphus Brito's *Ars Vetus* in Greek Translation", *Classica et Mediaevalia*, 33 (1981–1982), 263–319, at 307–09. He retained this rendering in his commentary on Thomas Aquinas' *De Esse et Essentia* of 1445–1450; see G. Scholarius, *Oeuvres complètes*, ed. L. Petit, X. A. Sidéridès,

To Latins and to a Greek such as Argyropoulos trained in Latin scholasticism second intentions were not simply concepts, but concepts of concepts; they were second order concepts.[34] Man, dog, rain, and table, as grasped and abstracted by the human mind, are first intentions or first order concepts of extra-mental things; species, genus, *differentia*, accident, and individual are second intentions created by the human mind as it reflects on its first intentions. In the sentence, "man is a rational animal," the subject *man* is a first intention and the predicate *rational animal* a second intention.[35] Bessarion apparently made the mistake of understanding a term such as "man" to be a second intention when taken as a universal or species. He thus identified it with forms of things. Consequently, adapting his Latin to what he took to be the Latin way of thinking, Bessarion asked whether forms are inseparable or, if separable, whether they are self-subsistent or are located in second intentions.

In 1469, Bessarion published the *In Calumniatorem Platonis* in the Latin of Niccolò Perotti.[36] But in the passage that concerns us Perotti changed very little.[37] Most importantly, he kept Bessarion's "in secundis animi conceptibus." But he did add an equivocation. He changed Bessarion's *omnino* ("completely" translating the πάντῃ of the Greek original) to *prorsus*, which could have the sense of "utterly,"[38] but also that of "truly." Hence the text Argyropoulos read in Perotti's rendering ran as follows:

and M. Jugie, 8 vols., Paris 1928–36, 6: 282.6; but in the slightly earlier attack on the followers of Acindynus (1445) he preferred δεύτερα νοητά (*ibid.* 3: 230.2, 7, 10, 17, 35).

[34] See R. W. Schmidt, *The Domain of Logic according to Saint Thomas Aquinas*, The Hague 1966, 94–129, especially 122–24; J. Pinborg, "Zum Begriff der Intentio Secunda", *CIMAGL* 13 (1974), 49–59; G. Leff, *William of Ockham*, Manchester 1975, 128–31; C. Knudsen, "Intentions and impositions", in *The Cambridge History of Later Medieval Philosophy*, eds. N. Kretzmann, A. Kenny, J. Pinborg, and E. Stump, Cambridge 1982, 479–95; and H. Mikkeli, *An Aristotelian Response to Renaissance Humanism: Jacopo Zabarella on the Nature of Arts and Sciences*, Helsinki 1992, 46–47.

[35] I take this example from A. Perreiah's introduction to his translation of Paulus Venetus, *Logica Parva*, Vienna 1984, 19.

[36] See Monfasani, "Bessarion Latinus", 167–69; and *idem*, "Still More on *Bessarion Latinus*", *Rinascimento*, ser. 2, 23 (1983), 217–35 (reprinted in *idem* 1995).

[37] See Appendix 1, item 5.

[38] Cf. Perotti's *Cornu Copiae* 7 vols., ed. J.-L. Charlet, G. Abbamonte, M. Furno, P. Harsting, M. Pade, J. Rammminger and F. Stok (Sassoferrato 1989-99), at 1:322 (*editio* 1:115): "omnino, quod significat prorsus, ..."; and at 11.5 (*editio* 5:75): "... et radicitus aduerbium, hoc est a radice. Et per metaphoram ponitur pro eo quod est prorsus, omnino." I wish to thank Marianne Pade for calling these passages to my attention.

"whether some forms are separated or are utterly/truly unseparated, but if they are separated, whether they self-subsist or are placed in second concepts of the soul."

*

Argyropoulos' letter does not survive. What we know of it derives from the little Bessarion tells us in his covering letter to Gaza's *Antirrheticon*, and from the passages Gaza chose to quote as part of his refutation. Gaza was not especially methodical. For instance, at the start of the *Antirrheticon*, he mocks Argyropoulos' doubts about the word *prorsus*, but only at the end does he actually quote Argyropoulos' words, which show that Argyropoulos correctly divined Bessarion's meaning despite the equivocation introduced by Perotti. It was also only at the end that Gaza gives Perotti's Latin text which was at the heart of the matter. Furthermore, it is difficult or impossible at times to follow Argyropoulos' argument from Gaza's quotations. It is as if Gaza really had only an audience of two: Bessarion and Argyropoulos, both of whom knew what the latter had written. All other readers had to be content with believing that Gaza's extensive arguments thoroughly refuted the cardinal's opponent.

On the other hand, Gaza did quote a considerable number of passages. By collating these quotations, one can get a fairly good idea of the main lines of Argyropoulos' criticism, even if not all the connections are clear. This is how Argyropoulos translated the offending passage back into Greek: [the question is] "whether some forms are separated or *prorsus* [sic] separable—alternatively, completely separable—, and if separated, whether they self-subsist or reside in second concepts."[39] Gaza made fun of Argyropoulos' initial puzzlement with *prorsus*,[40] but in fact, as Gaza had eventually to admit,[41] Argyropoulos rightly divined that behind Perotti's *prorsus* stood something like the Greek πάντα.[42] Argyropoulos had also guessed correctly that the Greek word which *concepta* translated was *epinoiai*. Gaza derided Argyropoulos' rendering of Bessarion's *secundum conceptum* as *deutera epinoia* as equivalent to saying *deutera deutera*

---

[39] Appendix 1, item 6 = Appendix 2, items 4 and 40.
[40] Appendix 2, item 5.
[41] Appendix 2, item 40.
[42] *Ibid*. Bessarion had actually written πάντῃ; compare Appendix 1, items 3 and 6.

ennoia [sic] to a Greek speaker.[43] But Gaza's refutation presumes that Greeks traditionally understood *epinoia* as equivalent to a what the Latins called a second intention, which is not the case. The only distinction the Greek commentators on Porphyry make is between *epinoia*, explained as the concept of a real thing, and *psilos epinoia*, explained as the concept of a fiction impossible in nature.[44] Assuming as true what he was supposed to prove, Gaza had taken Bessarion's rendering as normative when it actually was a dubious novelty. So, despite Gaza's carping, Argyropoulos had actually acquitted himself well in turning Perotti's Latin back into Greek.

Argyropoulos made three basic criticisms.[45] First, he argued that the second of Bessarion's two alternatives (i. e., "if separated, whether they self-subsist or reside in second concepts") was logically defective on the grounds that what resides in another is by definition not separated.[46] Second, he could not understand Bessarion's use of the term "second concepts." Argyropoulos attributed the distinction between first and second concepts to "some of the ancients" who considered "man" a first concept and "species" and "genus" second concepts.[47] What does "separated" mean, he asked, in the case of a particular animal or of second level concept "animal"?[48] The use of second concepts makes no sense here and carries no special distinction in relation to first concepts.[49] What was necessary to ask is whether forms subsist or reside only in "simple concepts" (i. e., as Porphyry asked).[50] Argyropoulos seems also to have argued that ultimately the question Bessarion wanted to ask was about the being or

---

[43] Mohler, 3: 235.6–8: "ὁ δὲ δευτέραν ἐπίνοιαν ἑρμηνεύων εἶπε καὶ ἀδολεσχεῖ, δευτέραν δευτέραν ἔννοιαν λέγων τοῖς Ἕλλησι καὶ τὴν φωνὴν συνετοῖς."

[44] Cf. Elias, *In Porphyrii Isagogen et Aristotelis Categorias Commentaria*, ed. A. Busse (*Commentaria in Aristotelem Graeca*, [= *CAG*] 18.1), Berlin 1900, 49.16–20; and David, *Prolegomena et In Porphyrii Isagogen Commentarium*, ed. A. Busse (*CAG*, 18.2) Berlin 1904, 119.17–24.

[45] Gaza says that Agyropoulos proceeded by a series of disjunctive syllogisms. Quite apart from the question of whether Gaza's characterization is fair, it is would be hazardous to recreate the sequence from Gaza's quotations; see Appendix 2, item 36.

[46] Appendix 2, items 6–7, 9–10, 12–19, 21–23.

[47] *Ibid.*, item 13.

[48] *Ibid.*

[49] *Ibid.*, items 14–15, 18–20, 32.

[50] *Ibid.*, items 15–16; item 15 seems also to suggest a preference for "whether forms subsist or have their existence in another."

non-being of things, including the forms.⁵¹ Third, Argyropoulos lectured Bessarion on the difference between being separated and being subsistent, for Bessarion's second question seems to presume that being subsistent is a sub-category of being separated when in fact the opposite is true.⁵² He also lectured Bessarion on the relationship between being a substance and being subsistent,⁵³ but I am not sure how that relates to his criticism of Bessarion. There are several quotations where the context is not clear. He spoke in a logical vein (though Gaza did not understand this) of essential and accidental things being "in" accidents (e. g., the dog is white; the dog thus is thus encompassed by white).⁵⁴ Gaza says Argyropoulos also criticized Porphyry for not stating whether he believed the second concepts of genus and species themselves existed as individual entities (i. e., as Platonic forms).⁵⁵

Finally, Argyropoulos' letter seems to have discussed at least two issues not bearing directly on the passage at the start of the *In Calumniatorem Platonis*. Argyropoulos rejected Aristotle's view that all animals lead with their right limb in locomotion.⁵⁶ He also opposed Aristotle concerning the imagination, taking the side of the Latins,⁵⁷ who said that imagination resided in the brain and that the imagination used the brain as its organ,

---

⁵¹ *Ibid.*, items 2, 19, 36–38. This argument seems to have especially irked Bessarion since he alludes to it (item 2).

⁵² *Ibid.*, items 21.

⁵³ *Ibid.*, items 27 and 29.

⁵⁴ *Ibid.*, item 30.

⁵⁵ *Ibid.*, items 34–35. I would add a negative before ἐν τοῖς αἰσθητοῖς in Mohler, 3: 230.6 to match the negative in Mohler, 3: 230.26.

⁵⁶ *Ibid.*, items 22 and 39. See Arist.*De Caelo* 2.284b28; *Hist. Animal.* 2.498b6–7; *De Part. Animal.* 4.684a27–28 (cf. *ibid.* 3.671b29–31 and 672a23–24); *De Inces. Animal.* 705b30, 706b17, 712a25–28. Albertus Magnus endorsed this view; see his commentary on the *De Caelo*, Bk. 2, tr. 1, cc. 5–6, in his *Opera Omnia*, ed. A. Borgnet, vol. 4, Paris 1890, 133–42; and his commentary *De Motu Animal.*, Bk. 2, tr. 1, c. 2, in *ibid.*, vol. 9 (Paris, 1890), 286–88.

⁵⁷ The Latins received their *opinio communis* from Arab authorities such as Razes and Avicenna; see E. R. Harvey, *The Inward Wits: Psychological Theory in the Middle Ages and the Renaissance*, London 1975, 10, 12, 43, 55; N. H. Steneck, "Albert on the Psychology of Sense Perception", in J. A. Weisheipl, ed., *Albertus Magnus and the Sciences: Commemorative Essays, 1980*, Toronto 1980, 263–90, at 277; and K. Park, "The Organic Soul", in *The Cambridge History of Renaissance Philosophy*, ed. C. B. Schmitt, Q. Skinner, E. Kessler, and J. Kraye, Cambridge 1988, 464–84, at 471.

against Aristotle, who said that imagination resided in the heart.[58] The raising of these issues suggests that Bessarion had engaged Argyropoulos in some sort of scientific dialogue and that Argyropoulos had taken the opportunity to correct the cardinal. Gaza defended Bessarion by saying that the cardinal wrote in defense of Plato when he argued "that the imagination uses an organ which is like that which each of the sensitive faculties uses."[59] I could not find this argument in the *In Calumniatorem Platonis*, but Gaza's words at least confirm that Bessarion and Argyropoulos were discussing arguments the former should use in the Plato-Aristotle controversy.

*

Theodore Gaza's *Antirrheticon* in refutation of Argyropoulos is a nearly continuous stream of irrelevancies and sophistries. He first argued from the equivocation of terms.[60] He explained that "separable" is an equivocal term, that it can mean what is separable by abstraction as well as what is separable because it subsists by itself apart from matter. This, of course, is true. But Gaza was thus admitting the absurdity of Bessarion's double question. For in the first question Bessarion asked whether forms are separable or completely inseparable; in the second, on the assumption that they are separable, he asked whether they self-subsist or reside only in concepts. But in the latter instance they are separable only by abstraction and therefore are completely inseparable. Bessarion did not ask two questions, but one question, resorting to an equivocation, as Gaza admits, to make them seem like two questions. After the first question Bessarion should have substituted "id est" for "et si separatae" since the second question is a restatement of the first in different terms. Gaza seems not to

---

[58] Appendix 2, item 39 (πυθόμενος δέ φησι καὶ τῶν ἐν Εὐρώπῃ φιλοσοφούντων). For Aristotle's position on the heart as the organ of the imagination see the passages cited by D. Ross, *Aristotle*, 5th edition, London 1949, 143 n. 1.

[59] Mohler, 3: 232.36–233.1.

[60] Mohler, 3: 208.4–211.17. At 211.2–3, in arguing that "form" also is an equivocal term, he attributes to Porphyry a distinction between divine, physical, and logical form, which is a distinction not to be found in Pophyry; cf. Porphyry's discussion of form in his *Isagoge*, ed. Adolph Busse (*CAG*, 4.1), Berlin 1887: 4.11–12; and *In Aristotelis Categorias*, *ibid.*, 82.10–11. Gaza also cites "the Arab Averroes" for the opinion that divine form is a universal (Mohler, 3: 211.5–6).

have understood that he was justifying Argyropoulos' condemnation of the second question.

Gaza next explained that according to the Greek commentators, Averroes, and "the Italians," logic deals with concepts, not with extra-mental realities.[61] This again is true. But he then goes on to argue that "concept," *epinoia* in Greek, is what contemporary Latins mean by "second concept" and what the Stoics called "second apprehension" (*deutera katalepsis*) while the thought (*ennoema*) of primary perceptions (*prota noemata*) is what the Stoics called "first apprehension."[62] Thus, the way Argyropoulos used the terms "first concept" and "second concept" (*ennoia*) has no basis in Greek and Latin vocabulary.[63] Gaza is guilty of breathtaking confusion and fiction here. *Katalepsis* and *ennoema* are Stoic technical terms. However, by *katalepsis* the Stoics meant the valid intellectual apprehension of an extra-mental object.[64] It was not itself a thought. Furthermore, the Stoics never distinguished between first and second *katalepses*.[65] Stoic *ennoemata* and *ennoiai* would also qualify as first intentions, as Gaza suggests, since the Stoics considered them "phantasies" of the mind and the ideas which Plato mistakenly made into extra-mental immaterial realities.[66] Thus, contrary to Gaza's argument, *ennoemata* as well as *ennoiai* would also qualify as second order concepts such as

---

[61] *Ibid.*, 211.18–30. Knudsen, 479–80, traces the Arab tradition back to Alfarabi and Avicenna.

[62] Gaza's stated source was Diogenes Laertius (7.60–61 = H. von Arnim, *Stoicorum Veterum Fragmenta*, 4 vols., Leipzig 1903–1924 [reprint, Stuttgart 1964], 2: frag. 226, and 1: frag. 65; see Mohler, 3: 212.9–13 (. . . ὡς ὁ Λαέρτιος Διογένης ἀναγέγραφεν, ἐννόημα ἔφασκον εἶναι φάντασμα διανοίας . . .), from which Gaza concluded (*ibid.*, 212.13–15): "κείσθω δή, εἰ δοκεῖ, ἔννοια τὸ ἀντικείμενον, καὶ δύο ταῦτα ἔννοιαν καὶ ἐπίνοιαν λέγομεν ἀποδιδόντες δυσὶ τῇ τε πρώτῃ καὶ δευτέρᾳ καταλήψει, ὡς Λατῖνοι προσαγορεύουσι."

[63] See the previous note and *ibid.*, 211.30–37: "['Ιταλιωτῶν τε οἱ τὰς ἐπιστήμας μετιόντες ἅπαντες] καλοῦσι δὲ τὴν μὲν ἐπίνοιαν, ὡς ἄν τις αὐτολεξεὶ μεταφράζων λέγοι, δευτέραν κατάληψιν, τὴν δὲ τῶν πρώτων καὶ ἁπλῶς νοημάτων ἔννοιαν πρώτην κατάληψιν λαβόντες, ὡς ἔοικε τοὔνομα παρὰ τῶν Στωικῶν, καθάπερ καὶ ἄλλα συχνὰ τῶν περὶ τοὺς ὅρους. ἐκεῖνοι γὰρ τὸ καταληπτικὸν καὶ ἀκατάληπτον ἐπὶ τούτοις ἔλεγον. τὸ δὲ πρώτη καὶ δευτέρα ἐπίνοια, ὡς ὁ ἀντιλέγων μεταβάλλει, οὔτε τῶν ἑλληνικῶν οὔτε τῶν ῥωμαϊκῶν ὀνομάτων ἐστίν. ἡμεῖς δὲ ἐπίνοιαν μὲν λέγοντες τὴν τούτοις δευτέραν κατάληψιν."

[64] See P. O. Kristeller, *Greek Philosophers of the Hellenistic Age*, New York 1991, 25; Arnim, 1: frag. 60.

[65] Nothing to this effect can be found in the *Index verborum* in Arnim, 4.

[66] Kristeller, *Greek Philosophers*, 27 and 62; Arnim, 1: frag. 65 and 2: frag. 83; see also Arnim 4: *Index verborum*, s. v. ἐννόημα and ἔννοια.

"genus" and "species." But the term Bessarion himself used was *epinoia*. Stoics defined *epinoia* as "recollected thought" as distinct to thought which was a "rational phantasy".[67] One can see why Gaza guessed that "recollected thoughts" were Stoic second intentions. But this definition signifies thought recollected from memory and not thought created by reflection on thoughts; it is not the product of a second *katalepsis* nor a second order concept. The problem for Gaza was that he was trying to create distinctions in Stoic logic that did not exist. Nor was Gaza right to presume that the Stoics took *ennoiai* to be the subject of logic. Rather, they defined the subject of logic to be signifiers (*semainonta*) and significants "(*semainomena*).[68] Finally, while insisting without demonstration that *epinoiai* is the correct translation of what "Italians" call second intentions,[69] Gaza wrongly refused to acknowledge that Argyropoulos was using the terms first and second "concepts" in accordance with current Latin usage.

After making some unobjectable comments (on equivocation, the need for definition and a sense of context, and the nature of disjunctives), Gaza next explained that Bessarion intended two antitheses: the first between separable and inseparable, the second between self-subsisting and subsisting in a concept (*epinoia*).[70] This is surely the case, but the fact remains that Bessarion confused matters by translating *epinoiai* as *secunda concepta* while his second antithesis remains pointless since it is a restatement of the first. Consequently when Gaza continued on about the different meanings of "separable" and concluded that Bessarion used these multiple senses,[71] he really was not answering Argyropoulos' criticism.

In the next section of the *Antirrheticon*, Gaza gave extensive quotations from Argyropoulos' letter and attempted to answer them, his essential point being that the critic failed to grasp how Bessarion used words such as "separable" and "subsistent" in both an absolute sense and in a relative sense. The critic also did not know the true contraries of "self-subsisting" although this knowledge is necessary in order to understand what

---

[67] Arnim, 2: frag. 89 (Galen *Defin. Medicae* 125, which Gaza may have very well read): ἐπίνοιά ἐστιν ἐναποκειμένη νόησις· δὲ λογικὴ φαντασία.

[68] See J. Gould, *The Philosophy of Chrysippus*, Leiden and Albany, N.Y. 1970, 68; Arnim, 2, frs. 122 and 166.

[69] See the discussion of Gaza's criticism of Argyropoulos' translation on p. 69 above for another instance of Gaza's commission of the sin of *petitio principii*.

[70] Mohler, 3: 214.24–26.

[71] *Ibid.*, 216.8–11.

Bessarion was doing. Interestingly, after quoting Argyropoulos to the effect that a second intention is an *atomos* (i. e., uncompounded, not an entity composed of matter and form),[72] Gaza says that it is easy to refute for anyone trained in the logic of the "moderns" (*neoi*) and explains *inter alia* that an *atomos* is a second "thought" (*deuteron noema*) and therefore resides in a concept (*epinoia*) and is the object of logic (*dialektike theoria*).[73] Whatever the validity of Gaza's interpretation of *noema* and *epinoia*, the passage confirms that Gaza was familiar with contemporary Latin logic. He even endorsed the standard view among Latins that the object of logic is second intentions.

I have already made use of parts of the rest of the *Antirrheticon*. Short of a complete translation, which does not befit an article,[74] a passage-by-passage analysis would be tedious and unproductive. So let me pick out five passages of interest in the remainder of the treatise that I have yet to discuss.

Against Argyropoulos' comment that "subsistent" is a more comprehensive term than "separated,"[75] Gaza strangely maintained that "the subsistent is equal to the separable and exists in a similar way as the separable,"[76] which he can only render plausible by going on about the absolute and relative meanings of separable and subsistent. Against Agyropoulos' argument that Bessarion's two questions are really indistinguishable from each other,[77] Gaza gave an array of examples showing how logical, physical, and ontological distinctions can be drawn, but he never really refuted Argyropoulos.[78] Argyropoulos had made the analogy that subsistent is to being as the non-subsistent is to non-being.[79] I am not sure what was the point of Argyropoulos' argument here, but Gaza reacted with the bizarre counter thesis that "the subsistent is prior to and of wider extent in some way than beings, and therefore the non-subsistent will be

---

[72] Appendix 2, item 19.
[73] Mohler, 3. 222.9–13. Note that at 222.12 one should read κατ' αὐτοῦ (as in MS Laur. 55, 13) instead of Mohler's κατ' οὐ.
[74] I have prepared an English translation for a future monographic study of Gaza.
[75] Appendix 2, item 21.
[76] Mohler, 3: 223.7–8: "τό γε γὰρ ὑφεστηκὸς ἐπ' ἴσης τῷ χωριστῷ καὶ ὁμοίως ἔχον."
[77] Appendix 2, item 23.
[78] Mohler, 3: 223.24 sq.
[79] Appendix 2, item 28.

prior to and of wider extent in some way than non-beings."⁸⁰ Gaza could not understand why Agryropoulos said that Bessarion's distinction between first and second intentions made no sense in the context of his second question.⁸¹ Argyropoulos' assertion that the Ideas were either self-subsistent or existed in something else⁸² provoked Gaza into a dissertation on the presence of the Ideas in God and therefore of their not being in place or time and that they are not "together" in the sense that elements in the same genus are together or as convertible as a consequent of their being.⁸³ The relevancy of all this is not clear.

But perhaps the oddest moment in the *Antirrheticon* comes in the last passage I shall discuss, where Gaza refuted what he said was Argyropoulos' attack on Porphyry for not asking whether the concepts *genera* and *species* are independent entities.⁸⁴ Gaza responded by accusing Argyropoulos of deriving his argument from the Scotists, who "atomize" divine entities and who teach that immaterial forms are distinguished from each other by the principle of *haeceitas* [sic; read *haecceitas*], which Gaza transliterates as αἰκέϊτας and translates as τουτότης.⁸⁵ Gaza rightly points out that there are only two theological schools among the Italians, that of the Scotists and that of the Thomists.⁸⁶ Ockhamist theology did not exist for him.⁸⁷ Gaza himself disapproved of the Scotist doctrine of the real distinctions in the divine essence (which is what he interpreted as immaterial atoms). He considered the Thomists to have "more persuasive things to say."⁸⁸ His patron Bessarion, on the other hand, was favorably inclined to *haeceitas* [sic; his spelling] in the *In Calumniatorem Platonis* as a way of explaining spiritual individuation. Probably on the advice of one or more scholastics

---

⁸⁰ Mohler, 3: 226.29–31: "ἀλλὰ μὲν πρότερον τῇ φύσει καὶ ἐπὶ πλέον τῶν ὄντων οὑτινοσοῦν τὸ ὑφεστηκός. καὶ τὸ μὴ ὑφεστηκὸς ἄρα πρότερον καὶ ἐπὶ πλέον ἔσται οὑτινοσοῦν τῶν μὴ ὄντων."

⁸¹ See Appendix 2, item 32, and Mohler, 3: 227.35 sq.

⁸² Appendix 2, item 33.

⁸³ Mohler, 3: 229.6 sq.

⁸⁴ See note 55 above.

⁸⁵ Mohler, 3: 230.7 sq.

⁸⁶ *Ibid.* 230.9–10.

⁸⁷ On this state of affairs see J. Monfasani, "Aristotelians, Platonists, and the Missing Ockhamists: Philosophical Liberty in Pre-Reformation Italy", *Renaissance Quarterly*, 46 (1993), 247–76.

⁸⁸ Mohler, 3: 230.28.

in his household, Bessarion contended that Thomas Aquinas agreed with the theory behind the doctrine of *haecceitas* because of the influence of Avicenna.[89] Even the Thomist George Scholarius professed a liking for the Scotist doctrines of *haecceitas* and the real distinction because they lent comfort to the Greek Hesychasts' understanding of the divine energies.[90]

In sum, Gaza did the job Bessarion assigned him: to refute Argyropoulos in a substantial treatise. Argyropoulos was imprudent to correct the cardinal on such a minor matter. But since his criticisms were correct, Gaza had a hard row to hoe. Gaza's treatise shows him an intellectual courtier. It has real historical interest but does Gaza's reputation as a philosopher no good.

Appendix 1
Variant Versions of Porphyry's Questions in Chronological Order

1. Porphyry, *Isagoge*, : "αὐτίκα περὶ τῶν γεννῶν τε καὶ εἰδῶν τὸ μὲν εἴτε ὑφέστηκεν εἴτε καὶ ἐν μόναις ψιλαῖς ἐπινοίαις κεῖται εἴτε καὶ ὑφεστηκότα σώματά ἐστιν ἢ ἀσώματα καὶ πότερον χωριστὰ ἢ ἐν τοῖς αἰσθητοῖς καὶ περὶ ταῦτα ὑφεστῶτα, παραιτήσομαι λέγειν βαθυτάτης οὔσης τῆς τοιαύτης πραγματείας καὶ ἄλλης μείζονος δεομένης ἐξετάσεως" [ed. Busse, 1.9–14].
2. Boethius's Latin translation of Porphyry: "Mox de generibus ac speciebus illud quidem sive subsistunt sive in solis nudisque intellectibus posita sunt sive subsistentia corporalia sunt an incorporalia, et utrum separata a sensibilibus an in sensibilibus posita et circa ea constantia dicere recusabo, altissimum enim est huiusmodi negotium et maioris egens inquisitionis" [ed. Busse, 25.10–14].
3. Bessarion's original Greek text: "καὶ εἴ τινα χωριστὰ εἰσὶν εἴδη ἢ πάντη ἀχώριστα καὶ εἰ χωριστά, πότερον καθ' αὑτὰ ὑφεστῶτα ἢ ἐν ψιλαῖς κείμενα ἐπινοίαις" [Mohler, 2: 2.15–17].
4. Bessarion's own Latin translation: "An formae aliquae separatae sint aut omnino inseparatae, et si separatae, utrum per se subsistant an in secundis

---

[89] Mohler, 2: 401.23–25.

[90] See M. Jugie, "Palamite (Controverse)", *Dictionnaire de théologie catholique*, 11 (Paris, 1931–1932), 1777–1818, at 1800–01; S. Guichardan, *Le Probléme de la simplicité divine en Orient et en Occident aux XIVᵉ et XVᵉ siècles: Grégoire Palamas, Duns Scot, Georges Scholarios*, Paris 1933, 188–90, 197, 201–02, 204. Scholarius translated the formal distinction as εἰδικὴ διάκρισις; see Scholarius, *Oeuvres complètes*, 3: 226.14.

animi conceptibus collocentur" [MS Venice, Bibl. Marc., Zan. Lat. 230, f. 4r].
5. Niccolò Perotti's Latin translation: "An formae aliquae separatae sint an prorsus inseparatae, quodsi separatae sunt, utrum per se substent an in secundis animi conceptibus positae sint" [1469 ed., fol. (15r); 1503 ed., sign. b 1r; ed.Mohler, 2: 3.18–19].
6. John Argyropoulos's Greek translation of Perotti's Latin: "πότερόν τινα εἴδη ἐστὶ κεχωρισμένα ἢ πρόρσους ἀχώριστα – ἢ πάντα ἀχώριστα –, καὶ εἰ κεχωρισμένα, πότερον καθ᾽ αὑτὰ ὑφέστηκεν ἢ ἐν δευτέραις ἐπινοίαις κεῖται" [Th. Gaza, Antirrheticon, ed.Mohler, 3: 207.15–16 for almost all of the lemma, and 234.38-39 for the three words between the long dashes].

Appendix 2
Lemmata and Descriptions of John Argyropoulos' Letter to Cardinal Bessarion

Since all these passages come from one easily accessible source, vol. 3 of Ludwig Mohler's *Kardinal Bessarion*, I did not see the value of reproducing the lemmata *in toto*. So I give the text of only a few short items. But a list is necessary since Mohler did not identify all the lemmata. I include (1) Argyropoulos' *ipsissima verba* as quoted by Gaza, (2) paraphrases by Gaza, and (3) words of Gaza supplying the context to (1) and (2). All references are to volume 3 of Mohler.
1. Bessarion's letter, 545.18 (recte 545.6): "τοσοῦτον λόγων πλῆθος ἀντέθηκας."
2. *Ibid.*, 545.27–28 (recte, 545.15–16): "εἰ τὰ ἡμῖν εἰρημένα οὔτ᾽ ἐπὶ τῶν ὄντων, οὔτ᾽ ἐπὶ τῶν μὴ ὄντων ἀληθεύει, ὡς φής."
3. *Ibid.*, 546.10: "δέον πρὸ πάντων ἡμῖν, εἰ ἀπ᾽ εὐνοίας, ὡς φής, ἐγεγόνει."
4. Th. Gaza's *Antirrheticon*, 207.14–16, the last part of which is repeated in Appendix 1, item 6: "γράφων ἑλληνιστὶ καὶ μεταβάλλων οὑτοσὶ τὸ ῥωμαϊκὸν γράμμα· «πότερόν τινα εἴδη ἐστὶ κεχωρισμένα ἢ πρόρσους ἀχώριστα, καὶ εἰ κεχωρισμένα, πότερον καθ᾽ αὑτὰ ὑφέστηκεν ἢ ἐν δευτέραις ἐπινοίαις κεῖται.»"

5. 213.15–17.
6. 216.24–26.
7. 216.35–37.
8. 217.6–8.
9. 217.22–32.
10. 218.10–12.
11. 218.28–29.
12. 218.36–39.
13. 219.3–15.
14. 220.32–34.
15. 221.8–11.
16. 221.14–15.
17. 221.23 = partial repeat of item 15.
18. 221.28–31.
19. 222.4–8.
20. 222.17–18.
21. 222.25–35.
22. 223.23–24.
23. 224.5–9.
24. 224.17.
25. 225.10–14.
26. 225.27–30.
27. 226.14–21.
28. 226.28–29.
29. 227.1–5.
30. 227.12–16.
31. 227.18–21.
32. 527.29–36.
33. 228.31–32.
34. 230.6–8.
35. 230.20–24.
36. 231.4–16.
37. 231.25–29.
38. 231.38–39.
39. 232.10–21.
40. 234.38-39 = Appendix 1, item 6.

Metaphysics or Empirical Science? The two Faces of Aristotelian Natural Philosophy in the Sixteenth Century

by Eckhard Keßler

The order of Aristotelian writings on the philosophy of nature – as arranged by Andronikos of Rhodes, followed by Neoplatonic and scholastic teaching and preserved up to Bekker's edition – starts with the *Physics*, continues with the treatises *On the Heavens*, *On Generation and Corruption* and the four books on *Meteorology*, and ends with the *De Anima* and the *Parva naturalia*, which are followed by the various zoological treatises. This order leads from the more general to the more particular, allows for deductive teaching and, what is even more important, agrees with the Aristotelian theory of science. That does not mean, however, that whoever reads Aristotle in this order gets a clear and consistent impression of his teaching. For obviously, contrary to what for centuries his adherents believed, Aristotle did not write his books in a deductive, systematic way; his thought and writing were the result of his intellectual development and therefore are not free from contradictions and inconsistencies.

One of the most conspicuous incoherences in Aristotle's writings on natural philosophy is his twofold approach towards natural beings. The first approach is that of the *Physics*, where he defines the object of physics as the movable body or being, *ens* or *corpus mobile*, reflects on the prerequisites for any kind of motion and change, and arrives at matter, form, privation and the four causes as the general principles of nature. The second is found in the treatise *On Generation and Corruption* and in the fourth book of *Meteorology*, where he defines the object of natural philosophy as being the potentially perceptible body, *corpus potentia sensibile*,[1] asks what might be the most basic object of sense-perception, and concludes that touch is the most fundamental sense and hot and cold, moist and dry, the fundamental first qualities. These qualities in different

---

[1] See Aristotle, *De generatione et corruptione* II,1; 329 a 33.

combinations constitute the simple bodies of the four elements, which in their turn, thanks to the interaction of the first qualities, constitute the various species of mixed bodies. The first approach may be called a *metaphysical* one, since it is based on the purely rational analysis of the concept of a movable body or being – and, indeed, corresponding reflections are to be found in Aristotle's *Metaphysics*; the second approach, which is based on an empirical analysis of what is or seems to be given in sense-perception, may be considered a *naturalistic* one.

Now the mere fact that one and the same object is analysed in different disciplines and from different points of view would not disturb scientific consistency, as long as the perspectives and the results are compatible with each other. In the case of the metaphysical and the naturalistic approach to nature, however, they obviously do not conform. For the metaphysical approach concentrates on the determinate essence of natural beings and teaches that not the form, but the composite of matter and form is generated, so that generation turns into an instantaneous act of composition; the naturalistic approach, on the other hand, concentrates on the process of coming to be and teaches the continuous interaction of the elementary first qualities, in the course of which the different species of mixed bodies emerge. Further, according to the metaphysical approach generation understood as an instantaneous act would not imply continuous motion and consequently would not explain the process of coming to be in its proper sense; but according to the naturalistic approach form itself would be subject to the process of generation and therefore would be inadequate to account for the determinate essence of natural beings. In the tradition of Aristotelian natural philosophy, therefore, the question of how to cope with this inconsistency between the metaphysical and the naturalistic approach became a constant problem as soon as people started to interpret Aristotle systematically.

As Anneliese Maier has shown in one of her most important papers, entitled *Die Struktur der materiellen Substanz*,[2] scholastic philosophy in general tried to overcome this problem through the notion of substantial form, *forma substantialis*. On the one hand the substantial form is meant to determine the very essence of natural beings and therefore corresponds to the metaphysical concept of form. On the other hand it requires for its

---

[2] Anneliese Maier, "Die Struktur der materiellen Substanz", in *eadem, An der Grenze von Scholastik und Naturwissenschaft*, 2 Roma 1952, 1-140.

introduction into matter a certain preparation, an adequate *dispositio* or *complexio*, in the receiving material subject, which results from the interaction of the first qualities, so that the naturalistic concept of generation through mixture of the elementary qualities is honoured as well. Finally most of the scholastic philosophers, following the example of Avicenna, suppose some kind of celestial or divine *dator formarum* to act as the efficient cause for the introduction of the substantial form into the well disposed matter, and thereby make natural coming to be dependent on a supernatural agent.[3]

It is not my intention to report Anneliese Maier's painstaking analysis of the various turns which this discussion took in the course of the Middle Ages, or to discuss her conclusion that scholastic philosophy remained stuck between these two approaches until the end of the fourteenth century. It is my intention, however, to question her final statement, that this situation still did not change after Albert of Saxony and Marsilius of Inghen in the fourteenth century until in the seventeenth century the new atomism got rid of the qualitative concept of element and – consequently – of the concept of substantial form, and thus freed natural philosophy from the domination of metaphysics.[4] To put the matter more positively, I intend to argue that in fact the emancipation of natural philosophy from metaphysics did not start with the revival of atomism in the seventeenth century, but with the revival of a strong naturalistic tendency as early as the beginning of the sixteenth century.

Paradoxically, the origin of this sudden invigoration of natural philosophy seems to have been Florentine Neoplatonism, which did not just teach an alternative philosophical doctrine, but propagated the universal concept of

---

[3] See Anneliese Maier, *op. cit.* (n. 2) 23 ff.; Avicenna Latinus, *Liber Tertius Naturalium. De generatione et corruptione* XIV, 39 ff., ed. S. van Riet, Leiden 1987, 139 f.: "Et quodlibet istorum elementorum habet latitudinem in sua qualitate secundum magis et minus, quia sua qualitas naturalis vel accidentalis poterit intendi et remitti, observando adhuc formam et speciem suam. Nihilominus, ista intensio et remissio habent terminos limitatos quos, quando transcendit, deperditur completa dispositio quae est in materia ad illam formam et disponitur dispositione completa ad aliam formam. Et de usu materiae est, quando disponitur dispositione completa ad recipiendum formam, quod scilicet influatur illa forma super eam a datore formarum in materiebus, <et recipit eam> et amovet alias… (l.62 f.:) Et diversificantur complexiones istorum compositorum propter diversitatem qualitatum elementorum in ipsis"

[4] See Anneliese Maier, *op. cit.* (n. 2), 137 ff.

prisca philosophia, bringing all philosophical sects and all true religious teachings under the roof of one and the same spiritual tradition.[5] Thus Florentine Neoplatonism did not fight Aristotle, as one might have expected, but integrated him into its general concept of philosophy as the *physicus*, the most subtle and sophisticated explorer of the material world.[6] At the same time it acknowledged neither the superiority of the Aristotelian tradition in natural philosophy nor that of the scholastic tradition in the realm of theology, but claimed to be in possession of a more comprehensive theology and a more comprehensive understanding of nature, as taught under the headings of *theologia platonica*[7] and *magic*, both *spiritual* and *demonic*.[8]

It seems to have been in response to these claims that a decisive turn took place in the concept of natural philosophy. For both scholastic theologians and scholastic philosophers seem to have accepted the Neoplatonic notion of Aristotle as the *physicus* but to have denied the Neoplatonic demand for leadership in matters of theology as well as natural philosophy.

The typical example is the Bolognese Dominican Chrysostomus Javelli, who at the beginning of the sixteenth century writes:

> Plato descends from the superior to the sensible, thereby rather accepting opinions about the divine beings – as if they were sent from the heavens – than proving them. For this way of arguing is appropriate only to the theologian, who is occupied with divine revelation; to the philosopher, however, who deals with the human world, it is almost alien. Aristotle, however, being the most sophisticated explorer of nature, rises step by step from the sensible and the better known to the immaterial ... As long as he rose from sense-perception, he was able to philosophize determinately and coherently. As soon as he lost the leading hand of the senses, his intellect began to darken... For philosophy and Aristotelian philosophy are not

---

[5] See Giovanni Pico della Mirandola, *Conclusiones nongentae / Le novecento Tesi dell'anno 1486*, a cura di A. Biondi, Firenze 1995; Frances A. Yates, *Giordano Bruno and the Hermetic Tradition*, London 1964; Cesare Vasoli, "La prisca teologia e il neoplatonismo religioso", in P. Prini (ed.), *Il neoplatonismo del Rinascimento*, Firenze 1993, 83-201.

[6] M. Ficino, *Theologia Platonica de immortalitate animorum* VI,1, 3 vols., ed. R. Marcel, Paris 1964-1970, vol. I, 224: "... sicut nos docent prisci theologi: Zoroaster, Mercurius, Orpheus, Aglaophemus, Pythagoras, Plato, quorum vestigia sequitur plurimum physicus Aristoteles".

[7] See Ficino's *Theologia Platonica...*, *op. cit.* (n. 6).

[8] See Ficino, *De vita*, a cura di A. Biondi / G. Pisani, Pordenone 1991; D.P. Walker, *Spiritual and Demonic Magic from Ficino to Campanella*, London 1958.

identical – since philosophy as such is the science of pure truth, which, being a divine possession, is sent to us by the father of lights.[9]

Javelli, the theologian, uses the reduction of the *philosopher* to a mere *physicus* as a pretext to reduce human philosophy in general to a pure enterprise of natural reason and to seize upon metaphysics as his own supernatural realm of theology. Pomponazzi, the Aristotelian philosopher, whom Javelli defends against his Neoplatonic adversaries, makes use of the same reduction in order to philosophize undisturbed by objections whether arising from theology or from metaphysics,[10] and strenuously defends nature from the interference of supernatural and occult causes.[11]

With Javelli, as Charles Lohr has proved, the *Second Scholastics* begin and, though this was not the purpose, natural philosophy is emancipated from the tyranny of metaphysics.[12] With Pomponazzi a new naturalistic approach towards nature is developed, which in the course of the century helps to resolve the duality in Aristotelian natural philosophy.

---

[9] Chrysostomus Javelli, "Solutiones Rationum animi mortalitatem probantium quae in defensorio contra Niphum excellentissimi domini Petri Pomponatii formantur", in Pomponazzi, *Tractatus acutissimi, utillimi et mere peripatetici*, Venetie 1525, f. 108 v (Epist. dedic.): "Plato a superioribus descendit ad sensum, sententias de divinis entibus veluti ab alto demissas magis acceptans quam probans. Qui nempe modus soli theologo innitenti divinae revelationi proprie convenit, philosopho autem in humanis versanti fere extraneus. Aristoteles autem veluti calidissimus naturae scrutator, a sensatis et notioribus paulatim se ad immaterialia elevat... Quantum ex sensu elevatus, tantum determinate et constanter philosophari potuit. At quamprimum manuductio ex sensu defecit, caligavit eius intellectus... Neque enim philosophia et Aristotelis philosophia convertuntur. Philosophia si quidem in se est scientia mere veritatis, quae est divina possessio nobis a patre luminum demissa."

[10] See Pomponazzi, "Defensorium", in *Tractatus acutissimi, op. cit.* (n. 9) f. 104 ra: "... quod queritur est *quid senserit Aristoteles quidve per rationes naturales de hoc haberi potest* ... Ex mandato enim Leonis decimi et Senatus Bononiensis teneor legere, interpretari et secundum iudicium meum sententiare, *quid senserit Aristoteles quid per principia naturalia haberi potest* ... Mandata sequor, iuramentum observo."

[11] Eckhard Keßler, "Pietro Pomponazzi: Zur Einheit seines philosophischen Lebenswerkes", in Tamara Albertini (Ed.): *Verum et Factum. Beiträge zur Geistesgeschichte und Philosophie der Renaissance zum 60. Geburtstag von Stephan Otto*, Frankfurt a.M. etc. 1993, 397-420.

[12] See. Charles H. Lohr, "The Sixteenth-Century Transformation of the Aristotelian Natural Philosophy", in *Aristotelismus und Renaissance. In memoriam Ch.B. Schmitt*, edd. E. Keßler et al., Wiesbaden 1988, 89-99, esp. 99.

In order to understand what was actually going on, we therefore have to take a closer look at Pomponazzi, who is best known for his denial of the immortality of the individual human soul and the scandal which resulted from this denial.[13] We shall not deal here with the significance of his denial in the ongoing psychological discussion of the Middle Ages and the Renaissance,[14] or with his argumentation as such, which, of course, is mostly a report and analysis of and a response to the traditional discussion. We shall, however, reconsider for a moment the formal principle which determines Pomponazzi to argue in favour of Alexander of Aphrodisias' denial of an immortal human soul, both in the famous *Tractatus de immortalitate animae* of 1516 and in the preceding *Quaestiones* of 1504/05.

In the latter, he concludes the discussion of the various interpretations of Aristotle's psychology with the statement that *stando in puris naturalibus opinio Alexandri multum quadrat* – "as long as we remain within the purely natural, Alexander's opinion agrees very well",[15] defining the *pura naturalia*, the purely natural, as the general basis of his argumentation. What is meant by these *pura naturalia* seems to be more exactly explained in the course of the argument itself, when Pomponazzi refers to sense-perception as opposed to the absurdity of metaphysical speculation,[16] to

---

[13] See his *Tractatus de immortalitate animae* (1516), ed. G. Morra, Bologna 1954; Etienne Gilson, "Autour de Pomponazzi: Problématique de l'immortalité de l'âme en Italie au début du XVIème siècle", *Archives d'histoire doctrinale et littéraire du moyen âge* 28 (1961) 163-279.

[14] This has been done in Olaf Pluta, *Kritiker der Unsterblichkeitsdoktrin in Mittelalter und Renaissance*, Amsterdam 1986; Eckhard Keßler, "The Intellective Soul", in Ch.B. Schmitt et al. (eds.), *The Cambridge History of Renaissance Philosophy*, Cambridge 1988, 485-534.

[15] P. Pomponazzi, *Corsi inediti dell'insegnamento Padovano II (Quaestiones physicae et animasticae decem, 1499-1500; 1503-1504)*, ed. Antonino Poppi, Padua 1970, 93, 2-4: "ideo, ut dixi, stando in puris naturalibus opinio Alexandri multum quadrat"; see also *ibid.*, 60, 21 ff.: "Sed domini, advertatis hic quod, ut dixi, stando in puris naturalibus non videtur dissona opinio Alexandri... Dico tamen quod opinio ista Alexandri est falsissima."

[16] See P. Pomponazzi, *Corsi inediti, op. cit.* (n. 15) 9,11 ff.: "Amplius, si ipsa anima intellectiva separatur a corpore, cum sit unum ens per se, quomodo cum corpore faciet unum per se? Videtur, quod unum per accidens faciet, et ipse Alexander multum deridet istam opinionem sic dicentem, scilicet quod anima intellectiva det esse materiae et extensa etc., et tamen separari possit a corpore, et esse immortalis. Amplius, hoc videtur esse contra sensum, nam nos videmus homines esse sicut alia animalia, unde alia animalia habent carnes, ossa, intestina multum bene ordinata et distincta sicut nos homines; et si aliquis hominis carnes comederet, sicut aliorum animalium, carnes saperent sicut et aliae carnes, quare videtur quod ita sit de hominum anima sicut de aliorum animalium anima."

reason as opposed to blind submission to authority[17], and to natural principles, *principia naturalia*, as opposed to rhetorical or occult reasoning.[18] Apparently the "purely natural", the *pura naturalia*, which serve as the basis of Pomponazzi's psychological argumentation, comprise both arguments which are acceptable in the context of natural philosophy, and principles which can be admitted as working within the realm of natural beings.

Thus, for further clarification, we have to take a look at Pomponazzi's concept of natural philosophy and of nature itself. Regarding the first, in a short chapter entitled *De modo procedendi in naturalibus*, "On the method of proceeding in natural matters", he makes it quite clear that knowledge of nature and natural objects can be attained only by sense-perception and arguments derived immediately from it, and that whenever reason seems to contradict sense-perception, the former has to give way to the latter.[19] Consequently we may say that for Pomponazzi natural philosophy has become an empirical discipline, and that according to him in order to be appropriate to the realm of nature arguments have to be based on sense-perception and exclude all types of metaphysical speculation.

Regarding the concept of nature itself, in the short treatise entitled *De actione reali*, "On real action", Pomponazzi develops a universal theory of

---

[17] See P. Pomponazzi, *Corsi inediti, op. cit.* (n. 15) 11, 11 ff.: "Auctoritates, etsi glosari possint, tamen expeditius non admittantur; tantum enim rationibus innitor et, domini, si sunt plures modi respondendi secundum Alexandrum ad Philosophi rationes, tamen volo habere unum modum respondendi."

[18] See P. Pomponazzi, *Corsi inediti, op. cit.* (n. 15) 2, 4 ff.: "Unde debetis, domini, scire quod in ista materia tot et tanta dicuntur a doctoribus et naturalia et astronomica et rhetorica, ut temporis angustia non petit (sic!) omnia dicta illorum dicere; tantum enim secundum principia naturalia opinionem istam pertractabo."

[19] See Pomponazzi, "De modo procedendi in naturalibus" (De reactione II,1), in *Tractatus acutissimi, ibid.* (n. 9) f. 30 vb: "Etenim cum omnis naturalis cognitio aut per sensum aut per rationem conformem sensui habeatur, ut et octavo *Physicorum* (253 a 33) et nono capite tertii de generatione animalium (760 b 31) dicit Aristoteles: ideo quae sensui manifesta sunt, a naturali sine ratione aliqua sunt accipienda; quod si aliquae sunt rationes, quae sensui contradicant, quantumcumque sint validissimae, sensui et non rationi adhibenda est fides." See also Eckhard Keßler, "Physik oder Metaphysik. Beobachtungen zum Begriff der Naturwissenschaft in der Methodendiskussion des 16. Jahrhunderts", in *Aristotelica et Lulliana magistro doctissimo Charles Lohr septuagesimum annum feliciter agenti dedicata* [Essays in honour of Charles H. Lohr] (Instrumenta Patristica XXVI), edd. Fernando Domínguez, Ruedi Imbach, Theodor Pindl et Peter Walter, Steenbrugis 1995, 223-244.

local motion, which acts as the inherent dynamic principle of the whole universe from the celestial bodies of the stars to the ethereal spirits in the animals, and which causes all kinds of coming to be and passing away.[20] In consequence, nature according to Pomponazzi does not allow for instantaneous processes of formation, as would be required in the theory of generation through composition of matter and substantial form, but results exclusively from continuous processes of change, as supposed in the theory of generation through the interaction of first qualities and the mixture of elements.

If we take the approach from sense-perception and the reduction of natural processes to local motion together, it becomes evident that the *pura naturalia*, the "purely natural", on the basis of which Pomponazzi feels entitled to defend Alexander's psychological position, represent a concept of natural philosophy which, while abandoning metaphysical principles and argumentation as used in the tradition of the Aristotelian *Physics*, is dedicated to a purely empirical explanation of the sensible world of material reality, in the tradition of the Aristotelian treatise *On Generation and Corruption*.

Now such a combination of materialistic psychology and empirical, naturalistic philosophy of nature does not seem to be all that original.

---

[20] Pomponazzi, "De actione reali", in *Tractatus acutissimi, op. cit.* (n. 9) f. 38 rb: "Aristotelis autem sententia huic opponitur. Credit enim numerum intelligentiarum coaequari numero corporum caelestium, ab ipsaque intelligentia nihil immediate provenire posse nisi motus localis (sic!) corporum caelestium, per quem omnia haec inferiora generantur et corrumpuntur, ut satis et ex octavo *Physicorum* (265 a 13 ff.) et ex secundo *De generatione* (338 a 4 ff.) patet; caelumque esse nexum inter immaterialia et materialia posuit, quoniam ab agente omnino immobili nihil provenire potest nisi mediante motu aeterno et non esset multiplicitas effectuum, ut ipse secundo *De generatione* (336 a 15 ff.) manifestat. Sic itaque secundum Aristotelem etsi in intelligentiis sint species factivae rerum, tamen per tales species non possunt immediate producere nisi motu, quo mediante fiunt generationes et corruptiones et denique haec omnia inferiora"; *ibid.* f. 38 vb: "Species igitur caliditatis secundum dictum modum sive sit in intellectu practico sive in virtute imaginativa immediate et per se non potest producere caliditatem, sed solum mediante motu locali secundum declaratum modum. Et ita dicatur de specie frigiditatis, coloris, saporis, odoris et reliquis. Et erit convenientia inter inferiora et superiora. Dictum namque est, quod intelligentia per speciem suam caliditatis vel alterius non posset immediate calefacere, sed solum movendo caelum, per cuius motum cuncta generantur. Sic et in animalibus species rerum non possunt immediate illas res producere nisi mediante motu locali spirituum et instrumentorum, nisi forte dicamus quod species motus localis cum appetitu immediate localiter movent spiritus."

Pomponazzi could have read in Averroes' commentary to the *De anima* that Alexander had maintained the mortality of the material intellect because this position seemed to conform closely with the *naturalia*, the natural;[21] and he could have found that these *naturalia* were meant to signify the first qualities, the elements and their mixtures, as represented in the *De generatione et corruptione*.[22] And when later, after the publication of Girolamo Donato's Latin translation,[23] Pomponazzi had access to Alexander's psychological treatise itself, he could have found the verification of what he had read in Averroes. There Alexander postulates that in order to understand the miracle of the soul, the psychologist should first study the miracles of nature, especially the structure and organisation of the human body;[24] he subordinates the metaphysical matter/form paradigm of the *Physics* to the naturalistic principle of the sensible body from the *De generatione*,[25] and changes the form into a kind of quality[26] and the composition of form and matter into a mixture of elements;[27] and he reduces the various kinds of different motions and processes to the local

---

[21] Averrois Cordubensis *Commentarium Magnum in Aristotelis De Anima Libros* (III, c. 5), ed. F. Stuart Crawford (*Corpus Commentariorum Averrois in Aristotelem* VI,1), Cambridge, Mass., 1953, 393, 196 ff.: "Alexander autem sustentatur super hunc sermonem postremum, et dicit quod magis convenit Naturalibus, scilicet sermonem concludentem quod intellectus materialis est virtus generata, ita quod existimamus de eo quod opinatur et in aliis virtutibus anime, esse preparationes factas in corpore per se a mixtione et complexione."

[22] Averrois Cordubensis *Commentarium Magnum in Aristotelis De Anima Libros* (III, c. 5), *op. cit.* (n. 21) 394, 202 ff.: "Et dicit hoc non esse inopinabile, scilicet ut ex mixtione elementorum fiat tale esse nobile mirabile, licet sit remotum a substantia elementorum propter maximam mixtionem. Et dat testimonium super hoc esse possibile ex hoc quod apparet quod compositio que primo cecidit in elementis, scilicet compositio quatuor qualitatum simplicium, cum hoc quod est parva illa compositio, est causa maxime diversitatis in tantum quod unum est ignis et aliud est aer. Et cum ita sit, non est remotum ut per multitudinem compositionis que est in homine et in animalibus fiant illic virtutes diverse in tantum a substantia elementorum."

[23] Alexander of Aphrodisias, *Enarratio de anima ex Aristotelis institutione*, interprete Hieronymo Donato, Brescia 1495.

[24] Alexandri Aphrodisiensis *De anima liber cum Mantissa*, ed. I. Bruns (Supplementum Aristotelicum II,1), Berlin 1887, 2,10-25.

[25] *Ibid.* 2,25 – 3,2.

[26] *Ibid.* 17,17 f.

[27] *Ibid.* 8,1-25.

motion of elementary simple bodies,[28] and the differences between natural beings to the different mixtures of the underlying elements.[29]

We may conclude, therefore, that it is not by chance that Pomponazzi's "naturalistic" psychology, which claims to be based on the *pura naturalia*, is accompanied by a "naturalistic" philosophy of nature based on Aristotle's teaching in the *De generatione et corruptione*.[30] It would not be surprising either, if those who followed Pomponazzi were to regard the separability of the human intellect as being linked to the acceptability of metaphysical principles and supernatural substantial forms in the world of nature, and if those who rejected metaphysical principles in nature also rejected the immortality of the soul and vice versa.

Whether this was indeed generally the case, I am not yet able to prove. But the few instances which I am able to offer at the moment seem sufficient to prove at least that as a consequence of the new reception of Alexander[31] an attempt was made to overcome the incoherence between the metaphysical and the naturalistic approach in the Aristotelian tradition of natural philosophy; that a new way of understanding Aristotle's natural philosophy was tried, which separated the "metaphysical" *Physics* from the "naturalistic" *De generatione et corruptione* and concentrated on the latter; and that this new way of reading Aristotle paved the way for a new reading of the book of nature itself.

In order to get an impression of what was going on in the philosophy of nature in the sixteenth century, it may be useful to distinguish between two

---

[28] *Ibid.* 7,14-8,1.

[29] *Ibid.* 8,25 ff.

[30] As the bibliography in Charles H. Lohr, *Latin Aristotle Commentaries II: Renaissance Authors*, Florence 1988, 347-362, proves, Pomponazzi fulfilled his statuary obligations as professor of natural philosophy by commenting on the *Physics* as well as – indeed, more often than – on the *De generatione et corruptione* and the *Meteorologica*. Yet his basic statements on the principles of nature and natural philosophy are uttered in the context of treatises and questions dealing with the interaction of first qualities, and of his expositions of the Aristotelian teaching the only one published during the Renaissance was the *Dubitationes in Quartum Meteorologicorum librum* (Venice 1563), which deals with the theory of active qualities as well as elementary mixtures.

[31] According to F. Edward Cranz ("Alexander Aphrodisiensis" in *Catalogus Translationum et Commentariorum. Medieval and Renaissance Latin Translations and Commentaries*, ed. P.O. Kristeller, vol. I, Washington 1960, 81) the Latin translation of Alexander's *De anima* went through twelve editions between 1495 and 1559 and that of his *De mixtione* and of his commentary to the *Meteorologica* appeared in five editions between 1540 and 1559.

kinds of philosophers: that is between those who taught as professors of natural philosophy in high schools and universities and consequently had to meet the requirements of the relevant statutes, and those who did not earn their living by teaching philosophy and thus were free to philosophise according to the best of their ability.

The members of the first group obviously could not avoid commenting on the "metaphysical" principles of nature as taught in the Aristotelian *Physics*, which traditionally served as the first introduction to natural philosophy in schools and universities from the times of Neoplatonism in late Antiquity throughout the Middle Ages and the Renaissance up to the *cursus philosophici* of the late sixteenth and the seventeenth centuries. What they could do, however, was to underline the differences between the two approaches, and thus virtually divide natural philosophy into two disciplines and gain autonomy for the empirical, "naturalistic" parts of the Aristotelian tradition. Thus we can observe that, as Kees Leijenhorst has recently established,[32] the traditional hierarchical distinction made by some philosophers of the later sixteenth century between the *Physics* as the *physica generalis* and the other Aristotelian treatises on nature as the *physica particularis* was taken as a methodological one, so that the *Physics* were counted among the metaphysical disciplines and the former *physica particularis*, honoured with the status of natural philosophy, was turned into a discipline in its own right. Even though leading representatives of Renaissance scholastic philosophy do not hesitate to reject this new distinction, the mere fact that they find it necessary to discuss proves its actuality. When Hobbes later uses this same distinction in organising his *De corpore*, it becomes manifest that they had not succeeded in repressing it.[33]

Furthermore, without offending against the statutes of the school, philosophy teachers could shift the emphasis both in teaching and in

---

[32] Kees Leijenhorst, *Hobbes and the Aristotelians. The Aristotelian Setting of Thomas Hobbes's Natural Philosophy*, Utrecht 1998.

[33] See e.g. Benedicti Pererii S.J. *De Communibus omnium rerum naturalium Principiis & Affectionibus libri XV*, II,7, Lyon 1588, 90: "Caeterum, quoniam nonnulli aetatis nostrae Philosophi praestantes ingenio & scientia Philosophiae Aristotelicae (sc. Antonius Mirandulanus) pugnacissime contendunt octo libros Physices (in quibus agitur de principiis & affectionibus rerum naturalium) omnino removendos esse a partibus Physicae & referendos esse ad Metaphysicam, initium autem Philosophiae naturalis sumendum esse ex libris de Caelo, age hanc etiam opinionem obiter refellamus." See Kees Leijenhorst, *Hobbes and the Aristotelians... op. cit.* (n. 32) 39 ff.

publishing from one part of the prescribed course to the other, in our case from the *Physics* to the *De generatione et corruptione*, and by doing so adjust their teaching to new philosophical developments. As a statistical analysis by Paul Richard Blum seems to prove, the most surprising novelty in the philosophy teaching of the religious orders at the turn of the sixteenth and seventeenth century was the growing attention paid to the treatises on and problems of the "naturalistic" approach to nature.[34]

Finally, the most radical strategy was to deal with the *Physics* in a "naturalistic" way and adapt it to the principles of the *De generatione et corruptione*, according to the example of Alexander in his treatise on the soul. This was the approach taken by Simon Portius, a former student of Achillini and Pomponazzi at Bologna, and professor of natural philosophy at Naples and Pisa.[35]

Like his teacher Pomponazzi, Portius in a "Disputation on the human mind", *De humana mente disputatio*, had denied the immortality of the human soul for the simple reason that the soul is defined to be the form or the first entelechy, *entelécheia*, of an organic natural body.[36] For according to Portius form or entelechy signifies an end, *finis*, that is gained or possessed as the result of a preceding motion,[37] and that means that it is subjected to generation and corruption.

When two years later, in 1553, he published two books "On the Principles of Natural Beings", *De rerum naturalium principiis libri duo*, he promised to comment on the first two books of Aristotle's *Physics* from the perspective of Alexander, that is on the hypothesis of the overall non-

---

[34] See Paul Richard Blum, "Der Standardkurs der katholischen Schulphilosophie im 17. Jahrhundert", in *Aristotelismus und Renaissance, op. cit.* (n. 12) 127-148, esp. 132.

[35] For Simon Portius (1496-1554) see Charles H. Lohr, *Latin Aristotle Commentaries II: Renaissance Authors*, Florence 1988, 364-366.

[36] See Aristotle, *De anima* II,1; 412 a 19-21; 412 b 5 f. (in the translation of Argyropulos, see *Aristoteles latine, interpretibus variis*, ed. Academia Regia Borussica, Berlin 1831, reprint München 1995, 209-226): "necesse est igitur animam substantiam esse, perinde atque *formam*, corporis naturalis potentia vitam habentis ... si igitur commune quid de omni anima sit dicendum, ipsa perfectio prima primusque actus [=*entelécheia*] est corporis naturalis, cuius partes sunt instrumenta."

[37] Simon Portius, *De humana mente disputatio* I, Florentiae 1551, p. 8: "Entelechia peculiari significatione perfectionem & finem postremum per motionem partum significat"; p. 9: "Forma finis habitus per motum appellatur & hoc pacto dicitur entelechia"; p. 10: "Anima rationalis ... quandoquidem anima, est forma et corporis perfectio." See Eckhard Keßler, "The intellective soul", *op. cit.* (n. 14) 519-521.

contradictory coherence of Aristotle's teaching, and on the basis of Alexander's scattered remnants on natural philosophy.[38] Both principles seem to amount to one and the same approach: to read the *Physics* in the light of Aristotle's later writings *On generation and corruption* and of Alexander's various expositions of these writings in the treatises *On the soul*, *On mixture* and the *Commentary to the "Meteorologica"*.[39]

The basis of this interpretation is laid down in the first chapter of the first book, where Portius assigns to each of the two books a special subject and a corresponding method.

The subject matter of the first book is matter, form and privation, defined as the principles of how natural entities come to be, *ut res fiunt*, and its method is said to be the "division", *divisio*, of what hitherto is known only in a confused way. This method is described as being familiar not only to the natural philosopher but also to the metaphysician. To the second book Portius assigns as subject matter the causes on account of which natural beings are how they are, *causae ut sunt*, and, as the corresponding method, inference from the effects or signs to the causes or, better, from the sensible to the purely conceptual.[40]

---

[38] Simon Portius, *De rerum naturalium principiis libri II*, I,1, Neapoli 1553, 4: "Id interpretes aliter atque aliter... prout quisque rectus (sic!) iudicavit, explicare conantur. Verum enimvero dum hi temere ac pro lubito Philosophum oculatissimum multa, quae deinde tractando non persequitur, proponere autumnant, miris ambagibus ac tricis, unde se extricare nequeant, sese irretiunt: quas facile effugiet is, qui id proponi a Philosopho, quod postea pertractet, existimabit. Atque id solus ut mea fert opinio, Alexander probe perspexit. Si quidem ipse Aristoteles sibi ipsi constare, atque id, quod initio proposuit, tractando exequi, sua interpretatione edocet. Caeterum cum Alexandri verba concise admodum a Simplicio citentur ... illa explicare nitemur et quae alibi, ubi haec Aristotelis verba enucleare voluit, tradidit, unum in locum congerere conabimur, quo tum Philosophi, tum Alexandri sententia clarior elucescat."

[39] See above, n. 31.

[40] Simon Portius, *De rerum naturalium principiis* I,1, *op. cit.* (n. 38) 3: "Ut res Naturales accurate Aristoteles tractaret, duos ad exquisitam earum cognitionem Libros conscripsit; primum videlicet ac secundum Physicae auscultationis: atque id hoc consilio factum ab illo fuisse suspicor, quia rerum naturalium principia duplici via indagare possimus; una ut fiunt: altera ut sunt: et ut res fiunt tribus principiis materia, privatione, ac forma constant: ut vero sunt, natura, causisque naturalibus coalescunt. Proinde primo libro, rerum primordia ut fiunt scrutatur: atque in secundo earundem ut iam sunt, originem investigat: verum diversa tractandi ratione: namque in illo via, et naturali, et primo philosopho trita, per confusa, quae sunt disiuncta, dividendo incedit; et hoc pacto ea quae sunt circa principia inquirit, ut eorum cognitionem venetur: In hoc autem ab effectis quod est a signo, rerum causas rimatur."

At first glance, however, Portius does not seem to follow his own division, since, as a look at the chapter headings of the first book proves,[41] the only topic that gets discussed in that book is matter; and at the beginning of the second book, instead of turning to the subject he had announced, he continues with what was said to belong to the first book and discusses the natural principle of form[42]. But the first glance is misleading. For when Portius deals with the form, he does not treat it as a self-subsisting part of the composite of form and matter, but as the efficient cause for natural beings to be the way they are, as *causa ut sunt*.[43] In this connection he asks whether it is necessary or even possible to consider form to be a substance apart from the two ways in which matter can be substance, namely the simple and the composite.[44] In other words he asks

---

[41] See the following chapter headings from the first book, Cap.1 (p. 3): Qua Methodo Investiganda sunt rerum naturalium Principia ex Aristotele; Cap.2 (p. 24): De materia prima; Cap.3 (p. 26): Quid significet materia et subiectum; Cap. 4 (p. 29): An materia, cum sit omnes formae potentia, nullamque sibi vendicet propriam, sit substantia actu; Cap. 5 (p. 35): De potentia et materiae Indeterminatione; Cap. 6 (p. 45): An in materia forma quaedam existat, ante quam forma producatur; Cap. 7 (p. 50): An prima materia sit omnium generabilium et corruptibilium una; Cap. 8 (p. 61): An reperiatur aliud corpus praeter naturale et mathematicum; Cap. 9 (p. 63): An materia appetitu naturali expetat formam; Cap.10 (p. 69): An materia sit principium Individui; Cap.11 (p. 76): An materia sit pars, ut latini loquuntur, quiditatis.

[42] See the chapter headings of the second book: Cap. 1 (p. 81): An forma sit substantia, et an Aristotelis rationes probari possint, reperiri formam substantiae; Cap. 2 (p. 85): De natura, quid sit; Cap. 3 (p. 93): Quare definierit naturam Philosophus cum sit nota per se; Cap. 4 (p. 99): Utrum causa efficiens possit appellari natura secundum Aristotelem; Cap. 5 (p. 101): De causa finali; Cap. 6 (p. 108): An finis sit naturae actionum terminus sub boni specie; Cap. 7 (p. 114): An idem sit agens, quod per electionem et quod per cognitionem agit; Cap. 8 (p. 118): An omnia bonum expetant; Cap. 9 (p. 122): De causis rerum naturalium efficientibus; Cap.10 (p.125): Utrum cum reddimus rationem alicuius effectus naturalis, per quam generatur scientia, opus sit omnes causas per se reddere; Cap.11 (p. 142): An fatum sit; Cap.12 (p. 143): Sententia Platonis de nomine fati; Cap.13 (p. 144): Quae ambigua sint in sententia Platonis; Cap.14 (p. 146): Quid Plotinus senserit de fato; Cap.15 (p. 148): Quid sit in Plotini sententia ambiguum; Cap.16 (p. 150): Chrysippi de fato sententia; Cap.17 (p. 152): Quid sit controversum ac dubium in Chrysippi placito; Cap.18 (p. 153): Quid sentiat Aristoteles de fato.

[43] Simon Portius, *De rerum naturalium principiis* II,1, *op. cit.* (n. 38) 21: "Nec secundus (sc. liber) a primo distrahi debet, ut graecis placet, quasi in primo de materia potius quam de aliis principiis, atque in secundo de efficiente, vel de forma magis quam de aliis pertractetur. nam uterque eadem proponit, licet diversa explicandi ratione, ut antea diximus, & in primo materiam, in secundo vero formam, quae cum efficiente similitudinem obtinet, investigat".

[44] Simon Portius, *De rerum naturalium principiis* II,1, *op. cit.* (n. 40) 81: "Cum Aristoteles substantiam de tribus dici asserat, de materia, forma, & quod ex his constare videtur,

whether it is necessary or even possible to suppose something like a substantial form to be the cause of the essence of natural beings.

To answer this question, he searches the hierarchy of natural beings from the elements through all kinds of mixed bodies up to the animals and men – following Alexander's example in the introductory part of his treatise *On the soul*[45] – with the result that at every step the specific nature and virtue of the entities examined can be explained in terms of accidental qualities, their mixtures, temperaments and complexions, and that no such thing as a substantial form is necessary to serve as efficient cause for natural beings to be what they are and to act as they do.[46]

Thus the *Physics* in Portius is no longer a "metaphysical" treatise. The only "metaphysical" part is the first book, which deals with the substance or underlying matter, the ontological basis of all real being which, although it cannot be the object of sense-perception itself, can be reached through the analysis of sensible objects.[47] Everything else, however, since it already has the determinate essence of a concrete being, a *concretum accidentale*, is

---

composito naturali: de materia quidem, ut substernitur contrariis eaque recipit: de forma vero, ut qua composita habent esse simpliciter habentque nomen ac definitionem: et postremo de composito, ut per se existit, et ex illis conflatur, quod etiam proprie ac primo dicitur substantia omnibus conspicua perscrutandum est, an tria substantiarum genera inveniri contingat. Antiquiores duas solum substantias probarunt (caetera enim omnia accidentia esse dicebant)... Verum cum accidens aliud sit separabile, aliud minime... hoc accidens (sc. inseparabile) Peripatetici vocarunt formam substantiae; antiqui autem, qualitatem materiae, quae materia tantum erat substantia, et per eam composita."

[45] See Simon Portius, *De rerum naturalium principiis* II,1, *op. cit.* (n. 38) 82; Alexandri Aphrodisiensis *De anima liber cum Mantissa*, ed. I. Bruns (*Supplementum Aristotelicum* II,1), Berlin 1887, 2,25-11,13.

[46] Simon Portius, *De rerum naturalium principiis* II,1, *op. cit.* (n. 38) 82: "Sic nec aliquis elementorum motus, formas ut substantias dicamus esse cogit ... Porro in inanimatis, puta metallis, primorum corporum mixtio, et forma propria, quae nichil aliud est quam complexio, illorumque temperamentum quo inter se distant ... In plantis autem, est mixtio corporum et earum vita est temperamentum, quo nutriuntur, crescunt et generant ... At vero Animalia rationis expertia, forma propria est sensus, quae est temperies quaedam qualitatum ... Est et ratio, quae nec ipsa est substantia, quoniam intelligere et velle haudquaquam a substantia oritur, sed a nobilissimo perfectissimoque temperamento. et huic sententiae Alexander quoque astipulatur."

[47] Simon Portius, *De rerum naturalium principiis* I,1, *op. cit.* (n. 38) 6: "Et si in fine eius libri dicat, oportere primum considerare quid sit natura: tamen per naturam nihil aliud innuit quam rerum naturalium cognitionem, quae praecedere primam philosophiam debet, ut ipsa quoque libri inscriptio docet, quae est *tôn metà tà physiká*."

subject to sense-perception[48] and therefore to empirical investigation from the effects to the causes according to the processes of qualitative interactions and elementary mixtures. There is no need to have recourse to abstract formal causes, which have only an intentional and therefore secondary being.[49]

I have said that the background of Portius' transformation of the Aristotelian *Physics*, and consequently of his "naturalistic" philosophy and psychology in general, was Alexander. This is not the whole truth. For Portius does not only quote Alexander, but refers again and again with similar reverence to Hippocrates and Galen. The medical tradition, as is well known, acquires in the course of the sixteenth century an increasing influence on philosophical discussion.[50] It seems that at least some representatives of the new, non-metaphysical philosophy of nature, who did not teach philosophy in schools and universities and thus were not restricted to teaching statutes, belonged to this tradition.[51] It may well have been that the Alexandristic turn which we found in school philosophers

---

[48] Simon Portius, *De rerum naturalium principiis* I,1, *op. cit.* (n. 38) 22: "Quod si planius explicari cupis, quid sit quod in notitia vocata occursoria, primum se offert ... aio id quod primum in notitia fit obvium, esse concretum accidentale, quemadmodum meo quidem iudicio, ut ad naeotericos descendamus, Hervaeus rectius quam caeteri, animadvertit. id enim primum a sensibus intellectus recipit."

[49] Simon Portius, *De rerum naturalium principiis* II,1, *op. cit.* (n. 38) 85: "Attamen in praedicamentis, primam ac precipuam substantiam facit compositum atque ad hanc magis accedit species quam genus. Quare species magis dicuntur substantia quam genera. quod propter Platonicos dicitur, qui formas et ideas, priores ac nobiliores substantias esse asseverabant. Sed ab illis dissentit Aristoteles, qui compositum praecipuas facit substantias. nam formae abstractae, quas genera et species appellat, et si nobilius esse obtineant: habent tamen esse tenuissimum, utpote in intellectu; non autem obtinent esse lapidis vel ligni, perfectius enim esse est ligni compositi quam quod est in mente, licet aliter cuipiam videri possit, et quod sit in mente nobilius et praestantius haberi. Non est igitur dicendum hoc esse in mente esse praestabilius ligno in re. quemadmodum medici de sanitate sentiunt. eadem enim sanitas est in mente et in re tamen ea quae in re vera dicitur sanitas, ea vero in mente, et si obtineat esse nobilius, non tamen vera et absoluta sanitas nuncupatur. Eodem modo se res habet in ideis, quae etiam si possideant nobiliorem essendi modum in intellectu divino et in intellectibus nostris atque aeternis rationibus, verius tamen esse est in materia."

[50] For the influence of the medical discussion on natural philosophy in the sixteenth century see the hitherto unpublished *Habilitationsschrift* of Michaela Boenke, *Körper, spiritus, Geist. Psychologie vor Descartes*, München 1997.

[51] See Alfonso Ingegno, "The new philosophy of nature", in *The Cambridge history of Renaissance Philosphy, op. cit.* (n. 14) 236-263.

like Pomponazzi and Portius encouraged medical professors to trust in the philosophical relevance of their traditional naturalistic paradigm of nature.

I shall try to give a brief outline of three of them, Girolamo Fracastoro, Girolamo Cardano and Bernardino Telesio. The two Girolamos were medical doctors themselves and the third, Telesio, dedicated his whole life to writing his only book on nature in the medical tradition.

Fracastoro, who was born in Verona in 1483 and died nearby in 1553, had studied with Pomponazzi in Padua. In his most basic treatise on natural philosophy, the *De sympathia et antipathia rerum* of 1546, he analyses the concept of general sympathy and antipathy between natural beings, which contemporary Neoplatonists regarded as an effect of occult causes and used as a principle to account for apparently supernatural phenomena.[52] Fracastoro tries to describe this principle in terms of a general potential common to the attraction and repulsion between similar and dissimilar bodies[53] and to the interaction between the first qualities[54], and thus succeeds in reintegrating occult or "meta-physical" phenomena, hitherto explained through *sympathia* and *antipathia*, into a naturalistic concept of nature.

At the same time, he develops a new general theory of nature, including even the soul and its intentional actions, which is based exclusively on the principles of interaction and mixture as derived from the tradition of *De generatione et corruptione*. It will be no surprise that besides Hippocrates and Galen he also quotes Alexander of Aphrodisias.[55]

---

[52] Girolamo Fracastoro, *De sympathia et antipathia rerum*, Praefatio, in *Opera, pars prior*, Lyon 1591.

[53] Girolamo Fracastoro, *De sympathia et antipathia rerum*, Cap.V, *op. cit.* (n. 52) 19: "Sicut autem inter similia mutua versatur attractio, ita et inter dissimilia et contraria versari propulsationem quandam mutuam consentaneum est credere."

[54] Girolamo Fracastoro, *De sympathia et antipathia rerum*, Cap. VI, *op. cit.* (n. 52) 19 f.: "Est autem et alia magnopere admiranda elementorum Sympathia et Antipathia circa eas qualitates, quae contrariae inter se sunt, ut caliditas, frigiditas, humiditas et siccitas: nam has quidem contrarias esse et sese mutuo destruere atque interimere manifestum est, at vero quis non miretur, quum nihilominus videamus certos unius contrarii gradus stare ac quodammodo congaudere cum certis alterius, quosdam vero cum quibusdam non posse consistere."

[55] See e.g. Girolamo Fracastoro, *De sympathia et antipathia rerum*, Cap. V, *op. cit.* (n. 52) 18: "Ad quae si quis respiciat, non alienum fortasse et veluti paradoxum quoddam existimabit, quod Alexander dixit attractionem omnem a calore esse."

Cardano, who was born in Milan in 1501 and died in Rome in 1576, was to become one of the most curious personalities of the Renaissance.[56] His very dense treatise on nature, *De natura*, starts with a metaphysical reflection on the Aristotelian principle of matter as *prima materia*. Cardano realizes that primary matter cannot be subject to sense-perception,[57] that it cannot be defended as a natural principle[58], and that it is better to discuss nature on the basis of the elements.[59] Thus he tries to develop, rather tentatively, a theory of natural generation whether caused by the primary quality of celestial warmth in what he calls the passive, underlying elementary "form",[60] or by the interaction between celestial warmth and the humid, contained in the elements.[61] He emphazises that it has to be the form which is generated, for otherwise, if the form were eternal, there would be no generation but only composition.[62]

Consequently, according to Cardano, there can be neither matter nor anything like a substantial form. Since, however, without these two prin-

---

[56] For Cardano see Eckhard Keßler (ed.), *Girolamo Cardano. Philosoph, Naturforscher, Arzt*, Wiesbaden 1994; M. Baldi / G. Canziani (edd.), *Girolamo Cardano. Le opere, le fonti, la vita*, Milano 1999.

[57] Girolamo Cardano, "De natura", in *Opera omnia*, vol. II, ed. Spohn, Lyon 1662, Repr. New York and London 1967, 284b10 ff.: "Quaecumque etiam astruuntur vel ex ratione ac principiis deduci debent aut esse manifesta sensui: at sensus nullus eam (sc. primam materiam) cognoscit, quoniam actum non habet, et ubi actus deest, etiam motus deest, sensus autem omnis in motione consistit."

[58] Girolamo Cardano, "De natura", *op. cit.* (n. 57) 284b31 f.: "Neque enim illa materia ullo modo statui potest".

[59] Girolamo Cardano, "De natura", *op. cit.* (n. 57) 284b38 ff.: "Melius est ergo unam formam elementorum subiectum statuere generationi, agens autem ut instrumentum calorem coelestem, cum omnia sic generari videamus. Nam elementa frustra omnino essent. Si materia prima esset."

[60] See n. 59.

[61] Girolamo Cardano, "De natura", *op. cit.* (n. 57) 285a35 ff.: "Principia ergo omnium dico in his inferioribus calorem a coelestibus demissum et humidum quod est in ipsis elementis. At ubi desierit horum alterum fit quod corruptio vocatur: oportet enim esse id quod agat et id in quod agat."

[62] Girolamo Cardano, "De natura", *op. cit.* (n. 57) 285b9 ff.: "forma autem cum composito simul fit. Quod si non fiat forma, aeternam esse necesse est, non igitur fit compositum sed compaginatur ut diximus. Aut igitur forma non est principium quia fit, nemo enim principium fieri concedit: aut si non fit in idem redimus ne omnia compaginentur non generentur. Dicimus ergo omnia fieri ex calido et humido, quoniam quae fiunt aut corpora sunt aut in corpore, innatum est autem calidum et humidum cuncta cogere aut dissolvere aut mutare."

ciples there would be nothing left to account for the determinate essence and the oneness of natural bodies, the generation and persistence of a natural body would depend on mere chance. To solve this problem, which Averroes had already mentioned as following from Alexander's teaching,[63] Cardano asks at the beginning of *De natura* as well as in *De uno*, a treatise specifically dedicated to these questions, what brings about the oneness of natural beings. He arrives at some kind of immaterial and immortal soul as a metaphysical principle, which uses warmth as its instrument and guides its activities so as to constitute the different unities of the universe.[64]

Thus, if we may generalize from what can be seen in Cardano, the "animistic" character of many of the so called new philosophies of nature may well result from the effort to overcome the shortcomings of their Alexandristic tendencies. That this however is not invariably the case, is manifest in the last philosopher whom I intend to present: Bernardino Telesio.[65] He lived from 1509 to 1588, mostly in Cosenza, his birthplace, and devoted a large part of his life to the writing of his *De rerum natura iuxta propria principia*. There is much that could be said about him. I shall say only a few words.

We do not know whether he knew Pomponazzi's former student Portius, who published and for some time taught in Naples, but from the beginning of his book he makes it quite clear that he belongs to the "naturalistic" school of natural philosophy. In the first paragraphs of his proemium he promises that he will not deal with metaphysical principles of nature, which are the result of mere theoretical speculations, but that his philosophy of nature will be based on what is obvious to sense-perception or can be derived immediately from it. This was just what Pomponazzi had

---

[63] Averrois Cordubensis *Commentarium Magnum in Aristotelis De Anima Libros* (III, c. 5), *op. cit.* (n. 21) 398, 325 ff.: "Et ista opinio est similis opinioni negantium causas agentes et non concedentium nisi causas materiales; et sunt illi qui dicunt casum. Sed Alexander est maioris nobilitatis quam ut credat hoc."

[64] Cardano, "De uno", in *Somniorum Synesiorum omnis generis insomnia explicantes Libri IV*, Basel 1562, 247 f.: "Si igitur multa in unum tenderent, fortuitum esset, et aliquando aberraret. non ergo tendunt in unum, sed ab uno procedunt: sic enim non possunt aberrare. ab anima igitur sunt omnia: sed anima, si esset extensa, haberet aut partem in parte, et sic non totus homo sentiret aut videret: aut partem in toto, quare una parte sentiente altera sentiret ..."

[65] For Telesio see Martin Mulsow, *Frühneuzeitliche Selbsterhaltung. Telesio und die Naturphilosophie der Renaissance*, Tübingen 1998.

proposed.⁶⁶ In the following chapters of the nine books Telesio unfolds a universe, the principles of which – according to the first book⁶⁷ – are the two active principles of warmth, concentrated in the sun, and of cold, concentrated in the earth, which fight each other and use as the underlying material of their battle the totally passive mass, *moles*.⁶⁸ Everything that exists in this world is thus the result of the interaction between the active first qualities, which in Aristotle's *De generatione et corruptione* serve as the first and basic object of sense-perception and therefore constitute the primary object of natural philosophy, the potentially perceptible body, *corpus potentia sensibile*. There is no substantial form to determine the specific essence of the various species, and there is no soul to direct the antagonism between the qualities. There is only the capacity of the two active qualities to distinguish between what is similar and dissimilar, pleasing and displeasing to them, a capacity which guides their actions,⁶⁹

---

⁶⁶ Bernardino Telesio, *De rerum natura iuxta propria principia*. Prooemium, Lat. / Ital. ed. Luigi De Franco, 3 vols., Cosenza / Firenze 1965 – 1977, I, 26 f.: "Qui ante nos mundi hujus constructionem rerumque in eo contentarum naturam perscrutati sunt... nimis forte sibi ipsis confisi, nequaquam, quod oportebat, res ipsas earumque vires intuiti, eam rebus magnitudinem, ingeniumque et facultates quibus donatae videntur, indidere; sed veluti cum Deo de sapientia contendentes decertantesque, mundi ipsius principia et caussas ratione inquirere ausi, et, quae non invenerant, inventa ea sibi esse existimantes volentesque, veluti suo arbitratu mundum effinxere. Itaque corporibus, e quibus constare is videtur, nec magnitudinem positionemque, quam sortita apparent, nec dignitatem viresque quibus praedita videntur, sed quibus donari oportere propria ratio dictavit, largiti sunt... Nos non adeo nobis confisi, et tardiore ingenio et animo donati remissiore, et humanae omnino sapientiae amatores cultoresque (quae quidem vel ad summum pervenisse videri debet, si, quae sensus patefecerit et quae e rerum sensu perceptarum similitudine haberi possunt, inspexerit) mundum ipsum et singulas ejus partes, et partium rerumque in eo contentarum passiones, actiones, operationes et species intueri proposuimus."

⁶⁷ Bernardino Telesio, *De rerum natura iuxta propria principia* I,1 (chapter-heading), *op. cit.* (n. 66) 30: "Solem a calore, terram a frigore constitutam esse; et quae agendi operandique facultates speciesque et dispositio soli inditae sunt, a calore, quae vero terrae, a frigore inditas esse omnes: et entia omnia a caelo, terram oppugnante inverteteque, constituta esse".

⁶⁸ Bernardino Telesio, *De rerum natura iuxta propria principia*. I,2 (chapter-heading), *op. cit.* (n. 66) 40: "Calorem sui natura mobilem, frigus contra immobile esse; et propterea molem illi, quam subit, tenuem levemque, huic contra densam gravemque faciendi facultatem tributam esse; et albedinem omnem caloris speciem et veluti faciem esse."

⁶⁹ Bernardino Telesio, *De rerum natura iuxta propria principia*. I,6, *op. cit.* (n. 66) 64 f.: "Et quoniam insuper maxime contrariis, et quibus mutuo sese oppugnent perdantque, utrumque donatum est viribus: utique, si utrumque servandum fuit, utrique et sui ipsius passiones et alterius actiones viresque percipiendi, et propriarum similiumque, a quibus fovetur servaturque, perblandus; contrariarum vero dissimiliumque, a quibus obliditur

and the difference in magnitude and position, which results in different effects.[70]

Thus in Telesio the "naturalistic" approach from the Aristotelian tradition seems to have achieved its most radical realisation and the break with the "metaphysical" approach seems total. Yet this does not mean that the "naturalistic" approach is the only survivor. On the contrary, five years after Telesio had published the last and definitive version of his *De rerum natura iuxta propria principia*, Francesco Patrizi would publish his metaphysical response, the *Nova de universis philosophia*;[71] and during the same years Tommaso Campanella, while expressly defending his compatriot's new philosophy of nature, later came to see the need for a complementary new metaphysics.[72]

Therefore, even if the observations presented in this paper are correct, they cannot be considered representative of the discussion in sixteenth century natural philosophy as a whole, and do not allow us to draw a conclusion about its general character. But they suggest four hypotheses, which it may be worth keeping in mind:

(1) It is well known that the discussion on the immortality of the soul had a great impact on the disciplines of psychology, anthropology, epistemology, metaphysics, theology, moral philosophy and ethics. Now it appears that it also had an impact on the general concept of natural philosophy, of which in the Aristotelian tradition psychology is a part. Both psychology and natural philosophy should therefore be studied in their relation to one another, regardless of whether they are treated inside or outside the schools and universities.

---

perditurque maxime molestus indendus utrique fuit sensus, et manifeste inditus est."

[70] Bernardino Telesio, *De rerum natura iuxta propria principia*. I,10, *op. cit.* (n. 66) 94 ff.

[71] Francesco Patrizi, *Nova de universis philosophia, in qua Aristotelica methodo non per motum, sed per lucem & lumina ad primam causam ascenditur. Deinde propria Patricii methodo tota in contemplationem venit Divinitas. Postremo methodo Platonica rerum universitas a conditore Deo deducitur*, Ferrara 1591; for Patrizi's open critique of Telesio see Bernardino Telesio, *Varii de naturalibus rebus libelli*, ed. Luigi de Franco, Firenze 1981, 463-474.

[72] Thomae Campanellae *De sensu rerum et magia*, ed. Tobias Adami, Frankfurt 1520, Reprint in Tommaso Campanella, *Opera Latina, Francofurti impressa annis 1617-1630*, ed. L. Firpo, Torino 1975, vol. I, 87-371; (it.: Tommaso Campanella, *Il senso delle cose e la magia*, ed. Antonio Bruers, Bari 1925, Reprint Genova 1987; ed. L. De Franco, Cosenza 1987).

(2) There seems to be a close relation between the denial of the immortality of the soul and the "naturalistic" approach to nature in the tradition of Aristotle's *De generatione et corruptione*. Since this position can be traced back to Alexander of Aphrodisias and its defenders frequently refer to him, we seem justified in referring to Alexandrinism in sixteenth century Renaissance philosophy, using a concept coined by Ernest Renan in the nineteenth century which appeared to have lost its significance in the light of new research in the twentieth.[73]

(3) Parallel to the "naturalistic" Alexandrist position, which was based on sense-perception, there seems to have been another position, which combined the defence of the immortality of the soul with the "metaphysical" approach to nature in the tradition of Aristotle's *Physics*, and argued on the basis of intentional principles. We may perhaps trace the modern distinction between natural science and philosophy of nature back to these two positions in sixteenth century Renaissance Aristotelianism, which would thus have survived as the basic attitudes towards nature in modern times.

(4) Even though the propagation of the Alexandrist position by no means resulted in a total replacement of the metaphysical with the naturalistic approach towards nature, it seems to have opened the way to the development of empirical science as early as the beginning of the sixteenth century and in the very centre of the Aristotelian tradition. It was to be Francis Bacon himself, the harbinger of modern science, who, while criticizing Telesio for not keeping strictly to the limits of sense-perception,[74] would nevertheless praise him as being *primus novorum*

---

[73] See Ernest Renan, *Averroès et l'averroisme,* 3rd edn., Paris 1866; Paul Oskar Kristeller, "Paduan Averroism and Alexandrinism in the Light of Recent Studies", in *Aristotelismo Padovano e Filosofia Aristotelica* (Atti del XII Congresso Internazionale di Filosofia 1958), Florence 1960, 147-155.

[74] Francis Bacon, "*De principiis atque originibus...*", in *Opera*, edd. J. Spelling et al., 14 vols., London 1857-74, vol. III, 107: "Qua in parte Telesius non admodum feliciter perfungitur, sed more adversariorum suorum se gerit; qui cum prius opinantur quam experiuntur, ubi ad res particulares ventum est, ingenio et rebus abutuntur, atque tam ingenium quam res misere lacerant et torquent; et tamen alacres et (si ipsis credas) victores suo sensu utcunque abundant."

hominum, the first of the moderns,[75] and thus acknowledge the contribution which the naturalistic approach of Renaissance Aristotelianism made to the emergence of modern science.

---

[75] Francis Bacon, *op. cit.* (n. 74) 114: "De Telesio autem bene sentimus, atque eum ut amantem veritatis et scientiis utilem et nonnullorum placitorum emendatorem et novorum hominum primum agnoscimus."

The Aristotelian Classification of Knowledge in the Early Sixteenth Century

by Heikki Mikkeli

During the latter half of the fifteenth century Gregor Reisch (1467?-1525), prior of the Carthusian monastery of Freiburg, wrote a general treatise on the different fields of knowledge. This textbook in philosophy, entitled *Margarita philosophica*, was first published in Freiburg in 1503 and various editions of the treatise were printed in the course of the sixteenth century. Reisch began his book by presenting a diagram showing a classification of knowledge or philosophy. True to the traditional Aristotelian model, he divided the various fields into theoretical or speculative, and practical (see fig. 1).

Reisch further divided the theoretical subjects into real and rational. The former, in the conventional Aristotelian manner, comprised metaphysics, mathematics, and natural philosophy, the latter the tools of reasoning: grammar, rhetoric and logic. According to Aristotle himself, these logical disciplines did not possess the status of true sciences, being of an instrumental nature. They provided the means for studying other fields of knowledge; thus the demonstrative syllogisms taught in logic, for example, were a means of ensuring the degree of certainty required in the theoretical sciences.

Reisch classified practical philosophy as either active or productive. The practical sciences included ethics, politics, economics, monastics, and both civil and canon law. The productive or mechanical arts covered the subjects which aimed at the fashioning of an artefact or the attainment of an objective, such as fabric-making, navigation, agriculture and medicine. Though of vital importance to human life, these were not, according to Reisch, on a par with the theoretical or practical sciences.[1]

---

[1] G. Reisch, *Margarita philosophica*, Freiburg 1503, liber XI (Quorum differt ars et scientia et quae artes liberales et mechanicae): "Illae a tali opere ad exteriora recedere adulterari et mechari faciunt. Unde et mechanicae dicuntur. Sunt autem homini necessariae."

Fig. 1a. Classification of knowledge. From G. Reisch, *Margarita Philosophica* (Friborgi [i. B.], 1504).

The Aristotelian Classification of Knowledge in the Early 16. Century

Fig. 1b. From Gregor Reisch, *Margarita philosophica* (Freiburg 1504).
Here the young schoolboy Nicostramus is guided to tht "temple of learning". He knows already the alphabet and begins his studies with Latin, grammatics, logic and so on. At the top of the temple is the discipline of theology, and Petrus Lombardus who wrote the influential sentence commentaries.

This basically Aristotelian classification of knowledge as applied by Reisch represented one of three such classifications in use in Europe at the beginning of the modern era.[2] The second general classification was the division observed by the medieval universities into *trivium/quadrivium* subjects – the so-called seven liberal arts – and the mechanical arts, which stood below them in the hierarchy of knowledge and were not studied at the university. Reisch incorporated these liberal arts in his own scheme, referring to the rational subjects (grammar, rhetoric and logic) of the *trivium* and the sub-divisions of mathematics of the *quadrivium* (arithmetic, geometry, music and astronomy).[3] The third classification of knowledge was the Stoic-Platonic tripartition into logic, ethics and physics.[4]

Around the turn of the sixteenth century, however, scholars came under pressure to modify the medieval classification of knowledge, when the Aristotelian ideal stressing theoretical knowledge was confronted with the needs of practical life given priority by the humanists. The majority of articles on classifications of knowledge have glossed over the entire sixteenth century as being a period of only minor interest between the classifications developed at the medieval universities and the new principles put forward by Francis Bacon at the beginning of the seventeenth century.[5] If we consider the interest among humanists in the practical branches of knowledge, the mechanical arts constitute an extremely interesting group of subjects because they enjoyed a clear rise in status in the first half of the sixteenth century. In order to gain a better understanding of the changes taking place, it is first necessary to examine the status of the arts in the medieval university.

---

[2] Aristotle himself did not, in any of his works, present any systematic classification of knowledge. Focal passages in his works as regards the division of branches of learning are, however, *Nicomachean Ethics* VI,4 and *Metaphysics* VI,1.

[3] For the liberal arts in the medieval Aristotelian classification of knowledge see R. McInerny, "Beyond the Liberal Arts", *The Seven Liberal Arts in the Middle Ages*, ed. David L. Wagner, Bloomington 1986, 248-272.

[4] This division appears in the sixteenth century in, among others, the work *Libri VII de dialectica* (1537) by Symphorien Champier and in *De veris principiis* (1553) by Mario Nizolio.

[5] See e.g. R. Flint, *Philosophy as Scientia Scientiarum and a History of Classifications of the Sciences*, Edinburgh and London 1904, and N. Fisher, "The Classification of the Sciences", *Companion to the History of Modern Science*, edd. R.C. Olby, G.N. Cantor, J.R.R. Christie and M.J.S. Hodge, London and New York 1990, 853-868.

The mechanical arts in medieval classifications

Scholars in the twelfth and thirteenth centuries became more closely acquainted than their predecessors with the texts of many of the Classical authors, and consequently more interested in the classification of knowledge. The objective of most medieval classificatory systems was to demonstrate the relation between human knowledge and the knowledge of God. The ultimate goal was in most cases to underline the status of theology as the science to which all others were subordinated. As George Ovitt has pointed out: "the classifications of the sciences were intended to systematise what was known in order to ensure the primacy of what was believed."[6]

This seeking to achieve salvation was also very much to the fore in the *Didascalicon* written by Hugh of Saint Victor (1096?-1141) in Paris towards the end of the 1120s. In this work Hugh divides the branches of knowledge into four categories on the Aristotelian model: theoretical, practical, mechanical and logical. According to Hugh, the purpose of the theoretical sciences is to meditate on the truth, that of the practical sciences to meditate on moral precepts, that of the mechanical arts to regulate the practical workings of life on earth, and that of the logical disciplines to provide the knowledge necessary for communication and argumentation.

Hugh's text was of the utmost influence as regards the treatment of the mechanical arts and the status afforded them. He divided the mechanical arts into seven branches: fabric-making, armament, commerce, agriculture, hunting, medicine, and theatrics. The fact that he listed precisely seven mechanical arts is no coincidence, since their number clearly corresponds to that of the liberal arts:

> These sciences are called mechanical, that is, adulterate, because their concern is with the artificer's product, which borrows its form from nature. Similarly, the other seven are called liberal either because they require minds which are liberal, that is, liberated and practised (for these sciences pursue subtle inquiries into the causes of things), or because in antiquity only free and noble men were

---

[6] G. Ovitt Jr., "The Status of the Mechanical Arts in Medieval Classifications of Learning", *Viator* 14 (1983), 91. See also G. Ovitt Jr., *The Restoration of Perfection. Labor and Technology in Medieval Culture*, New Brunswick and London 1987, chapter 4 ("The Mechanical Arts in the Order of Knowledge"), and F. Alessio, *La filosofia e les 'artes mechanicae' nel secolo XII*, Spoleto 1984 (1965).

accustomed to study them, while the populace and the sons of men not free sought operative skill in things mechanical.[7]

Hugh thus includes the mechanical arts in his classification of knowledge, but, as was traditional, grants them only an adulterate status. There are, in his view, two reasons why they are lowly: firstly, their concern is with the artificer's product, and secondly, those who pursue them are illiberal and do not therefore enjoy the free status of those who practise the nobler arts. The liberal arts are thus the arts of the mind as opposed to the mechanical arts, the arts of the hand.

Hugh himself in no way looked upon the mechanical arts as useless, despite their humble status in the hierarchy of knowledge, since they were equally capable of preparing students for wisdom and salvation. However, as long as other subjects had metaphysical aims, i.e. were regarded as means of approaching God, the mechanical arts, being concerned with the material world here on earth, had no chance of acquiring a more elevated status. They were concerned with the condition of the body in the world, and could therefore serve only as a preliminary step in the journey towards salvation. Thus the mechanical arts could not offer those who pursued them any greater knowledge of God.[8]

The *De ortu scientiarum* written in the 1250s by Robert Kilwardby (c. 1215-1279) mainly agreed with Hugh's classification of knowledge, as far as the mechanical arts were concerned. But unlike Hugh, Robert Kilwardby did not make a strict distinction between the theoretical and the practical branches of learning. Instead he argued that each practical science and art needed to be backed by theory in order to achieve its goal. In the list of seven mechanical arts Kilwardby also replaced Hugh's theatrics with architecture and commerce with navigation.[9] Like Hugh, he considered the

---

[7] Hugh of Saint Victor, *Didascalicon*, trans. J. Taylor, New York 1991, 75. The Latin text (*Patrologia Latina 176*, 760) reads as follows: "Hae mechanicae appellantur, id est adulterinae: quia de opere artificis agunt quod a natura formam mutuatur. Sicut aliae septem liberales appellatae sunt; vel quia liberos, id est, expeditos et exercitatos animos requirunt, quia subtiliter de causis rerum disputant; vel quia liberi tantum antiquitus, id est, nobiles in eis studere consueverant: plebei vero et ignobilium filii in mechanicis propter peritiam operandi."

[8] Ovitt Jr. 1983, 95.

[9] R. Kilwardby O.P., *De ortu scientiarum*, ed. Albert G.Judy (Auctores Britannici Medii Aevi 4), London 1976, 127-33. The list given by Gregor Reisch falls somewhere in between the lists of mechanical arts presented by Hugh and Robert Kilwardby, for while Reisch replaced commerce by navigation, he still listed theatrics instead of architecture.

more abstract learning as of greater value than the less abstract, but he also thought that the status of the mechanical arts was partly determined by the scope of the methods and branches of learning they employed and not merely by their efficacy for salvation.[10]

The late fifteenth-century humanist classifications
As pointed out by James A. Weisheipl, the genre of literature dealing with the classification of knowledge virtually died out in the fourteenth century.[11] The scholastic university had by this time espoused the Aristotelian classification and in its teaching applied the division into seven free arts. No new ancient sources throwing any doubt on the accepted classification came to light at this stage in history. Thus the classification of the arts and sciences posed no problem and could be taken for granted. In fact, the question of the classification of learning and the criteria for such classification did not really arise again until the latter part of the fifteenth century, when the discovery of sources dating from antiquity and better editions of the ancient texts opened up new visions again.

The orations given in the universities at the beginning of academic years are an essential source for the investigation of the revival of interest in the classifications of knowledge. In 1476, a year after his move to Ferrara, Rudolph Agricola (1443-85) delivered his oration entitled *Oratio in laudem philosophiae et reliquarum artium* in the presence of Duke Ercole d'Este and the representatives of the university.[12] In this speech Agricola followed closely another oration by a fellow humanist Battista Guarino, entitled *Oratio de septem artibus liberalibus in inchoando felici Ferrariensi gymnasio habita*, given at the same *studio* in 1453.[13] In both of these orations philosophy is divided in traditional Stoic manner into physics, ethics, and logic.[14] Another humanist, Cristoforo Landino (1424-98), in a

---

[10] Ovitt Jr. 1983, 103.

[11] J.A. Weisheipl, "The Nature, Scope, and Classification of the Sciences", *Science in the Middle Ages*, ed. David C. Lindberg, Chicago and London 1978, 479.

[12] R. Agricolae, *Lucubrationes aliquot lectu dignissimae*, Cologne 1539, 145ff. A facsimile of this edition was published in Nieuwkoop in 1967.

[13] The text is printed in K. Müllner, "Acht Inauguralreden des Veronesers Guarino und seines Sohnes Battista". *Wiener Studien* XIX (1897), 126-143.

[14] For a more detailed discussion, see G. Tonelli, "Per una storia della classificazione delle scienze: due prolusioni di Battista Guarino e Rodolfo Agricola", *Filosofia*, 30 (1979), 312-13.

lecture on Cicero's *Tusculan Disputations* (1458), mentioned both the bipartite Aristotelian division of philosophy and the Stoic classification.[15]

Both Guarino and Agricola used the term physics (*physica*) as a synonym for the discipline of philosophy. In Aristotelian fashion physics (i.e. philosophy as a whole) can be divided further into theology (or metaphysics), mathematics, and natural philosophy (i.e. physics in the strict sense of the word).[16] Thus in Guarino's and Agricola's texts we find the Aristotelian division of the theoretical sciences (i.e. metaphysics, mathematics, and natural philosophy) as a subdivision of the principal Stoic tripartite division of all disciplines into physics, ethics, and logic.

An important phase in the rearrangement of knowledge was the increased value ascribed to natural philosophy in the latter part of the fifteenth century, even in humanist circles. In a famous passage of his *De sui ipsius et multorum ignorantia* Francesco Petrarca (1304-1374) had asked the question "what is the use of knowing the nature of quadrupeds, fowls, fishes, and serpents and not knowing or even neglecting man's nature, the purpose for which we are born, and whence and whereto we travel?"[17] However, in the latter part of the fifteenth century the Greek émigrés from Constantinople took a much broader view of Aristotelian philosophy. Thus Johannes Argyropoulos (c.1410-87), a Byzantine scholar who taught in Florence, began his course on Aristotle's *Physics* in 1458 by exclaiming: "How great is the nobility of this science, how great its perfection, its strength and power, and how great also is its beauty!"[18]

Angelo Poliziano's Panepistemon
On the eve of the 1490s Angelo Poliziano (1454-94), a humanist previously interested primarily in Platonic philosophy, embarked on a systematic appraisal of the works of Aristotle in a series of lectures at the University

---

[15] J-M. Mandosio, "Filosofia, arti e scienze: L'enciclopedismo di Angelo Poliziano", *Poliziano nel suo tempo*, a c. di Luisa Secchi Tarugi, Firenze 1996, 138-9.

[16] Tonelli 1979, 313.

[17] Francesco Petrarca, *On his own ignorance and that of many others*, in *The Renaissance Philosophy of Man*, edd. E. Cassirer, P.O. Kristeller and J.H. Randall Jr., Chicago and London 1948, 58-9.

[18] Cited from J. Kraye, "The Philosophy of the Italian Renaissance", *Routledge History of Philosophy, vol. IV: The Renaissance and the 17th Century Rationalism*, ed. G.H.R. Parkinson, London and New York 1993, 21. The Latin text is given in K. Müllner, *Reden und Briefe italienischer Humanisten*, München 1970 (1899), 43.

of Florence. He began his series in the academic year 1490-91 with the *Nicomachean Ethics*, continuing with logical works, the *Prior Analytics* and later the *Posterior Analytics* and the *Topics*. Each series had a preamble in which he presented an interesting outline of the fundamental issues of philosophy and learning. The introduction to the *Nicomachean Ethics* goes by the name of *Panepistemon*, a Greek word that may be freely translated as the systematisation of all the branches of knowledge.

Poliziano's encyclopaedic idea of learning is already visible in his work entitled *Miscellanea* which was published in 1489, a year before *Panepistemon* was written. In a well-known passage in *Miscellanea* 1.4 Poliziano points out that "it is not only the schools of philosophers which should be taken into account but also those of writers on law, medicine, dialectic, and the entire sphere of learning which we call *encyclia*; without forgetting the whole family of philology".[19]

Poliziano begins his lecture *Panepistemon* with a fascinating account of his chosen method. A scholar with a sovereign command of Latin, he nevertheless limits himself to a simple style in his introduction. He likens his work to the dissection carried out by an anatomist or the calculations of a tabulator whose objective is, by breaking philosophy down into its parts, to present the issues as lucidly as possible in order to make them easier to comprehend and remember.[20]

Poliziano's aim is to give a clear account of all the fields of human learning and not just of the theoretical and practical sciences. The *Panepistemon* is, therefore, probably the first Renaissance classification of knowledge explicitly designed to include the mechanical arts alongside

---

[19] A. Poliziano, *Miscellaneorum centuria prima*, in *Opera omnia*, Venice 1498, without page numbers: "Nec prospiciendae autem philosophorum modo familiae, sed et iureconsultorum, et medicorum item, et dialecticorum, et quicumque doctrinae illum orbem faciunt, quae vocamus Encyclia, sed et philologorum quoque omnium." In another passage of *Miscellanea* Poliziano also mentions the encyclopedic ideal of knowledge, and here he refers to Martianus Capella as his source, see Mandosio 1996, 144 (note 60). See also P. Godman, *From Poliziano to Machiavelli. Florentine Humanism in the High Renaissance*, Princeton 1998, 81.

[20] A. Poliziano, *Panepistemon*, in *Opera omnia*, Venice 1498, without page numbers: "Imitabor igitur sectiones illas medicorum, quas anatomas vocant. Imitabor et tabulariorum calculos. Nam et dividam singula prope minutatim, et in summa summarum redigam, quo possit ununquodque, vel facilius percipi, vel fidelius retineri."

rather than in subordination to the theoretical and practical subjects.²¹ Poliziano points out that his work is not confined exclusively to the traditional fields of learning and the liberal arts, and that it also includes the arts known as mechanical, considered to be of lower status but nevertheless indispensable to life.²²

Poliziano begins by dividing human knowledge into three categories: inspiration (*inspiratum*, i.e. theology), invention (*inventum*, i.e. philosophy), and mixture (*mixtum*, i.e. divination or prophecy).²³ He himself concentrates on philosophy, which he classifies in the conventional manner as theoretical, practical and rational.²⁴ Poliziano's approach was by no means rare in the Florentine *studio* of the latter half of the fifteenth century. Giovanni Argyropoulos (1415?-87), in his introduction to Aristotle's *Ethics* of 1456, had already divided philosophy into theoretical and practical and referred to this classification as being commonplace and familiar to all.²⁵

Unlike previous authors, Poliziano's approach nevertheless embraced a completely new dimension, emphasizing the nobility of the mechanical arts. His fundamental aim was an exposition of all the fields of learning necessary in order to understand the encyclopaedic and philosophical content of the works of the Classical poets. Poliziano therefore singled out the seven mechanical arts lauded by earlier writers. These were agriculture, the pasturing of cattle, hunting, architecture, graphics, cooking and theatrics. In addition to these seven, dealt with in some detail, there were

---

[21] A.F. Verde, *Lo studio fiorentino 1473-1503*, vol.4, tomo III, Firenze 1985, 945; Mandosio 1996, 147.

[22] Poliziano, *Panepistemon*: "Mihi vero nunc Aristotelis eiusdem libros de moribus interpretanti consilium est, ita divisionem istiusmodi aggredi, ut quoad eius fieri possit, non disciplinae modo, et artes vel liberales quae dicuntur, vel machinales, sed etiam sordidae illae, ac sellularie, quibus tamen vita indiget, intra huius ambitum distributionis colligantur."

[23] *Ibid.*: "Tria sunt igitur inter homines genera doctrinarum. Inspiratum, Inventum, Mixtum. In primo genere Theologia nostra. In secundo Mater artium philosophia. In tertio divinatio sita est."

[24] *Ibid.*: "Philosophia spectativa est, actualis, rationalis." Poliziano here uses slightly unusual terminology, but *spectativa*, for example, had been used by his friend the Venetian humanist Ermolao Barbaro, with reference to the theoretical and speculative sciences, in his translation, made in 1480, of Simplicius' commentary on Aristotle's *Physics*. See Mandosio 1996, 147.

[25] Mandosio 1996, 138-9.

a host of others which he was content merely to list as exhaustively as possible.[26]

It is no coincidence that Poliziano again arrived at precisely seven mechanical arts. For this corresponded to the number of liberal arts and also to the number of arts listed in one of his sources, the *Didascalicon* by Hugh of Saint Victor. What is interesting, however, is the fact that only three of the arts listed by Hugh and Poliziano are identical (agriculture, hunting and theatrics); otherwise the lists are different.[27] It is also clear that, in addition to the traditional seven mechanical arts, Poliziano was aiming to give as comprehensive a classification as possible of all the arts invented by man. At the end of his work, in his discussion of divination or prophecy, he is thus obliged to mention various divinatory arts, such as chiromancy and coscinomancy, although he personally regarded these as futile and ridiculous.[28]

An important source in the reassessment of the value of arts in the Renaissance was the pseudo-Platonic treatise entitled *Epinomis*. The text was first translated by the humanist George of Trebizond in 1451 and later by Marsilio Ficino in 1460s.[29] Thus *Epinomis* was well-known in the latter part of the fifteenth century and became a starting point for many discussions of the nature and divisions of arts. The text attempts to point out that all disciplines form a unity, an idea which comes very near to Poliziano's idea of *enkuklios paideia*, an encyclopaedic circle of learning.[30]

In *Epinomis* 974d-976c all the arts are divided into four categories: first, those which provide for our necessities, such as agriculture, hunting and divination; second, those which provide pleasure and recreation (i.e. the fine arts); third, those which are a defence against evils and dangers, such as medicine, navigation, and rhetoric; and, finally, a natural aptitude for

---

[26] Poliziano, *Panepistemon*: "Restant artifices varii, qui sic inter se permixti sunt, ut singuli singulis generibus subici nequeant. Itaque prius de his artibus breviter dicemus, quae sunt a scriptoribus celebratae, quales agricultura, pastio, venatio, Architectura, grafice, coquinaria, teatricae nonnullae, caeteras velut acervatim postea numeraturi."

[27] For further details of Poliziano's sources see Mandosio 1996, 153. In addition to these three Hugh mentions spinning and fabric-making, armament, navigation and medicine. Unlike Poliziano, however, Hugh does not stress the nobility of these mechanical arts.

[28] *Ibid.*: "Sed et chiromantia et item coscinomantia, multaque id genus alia vana prorsus, et de ridicula quaeque iam merito silentii nos admonent."

[29] A. Wesseling, "Introduction", A. Poliziano, *Lamia. Praelectio in Priora Aristotelis Analytica*. Leiden 1986, xxviii.

[30] Wesseling 1986, 54.

learning and for remembering and effectively utilizing acquired knowledge.[31] In his preface to Aristotle's *Prior Analytics*, entitled *Lamia*, Poliziano repeats this division, as does Ficino in his commentary on *Epinomis*.[32]

Comparison of Poliziano's treatment of the mechanical arts with the medieval classifications reveals some differences. To begin with, his classification is much broader in scope than those of Hugh of Saint Victor or Robert Kilwardby in that he attempts to identify all the human arts. Secondly, even though he too does not accord the mechanical arts a status equal to the higher arts, the form of the classification and its ideological objectives no longer determine the picture given of the mechanical arts as they still did in the Middle Ages. Now that the classification system no longer aspires to unite human knowledge with knowledge of God, and now that theology is no longer the science to which all others are subordinated, the mechanical arts, in Poliziano's system, are given greater significance as factors facilitating life on earth.

The place of medicine in the classifications
The relationships between the theoretical sciences and the practical arts and the changes taking place in these relationships are admirably revealed if we examine the position of medicine in the classifications made at the turn of the sixteenth century. As we can see from Gregor Reisch's diagram, the most common practice was to divide medicine into two parts, a theoretical and a practical. Theoretical medicine, which usually included physiology, semeiology and pathology, was counted as a theoretical science. In the opinion of many writers the theoretical principles of medicine have their roots in natural philosophy, so that theoretical medicine is a science subordinated to natural philosophy. This view of the relationship between medicine and natural philosophy is also clearly evident from Thomas Aquinas's commentary on Aristotle's *Sense and sensibilia* (*De sensu et sensato*) written in the year 1269:

> It is the task of the natural philosopher to investigate the primary and universal principles that govern health and illness; it is the physician's to put

---

[31] L. Tarán, *Academica: Plato, Philip of Opus, and the Pseudo-Platonic Epinomis* (Memoirs of the American Philosophical Society 107), Philadelphia 1975, 69-70; Wesseling 1986, 47-48.
[32] Wesseling 1986, 48.

these principles into practice, in keeping with the idea that he is the maker of health ... The physician should not limit himself to making use of medicines, but he should also be able to reflect upon the causes [of health and illness]. To this purpose, the good physician begins his training [with the study of] natural philosophy.[33]

The practical side of medicine as one of the mechanical arts, i.e. the art of providing medication or treatment, was usually thought to include hygiene and therapeutics, which in turn consisted of dietetics, pharmacy and surgery. Medicine as a whole thus had something of a dual role in these classifications of knowledge, which gave rise to some interesting discussion of its scientific status.

Throughout the fifteenth century Florence had been debating whether law was a nobler science than medicine.[34] Towards the end of the century the Aristotelian scholar Nicoletto Vernia (1420-99) spread the debate to his native town of Padua, by writing a tractate of his own on the subject.[35] In the foreword Vernia briefly touched on the classification of knowledge, presenting the conventional Aristotelian division into theoretical, practical and productive. He too named several mechanical arts: navigation, fabric-making, armament, agriculture, hunting, architecture and medicine.[36] Vernia's list is thus identical with that of Robert Kilwardby.

In the case of medicine, it was Vernia's intention to defend its noble status against the accusations of the legal scholars. He divided medicine into two as described above and admitted that applied medicine (*medicativa*) is a mechanical art, but claimed that since the nobler side of medicine, i.e. theoretical medicine (*medicina*), is part of natural philosophy, medicine

---

[33] Cited from L. García-Ballester, "Artifex factivus sanitatis: health and medical care in medieval Latin Galenism", *Knowledge and the Scholarly Medical Traditions*, ed. D. Bates, Cambridge 1995, 127-8.

[34] For this debate see C. Vasoli, "Le discipline e il sistema del sapere", *Sapere e/è potere. Discipline, dispute e professioni nell'università medievale e moderna*, ed. A. Cristiani, Bologna 1990, 11-36.

[35] N. Vernia, "Quaestio est, an medicina nobilior atque praestantior sit iure civili", *La disputa delle arti nel quattrocento*, a c. di E. Garin, Firenze 1947, 111-123. Vernia's treatise originally appeared as an introduction to Walter Burley's commentary on Aristotle's *Physics* (1482), a facsimile edition of which was published in 1972. See also E.P. Mahoney, "Philosophy and Science in Nicoletto Vernia and Agostino Nifo", *Scienza e filosofia all'università di Padova nel Quattrocento*, a c. di A. Poppi, Trieste, 1983, 155-9.

[36] N. Vernia, *Expositurus librum de phisico auditu Aristotelis*, in W. Burley, *In physicam Aristotelis expositio et quaestiones*, Hildesheim and New York 1972 (1482), f.2v.

as a whole is in fact a theoretical science and not an art. In Vernia's opinion, the two sides of medicine are founded on different parts of the mind: the practical side relies on the practical reason and the theoretical side on the speculative.[37]

As the sixteenth century progressed, reasoning such as this became a very common way of defending the status of medicine: its theoretical side was regarded as subordinate to theoretical natural philosophy, and medicine as a whole thus warranted the nobler status of a theoretical science. In his widely read *Tabula in dictis Aristotelis et Averrois*, Marcantonio Zimara (1475-1532) summed up the issue by saying that medicine derives its principles from natural philosophy, to which the theoretical side of medicine belongs.[38] Angelo Poliziano also alluded to this dual role of medicine in his *Panepistemon*. In speaking of the theoretical sciences he refers to the "pupil status" (*alumna*) of medicine in relation to natural philosophy.[39] In principle Poliziano looked upon medicine as a theoretical science; but in dealing with the numerous arts he mentioned various branches of nursing and medication practised by the peasants, such as the

---

[37] Vernia 1947 (1482), 117-118: "Pro declaratione primae est notandum quod medicina dupliciter sumitur: uno modo pro habitu scientifico per demonstrationem acquisito ... Verum tamen est quod ut plurimum procedit a posteriori, ut etiam contingit in scientia naturali; et sic sumendo medicinam, ipsa est naturali scientiae subalternata, a qua sua accipit principia... Secundo sumitur medicina pro habitu factivo, ex medicina primo modo sumpta generato, et sic sumendo est ars et non scientia, propria loquendo de scientia. Nam ars et scientia sunt habitus distincti, ut sexto *Ethicorum* ponit Aristoteles; et ista, non medicina, sed potius medicativa dici debet ... Medicina autem primo modo sumpta nullo modo ars mechanica dici potest, sed vera scientia, quae etiam subiecto differt a medicina secundo modo dicta, cum illa fundetur in intellecto practico, qui consiliativus a Philosopho sexto *Ethicorum* appellatur, prima vero in intellecto speculativo, sicut omnes aliae scientiae, et propterea a Philosopho scientifica appellatur."

[38] M. Zimara, *Tabula in dictis Aristotelis et Averrois*, Venice 1543, f.146r: "Medicina sumit principia sua a scientia naturali... Medicinae artis aliquod est speculativum, et illud est scientia naturalis, et aliquod practicum." For a broader treatment of Zimara's concept of knowledge see G. Dell'Anna, "Marco Antonio Zimara e l'aristotelismo: Il problema della scienza nei "Theoremata" (1523)", *Platonismo e aristotelismo nel Mezzogiorno d'Italia*, a c. di G. Roccaro, Palermo 1989, 55-77.

[39] Poliziano, *Panepistemon*: "Naturalis autem philosophiae quasi alumna medicina est, quam Theophilus graecus auctor in theoricen practicenque dividit." The *Theophilus graecus* to whom Poliziano refers was the Byzantine physician Theophilus Protospatarius who lived in the seventh century AD and wrote a commentary on the Hippocratic *Aphorisms*.

use of herbs and the preparation of aromatic substances, and the duties of barbers and bath attendants.⁴⁰

Another strategy for enhancing the status of medicine gained ground in the sixteenth century, one which helps to indicate the rise in status of the various arts. This approach accepted that medicine was an art rather than a science, but sought to prove that the arts founded on practice are no less noble than the sciences. The Paduan professor of medicine Giovanni Manardi (1462-1536), in his commentary on Galen's *Ars parva*, was anxious to retain the distinction between sciences and arts. He did not, however, consider it in the least derogatory to classify medicine as an art, especially since it was, in his opinion, the noblest of all the arts. Manardi likens medicine to a king who is not ashamed to be called a human even though this places him in the same species as the peasant.⁴¹

Rudolph Agricola, however, in the oration mentioned above, went even further in claiming that medicine is the noblest part of the whole philosophy of nature.⁴² Traditionally it had been assumed that the theoretical part of medicine was subordinated to natural philosophy. However, Agricola claimed that it is natural philosophy that is subordinated to medicine and not the other way round. Agricola's praise of medicine has been interpreted as a tribute to Niccolò Leoniceno (1428-1524), Ferrarese professor of medicine, and to his famous medical faculty,⁴³ but it can equally be considered a sign of the increased value attributed to the useful arts.

---

⁴⁰ *Ibid.*: "Sed et fructores, et lactarii, et pomarii, herbarii, et seplasiarii, et medicamentarii omnes, omnisque denique forensis turba. Quod genus et olitores ficitoresque sunt. Post hoc et ipsi corporis agentes curam, tonsores, balneatores."

⁴¹ G. Manardi, *In primum artis parvae Galeni librum commentaria*, Basel 1536, 43-44: "Nec velim vitio mihi verti, quasi de medicina pessime merito, quoniam eam in artium numero repono; quo leguleii infingere nobis solent; quasi vile sit artes profiteri vocarique, quod ipsi de dignantur, magistros. Nomen enim artem adeo nobilem signat, ut imperatoria quoque dignitas, qua nulla aliquando in terris maior fuit, Quintiliano teste, artis nomine censeatur. Nec dignitatem artis nomen abrogat medicinae, quia sit vilioribus communis; sicuti nec hominis nomen regibus, quia sit illis cum plebecula commune. Alioqui de se nobile quid ars repraesentat, cum qui arte pollent, ea carentibus semper praeponant. Non solum autem artem dicimus esse medicinam, sed artium nobilissimam."

⁴² Agricola 1967 (1539), 153: "Eam vero partem, quam proprie naturalem diximus vocari, tametsi multi varie, atque multipliciter usurpent: totam tamen sibi certissima illa salus atque praesidium rerum humanarum, medicina, iure quodam suo videtur vendicare."

⁴³ Tonelli 1979, 320.

In the latter half of the sixteenth century certain Aristotelian natural philosophers, such as Jacopo Zabarella (1533-1589) of Padua, while emphasising the supremacy of theoretical knowledge, nevertheless sought to refute the subordination of medicine to natural philosophy. Zabarella claimed that the most theoretical part of medicine, physiology, was not medicine at all, but natural philosophy, and that medicine as a whole was really an art. *Ibi incipit medicus, ubi desinit philosophus* (the physician begins where the natural philosopher ends) was an aphorism frequently heard in the debate on the relationship between natural philosophy and medicine.[44] Interpretations of this aphorism differed, however. To many of those writing about anatomy in the sixteenth century it emphasized the autonomous nature of the science, whereas Zabarella used it as a means of demonstrating the principal distinction between the practical arts and the speculative sciences of nobler status.[45]

Josse Clichtove's division of arts and sciences

The question of the status of the practical arts was also taken up north of the Alps in the early sixteenth century. In 1520 Josse Clichtove (Jodocus Clichtoveus, 1472-1543), a French humanist at the University of Paris, wrote a tractate on the division of arts and sciences entitled *De artium scientiarumque divisione introductio*. Clichtove based his own division both on the tripartite Aristotelian classification and on the division of *trivium* and *quadrivium* in the medieval university.

The most original feature of Clichtove's work is his presentation of the classification of knowledge in the form of a table. Whereas in speaking of the theoretical sciences and liberal arts he presents the objects and main authors of each, in dealing with the mechanical arts he specifies the

---

[44] For the origin and interpretations of the aphorism see Ch.B. Schmitt, "Aristotle among the Physicians", *The Medical Renaissance of the Sixteenth Century*, edd. A. Wear, R.K. French and I.M. Lonie, Cambridge 1985, 1-15. For the debate on the scientific nature of medicine in the Middle Ages see P.-G. Ottoson, *Scholastic Medicine and Philosophy*, Napoli 1984 (chapter 2), and in the Renaissance see H. Mikkeli, *An Aristotelian Response to Renaissance Humanism. Jacopo Zabarella on the Nature of Arts and Sciences*, Helsinki 1992 (chapter 6).

[45] For Zabarella's concept of knowledge see Mikkeli 1992 and H. Mikkeli, "The Foundation of an Autonomous Natural Philosophy: Zabarella on the Classification of Arts and Sciences", *Method and Order in Renaissance Philosophy of Nature. The Aristotle Commentary Tradition*, edd. D.A. di Liscia, E. Keßler and C. Methuen, Aldershot 1997, 211-228.

materials they use and their purposes. For example, the object of logic is argumentation and Aristotle is mentioned as the main author writing on the subject; but the material of fabric-making is wool and its object is to clothe the human body. Clichtove's table of the seven mechanical arts, their materials and purposes is as follows:

Artes mechanicae	Earum materiae	Earum fines
Lanificium	Lana	Indumentum corporis
Nemoraria	Arbores et ligna	Usus ignis
Militaria	Arma et bella	Suarum rerum defensio
Nautica	Navis et vela	Alimentum et mercatura
Agricultura	Agri et segetes	Nutrimentum hominis
Medicina	Vulnera	Sanatio hominis
Ars fabrilis	Ferrum et ligna	Habitatio hominum

Fig. 2: The mechanical arts according to J. Clichtove, *De artium scientiarumque divisione*. Paris 1520, f.17r.

Clichtove gives a traditional list of the seven mechanical arts: spinning and fabric-making (*lanificium*), the use of fire (*nemoraria*), warfare (*militaris*), navigation (*nautica*), agriculture (*agricultura*), medicine (*medicina*) and the art of building (*ars fabrilis*). He adds that some also list architecture as the eighth art, but he himself regards this as part of a greater entity, the art of building (*ars fabrilis*). In his opinion, therefore, architecture is not an art in its own right but merely an epithet of the art of building.[46] In the same context he addresses the dual nature of medicine in the classification of knowledge. Insofar as medicine is concerned with the curing of diseases in the human body, it ranks among the mechanical arts, but as a scientific

---

[46] Clichtove 1520, f.10v: "His ars fabrilis architectonica subsit: non id faciunt octavam aliquam speciem designantes. Non enim architectonica nova est artis species: sed nomen adiectuum et artis fabrilis epithetum significans in Latino idem quod praecipua vel principalis."

doctrine it belongs to the natural sciences.[47] Elsewhere Clichtove identifies this manual side of medicine with surgery.[48]

Taken as a whole, the mechanical arts are associated with manual skills and, according to Clichtove, have an inherently servile status: they serve other sciences as a slave his master or the body the soul.[49] He does not therefore attempt to grant these arts a status equal to that of the theoretical sciences. It is significant, however, that Clichtove gives the mechanical arts a table of their own, alongside that of the sciences, in which their usefulness and practical purposes are specially emphasized. Thus the mechanical arts are recognised in the classifications of knowledge, even though they still enjoy a lesser status.

Clichtove likewise classified the theoretical sciences and liberal arts according to their names, objects and main authors as follows:

Scientiarum nomina	Subiecta attributionis	Earum authores
Grammatica	Sermo latinus	Priscianus
Logica	Argumentatio	Aristoteles
Rhetorica	Oratio persuadens	Cicero
Musica	Numerus harmonicus	Boetius
Arithmetica	Numerus	Pythagoras
Geometria	Magnitudo	Euclides
Astronomia	Magnitudo celestis	Ptolomeus
Ethica	Bonum hominis	Aristoteles
Economica	Bonum domus	Aristoteles
Polytica	Bonum reipublice	Aristoteles
Physica	Res naturalis	Aristoteles
Medicina	Bonum corporis humani	Hippocrates
Metaphysica	Primum ens	Aristoteles
Theologia	Deus superbenedictus	Prophete et apostoli

Fig. 3: The theoretical sciences and liberal arts according to Clichtove 1520, f.17r.

---

[47] *Ibid.*: "Medicina autem sexta artis mechanice species non hic per ea sumitur scientia que humani corporis complexione morbosque considerat. Nam illa ars doctrinalis est et in nona divisione sub arte naturali collocatur: sed pro illa que vulnera et exteriores corporis lesiones curat."

[48] *Ibid.*, f.11v: "Et eadem chirurgia greco nomine dicitur, id est manualis: quae exteriore manuum applicatione officioque exerceatur."

[49] *Ibid.*, f.11r.

This table of sciences and liberal arts is a combination of the Aristotelian classification and the division into *trivium* and *quadrivium*. What is interesting is the choice of authors. For example, as the author on the theoretical side of medicine Clichtove names Hippocrates and not Galen. It is also interesting to note that metaphysics and theology are classified as different sciences, with Aristotle as the author for the former and Biblical sources for the latter.

The defence of the theoretical sciences
However, not all scholars and teachers in the late fifteenth and early sixteenth centuries were prepared to follow Poliziano's and Clichtove's example and expand the field of knowledge to include the arts. The Italian humanist Giorgio Valla (c.1413-1500) wrote his encyclopaedic work *De expetendis et fugiendis rebus* at the beginning of the 1490s, though it was not published until 1501. The subject of chapter one of volume 31, dealing with grammar, is the classification of knowledge. Chapter two draws a distinction between the liberal and mechanical arts and lists a number of occupations based on mechanical arts which Valla considers useful, mentioning for example bakers, potters, navigators, smiths, goldsmiths and carpenters.[50] The subject does not, however, appear to interest Valla greatly, and he does not devote many pages to it.

Valla's namesake, the humanist Lorenzo Valla (1407-57), expressed a more favourable view of the mechanical arts in his treatise *De voluptate* (c.1430). Lorenzo Valla emphasized the usefulness and, above all, the pleasure that all the human arts could give to mankind. He wrote: "The arts, and not only the liberal arts, tend to satisfy fundamental needs, and they aim at rendering life decorative and elegant. Such are agriculture, architecture, arts of weaving, of painting, of dyeing with purple, of sculpting, of fitting ships."[51]

---

[50] G. Valla, *De expetendis et fugiendibus rebus*, Venice 1501, Book 31, chapter 2, f.S5r: "Artis autem duae sunt species. Una quidem Moechanica, Altera vero liberalis. Ars Moechanica est quae suo nos aliquo captat emolumento, quo in genere Phrygiones, Fullones, Pistores, Figuli, Marmorarii, Naviculari, Fabri ferrarii, Fabri argentarii, Fabri tignarii, caeterique opifices in hoc genere, vulgo notiores, quam ut pluribus explicare necesse sit."
[51] L. Valla, *De voluptate* (c. 1430), in L. Valla, *Opera omnia*, a cura di E. Garin, facsimile of Basle-edition of 1543, Torino 1962, vol.II, 39.

In 1510 Johannes Murmellius (1480-1517), a humanist of note in Holland and Germany, published a book entitled *Didascalici libri duo*, a work he would appear to have written a few years earlier. The two volumes each address different subjects: the first reflects on the division and definition of the liberal and mechanical arts, while the second provides instruction for students. Murmellius cannot condone the rise in status of the mechanical subjects because they are servile and those pursuing them illiberal; hence the subjects are not worthy of closer study. Subscribing to the established division, he considers that those who pursue the liberal arts concentrate on the workings of the reason and human actions, whereas those engaged in the mechanical arts work with their hands, tools and machines. Murmellius also speaks of the definition and number of these mechanical arts and refers to the seven arts listed by Hugh of Saint Victor. But he is critical of Hugh's classifications, calling him a "philosophiser" (Lat. *philosophaster*) rather than a true philosopher.[52]

One tendency observable in the first half of the sixteenth century is the gradual disappearance of the medieval classification of knowledge founded on the liberal arts (i.e. the division of *trivium* and *quadrivium*). Ludovico Boccadiferro (Buccaferrea, 1482-1545), a professor of natural philosophy at the University of Bologna, provides an explicit reason for this development. In his commentary on book one of Aristotle's *Physics* he contends that the division is no longer applicable to the classification of knowledge because it makes no mention of the speculative sciences, such as metaphysics and natural philosophy.[53] Instead, Boccadiferro preferred to replace what he regarded as a medieval classification with the tripartite division of Aristotle, which he felt raised the theoretical sciences to the status they deserved. But he could not accept the idea of making the mechanical arts objects of philosophical reasoning, because philosophy, in debating external matters, would then become alienated from its primary task of speculative reasoning.[54]

---

[52] J.V. Mehl, "Johannes Murmellius's Approach to the Artes Liberales and Advice to Students in his "Didascalici libri duo" (1510)", *Acta Conventus Neo-Latini Hafniensis*, ed. Rhoda Schnur, Binghamton, N. Y. 1994, 648.

[53] L. Boccadifero, *Explanatio libri I physicorum Aristotelis*, Venice 1558, f.2r: "Ex his colligitur, perfectam esse Simplicii divisionem, Boetii vero mancam, quae naturalem ac divinam philosophiae partem praetermisit."

[54] *Ibid.*: "Vocantur etiam mechanicae, non quidem ut Parisienses philosophi interpretantur, quod faciunt intellectum moechari, hoc est rebus externis commisceri, a proprioque sui

Juan Luis Vives and the praise of the mechanical arts

Some authors writing outside the universities around the turn of the sixteenth century challenged the supremacy of the theoretical sciences over the arts. The most famous was probably Leonardo da Vinci and his contribution in the *Paragone* debate on the position of the visual arts in the classification of knowledge.[55] Leonardo personally described himself as a man without formal education, *un uomo senza lettere*. Examining the relationship between the mechanical arts and the theoretical sciences, he wrote:

> They say that knowledge born of experience is mechanical, but that knowledge born and consummated in the mind is scientific... But to me it seems that all sciences are vain and full of errors that are not born of experience, mother of all certainty, and that are not tested by experience, that is to say, that do not at their origin, middle or end pass through any of the five senses.[56]

Leonardo here specifically links the certainty of knowledge with the experience on which it is founded, and not with the certainty afforded by demonstrative reasoning.

Leonardo's treatise was not printed until the 1540s. At about this time Benedetto Varchi (1503-1565), an Aristotelian who had returned from Padua to Florence, gave a series of lectures on the subject at the Florentine Academy.[57] According to him, medicine is the noblest of all the arts because its purpose, health, is nobler than the purposes of the other arts; and medicine is immediately followed by architecture.[58] Varchi also wrote a tractate on the division of the sciences and arts in which he made an interesting distinction between the nobility of the branches of learning and the skill of those pursuing them. Just as sciences may in poor hands lose their nobility, so the mechanical arts may, in the hands of skilled craftsmen, become the noblest of subjects even though they are by nature lacking in

---

munere alienari."

[55] For these debates see C. Farago, "The Classification of the Visual Arts in the Renaissance", *The Shapes of Knowledge from the Renaissance to the Enlightenment*, edd. D.R. Kelley and R.H. Popkin, Dordrecht 1991, 23-47.

[56] L. da Vinci, *Paragone*, trans. I. Richter, London 1949, 25-6.

[57] For this series of lectures see F. Quiviger, "Benedetto Varchi and the Visual Arts", *Journal of the Warburg and Courtauld Institutes,* 50 (1987), 219-224.

[58] B. Varchi, "Della maggioranza delle arti (1547)", *Scritti d'arte del cinquecento*, a. c. di P. Barocchi, Torino 1977, 138-141.

status and nobility.⁵⁹ Varchi claimed that while grammar, for example, is in itself nobler than the arts, a good smith is in practice nobler than a poor grammarian. He thus raised the issue to a new plane and did not deny the benefit of the mechanical arts to human life. Yet at the same time he tried to adhere to the traditional Aristotelian hierarchy of knowledge, giving theoretical sciences the highest status.

One of the most notable defences of the arts during the first half of the sixteenth century is to be found in *De disciplinis*, a work written in 1531 by the Spanish humanist Juan Luis Vives (1492-1540) who was later influential in the Netherlands. The work is in two volumes: the first, entitled *De causis corruptarum artium*, deals with the reasons for the poor state of the sciences and arts, and the second, *De tradendis disciplinis*, discusses in a more conventional manner the classifications of knowledge and systems of teaching. One of Vives's basic beliefs was his view of the comprehensive, encyclopaedic nature of classical knowledge as something to which the differentiated, fragmented knowledge of his own day should once again aspire.⁶⁰

In the volume entitled *De tradendis disciplinis* Vives urged scholars to pay far more attention to the technical problems arising from the pursuit of the mechanical arts. He advised them to lower their gaze to the work of artisans so that they, the scholars, might also learn how the different arts were invented, and how they were practised and developed so as to be of the greatest benefit to mankind. Scholars, Vives claimed, should overcome the contempt they felt for the skills of the ordinary man and should not be ashamed of entering artisans' workshops in order to acquaint themselves with the skills they employ in the production of their artefacts. Vives reminded scholars what a great contribution they could make to human knowledge by recording what the manual workers did in their workshops and thus passing on their knowledge and skills to future generations. He also expressed his astonishment that in many ways his learned

---

⁵⁹ B. Varchi, "Divisione della filosofia", in *Opere* II Trieste 1859, 795: "È ancora da notare che come tutte le scienze possono, non già per loro stesse, ma solo per colpa di coloro che l'esercitano, diventare vili e meccaniche, cosi l'arti possono, non per sè ma per virtù di chi l'opera, divenire non solo laudevoli ma eziandio onoratissime, quantunque di sua natura fussero basse e disonorate."

⁶⁰ For this theme see V. Del Nero, *Linguaggio e filosofia in Vives. L'organizzazione del sapere nel "De disciplinis" (1531)*, Bologna 1991, 28-41.

contemporaries knew more about everyday life in the days of Cicero and Pliny than in their own times.[61]

Vives had already pointed out in the previous volume (*De causis corruptarum artium*) that knowledge of nature is by no means the exclusive domain of philosophy, and that the peasants and artisans in fact knew much more about nature than the great philosophers. For the philosophers devised a host of imaginary concepts while the peasants and artisans operated within nature and on its terms.[62] Vives thus clearly placed the mechanical arts on a par with the theoretical and practical sciences, on the grounds that the arts were useful and that the skills of those pursuing them benefited man in his practical everyday life. In this respect he differed from Poliziano and Clichtove who, while eager to list and describe the mechanical arts, still insisted on the primary status of the theoretical and practical sciences.

Vives' ideas on the significance of the practical nature of knowledge are also revealed in his attitude to the maker's knowledge tradition. So far as is known, he was the first Renaissance scholar to formulate the theory inherited from Antiquity that "man knows as far as he can make" (*tantum scis, quantum operaris*), as he wrote in his *Satellitia vel symbola*.[63] According to this view, which stresses the practical significance of knowledge, the most certain knowledge is attained not by means of demonstrative syllogisms in the theoretical sciences but in the practical

---

[61] J.L. Vives, "De tradendis disciplinis", in *De disciplinis libri XII*, Lyon 1636, 592-3: "Iam vir aetate, ingenio, rerum cognitione atque experimentis instructior, ac maturior paulo, considerare vitam humanam attentius incipiet, et hominum artes ac inventa ... Haec omnia persequetur qua ratione ac modo sint inventa, quaesita, aucta, conservata, applicata usui et emolumentis nostris ... Ideo nihil est hic opus schola, sed aviditate audiendi et cognoscendi: ut non erubescat etiam in tabernas et officinas venire, et ab opificibus de suis operibus sciscitari, ac edoceri: quod quia dedignati sunt iam olim docti homines facere, idcirco haec quae teneri, ac sciri tantopere referebat vitae, incognita illis penitus relicta sunt, ac praetermissa: eaque ignorantia in sequentibus adhuc seculis increvit, nihilque his annis quam plurimis annotatum est de moribus, ac ratione vitae, ut melius aetatem Ciceronis, aut Plinii noverimus, quam nostrorum avorum, quis tum victus, vestitus, cultus, habitatio."

[62] J.L. Vives, *Über die Gründe des Verfalls der Künste. De causis corruptarum artium*, E. Hidalgo-Serna, Hrsg., München 1990, 488: "Sunt enim earum rerum inexperti prorsus, et hujus naturae, quam melius agricolae et fabri norunt quam ipsi tanti philosophi, qui naturae huic, quam ignorarent, irati, aliam sibi confinxerunt." See also P. Rossi, *Philosophy, Technology and the Arts in Early Modern Europe*, New York 1970, 5-6.

[63] J.L. Vives, *Opera omnia*, ed. G. Mayans, vol. IV, Valencia 1783, 63.

sciences within the sphere of human action. This view was later expressed even more explicitly in the philosophy of Francis Bacon.[64]

Conclusion

In an important article Eckhard Keßler has recently examined the way in which Jacques Lefèvre d'Étaples (Jacobus Stapulensis, 1460-1536) and his circle tried to develop a new reading of Aristotle's works at the University of Paris in the early sixteenth century.[65] Lefèvre d'Etaples set out to lead humanistic text criticism in a direction which Keßler himself calls "the humanistic method of grammatical reading of Aristotle's texts". The vital aspect of this method compared with scholastic interpretations was that Aristotle was no longer the philosopher above all others but simply one among many. The aim was not so much to acquire an understanding of the entire Aristotelian *corpus* and to solve the incongruities in his works as to clarify the philosophical problems posed in them and to arrive at a teaching method of the maximum clarity. The logical structure of the Aristotelian works thus disintegrates, and a number of disparate Aristotelianisms emerge in the sixteenth century for widely different purposes.[66]

Lefèvre d'Etaples had visited Italy in the 1490s, met Angelo Poliziano there and been influenced by him in developing his new text-critical reading. A little later, Josse Clichtove was also a member of the circle of humanists in Paris. Thus many of the scholars mentioned by Keßler also took part in the debate on the classification of knowledge and specifically tried to widen the scope of knowledge to take in the mechanical arts. One consequence of the new humanistic interpretation of Aristotle developed by these scholars was the radical opening up of the field of knowledge. In this process, the worldly objectives of the mechanical arts – and the interest of knowledge aiming at practical benefit in general – were more clearly placed alongside the scholastic speculations aiming at purely theoretical

---

[64] For Bacon and the maker's knowledge tradition see A. Pérez-Ramos, *Francis Bacon's Idea of Science and the Maker's Knowledge Tradition*, Oxford 1988; for Bacon and the new principles of classifying knowledge see S. Kusukawa, "Bacon's Classification of Knowledge", *The Cambridge Companion to Bacon*, ed. M. Peltonen, Cambridge 1996, 47-74.

[65] See E. Keßler, "Introducing Aristotle to the Sixteenth Century: The Lefèvre Enterprise," in, *Philosophy in the Sixteenth and Seventeenth Centuries. Conversations with Aristotle'*, ed. C. Blackwell and S. Kusukawa, Aldershot 1999, 1-21.

[66] For an introduction to sixteenthth-century Aristotelianisms see Ch.B. Schmitt, *Aristotle and the Renaissance*. Cambridge, Ma. and London 1983.

knowledge. Both d'Etaples and his circle in Paris and Poliziano and his followers in Italy can thus be regarded as links between the humanism of the fifteenth century and the phenomenon customarily known as the seventeenth century scientific revolution.

GIOVAN FRANCESCO PICO E I PRESUPPOSTI DELLA SUA CRITICA AD ARISTOTELE

di Cesare Vasoli

1. Intorno alla singolare personalità di Giovan Francesco Pico è cresciuto, nel corso degli ultimi decenni, l'interesse degli studiosi della storia delle idee religiose, volti ad accertare quale fu il suo rapporto con la tradizione savonaroliana, prima e dopo la morte del Frate, quanto fu estesa e influente la diffusione della sua celebre *Vita Fratris Hieronymi Savonarolae* e di altri suoi scritti religiosi[1] e quale fu il carattere del suo legame spirituale con alcune veggenti e taumaturghe domenicane, la Beata Osanna Andreasi e la Beata Caterina da Racconigi.[2] Ma anche i filologi e gli storici della filosofia e della cultura hanno preso a studiare, con rinnovata attenzione, altre sue opere, come il *De studio divinae et humanae philosophiae*, il *De imaginatione*, il *De rerum praenotione*, il *De providentia Dei* e, soprattutto, l'*Examen vanitatis doctrinae gentium et veritatis Christianae disciplinae*, attratti sia dal suo vasto uso delle argomentazioni scettiche di Sesto Empirico, sia dalla sua critica radicale della filosofia aristotelica e della tradizione dottrinale "peripatetica" che ne era derivata.[3] É giustamente ben

---

[1] Cfr. Ch. B. Schmitt, *Gianfrancesco Pico della Mirandola (1469-1533) and his critique of Aristotle*, The Hague 1967, 186 sgg. Ma v. anche W. Cavini, "Un inedito di Giovan Francesco Pico della Mirandola: la *quaestio de falsitate astrologiae*", Rinascimento, S. II, 13 (1973), 133-71.

[2] Cfr., a questo proposito, C. Dionisotti, *Ermolao Barbaro e la fortuna di Suisseth*, in *Medioevo e Rinascimento. Studi in onore di Bruno Nardi*, Firenze 1955, I, pp. 217-53, part., p. 223; ma v. A. L. Radigonda, *Andreasi, Osanna*, in *Dizionario biografico degli Italiani*, III, Roma 1961, 131-32; G. Cappelluti, *Andreasi Osanna, beata* in *Bibliotheca Sanctorum*, I, Roma s.d. (ma 1965 ?), coll. 1170-1174; A. Guarienti, *Caterina da Racconigi, beata, Ibid.*, II, Roma s.d. (ma 1967 ?), coll. 992-993; G. Zarri, *Le sante vive: cultura e religiosità femminile nella prima età moderna*, Torino 1990, ad ind. Sull'intenso savonarolismo del Pico, cfr. R. Ridolfi, *Vita di Girolamo Savonarola*, Firenze 1997, VI ed., rist., ad ind.; G. C. Garfagnini, "Savonarola tra Giovanni Pico e Gianfrancesco Pico", in *Giovanni Pico della Mirandola. Convegno internazionale di studi nel cinquecentesimo anniversario della morte (1494)*, a cura di G. C. Garfagnini, Firenze 1997, I, pp. 237-79.

[3] Cfr. principalmente, Ch. B. Schmitt, *Cicero scepticus. A Study of the Influence of the "Academica" in the Renaissance*, The Hague 1972, ad ind.; W. Cavini, "Appunti sulla prima

noto il lavoro di Charles Schmitt che, nel 1967, dedicò proprio all' *Examen* un' importante volume monografico e, poi, anche in altri studi, tornò a indagare quest' aspetto della complessa attività speculativa dello sventurato Conte della Mirandola. Sono altrettanto conosciuti altri contributi che si sono aggiunti, specie nel corso degli ultimi anni, in occasione della vicina ricorrenza del quinto centenario della morte dello zio, alcuni dei quali compaiono appunto nei volumi degli atti del Convegno mirandolano del 1994, usciti proprio in questi giorni.[4] Nè occorrerà ricordare le indagini che, nel corso degli ultimi trent' anni, sono state condotte non solo sulla fortuna umanistica delle dottrine scettiche, ma pure sui maggiori protagonisti della crescente polemica antiaristotelica quattrocentesca e cinquecentesca, dal Petrarca al Valla ed ai maggiori rappresentanti della *renovatio* platonica, da Pierre de la Ramée a Francesco Patrizi. Sicchè non sarà inopportuno riprendere in esame, anche alla luce di queste nuove ricerche, proprio quella parte dell' *Examen* che può maggiormente interessare gli studiosi dell' aristotelismo nel Rinascimento e che, d' altro canto, permette di verificare, sia la continuità di temi già proposti dai critici umanisti, sia l' influenza diretta o indiretta di quell' opera sulle più tarde e maggiori polemiche del pieno e tardo Cinquecento.[5]

---

diffusione in Occidente delle opere di Sesto Empirico", *Medioevo*, 3 (1977), 1-20; L. Cesarini Martinelli, "Sesto Empirico e una dispersa enciclopedia delle arti e delle scienze di Angelo Poliziano", *Rinascimento*, S.II, 20 (1980), 327-58; Ch. B. Schmitt, "The rediscovery of ancient skepticism in modern times", in *The Skeptical Tradition*, ed. by M. F. Burnyeat, Berkeley – Los Angeles – London 1983, 225-51; G. M. Cao, "L' eredità pichiana: Gianfrancesco Pico tra Sesto Empirico e Savonarola", in *Pico, Poliziano e l' Umanesimo di fine Quattrocento*. Biblioteca Medicea Laurenziana. 4 novembre – 31 dicembre 1994. Catalogo a cura di P. Viti, Firenze 1994, 231-45.

[4] Cfr., in particolare, G. C. Garfagnini, *op. cit.*; F. Tateo, *I due Pico e la retorica*; J. Jacobelli, "Continuità o discontinuità fra quei due Pico della Mirandola ?", in *Giovanni Pico della Mirandola*, cit., II, pp. 451-63; 543-50.

[5] Cfr. Ch.B. Schmitt, *Aristotle in the Renaissance*, Cambridge, Mass. 1983; M.J. Willmott, *Francesco Patrizi da Cherso's Humanist Critique of Aristotle*, London 1984; Id., "'Aristoteles exotericus, acroamaticus, mysticus': two interpretations of the typological classification of the 'corpus aristotelicum' by Francesco Patrizi Patrizi da Cherso", *Nouvelles de la République des Lettres*, I (1985), 67-95; C. Vasoli, "De Pierre de la Ramée à François Patrizi. Thèmes et raison de la polémique autour d' Aristote", in *Revue des Sciences philosophiques et théologiques*, 70 (1986), 87*b*-98; *Aristotelismus und Renaissance: in memoriam Ch.B. Schmitt*, Hrsg. von E. Keßler, Ch. Lohr und W. Sparn, Wiesbaden 1988; M. Muccillo, *Platonismo, ermetismo e "prisca theologia". Ricerche di storiografia filosofica rinascimentale*, Firenze 1996, 73-193; C. Vasoli, "La critica di Francesco Patrizi ai 'principi' aristotelici", *Rivista di storia della filosofia*, 51 (1996), 713-87.

Naturalmente, data la brevità del tempo, potrò indicare solo alcuni argomenti che ritengo particolarmente importanti, limitandomi, peraltro, a prendere in considerazione alcuni capitoli del IV libro che, però, espongono in modo esauriente le ragioni di fondo di una critica suggerita, senza dubbio, sia dall' assoluto e meditato fideismo del Pico, diffidente e, addirittura, deciso avversario delle filosofie degli antichi "pagani", sia dal suo scrupolo filologico di studioso formato nella disciplina intellettuale umanistica, sia da una fondamentale esigenza di chiarezza espositiva, di rigore logico e di coerenza dottrinale che è alle origini di talune rilevanti critiche quattrocentesche come di altre celebri polemiche "antiperipatetiche" del XVI secolo.[6]

2. Non a caso, nel "proemio" di quel libro, viene riconosciuta la ricchezza e complessità dell' eccezionale "enciclopedia" aristotelica, l' eleganza erudita del suo stile, lodato non solo dai greci, ma anche dai latini che conoscono quella lingua e, persino, dallo stesso Cicerone. Il Pico è addirittura disposto ad ammettere che il Filosofo ha saputo suddividere così bene la "materia" della sua scienza da riuscire a trattare, con esatta diligenza, tutto il sapere naturale, sino alle minime cose. Ma non si è limitato a far questo; anzi, con la sua dottrina così "molteplice", ha voluto insegnare non solo ai filosofi, bensì pure ai retori, ai poeti ed agli storici quale sia la loro arte e come debbano usarla. Sicchè egli ha fornito a tutti sia il "terreno" in cui possono raccogliere ottime messi, sia anche gli strumenti per mieterle.[7] Ciononostante, i suoi seguaci sono sicuramente in errore, quando non vogliono riconoscere le sue inevitabili pecche, o si sforzano di ridurle al minimo. Accade, infatti, che si affrettino a scusarlo anche della sua ingratitudine contro il maestro Platone, da lui severamente confutato, ripreso e attaccato, con il pretesto che l' amore della verità deve precedere ogni altra ragione e che, solo per restar fedele a questo principio, Aristotele

---

[6] Com' è ben noto, queste esigenze erano state già proposte, con particolare insistenza, da Lorenzo Valla, nella sua critica dei fondamenti della logica aristotelica, cfr. Laurentii Valle *Repastinatio dialectice et philosophie.* Edidit G. Zippel, Padova 1982, I, pp. 1 sgg.; II, pp. 360 sgg. Gli stessi motivi sono largamente presenti anche nelle opere polemiche di Pietro Ramo e nelle *Discussiones peripateticae* di Francesco Patrizi.

[7] Cfr. Ioannis Francisci Pici Mirandulae Domini et Concordiae Comitis *In examen vanitatis doctrinae Gentium et veritatis Christianae disciplinae, qui et primus est adversus Doctrinam Aristotelis,* Lib. IIII, Proemium, in *Opera omnia* Ioannis Pici Mirandulae Domini, Concordiaeque Comitis, Tomus Secundus, Basileae, ex Officina Henricpetrina 1557, pp. 1011-15, indicato poi sempre come *Examen.*

non ha risparmiato le critiche al suo *praeceptor*. Non esitano neppure a celebrare le sue "virtù", a difendere certi comportamenti che molti giudicherebbero colpe (*crimina*), e, persino, a trasformare l'ingratitudine in una ragione di lode.[8]

Per quanto lo riguarda, il Pico chiederà, invece, a quei lodatori eccessivi di Aristotele che non mancano anche nella Chiesa cattolica, di scusarlo se, dopo aver tanto appreso da quel filosofo, di cui ha studiato per vent'anni le opere, al solo scopo di conoscere la verità, affermerà che la sua dottrina non ha quel peso attribuitole dalla maggior parte di loro; e se dimostrerà che essa è ingannevole quando tratta del vero fine della filosofia, ed è incerta e falsa in molte altre parti. In ogni caso, i suoi fedeli seguaci dovranno riconoscere che la sua critica è solo dettata dall'amore della verità e della *pietas*. Filosofi che si dichiarano cristiani e fratelli partecipi dell'unica vera religione, non potranno certo negargli quanto hanno concesso, senza che nessuno intercedesse per lui, ad un uomo, certo grande, ma estraneo alla verità cristiana e soggetto alle "superstizioni" profane dei Gentili. E, del resto, come può un cristiano tollerare che le opere di quel filosofo siano, se non addirittura preferite, per lo meno uguagliate al vangelo di Cristo, e talmente onorate e stimate che, tra quei dotti superbi, non manca, addirittura, chi preferisce esser chiamato aristotelico piuttosto che cristiano?[9] Con insistente e decisa polemica, il Pico attacca quei maestri, divenuti ormai così rozzi, privi di vera ragione e addirittura "deliranti" da ritenere che tutti gli insegnamenti del Filosofo siano veri ed incrollabili e che, addirittura, non esista alcuna dottrina più certa e più ricca di verità. Ora, egli stesso non nega che in Aristotele si trovino molte verità; le ritiene, però, mescolate ad altrettante "vanità"[10] che vanno ben separate, così come si usa fare per liberare il grano dalla paglia. Per questo, da strenuo seguace della spiritualità savonaroliana, invita costoro ad allontanarsi da Aristotele, per cercare delle verità migliori e ad innalzarsi dalle cose umane a quelle divine, sulle ali della fede e dell'amore. Ricordino che, già tra gli stessi greci, Teocrito di Chio lo ha accusato di "vanità", e che, d'altro canto, il *Liber Sapientiae* della Scrittura considera "vanità" tutto ciò che è privo

---

[8] *Examen*, p. 1011.
[9] *Ibid.*, p. 1012.
[10] *Ibid.*

della scienza di Dio e, dunque, persino questo suo studio, che pure è inteso soltanto ad indurli alla ricerca della verità suprema.[11]

D' altro canto, lo stesso Pico riconosce di aver accolto talune verità aristoteliche, come quelle concernenti l'anima razionale e l' "appetito" della materia prima; di aver difeso il Filosofo dalle false accuse di chi, come alcuni antichi e, più di recente, Lorenzo Valla, gli aveva imputato di negare assolutamente la Provvidenza divina; e di averlo, addirittura, seguito, come ottimo *naturae interpres*, nel suo *De imaginatione*.[12] Ma non è mai stato un seguace così ardente di Aristotele o di qualsiasi altro filosofo da non rendersi conto che la loro dottrina è spesso assai falsa ed erra su molti argomenti. Lo testimoniano i libri che egli ha scritto (*De studio divinae et humanae philosophiae*, *Theoremata de fide*, *Logicae Institutiones*), tutti ispirati alla ricerca della verità, per la cui difesa è pronto non solo a scrivere contro il Filosofo, ma persino contro se stesso, quando si scoprirà in errore. Sa bene di non esser affatto superiore ad Agostino, pronto a ritrattare ed emendare i suoi scritti già resi pubblici, a Girolamo, che corresse i suoi commenti ad Isaia e Abdia, ed allo zio, Giovanni Pico, che riconobbe di aver errato nella sua prima giovinezza e nutrì, da giovanissimo e poi negli anni più avanzati, opinioni tra loro assai diverse sull' astrologia e la magia naturale. Del resto l' onestà impone di riconoscere ed eliminare i propri errori, come fecero tanti illustri antichi e, tra questi, lo stesso Aristotele, che, sebbene criticasse spesso Platone, scrisse un' orazione in sua lode e gli innalzò un' ara. Ma, se ha lodato e talvolta difeso il Filosofo per rispetto della verità, non ha mai sostenuto che la sua dottrina fosse religiosa, profondamente certa e assolutamente vera. Anzi, ha spesso sottolineato che essa non è affatto certa, bensì soltanto "probabile", che non è vera in modo assoluto e, in qualche sua parte, senz' altro falsa, o, peggio ancora, corrotta dalla superstizione, com' era inevitabile nel caso di un uomo, grande e forse massimo tra i pagani, ma tuttavia sempre uomo e ignaro della "vera luce" e della "vera religione". Lo mostrerà, appunto, nel prosieguo di questo libro scritto proprio per indurre a scegliere un' altra via i molti filosofi che accettano Aristotele come il Vangelo.

Vi chiarirà, infatti, che ogni verità riconosciuta da Aristotele e non ignorata da altri filosofi, è derivata da Dio, elargitore e illuminatore dell' intelletto, e che quelle più illustri non furono scoperte da lui, ma da Platone

---

[11] *Ibid.*
[12] *Ibid.*, p. 1013.

e dai Pitagorici, discepoli di Mosè, in Egitto. Alcune verità sono, certo, veramente del tutto sue; ma non furono tanto il frutto di dottrina, quanto, piuttosto, di un' estrema cura e di diligenti esperienze, come si può ben vedere nei *Libri de animalibus*, considerati, da molti, i più illustri tra quanti scrisse. Eppure, non sono pochi i filosofi convinti che anche quest' opera non sia immune da errori: un giudizio al quale si deve consentire, almeno per alcune cose particolari. Sarà, dunque, del tutto lecito soppesare scrupolosamente anche questa filosofia oggi tanto apprezzata, in modo da riconoscervi, per esclusivo merito del *luminum pater*, quanto in essa è vanità o leggerezza.[13]

3. Con ostentata umiltà, il Pico afferma di aver scritto questo e i libri seguenti, non perchè si ritenesse adatto a sostenere un tale compito, ma solo per amore della verità. E ricorda che tutta l' opera è stata stesa, durante i primi tempi del suo "iniquissimo" esilio, mentre era impegnato a resistere con le armi agli ingiusti, ad implorare la potenza dei re e dei principi e l' amicizia dei suoi uguali.[14] Restituito finalmente al suo dominio, dopo quattro anni di guerra, si è trovato impegnato in non minori difficoltà e fatiche, ma non gli è mancato l' aiuto divino per concluderla, così come, tra i pericoli della guerra e nelle sue lunghe peregrinazioni in terre straniere, non gli era mai venuta meno la necessaria tranquillità e la pace dell' animo, beni che provengono solo dalla suprema fonte della verità e della bontà. Gli è stata così concessa la possibilità di mostrare, in questo quarto libro, in che consista, in generale, la "vanità" di Aristotele.[15]

Come si vede, Gianfrancesco non nasconde affatto ed anzi dichiara apertamente l' intento apologetico del suo scritto e la sua fondamentale ispirazione religiosa. Sicchè non meraviglia che l' attacco ad Aristotele si apra con il diretto richiamo a quelle pagine del "Proemio" generale dell' *Examen*, dove la "vanità" delle filosofie pagane era stata subito individuata

---

[13] *Ibid.*, p. 1014.

[14] *Ibid.*, pp. 1014-15. Il Pico si riferisce al suo primo esilio, quando, nel giugno del 1502, i suoi fratelli Ludovico e Federico mossero contro Mirandola, l' assediarono e se ne impadronirono il 6 agosto. Gianfrancesco, catturato, fu costretto ad abbandonare la città, dove potè rientrare, riassumendone il dominio, solo dopo il 20 gennaio del 1511, quando Papa Giulio II se ne impadronì, dopo un mese di assedio. Durante l' esilio, nel 1509, Gianfrancesco fu prima al servizio dell' Imperatore Massimiliano I e anche di Giulio II, durante la guerra contro Venezia sostenuta dalla Lega di Cambrai; quindi, tra il '10 e l' 11, servì ancora il Papa nella guerra contro Luigi XII.

[15] *Ibid.*, p. 1015.

nella loro inevitabile "superstizione", "incertezza" e "falsità", che le poneva in assoluto contrasto con la pura "verità" della religione cristiana. Il Conte conferma, quindi, che, anche nel caso del Filosofo per eccellenza, inizierà la sua discussione dall' accertamento della vanità del fondamento iniziale e del "fine" di quella dottrina, nonchè dei *media* fallaci di cui si serve per avvalorare la sua falsa verità.[16]

Certo, pure Aristotele riconosce, come tutti gli uomini, siano essi eruditi o *rudes*, che il "principio" della filosofia discende dal "sommo bene" e che il suo fine consiste proprio nell' ottenimento di quel bene; e, infatti, afferma che nessun uomo può non desiderare un tale bene, il cui possesso, secondo il comune consenso dei dotti, non è però raggiungibile al di fuori della religione (*praeterquam religionem*). Il Filosofo ne è anzi tanto convinto che, nell' *Ethica*, nella *Politica* e nell' *Oeconomica*, insegna appunto ad esser religiosi.[17] Ma proprio l' esame del suo atteggiamento teorico e pratico nei confronti della divinità, condotto sul fondamento delle sue stesse parole e di solidi testimoni, ne conferma la "vanità", sia nel modo di assumere il "principio" e di individuare il "fine", sia nel servirsi di un "medio" non adeguato. Il Filopono, autore della sua biografia ed espositore delle sue opere, ha infatti dichiarato che Aristotele fu indotto a filosofare non da Dio, ma da un "cacodemone", la Pizia, che gli ordinò di recarsi, proprio per questo, ad Atene. Si trattava, appunto, della custode del tempio di Apollo, spinta ed eccitata da un demone, considerato, anche da Aristotele e da molti altri, un dio conoscitore degli eventi futuri. E si sa che, a quel tempo, era costume comune chiedere proprio ad Apollo la facoltà di filosofare *facile et tuto*. Non può, dunque, stupire che anche lo Stagirita non solo credesse ai poteri divinatori di Apollo, ma innalzasse voti anche a Giove ed a Giunone, considerati *dei salutares*.[18]

Per il Pico, un filosofo che considera Dio in modo così ambiguo da parlarne, talvolta, come se fosse un' unica e assoluta divinità, ma senza esitare a onorare con il suo culto gli dei pagani, è, perlomeno, un uomo incostante e incerto; la sua religione è solo "superstizione" e mera "vanità", soggetta o almeno mista all' idolatria. Lo dimostra il fatto che onorò persino gli "eroi" pagani e che, per compiacere una donna amata, sacrificò alle divinità eleusine.

---

[16] *Ibid.*; e cfr. pp. 717-22.
[17] *Ibid.*, p. 1016.
[18] *Ibid.*

Come altri critici di Aristotele, passati e futuri, anche il Pico si serve della varia anedottica sulle "colpe" e le "infamie" di Aristotele, per aggravare questo giudizio, dettato da preoccupazioni esclusivamente religiose. Ma, più seriamente, preferisce proporre un elenco di passi che confermerebbero, insieme alla sua perenne incertezza, anche il suo paganesimo "superstizioso". Dio è, infatti, per lui, secondo i vari contesti, un *animal sempiternum optimum* (una frase spesso ripetuta anche dai suoi discepoli, in particolare da Temistio, e che forse ha indotto Alessandro di Afrodisia a identificare Dio con il mondo), oppure, semplicemente, la "prima mente" eterna che fa ruotare il primo cielo: un' idea, anche questa, del tutto estranea alla verità di fede. Né avrebbe senso cercare di nascondere, con traduzioni false, oppure con interpretazioni distorte o errate, le vere e certe parole di Aristotele che non lasciano , su questo punto, neppure un' ombra di dubbio.[19]

Comunque, Giovan Francesco non vuole affrontare, per il momento, una questione sulla quale tornerà più tardi, anche se non tace l' opinione di Atenagora, ben fermo nel ritenere che, per Aristotele, Dio fosse un "animale costituito di corpo e di anima", e quella , non diversa, di Galeno.[20] È, però, del tutto convinto che il Filosofo non abbia mai avuto una vera "scienza di Dio"; e che, proprio per questo, la sua dottrina sia assolutamente "vana" e nei suoi scritti, non si trovi alcuna "religione", ma soltanto e sempre "superstizione". Basti pensare che, nei libri VI e VII della *Politica*, parla di come elevare i templi agli dei ed agli "eroi" pagani ed istituire i loro sacerdoti, imponendo ai cittadini di onorarli. Anche chi lo difende dall' accusa di empietà e insegna che i suoi scritti hanno tramandato ai posteri il culto di Dio e l'idea della Provvidenza, dovrà, dunque, riconoscere che non lo fece in modo schietto e religioso, se è vero che, come tutti i "gentili", credeva agli oracoli dei demoni e riconosceva nei loro vaticini le cause di eventi fuori delle leggi naturali. Coloro che onorano Aristotele sappiano, insomma, che prestano il loro omaggio a un idolatra non diverso dagli altri pagani.[21]

---

[19] *Ibid.*, p. 1017.

[20] *Ibid.*, p. 1019. Prima (pp. 1018-19), il Pico ha citato il teologo carmelitano Giovanni Baconthorp, il francescano Erveo di Nédellec e Pietro Aureolo che hanno mostrato come Aristotele non abbia mai concepito Dio quale "*mens infinitae perfectionis*" e come il suo concetto di "atto puro" e di "motore primo" non si riferisca all' *omnino primus*, bensì alla dottrina dei "motori" e delle "sostanze separate", del tutto repugnante alla verità cristiana.

[21] *Ibid.* p. 1020.

Anche le notizie anedottiche sulla morte di Aristotele, sono utilizzate dal Pico per ribadire questa sua convinzione ed ammonire gli aristotelici troppo entusiasti del loro maestro a ricordare, piuttosto, i precetti apostolici, guardandosi dall'inganno di una filosofia che – come ripete, con implacabile monotonia – è del tutto "vana". Perchè, se fu cattivo l'"inizio" di Aristotele, lo fu pure non solo la fine della sua vita, bensì il "fine" stesso della sua dottrina, incapace di condurre, con sincerità, al vero ed ottimo scopo dell'uomo, e che, come "medio" per raggiungerlo, non indica la religione, ma piuttosto la superstizione.[22]

4. Sin qui il discorso del Pico non sembra distinguersi molto da una lunga e tradizionale polemica contro gli "errori" e la "falsità" dei filosofi antichi, di cui sarebbe facile ricostruire la lunga e varia fortuna medievale. Ma la sua "requisitoria" muta di tono quando, da questi argomenti, passa alla ripresa di alcuni tipici temi già sviluppati dalla critica umanista e intesi a verificare l'effettiva "paternità" delle opere raccolte nel *corpus* aristotelico pervenuto in Occidente, sceverando i testi presumibilmente autentici da quelli spuri o dubbi.[23] Il Pico scrive, infatti, che se anche i testi aristotelici sui quali si discute fossero davvero del tutto autentici e certi, sarebbe sempre facile dimostrare che il loro autore mescola, in ogni occasione, ad argomentazioni del tutto discutibili una "certezza" promessa però con il ricorso a prove incerte, ambigue e fondate sul ricorso a molte *auctoritates*. Si potrà, dunque, concludere che Aristotele ha spesso insegnato il falso in luogo del vero, così come ha commesso numerosi errori imperdonabili. Ma, per rispettare le buone regole del filosofare, il Conte dichiara che procederà ordinatamente, cominciando con lo spiegare come e donde sia sorta la grande autorità di cui ora gode il Filosofo "per eccellenza". Mostrerà, poi, che il *corpus* della sua opera è composto da opere d'incerta attribuzione e, addirittura, da non pochi scritti sicuramente apocrifi. Insomma: come si

---

[22] *Ibid.*

[23] *Ibid.*, pp. 1020. Anche la discussione critica e polemica sull'incertezza e oscurità della tradizione antica delle opere aristoteliche e sul carattere spesso "spurio" e, comunque, "corrotto" delle versioni latine medievali di Aristotele sono *topoi* costanti della cultura filosofica umanistica, dal Petrarca al Bruni, al Valla, agli autori delle nuove traduzioni dal greco di quei testi e, più tardi, alla prolissa, ma radicale contestazione di Francesco Patrizi (cfr. n. 5, e, in particolare, il lavoro della Muccillo). Il Pico (*ibid.*, pp. 1021-26) ne riprende e riassume gli argomenti essenziali, ricordando anche la polemica antiaristotelica di Rabbi Hasdai Crescas, e ripetendo la condanna di Averroè e dell'averroismo, già pronunziata, con particolare enfasi, anche dal Petrarca, da Giorgio Gemisto Pletone e dal Ficino.

costuma di solito nelle battaglie, inizierà la sua guerra filosofica con un combattimento affidato alla "fanteria leggera", in modo da insegnare agli accesi seguaci di Aristotele, che conoscono poco i libri stesi in altre lingue e per nulla quelli scritti in greco, quale sia il principio e l'ordine della loro "suprema" autorità e quali le dottrine che effettivamente professano.[24]

Per prima cosa, la sua critica dimostrerà che, nei secoli precedenti, la considerazione di Aristotele non fu così alta come lo è ora. Subito dopo, rivelerà che sono d' incerta attribuzione proprio i suoi libri oggi massimamente apprezzati, e che anzi non si è neppure certi di possederne davvero uno solo che sia sicuramente opera sua. Ma ciò significa che il Pico non è affatto disposto ad attribuirgli, senza una seria ed approfondita discussione, le dottrine che sono contenute in testi così dubbiosi e insicuri.[25]

Questi preliminari serviranno, comunque, a stabilire quali siano le dottrine da riconoscere veramente come opera di Aristotele, e che non gli siano state attribuite in modo falso o illegittimo. Eseguito questo accertamento, il Pico si propone di servirsi dell' autorità dei suoi stessi seguaci, del *modus scribendi* proprio di Aristotele, del continuo conflitto tra i suoi esegeti e del giudizio di teologi cristiani di grande fama, per mostrare quanto siano pericolosi i suoi errori e fallaci i significati delle sue argomentazioni, secondo la sua stessa testimonianza. A questa discussione sarà dedicato il quinto libro, mentre, nel sesto, verranno rilevati i "vizi" del procedimento dimostrativo aristotelico e la scarsa certezza della sua "arte conoscitiva". Nel settimo libro, sarà, invece, raccolta e registrata la gran massa degli errori del Filosofo, in modo che i lettori, ammoniti da questa triplice vanità, possano cercare, con maggiore avidità ed ardore, una dottrina del tutto vera.[26]

Non mi soffermerò a lungo sull' esame delle ragioni che, secondo il Pico, hanno permesso che si affermasse la grande e dominante "autorità" di Aristotele: un esame svolto con pedantesca prolissità, ma che, nondimeno, costituisce un'interessante e precoce tentativo di ricostruzione storica della fortuna del "peripatetismo". Basterà, comunque, notare la particolare insistenza del Pico nel ricordare che, nei tempi più vicini al suo insegnamento, anche alcuni dei migliori discepoli, Teofrasto e Andronico,

---

[24] *Ibid.*, p. 1021.
[25] *Ibid.*
[26] *Ibid.*

Filopono e Simplicio, non si peritarono di criticare talune dottrine del Maestro. Sicchè la vera origine del culto superstizioso di Aristotele dovrebbe essere attribuita all' incolta barbarie e rozzezza di quegli Arabi e "Mauri" che, non comprendendo bene quanto leggevano, si limitarono a ripetere meccanicamente le sue parole. In realtà, sinchè Atene poté resistere, il primato dei Peripatetici non fu mai assoluto, perchè continuarono ad esistere pure le varie scuole filosofiche dell' antichità, la Platonica, la Stoica, insieme a tutte le altre. Non diversamente, pure a Roma, dove Platone ebbe molto seguito, vennero assai celebrati gli Stoici ed anche Pirrone godé una notevole fortuna. Lo dimostra la filosofia di Cicerone, pronta ad accogliere dottrine della Nuova Accademia e dello stesso Platone, ma più vicina agli Stoici e, d' altro canto, disposta spesso a lodare ed anche a discutere i seguaci di Aristotele. É vero che, dopo la conquista di Atene, Silla portò a Roma l' intera "biblioteca" di Aristotele. Però il Pico sottolinea che, per tutta l' età imperiale, le varie scuole filosofiche dell' antichità trovarono numerosi seguaci; e cita Seneca, Epitteto, Sesto Empirico, Jerocle, Numenio, Giamblico, Plotino, Proclo ed Ermia, Alcinoo ed Albino, per mostrare come vigesse una piena *libertas philosophandi*. Certo, un celebre maestro, Alessandro di Afrodisia, esaltò molto Aristotele; ma, in compenso, Galeno fu assai critico nei suoi riguardi. E, pure al tempo di Agostino, schietto ammiratore di Platone, furono ancora sempre numerosi quei filosofi che si dichiaravano platonici o cinici. Persino dopo la caduta dell' Impero, Boezio, se tradusse Aristotele, studiò assai anche Platone, autore preferito pure da molti Padri latini e greci.[27]

Come vari altri autori umanistici, dal Petrarca al Bruni, dal Valla a Giorgio Gemisto Pletone ed al Ficino, anche il Pico è, insomma, convinto che il trionfo "scolastico" di Aristotele sia coinciso con l' età dei "barbari" e il progressivo oscuramento delle tradizioni filosofiche classiche, da lui, del resto, tutte severamente giudicate. Scrive, perciò, che solo dopo la chiusura della Scuola di Atene e la caduta di Roma in mano ai barbari, i libri dei filosofi greci e, in particolare, quelli di Aristotele, emigrarono presso gli Arabi, i "Mauri" e quegli "spagnoli" che si esprimevano in arabo. Ricorda, naturalmente, Alfarabi, Averroè e Avicenna (di cui non tace certe evidenti propensioni platoniche), per affermare che proprio i filosofi arabi, privi dei libri degli altri filosofi antichi, o mal persuasi che solo Aristotele possedesse la "luce della verità", dedicarono tutto il loro ingegno a studiarlo ed

---

[27] *Ibid.*, pp. 1021-23.

interpretarlo. Poi, al tempo di Alfonso il Savio, le loro opere passarono dalle terre musulmane della Spagna a quelle cristiane, ove furono accolte e tradotte, prima di giungere a Parigi, dove fioriva lo studio della filosofia e, sino dal tempo di Carlomagno, Giovanni Scoto aveva tradotto i testi dionisiani. Neppure gli Ebrei rimasero estranei alla crescente influenza di Aristotele: in particolare, Mosè Maimonide tentò di esporre "da filosofo" l'Antico Testamento, accettando in gran parte le sue dottrine. Un tale atteggiamento suscitò molte critiche da parte di diversi dotti ebrei, e tra queste il Pico cita soprattutto quelle di Hasdai Crescas, un autore che – com' è noto – utilizzerà ampiamente nella critica di alcune dottrine aristoteliche capitali.

Come avevano già fatto il Petrarca, Gemisto ed il Ficino, anche il Conte riserva però il suo giudizio più duro ad Averroè ed agli averroisti che, come il loro maestro, non sono disposti ad ammettere l' esistenza di alcun errore nelle opere di Aristotele, e che, comunque, si sono fatti seguaci di un uomo disposto ad accettare l' empia e *delira* religione di Maometto. Ad Averroè contesta, inoltre, che, considerando la relativa brevità della sua vita, non potè certo leggere probabilmente tutte le opere del Filosofo e, in ogni caso, non tenne conto neppure degli errori già messi in luce dai suoi seguaci e commentatori greci, Teofrasto, Andronico, Filopono e Simplicio, accettando, senza respingerli, anche le "vanità" e gli equivoci più evidenti. Non basta: facendo proprio un altro tipico *topos* umanistico, insiste pure sulla pessima qualità delle traduzioni in arabo e dall' arabo dei testi aristotelici e degli stessi commenti averroistici, volti in un latino barbaro, non "fedele" e non "nitido". Ciò non ha impedito, tuttavia, che Averroè ed il "suo" Aristotele venissero presto accolti ed esaltati nell'Occidente cristiano e che, per oltre due secoli, fossero identificati con la "verità" filosofica.[28]

Solo ai tempi di Eugenio IV e di Niccolò V, Giorgio Gemisto Pletone ed il Bessarione tornarono a restituire al mondo cristiano occidentale le dottrine platoniche; e negli stessi anni, anche Niccolò Cusano fu piuttosto attratto da Platone, già prima che il Ficino ne traducesse tutte le opere in buon latino, illustrandole con i suoi vasti commenti. Però molti altri filosofi restarono fedeli ad Aristotele che, addirittura, ritenevano meno "dissonante" dalla religione cristiana di quanto non lo fosse Platone, considerato un

---

[28] *Ibid.*, pp. 1023-25.

pericoloso veicolo di dottrine eterodosse.[29] Infine, Giovanni Pico si propose di "concordare" le filosofie dei due massimi pensatori del mondo antico: un' ardua impresa che avrebbe forse compiuto, se la sua vita non fosse stata così breve.[30]

Il nipote non esita, però, a dichiarare, nel modo più esplicito, che il suo proposito è del tutto diverso: *non conciliare, sed infirmare universam Gentium doctrinam*, affinchè, sull' esempio degli antichi teologi, i dotti cristiani tornino a dedicarsi allo studio della Scrittura e della suprema ed unica sapienza. Perchè la sola verissima filosofia, che non è di questo mondo, è raggiungibile – come afferma Agostino – solo quando le anime tornano a se stesse e, nel loro segreto, possono *respicere patriam sine disputationum concertatione*. Un programma che, di nuovo, sembra ispirato all' esempio del Savonarola e che lo stesso Gianfrancesco aveva delineato, sin dal 1496, nel *De studio divinae et humanae philosophiae*,[31] e ribadì, nel 1514/ 15, in alcuni passi della *De reformandis moribus oratio*, rivolta a Leone X ed ai Padri del quinto Concilio Lateranense.[32]

5. Stabiliti così tutti i presupposti della sua critica, il Pico può quindi procedere, nel capitolo terzo del IV Libro, alla lunga elencazione delle obiezioni mosse ad Aristotele dai suoi stessi seguaci e dai maggiori filosofi dell' antichità, concordi, in sostanza, nel ritenere che, in molti casi, la sua dottrina è incerta o ambigua. Ma più che questa dimostrazione delle sue vaste conoscenze filosofiche, forse più indirette che dirette, interessa notare come, nel IV capitolo, riprenda proprio il tema dell' incerta paternità delle opere aristoteliche, per dichiarare che non si conosce alcun libro di cui si possa verificare l' effettivo possesso da parte del Filosofo, o, per parlar più chiaramente, l' effettiva derivazione dai suoi "esemplari" o da testi da lui veramente composti ed editi. Si tratta, insomma, di un dubbio di grande

---

[29] Il Pico sembra qui alludere principalmente alla nota polemica antiplatonica di Giorgio Trapezunzio; e cfr. J. Monfasani, *George of Trebizond. A Biography and a Study of his Rhetoric and Logic*, Leiden 1976, part. pp. 201-29.

[30] *Ibid.*, pp. 1025-26.

[31] Cfr. *Ioannis Francisci Pici Mirandulae de morte Christi et propria cogitanda libri tres. Eiusdem de studio divinae et humanae philosophiae libri duo*, Bononiae, Benedictus Hector 1497.

[32] Cfr. *Ioannis Francisci PICI Mirandulae Domini et Concordiae Comitis ad Leonem Pontificem Maximum et Concilium Lateranensem de reformandis moribus oratio. Eiusdem hymni tres D. Martino, Magdalenae et Antonio decantanti*, Hagenau, Thomas Amshelm 1520.

rilevanza, sollecitato proprio dall'estrema diversità delle opinioni degli stessi filosofi o storiografi antichi a proposito della presentazione, disposizione e ordinamento del *corpus*. Basti dire che Diogene Laerzio dissente, in gran parte, da coloro che scrissero prima della composizione delle sue *Vitae philosophorum*, e che gli autori posteriori contrastano, a loro volta, sia con lui, sia con gli altri. Proprio il Laerzio, a proposito delle opere di logica, cita scritti che al tempo del Pico non si possedevano più, mentre tace di altri che erano, invece, conosciuti e letti.[33]

Ma non basta: chi segua le lunghe dispute intorno a questo argomento, non ha difficoltà a riconoscere che il problema dell'attribuzione è stato, da lungo tempo, l'oggetto di un serrato dibattito, mai davvero conchiuso o chiarito. Lo confermano le numerose citazioni tratte dallo stesso Laerzio, da Ammonio, Teofrasto, Ateneo, Temistio, Plinio, Quintiliano e persino da Tommaso d'Aquino che, secondo il Pico, accrescono i dubbi e le confusioni e lasciano nella massima incertezza. Senza dubbio, una situazione così imbarazzante per i più stretti seguaci di Aristotele può essere spiegata con buone ragioni : e, cioè, in primo luogo, con l'esistenza di diversi filosofi – otto, secondo lo stesso Laerzio – che si chiamavano ugualmente Aristotele; e, ancora, con la scarsità d'intitolazioni chiare e concordi che ha permesso ad alcuni di attribuire falsamente taluni scritti al Filosofo. Il Pico ricorda che qualcosa di simile è accaduto, del resto, anche in tempi più recenti, quando i Frati Minori e i Domenicani hanno attribuito il medesimo commento ai Salmi, rispettivamente a Alessandro di Hales e ad Ugo di San Vittore: una questione risolta, a suo modo, solo quando il Patriarca di Venezia ha ordinato che fosse stampato senza alcuna attribuzione. Ma aggiunge una nuova, diversa causa: l'esistenza indubbia di certe opere dei maestri peripatetici che imitavano quelle di Aristotele e che sono state poi confuse con le sue, come può dimostrare una notevole casistica subito citata. Né stupisce che il Conte ponga in particolare risalto il caso del commento alla *Physica* di Temistio, un'opera preceduta, nella versione latina di Ermolao Barbaro, da un ampio proemio attribuito allo stesso autore, che però si può leggere del tutto identico anche nel testo greco del commento di Simplicio. Può darsi che Simplicio abbia plagiato da Temistio quel proemio, parola per parola; ma è un'ipotesi poco credibile, perché un simile comportamento sarebbe stato troppo rischioso. Eppure, sembra ancor più impossibile che egli abbia potuto scrivere lo stesso testo, in modo

---

[33] *Examen*, cit., pp. 1029-30.

del tutto identico. Comunque, il rilievo del Pico è giusto e ben fondato; e trova la sua spiegazione nel dato ormai acquisito che il Barbaro si era servito per la sua versione di uno di quei codici greci che premettono, senza dirlo, il proemio di Simplicio al commento di Temistio.[34]

A ciò si aggiunga che Tolomeo Filadelfo, Re d' Egitto, un sovrano desideroso di conoscere la filosofia di Aristotele, offrì congrui premi a chiunque recava alla biblioteca di Alessandria un libro di Aristotele, con il risultato di corrompere l' integrità dei testi aristotelici, sino al punto di far correre sotto il suo nome ben quaranta Libri di *Analytici*. Il Pico cita, poi, diversi esempi, tratti sia dalla tradizione aristotelica, sia da altri casi simili di diffusione di scritti classici, per i quali si possono proporre ragioni e spiegazioni simili.[35] Resta, insomma, il fatto indubbio che tutti i libri di Aristotele sono adesso incerti, e che neppure si può ben distinguere la loro paternità dallo stile. In realtà, anche seguendo questa via, è praticamente impossibile trovare un solido criterio di distinzione tra opere edite nello stesso secolo da autori che usavano lo stesso modo di scrivere, soprattutto quando costoro erano dei discepoli che si sforzavano d' imitare i loro maestri anche nello stile.[36] Lo confermano i vari casi di libri, tra i più importanti attribuiti ad Aristotele, la cui paternità è stata smentita da alcuni tra i maggiori e più autorevoli "peripatetici".[37]

6. Giovan Francesco vuole, tuttavia, dimostrarsi talmente equo nei confronti di Aristotele da concedere che tutti i libri attribuitigli siano "legittimi", non vi sia mai stata confusione tra i suoi scritti e quelli dei discepoli, non sia mai stata messa in dubbio l' autenticità dei *Praedicamenta*, del *De interpretatione* e degli *Analytici* e non si sia mai verificata la massima confusione nei titoli e nella successione dei singoli libri e capitoli. Ciò non toglie, però, che quei testi ci siano pervenuti attraverso vicende estremamente complesse e addirittura romanzesche, qui ricostruite con puntigliosa insistenza, per mostrare come abbiano favorito l'inevitabile "interpolazione" e "corruzione", rivelate dalle numerose e vistose diversità dei "testi-

---

[34] *Ibid.*, pp. 1030-32. E cfr. per la spiegazione di questa confusione tra i due commentatori, la prefazione di H. Schenkel a Themistius, *In Aristotelis physica paraphrasis*, CAG, V, p. XIX.
[35] *Ibid.*, pp. 1032-34.
[36] *Ibid.*, p. 1033.
[37] *Ibid.*, pp. 1033-34.

moni" antichi che ci sono pervenuti.[38] Del resto, quando Silla, duecento anni dopo la morte del Filosofo, recò a Roma da Atene la biblioteca di Apellicone Teio, ricca di molte opere di Aristotele e di Teofrasto prima ignote, quegli scritti erano talmente guasti e già cosí corrotti che si dové affidarli al grammatico Tirannione perchè li emendasse e integrasse; e pure Andronico di Rodi lavorò a distinguerli, ricomporli e ristabilirne l'ordine. Neppure l'impegno di quei dotti impedí che circolassero poi diversi ordinamenti dei libri aristotelici e testi assai diversi e d'incerta origine. Il Pico cita, ad esempio, il caso dell'inizio del III Libro *De anima*, a proposito del quale le opinioni dei vari lettori e commentatori greci e latini sono le più diverse e contrastanti; e continua poi ad enumerare un'altra serie di dubbi e incertezze simili che rendono difficilissimo sapere quale fosse l'esatta struttura di quei testi aristotelici, se essi ci siano pervenuti come li scrisse il Filosofo, o se, invece, siano stati del tutto manipolati, interpolati e mutati.[39] Si tratta, del resto, di vicende comuni anche a molti altri libri di varia e lunga tradizione, come conferma il caso del *Corano*, le cui peripezie, diversità testuali profonde, dubbi sull'autenticità e sulla stessa identificazione del suo autore sono stati bene esposti dal Cusano, nella *Cribatio Alchorani*.[40]

D'altro canto, anche chi sostenesse che i testi greci delle opere di Aristotele, quali ci sono pervenuti, siano genuini e trasmettano veramente le idee del loro autore, dovrà pure riconosce che le loro versioni latine non sono affatto fedeli. Il Pico esime da questo perentorio giudizio solo gli scritti aristotelici che sono stati tradotti da Teodoro Gaza, il quale, tuttavia, ha ammesso di essersi molto impegnato per riparare gli errori e le lacune dei codici. Ma, aderendo al giudizio comune degli umanisti, è altrettanto deciso nel considerare irreparabilmente corrotte le traduzioni dall'arabo, nelle quali, in sostanza, *tot pene errores, quot verba spectantur*.[41] Un simile giudizio dovrebbe bastare a dimostrare quale possa essere la fedeltà esegetica di un'interprete, Averroè, tanto esaltato dagli indotti, e in che conto si debba tenere quanto ha scritto nel Proemio della sua esposizione della "filosofia naturale". Costui afferma testualmente che, nel corso di

---

[38] *Ibid.*, pp. 1034.

[39] *Ibid.*, pp. 1035-38.

[40] *Ibid.*, p. 1038. Da queste peripezie è però esentato il testo della Bibbia conservato dagli Ebrei con tale cura da permettergli di evitare anche le conseguenze della cattività babilonese e delle devastazioni delle loro terre.

[41] *Ibid.*

millecinquecento anni, non è mai stato scoperto alcun errore negli scritti di Aristotele. Ma quanto può valere questa certezza di un uomo che ammetteva di non conoscere la lingua greca e, dunque, non aveva mai letto il "vero" Filosofo, bensì soltanto le versioni arabe piene di errori e di falsità, sulle quali condusse i suoi celebrati commenti ? E, in ogni caso, anche se avesse letto i testi greci, non avrebbe mai potuto attingere a quelli genuini di Aristotele, bensì solo ai rifacimenti di Apellicone Teio, di Tiranione e di coloro che poi si arrogarono il nome di Peripatetici.[42]

Sono queste le conclusioni estremamente scettiche sullo stato della tradizione aristotelica e sulla sua "verità" storica e filologica, alle quali si deve pervenire, dopo avere esaminato una storia così confusa ed incerta. E da esse il Pico prenderà le mosse per sostenere che, secondo la testimonianza di Teofrasto, di Andronico, di Simplicio, di Porfirio e di altri autori, la stessa dottrina "genuina" di Aristotele era ambigua, oscura, e, in taluni casi, falsa,[43] così com' era difficile e variamente interpretabile il suo modo di esprimerla.[44] Da questa originaria oscurità e incertezza è derivato il perenne dissenso tra tutti i suoi interpreti che ne hanno fornito le esegesi più contrastanti.[45] Sicchè i teologi cristiani di tutti i tempi non hanno errato, quando, indipendentemente da qualsiasi discussione esegetica, hanno sottoposto a severa critica le tesi aristoteliche fondamentali, ben consapevoli di quanto fossero discordanti dall' unica verità della rivelazione.[46]

La tenace critica di Gianfrancesco Pico potrà così procedere, nell' ultima parte dell' *Examen*, alla discussione sistematica dei concetti fondamentali della "fisica" aristotelica (le nozioni di "moto", "tempo", "spazio" e "vuoto"), richiamandosi soprattutto al Filopono ed al Crescas, per mostrare la "vanità" di una filosofia considerata la massima espressione della ragione, ma che, con i suoi errori, confermava l' impossibilità umana di raggiungere, con le sue forze, la *sincera veritas*.[47] In tal modo, il fedele seguace del tomista Savonarola giungerà a porre in seria discussione alcuni principi fondamentali della scienza scolastica e della sua *imago mundi* che, più tardi, avrebbe costituito uno dei baluardi del sistema ideologico della

---

[42] *Ibid.*, pp. 1038-39.
[43] *Ibid.*, pp. 1039-41.
[44] *Ibid.*, pp. 1042-45.
[45] *Ibid.*, pp. 1045-47.
[46] *Ibid.*, pp. 1048-53.
[47] *Ibid.*, pp. 1177 sgg.

Controrifoma. Non stupisce che taluni argomenti largamente sviluppati in questo libro fossero poi ripresi, con un ben diverso intento polemico, proprio dai *novatores*, già impegnati nella radicale dissoluzione della tradizione peripatetica. Un esito, questo, che un sincero fideista, apologeta della profezia, fermamente convinto dei nefasti poteri diabolici dei maghi e delle streghe, e impegnato a respingere le temibili lusinghe delle filosofie dei pagani, non si sarebbe certo mai atteso.

The Transformations of Alexander of Aphrodisias' Interpretation of Aristotle's Theory of the Soul[*]

by Olaf Pluta

In late antiquity and up to the thirteenth century Alexander of Aphrodisias (around 200 AD)[1] was the most influential commentator of Aristotle. His commentaries were considered so accurate and comprehensive that Alexander was simply referred to as "the Commentator" (ὁ ἐξηγητής)[2] – a title which Averroes (d. 1198) gained for himself in the later Middle Ages – and his own works were considered so enlightening and insightful that he was even called "the new Aristotle" and "the second Aristotle" (ὁ νεώτερος Ἀριστοτέλης, ὁ δεύτερος Ἀριστοτέλης).[3] Alexander of Aphrodisias dominated the intellectual life in such a way that Averroes, who heavily criticizes him on many occasions, tells us about his own contemporaries in his long commentary on the *De anima*: "nobody is considered a

---

[*] The writing of this article was made possible through financial support from the Netherlands Organization for Scientific Research (NWO), grant 200-22-295.

[1] Little is known of the life of Alexander of Aphrodisias. The only direct information concerning his life stems from the introduction to his *De fato* which he dedicated to Septimius Severus and Antonius Caracalla and which is hence to be dated between 198 and 209. We do not even know for certain in which Aphrodisias he was born, though his name probably links Alexander to the familiar city in the south-west of Asia Minor along the Aegean Sea.

[2] Cf. e.g. Simplicius, *In Physica* (Commentaria in Aristotelem Graeca = CAG 10), 1170, 13; 1176, 32; Olympiodorus, *In Meteorologica* (CAG 12.2), 263, 19-21. Further references can be found in R. W. Sharples, "Alexander of Aphrodisias: Scholasticism and Innovation", *Aufstieg und Niedergang der römischen Welt* (= ANRW) 2.36.2 (1987), 1176-1243, note 23.

[3] Cf. Syrianus, *In Metaphysica* (CAG 6.1), 100, 6; David (Elias), *In Categoriae* (CAG 18.1), 128, 13. Cf. E. Zeller, *Die Philosophie der Griechen in ihrer geschichtlichen Entwicklung*, III.1, Leipzig 1903, 805 n.2 (807). These passages have been interpreted by P. Moreaux, "Aristoteles, der Lehrer Alexanders von Aphrodisias", *Archiv für Geschichte der Philosophie* 49 (1967), 169-182, as referring to Aristotle of Mytilene; however, this interpretation has been criticized by P. Thillet (ed.), *Alexandre d'Aphrodise: Traité du Destin*, Paris 1984, xix-xxxi.

knowledgeable and complete person among them if he is not an Alexandrist" (*nullus enim est sciens et perfectus apud eos nisi qui est Alexandreus*).[4]

Throughout the later Middle Ages and the Renaissance Alexander was most famous – and infamous – for his theory of the human intellect; therefore my paper will focus on this topic.

My paper will have three parts. In the first, I will briefly survey the transmission and translation of his commentaries on Aristotle's *De anima* and his own works on Aristotelian psychology during the Middle Ages and the Renaissance. In the second part, I will focus on the reception and transformation of Alexander's thought by John Buridan and his school. In the third part, I will concentrate on Pietro Pomponazzi's commentaries on Aristotle's *De anima*. These writings were deeply rooted in the medieval discussions and cannot be fully understood without these sources, but they also further developed Alexander's views and came up with a more elaborate theory of the human intellect.

*

Alexander of Aphrodisias' works on psychology

Three psychological treatises are attributed to Alexander of Aphrodisias. From references in ancient commentators we know of the existence of a commentary on Aristotle's *De anima*.[5] While this commentary has not survived, we possess a treatise by Alexander, named *De anima* (Περὶ ψυχῆς).[6] Furthermore, we possess the *De intellectu* (Περὶ νοῦ), which is part of a collection of psychological writings known as the *Mantissa*,[7] which is also referred to as the second book of Alexander's *De anima*. However, the authenticity of this work was called into question in 1942 by Moreaux, who detected a great divergence of doctrine with the *De anima*. In contrast, some scholars have argued that the *De intellectu* is either a work of Alexander's youth or of his maturity. However, recent scholarship has reinforced

---

[4] Cf. Averroes, *Commentarium magnum in Aristotelis De anima libros*, ed. F. Stuart Crawford, Cambridge, Mass. 1953, 433, 150-151.

[5] Cf. Philoponus, *In De anima* (CAG 15), 21, 20-23; 118, 27f.; 159, 18-19; Michael of Ephesus, *In Parva Naturalia* (CAG 22.1), 135, 24-28.

[6] Edited by I. Bruns, *Alexandri Aphrodisiensis praeter commentaria scripta minora. De anima liber cum Mantissa* (Supplementum Aristotelicum 2.1), Berlin 1887, 1-100.

[7] Edited by I. Bruns under the title "De anima libri mantissa", *ibid.*, 101-186 (*De intellectu*, 106, 18-113, 24).

Moreaux's view and has made it evident that both the contents and the style of the *De intellectu* show that it is not an original work but a later compilation.[8] It may be noted that already Averroes has pointed to the apparent contradictions between the *De intellectu* and Alexander's *De anima*.[9]

In both treatises the potential or material intellect (*intellectus possibilis*, *intellectus materialis*) is identified with the human intellect. However, in the *De anima* the human intellect is a complete faculty, capable of abstracting form from matter, while in the *De intellectu* it is merely an embryonic form of the intellect that has yet to develop to this state. In both treatises the productive intellect (*intellectus agens*) is identified with the divine intellect. However, in the *De anima* the divine intellect only indirectly contributes to the formation of the human intellect by rendering the forms that are then independently abstracted from matter by the human intellect, while in the *De intellectu* the divine intellect directly takes part in the act of intellection.

Nevertheless, what is common to both treatises, aside from the apparent differences concerning the theory of human intellection, is the opinion that the human soul springs from a corporeal mixture and is hence mortal. It was this opinion, common to both texts, that was primarily connected with the name of Alexander of Aphrodisias in the Middle Ages and the Renaissance.

Of these two texts only the *De intellectu* was available in a Latin translation during the Middle Ages. This translation, which drew upon both Arabic and Greek sources, was made at the end of the twelfth century in Toledo and is commonly attributed to Gerard of Cremona. However, there is evidence that this translation was made by Dominicus Gundissalinus.[10] In the Italian Renaissance, the *De intellectu* was translated from

---

[8] The whole discussion concerning the authenticity of the *De intellectu* has been summarized in *Two Greek Aristotelian Commentators on the Intellect: The* De Intellectu *Attributed to Alexander of Aphrodisias and Themistius' Paraphrase of Aristotle* De anima *3.4-8*. Introduction, Translation, Commentary and Notes by F. M. Schroeder and R. B. Todd (Mediaeval Sources in Translation, 33), Toronto 1990, 6-22.

[9] "Quod autem dixit in quodam tractatu quem fecit de Intellectu Secundum Opinionem Aristotelis videtur contradicere ei quod dixit in libro de Anima. ... Et manifestum istius sermonis contradicit sermoni eius in libro de Anima, et est quod intellectus qui est in potentia non intelligit illum qui est in actu" (*op. cit.*, 483, 114-484, 127).

[10] Cf. M. Alonso, "Traducciones del arcediano Domingo Gundisalvo", *Al-Andalus* 12 (1947), 295-338; concerning Alexander von Aphrodisias see 315-317.

Greek into Latin by Girolamo Bagolino and published in Verona in 1516. The complete *Mantissa*, which contains the *De intellectu*, was translated into Latin by Angelo Canini and appeared in Venice in 1546.[11]

The theory of the *De intellectu* that the human soul is a material form and springs from a corporeal mixture immediately gained widespread acceptance as is apparent from a report given by William of Auvergne (d. 1249), also known as William of Paris, who writes in his own treatise *De anima*: "many people swallow down these positions, they take them in without any investigation through discussion and examination, they even accept them and hold them as most certain."[12] For William, Alexander's theory of the soul is not only entirely wrong but also extremely dangerous. Therefore, it must be stamped out with special endeavour (*studiosius et perscrutatius exterminanda est eius sententia*),[13] and not only by arguing against it, but also with fire and sword (*igne et gladio*).[14] Albert the Great (d. 1280) and Thomas Aquinas (d. 1274) also severely attacked the *opinio Alexandri* with harsh words.[15]

The sharpness of these polemical attacks against Alexander may be seen both as an indication of his influence and of the threat his thesis of the mortality of the soul posed to the Christian doctrine of immortality. The

---

[11] For the available translations see F.E. Cranz, "Alexander Aphrodisiensis", *Catalogus translationum et commentariorum: Mediaeval and Renaissance Latin Translations and Commentaries. Annotated Lists and Guides*, vol. I, ed. P. O. Kristeller, Washington, D.C. 1960, 77-135; idem, "Alexander Aphrodisiensis. Addenda et corrigenda", *ibid.*, vol.II, ed. P. O. Kristeller/F. E. Cranz, Washington, D.C. 1971, 411-422. Cf. also F. E. Cranz, "The Prefaces to the Greek Editions and Latin Translations of Alexander of Aphrodisias, 1450 to 1575", *Proceedings of the American Philosophical Society* 102 (1958), 510-546.

[12] "Et quoniam multi deglutiunt positiones istas (*i.e. Alexandri*) absque ulla investigatione discussionis et perscrutationis recipientes illas, et etiam consentientes illis et pro certissimis eas habentes, conveniens est de ipsis considerationes facere ..." (Guillelmus Alvernus, *De anima*, VII, 3; *Opera omnia*, II, Paris 1674, Reprint Frankfurt am Main 1963, 205b). All Latin spelling has been normalized. Cf. Gabriel Théry, *Autour du décret de 1210: II. – Alexandre d'Aphrodise. Aperçu sur l'influence de sa noétique*, Le Saulchoir 1926, 112.

[13] *Ibid.*, V, 3; *ed. cit.*, 114b.

[14] *Ibid.*, V, 5; *ed. cit.*, 119a.

[15] "Haec autem phantasia omnino est erronea" (Albertus Magnus, *De natura et origine animae*, II, 5; editio Coloniensis, XII, ed. B. Geyer, Münster in Westf. 1955, 24b, 98; cf. *ibid.*, 25b, 55-56, 64-65); "Ratio etiam sua frivola omnino est" (Thomas de Aquino, *Summa contra gentiles*, III, c.72; editio Leonina, XIV, Rome 1926, 108a).

condemnations of 1270 and 1277, which contain a number of Alexandrist theses,[16] also point in this direction.

This may explain why the Dominicans who at that time possessed the only Greek manuscript of Alexander's *De anima* in the Latin West, the famous Codex Graecus 258 of the Biblioteca Marciana in Venice,[17] did not make any effort to translate this important text – despite the fact that many people were interested in it.

Alexander's *De anima* was translated into Arabic (by Ishāq ibn Hunain) and published in Baghdad in the year 910. Thus, this text was easily available to Avicenna (Ibn Sınā) and Averroes (Ibn Rushd). However, there was no Latin translation available up to the year 1495 when the Venetian nobleman Girolamo Donato (Hieronymus Donatus) published a Latin translation of the text from the Greek original.[18]

However, some passages of Alexander's *De anima* are cited in full in Averroes' own long commentary. These few passages were the only authentic texts of Alexander on the theory of the soul available in the Latin West up to the end of the fifteenth century. It is obvious that the knowledge of Alexander's psychology which could be gained by reading these passages was fragmentary at best. Thus, the medieval thinkers had to partly reconstruct and reinvent Alexander's theory. It was John Buridan who made a big effort in this direction.

John Buridan and his school

John Buridan (d. 1360) was the most important natural and moral philosopher of his time. Just by looking at the sheer number of his commentaries on Aristotle and at the distribution of manuscripts throughout the fourteenth and fifteenth centuries it becomes apparent that John Buridan was one of the most influential philosophers of the later Middle

---

[16] "Quod anima, quae est forma hominis secundum quod homo, corrumpitur corrupto corpore", "Quod forma hominis non est ab extrinseco, sed educitur de potentia materiae", "Quod anima est inseparabilis a corpore; et quod ad corruptionem harmoniae corporalis corrumpitur anima" – 1270, prop. 7; 1277, prop. 105; 1277, prop. 116 (cf. *Chartularium Universitatis Parisiensis*, ed. H. Denifle/Ae. Chatelain, tomus I, Paris 1899, reprint Bruxelles 1964, 486-487 and 543-558).

[17] Cf. L. Labowsky, "William of Moerbeke's Manuscript of Alexander of Aphrodisias", *Mediaeval and Renaissance Studies* 5 (1961), 155-162. On f.1r of the Codex Graecus 258 one reads: "liber fratris guillelmi de morbeka ordinis predicatorum penitentiarii domini pape" (cf. *ibid.*, 156).

[18] See note 11 above.

Ages and beyond. His voluminous *Questions on the Ethics*, for example, appeared in print as late as 1637 when it was published in Oxford by H. Cripps.[19] In particular, his influence was overwhelming at the newly founded universities in central Europe, that is in Kraków, Vienna, Prague, Heidelberg, Cologne, Erfurt, Leipzig and Rostock.[20] Thus, a document, dated December 24, 1425, and now in the Historical Archive of Cologne rightfully labels the preceding century as *saeculum Buridani*.[21]

Buridan wrote both literal expositions (*expositiones*) and problem-oriented questions (*quaestiones*) on Aristotle's *De anima*. At least three redactions of these *Expositiones* and *Quaestiones* have survived.[22] We do not yet have critical editions of any of these texts.[23]

---

[19] Johannes Buridanus, *Quaestiones in decem libros Ethicorum Aristotelis ad Nicomachum*, ed. H. Forrest, H. Curtayne, J. Wilmot, Oxford 1637.

[20] This can be easily verified by referring to the repertories of commentaries on Aristotle for the libraries of these cities which have been compiled by the Polish scholars Korolec, Włodek and Markowski: M. Markowski, S. Włodek, *Repertorium commentariorum medii aevi in Aristotelem Latinorum quae in Bibliotheca Iagellonica Cracoviae asservantur*, Wrocław 1974; M. Markowski, *Repertorium commentariorum medii aevi in Aristotelem Latinorum quae in bibliothecis Wiennae asservantur*, Wrocław 1985; G. B. Korolec, *Repertorium commentariorum medii aevi in Aristotelem Latinorum quae in Bibliotheca olim Universitatis Pragensis nunc Státní Knihovna ČSR vocata asservantur*, Wrocław 1977; M. Markowski, *Repertorium commentariorum medii aevi in Aristotelem Latinorum quae in Bibliotheca Amploniana Erffordiae asservantur*, Wroclaw 1987. A repertorium for Leipzig is in preparation. Cf. also M. Markowski, *Buridanica quae in codicibus manu scriptis bibliothecarum Monacensium asservantur*, Wrocław 1981.

[21] Cf. E. A. Moody, *Studies in Medieval Philosophy, Science, and Logic. Collected Papers 1933-1969*, Berkeley 1975, 442. An edition of this document can be found in F. Ehrle, *Der Sentenzenkommentar Peters von Candia, des Pisaner Papstes Alexanders V. Ein Beitrag zur Scheidung der Schulen in der Scholastik des 14. Jahrhunderts und zur Geschichte des Wegestreites* (Franziskanische Studien, Beiheft 9), Münster 1925, 281-290.

[22] For the extant manuscripts see B. Michael, *Johannes Buridan: Studien zu seinem Leben, seinen Werken und zur Rezeption seiner Theorien im Europa des späten Mittelalters*, Histor. Diss. FU Berlin 1978, Berlin 1985, vol. 2, 677-735.

[23] The only texts which are fairly easily accessible are the second and third book of the last redaction of his Questions on Aristotle's *De anima*, which appeared as part of two dissertations, namely P. G. Sobol, *John Buridan on the soul and sensation. An edition of his commentary on Aristotle's book On the Soul with an introduction and a translation of question 18 on sensible species*, Phil. Diss. Indiana University 1984, Ann Arbor, Mich. 1992, and J. A. Zupko, *John Buridan's philosophy of mind. An edition and translation of Book III of his "Questions on Aristotle's De anima" (third redaction) with commentary and critical and interpretative essays*, Philos. Diss. Cornell University 1989, 2 vols., Ann Arbor, Mich. 1990. Both editions are based on only six manuscripts.

While most of Buridan's works have been printed in the fifteenth and sixteenth centuries, none of his *De anima* commentaries was ever printed. The text of Buridan's *Quaestiones de anima*, which appeared in Paris in 1516, and which was edited by the Scottish logician George Lokert,[24] who belonged to the circle of John Mair,[25] cannot be found in any of the extant manuscripts of Buridan's works. It is either a shortened version prepared by Lokert himself, or it represents the text of one of the numerous abbreviations of Buridan's works which were usually labelled *Quaestiones breves* or *Quaestiones brevissimae*.

Thus, to study Buridan's views on Aristotle's theory of the soul, one still has to rely for the most part on manuscript sources. Given this situation, it is no wonder that Buridan's psychological works have remained largely uncharted territory.

As has been shown in detail elsewhere, Buridan relies on Averroes' citations when he discusses Alexander's theory of the soul.[26] However, Buridan does not simply repeat Alexander's text, nor does he closely follow the interpretation given by Averroes. While he states that – according to Alexander – the intellect is a generable and corruptible form (*forma generabilis et corruptibilis*), a formulation which can also be found in Averroes, this form is further characterized as being educed from the potency of matter (*educta de potentia materiae*). It is this characterization which became commonplace in the later Middle Ages and was repeated

---

[24] Cf. B. Michael, *op. cit.*, 690-692. The later editions of 1518 and 1534 follow this print. The text of Lokert's edition is now easily accessible in B. Patar, *Le Traité de l'Âme de Jean Buridan [de prima lectura]* (Philosophes médiévaux, XXIX), Louvain-la-Neuve/Longueuil, Québec 1991, 495-695. The *Expositio* and *Quaestiones*, which were edited by Patar and attributed to John Buridan in this volume on pages 1-491, are of dubious authenticity.

[25] Cf. A. Broadie, *The Circle of John Mair. Logic and Logicians in Pre-Reformation Scotland*, Oxford 1985, and *idem*, *George Lokert: Late-Scholastic Logician*, Edinburgh 1983.

[26] Cf. O. Pluta, "Averroes als Vermittler der Gedanken des Alexander von Aphrodisias", ed. F. Niewöhner and L. Sturlese, *Averroismus im Mittelalter und in der Renaissance*, Zürich 1994, 201-221. This is also apparent from Buridan's own words. In the first redaction of his *Expositio de anima*, written before 1336, Buridan begins his presentation of Alexander's theory by referring to Averroes and saying: "Tunc recitat opinionem Alexandri". And in the last redaction of his *Quaestiones de anima* he begins a similar passage with the words: "Prima opinio fuit Alexandri, ut recitat Commentator" (cf. *ibid.*, 211).

over and over again by John Buridan and his many followers. It can also be found in Pomponazzi.[27]

The theory of *eductio formarum* and the wording "educta de potentia materiae" which is here used to describe Alexander's theory can also be found in the Latin Averroists, particularly in Siger of Brabant, who used it already in his earliest psychological writing, the *Quaestiones in tertium De anima*, written before 1270.[28] It can also be found in Siger's *De anima intellectiva*, most probably written in 1274,[29] and subsequently in the condemnation of 1277.[30]

The theory of *eductio formarum* can be further traced back to Albert the Great; however, the exact wording cannot be found in Albert.[31] Therefore, it seems safe to assume that Buridan has borrowed the terminology of his presentation of Alexander's position from Averroes and the Latin Averroists.

As Buridan states in the last redaction of his *Questions on the Physics*, one has to distinguish between *factio naturalis* and *creatio*. A form that is generated naturally depends not only on the Prime Agent but also on the underlying matter, therefore it is said to be educed from the potency of matter (*educitur de potentia materiae*). However, a form that is created apart from any natural influence depends only on God, therefore it is said

---

[27] Cf. Pomponazzi's question "Utrum anima sit mortalis vel immortalis," written in the academic year 1514-1515, edited by W. Van Dooren, "Pietro Pomponazzi: *Utrum anima sit mortalis vel immortalis*", Nouvelles de la Republique des Lettres I-II (1989), 71-135, in particular 94, 14 ("anima nostra est generabilis et corruptibilis"), 96, 15-16 ("educitur de potentia materiae"), 108, 19-20 ("voluit Alexander quod sit educta de potentia materiae").

[28] Cf. Siger de Brabant, *Quaestiones in tertium De anima. De anima intellectiva. De aeternitate mundi*, ed. B. Bazán (Philosophes médiévaux, XIII), Louvain/Paris 1972, 3, 50-52 ("Constat quod vegetativum et sensitivum educuntur de potentia materiae cum formatur progenitum."), 3, 54 ("educta de potentia materiae"), 10, 3-4 ("intellectus immediate educatur a Primo"), 14, 8 ("et quae de potentia materiae est educta, utitur organo sive instrumento"), 39, 97-98 ("nec intellectus materialis sine agente distincto potest educi ad actum"), 43, 91-92 ("educitur de potentia eius ad quod movetur"), 43, 94-96 ("Intelligibilia autem non educuntur de potentia intellectus, sed fluunt in eo ab extrinseco"). The term "educere" is also used in Siger's own description of Alexander's position (cf. *ibid.*, 11, 44-12, 58).

[29] Cf. *ibid.*, 110, 35 ("educta de potentia materiae").

[30] Cf. prop. 105 (see note 16 above).

[31] Cf. his *De anima*, III, 2, 4; editio Coloniensis, VII, 1, ed. Cl. Stroick, Münster in Westf. 1968, 182a, 15-183a, 45; *De natura et origine animae*, II, 5; editio Coloniensis, XII, ed. B. Geyer, Münster in Westf. 1955, 24b, 76-25b, 68.

not to be educed from the potency of matter (*non educitur de potentia materia*).³²

However, with respect to the human intellect the theory of *eductio formarum* can have a twofold meaning. The human intellect may be seen as directly educed from matter by the Prime Mover, or it may be seen as educed from matter without any special influence of the Primary Being. While in the first interpretation the superiority of the human intellect is maintained, the second interpretation leads to the conviction that the human soul comes into being in exactly the same way as all animal souls and is hence mortal.

Now, it is this last interpretation which Buridan attributes to Alexander. In the second redaction of his *Questiones de anima*, he writes that, according to Alexander, the human soul is generable and corruptible like the soul of a dog or a donkey (*sicut est anima canis aut asini*); and in the last redaction he states that, according to Alexander, the human soul is a material form, generable and corruptible, educed from the potency of matter and extended in the same way as matter, like the soul of an ox or a dog, and he explicitly adds that the human soul does not remain after death (*forma materialis, generabilis et corruptibilis, educta de potentia materiae et extensa extensione materiae, sicut anima bovis aut anima canis, et non est manens post mortem*).³³

---

³² "Ad aliam dico, quod differentia talis est inter factionem naturalem et creationem, quia forma, quae fit naturaliter, dependet in sui factione non solum ab agente, sed etiam a subiecto, in quo fit; ideo dicimus, quod *educitur de potentia materiae*. Sed quod creatur distincte a factione naturali, non dependet in sui factione nisi a deo; ideo dicimus, quod *non educitur de potentia materiae*." (*Quaestiones Physicorum* (ultima lectura), I, q.21; Copenhagen, Kongelige Bibliotek, Ny kgl. Saml. cod. 1801 fol., f.36rb).

³³ For these texts and their interpretation refer to A. Maier, "Das Prinzip der doppelten Wahrheit", eadem, *Metaphysische Hintergründe der spätscholastischen Naturphilosophie* (Studien zur Naturphilosophie der Spätscholastik, IV), Rome 1955, 20-27; O. Pluta, "*Homo sequens rationem naturalem* – die Entwicklung einer eigenständigen Anthropologie in der Philosophie des späten Mittelalters", ed. A. Zimmermann, *Mensch und Natur im Mittelalter* (Miscellanea Mediaevalia, 21/2), Berlin/New York 1992, 752-763; idem, "Ewigkeit der Welt, Sterblichkeit der Seele, Diesseitigkeit des Glücks – Elemente einer materialistischen Philosophie bei Johannes Buridan", ed. B. Mojsisch and O. Pluta, *Historia Philosophiae Medii Aevi. Studien zur Geschichte der Philosophie des Mittelalters. Festschrift für Kurt Flasch*, vol. 2, Amsterdam/Philadelphia 1992, 847-872; idem, "Einige Bemerkungen zur Deutung der Unsterblichkeitsdiskussion bei Johannes Buridan", ed. E. P. Bos and H. A. Krop, *John Buridan: A Master of Arts. Some Aspects of His Philosophy. Acts of the Second Symposium Organized by the Dutch Society for Medieval Philosophy Medium Aevum on the Occasion of its 15th Anniversary*, Leiden/Amsterdam (Vrije Universiteit), June 20-21,

In the second redaction Buridan further elaborates on Alexander's views by giving some examples that cannot be found in Averroes. Here Buridan states that according to Alexander some higher species of animals have the ability to think like a man or an ape (*sicut homo vel simia*), and that an ape can even be said to have some reason. The theory of the soul presented here is a materialistic theory, pure and simple.

Buridan's position as a regent master at the university of Paris did not allow him to affirm such a theory openly. The statute of April 1, 1270 had drastically curtailed the freedom of teaching by requesting that all masters of arts should refrain from discussing purely theological questions; and when they touched upon questions that belonged to both philosophy and theology, they were always to determine such questions in favour of the Catholic faith. This forced Buridan to structure his question in the following way.

After giving the introductory arguments *pro* and *contra*, and summarising the opinions of Alexander, Averroes, and the Catholic faith concerning the human intellect, Buridan lists all the arguments that Aristotle and Averroes used to demonstrate that the human soul is not a material form in the sense that it is educed from the potency of matter and extended in the same way as matter.

Buridan then proclaims that this conclusion is plainly true (*simpliciter vera*) and must be firmly believed, and that the arguments adduced for it are probable. Nevertheless, he states that it is not apparent to him that these arguments are evident on natural grounds, unless God would grant us this evidence by a grace outside the common course of nature.

After this confession the remaining part of the question is entirely devoted to a defence of Alexander's views. Buridan here speaks up for Alexander and brings forward the answers with which, in his opinion, Alexander would have countered (*Alexander sic respondisset ad illas rationes*).[34]

1991 (Artistarium, Supplementa VII), Nijmegen 1993, 101-111; *idem*, "Der Alexandrismus an den Universitäten im späten Mittelalter", *Bochumer Philosophisches Jahrbuch für Antike und Mittelalter* 1 (1996), 81-109.

[34] This procedure has annoyed Zupko, who writes: "Buridan uncharacteristically fails to reply to any of the N-arguments. What he gives us instead is a series of materialist replies to arguments on behalf of the thesis that the human intellect is not a material form – which is rather odd, since Buridan is not a materialist about the human intellect" (Zupko, *op. cit.*, vol. II, 458-459). However, it is exactly because Buridan affirms Alexander's materialistic

Buridan is the first medieval thinker to defend Alexander's theory of the soul. In the subsequent questions, he even approves it by saying that natural reason (*ratio naturalis*) dictates it, and that a pagan philosopher would hold the opinion of Alexander; the propositions of faith, on the other hand, can only be narrated but not demonstrated (*narrandae sunt sine probatione*).

Buridan's interpretation of Alexander was disseminated at the universities of the fourteenth and fifteenth centuries by his many followers, including Lawrence of Lindores, Marsilius of Inghen, Nicholas of Amsterdam, Biagio Pelacani of Parma and Benedikt Hesse of Kraków. These medieval reconstructions of Alexander's psychology became the basis for the discussions in the Italian Renaissance, particularly in Pietro Pomponazzi.

Pietro Pomponazzi

Pietro Pomponazzi hardly requires an introduction here. Suffice it to say that the discussion of Alexander's materialistic psychology culminated in Pomponazzi and in the famous immortality controversy that followed the publication of his treatise *De immortalitate animae* in 1516. This controversy, in which some of the leading Italian thinkers participated (in particular Gasparo Contarini, Agostino Nifo, Ambrosius Flandinus and Bartolomeo de Spina), lasted from 1516 until Pomponazzi's death on May 18, 1525.[35] The deathbed scene reported by one of the witnesses, Antonio Brocardo, strongly suggests that Pomponazzi personally did not believe in any kind of afterlife.[36]

In the last part of my paper I will deal with Pomponazzi's discussions of Alexander's theory of the soul. These discussions are especially elaborate in his early *Questions on the Soul*, read in the academic year 1503-1504 at the university of Padova, and in the lecture on the same topic which he gave in the academic year 1514-1515 at the university of Bologna, whereas these discussions have been omitted for the most part in his treatise *De immortalitate animae*. I will focus on the question "Utrum anima rationalis

---

theory of the soul that he attempts to defend him against his opponents.

[35] For this controversy see M. L. Pine, *Pietro Pomponazzi: Radical Philosopher of the Renaissance* (Saggi e testi, 21), Padova 1986, Chapter II: The Battle for the Soul: The Immortality Controversy, 124-234.

[36] Cf. Pine, *op. cit.*, 51f.

sit immaterialis et immortalis,"[37] which belongs to the earlier of the two lectures mentioned above, because at this stage of the development of his own psychological views the use of medieval sources is most apparent. This question also precedes the papal bull "Apostolici regiminis" of December 19, 1513, which formally condemned all those who claimed that the human soul is mortal. After this condemnation, Pomponazzi was even more cautious than before when he touched the question of immortality.

Pomponazzi makes use of the new translation of Alexander's *De anima* by Girolamo Donato here, to which he refers as the *Paraphrasis*. It is worth noting that Pomponazzi made attempts to obtain further new texts as becomes evident in the question where he mentions that while at Ferrara he made a certain Marco, probably the humanist Marco Musuro, translate a disgression of John the Grammarian (Ioannes Grammaticus) against Alexander for him.[38]

The general structure of this question, which is the first question of the lecture, is as follows: after some introductory words, Pomponazzi gives a number of arguments *pro* and *contra*; he attributes nearly all of the arguments against immortality to Alexander.[39]

Pomponazzi then proclaims that in this difficult question where there are most famous men on both sides, he would prefer to be a student rather than a professor, as he may perhaps be even more in doubt concerning this question than his students; he then goes on to declare that the resurrected Christ is the only demonstration of the immortality of the human soul.

After this confession Pomponazzi claims that his only intention in this first question is to check the validity of Aristotle's arguments in favour of the immortality of the soul and later on to destroy the opinion of Alexander with arguments. However, while he does the first in the remaining part of the question, one does not find any attempt to disprove Alexander's views. Instead, the last part of the question, which takes up more than half of the text, is entirely devoted to Alexander's refutation of Aristotle's arguments.[40] At the very end of the question Pomponazzi simply declares that Alexander's counter-arguments are false, that they

---

[37] Pietro Pomponazzi, *Corsi inediti dell'insegnamento padovano, II: «Quaestiones physicae et animasticae decem» (1499-1500; 1503-1504)*. Introduzione e testo a cura di Antonino Poppi (Saggi e testi, 9), Padova 1970, 1-25.
[38] Cf. *ibid.*, 11, 2-8.
[39] Cf. *ibid.*, 2, 12-9, 25.
[40] Cf. *ibid.*, 11, 18-25, 5.

cannot solve the arguments of Aristotle, and that he therefore sticks to the common belief in the immortality of the soul.

Thus, we have the same fundamental structure as in Buridan's question on the same subject: after a formal rejection of Alexander's views and a confession of the veracity of Christian doctrine, the majority of the question is devoted to a defence of Alexander's theory of the human soul. At the beginning of this last section, Pomponazzi explicitly says that he has taken these counter-arguments from others (*sumpsi ab aliis*). Now, what are his sources in this concluding section?

If one looks at the *Questions on the Soul* of Buridan and his followers it becomes evident, that most if not all of the counter-arguments can be found in these texts. *Causa brevitatis*, I cannot show this in detail for all the counter-arguments, but let us look at one of them.

In responding to this argument Pomponazzi again stresses the fact that he has taken the counter-argument from others by saying that he just acts as the prophet Mohammed who received some sayings and then compiled them into a whole.[41] And later he once again confirms his dependency on others by saying "hoc est illud quod dicunt moderni".[42]

The argument to which Pomponazzi later replies on behalf of Alexander is labelled as the argument "ex modo intelligendi" or "ex parte modi cognoscendi."[43] This argument is introduced by Pomponazzi as "potissima rationum quae possunt fieri in ista materia."[44] Upon trying to reply to this argument later in the question, he admits that this argument among all the others has always caused him the biggest problems.[45]

If the soul were a purely material form, as Alexander assumes, then it would be extended and located in a bodily organ. However, such a form, all agree, would be limited to a knowledge of singulars and would never be able to attain universal knowledge.

According to Alexander the argument is not valid. First of all, one has to acknowledge that animals are capable of abstracting and gaining universal knowledge to some degree, so it is not unreasonable to assume that the

---

[41] Cf. *ibid.*, 15, 7-12.

[42] Cf. *ibid.*, 17, 21.

[43] Cf. *ibid.*, 2, 18-19; 14, 16-17.

[44] Cf. *ibid.*, 3, 21-22.

[45] Cf. *ibid.*, 14, 18-19: "hoc argumentum inter omnia argumenta maximam mihi semper fecit difficultatem".

human intellect can rise to universal knowledge. Now, the human soul forms a composite of diverse functions. Some of these functions, like sensory perception, are directly linked to bodily organs whereas others, like the ability to abstract, proceed from the entire composite. Functions of this second type, which have a higher degree of complexity, are only indirectly dependent on bodily organs and can therefore elevate themselves above matter and attain universal knowledge.

Pomponazzi concludes: the human intellect in its functioning does not directly rely on a bodily organ; it does not need the body as subject (*non indiget corpore tamquam subiecto*), nevertheless it needs the body as object (*indiget tamen corpore tamquam obiecto*), that is, it relies in its functioning on the senses (*phantasmata*). This conclusion precisely anticipates Pomponazzi's solution of 1516.[46]

After all that has been said about the influence of Buridan and his school it will not come unexpected that we find a long discussion of this argument in Buridan who at this point explicitly argues against many contemporaries and more or less all of the ancient commentators.[47] Furthermore, Marsilius

---

[46] Cf. *ibid.*, 18, 8-15.

[47] The following manuscripts were used to establish the text below: Copenhagen, Kongelige Bibliotek, Ny kgl. Saml. cod. 1801 fol., written in Paris between 1377 and 1380 (= A), Frankfurt am Main, Stadt- und Universitätsbibliothek, Cod. Praed. 52 (= B), Vatican City, Biblioteca Apostolica, Cod. Vat. lat. 2163 (= C), Vienna, Österreichische Nationalbibliothek, Cod. 5367 (= D).

"Ad primam et secundam dubitationes (dubitationem BCD) dixerunt multi et quasi omnes expositores antiqui, quod ex eo intellectus apprehendit universaliter, quia (*add.* ipse BC) est separatus et immaterialis sic, quod non est eductus (deductus D) de potentia materiae nec extensus extensione materiae; ideo non recipit modo singulari, cum ex extensione et divisione materiae proveniat divisio et multitudo individuorum in rebus materialibus.

Ista opinio non videtur mihi sufficiens, primo, quia deus est summe separatus et immaterialis sic, quod non est eductus de potentia materiae, et tamen non intelligit modo universali sicut nos, quia, sicut dicit Commentator duodecimo *Metaphysicae*, hoc est intelligere res confuse et imperfecte, non intelligendo distinctionem singularium; deus autem (f.10rb A) omnia perfectissime et distincte intelligit, licet unica simplicissima intellectione. Sed de hoc est (f.9va B) videndum in duodecimo *Metaphysicae*.

Secundo non est verum, quod singularitas proveniat ex extensione vel materialitate, quia ita singulariter et distincte ab aliis existit deus et intellectus noster sicut aliquod extensum, immo etiam terminus universalis ita singulariter et distincte ab aliis existit in intellectu tuo vel meo sicut albedo in pariete.

Tertio, quia appetitus sensitivus ita est extensus et materialis sicut sensus, et tamen equus et canis per famem et sitim appetunt modo universali, non enim hanc aquam vel hanc avenam magis quam illam, sed quamlibet indifferenter; ideo quaecumque eis praesentetur,

of Inghen, as has been shown elsewhere, anticipates Pomponazzi's final conclusion in his question "Utrum intellectus utitur organo corporeo in intelligendo", in which he shows that the human intellect does not need a corporeal organ subjectively (*subiective*) because the act of knowledge itself is not contained in a bodily organ; nevertheless, the human intellect needs a bodily organ objectively (*obiective*) because it relies on the senses and receives the sensory perceptions like objects that are corporeal and require a bodily organ.[48]

*

bibunt eam vel comedunt. Et etiam intentio posita vel appetitus ignis ad calefaciendum est modo universali, scilicet non determinate ad hoc lignum, sed ad quodlibet lignum (*om*. BC) calefactibile indifferenter, licet actus (f.9ra C) calefaciendi determinetur ad certum singulare. Et ita etiam potentia visiva est modo universali ad videndum.

Dico igitur, sicut mihi videtur, quod una causa est in hoc, quod intellectus intelligit universaliter, licet existat singulariter et res intellecta singulariter et intellectio etiam singulariter. Et ratio huius (omne quod BD, omne aliud C) est, quia res intelliguntur non per hoc, quod sunt apud intellectum, sed per suam similitudinem existentem apud intellectum; res autem extra ex natura et essentia sua habent inter se convenientiam et similitudinem, ut suppono et postea declarabo. Modo si sit ita, quod sint multa invicem similia, omne (*add*. illud BC, illud D) quod est simile uni eorum quantum ad hoc, in quo sunt similia, est simile unicuique aliorum; ideo si omnes asini ex natura rei habent ad invicem convenientiam et similitudinem, oportet, quod quando species intelligibilis in intellectu existens repraesentabit per modum (f.6va D) similitudinis aliquem asinum, ipsa simul indifferenter repraesentabit quemlibet asinum nisi aliquod (aliud BCD) obstet, de quo postea dicetur. Ideo sic fiet universalis intellectio, et propter hoc etiam appetitus equi, qui est ratione carentiae cibi et potus, est modo universali, quia non est magis carentia huius quam illius, sed omnium indifferenter. Et ignis etiam per suam naturam intendit et appetit generare non sibi idem, sed sibi simile, quod non fieret magis in hoc ligno quam in illo; ideo intendit et appetit modo universali." (*Quaestiones Physicorum* (ultima lectura), I, q.7)

[48] Cf. O. Pluta, "Die Diskussion der Unsterblichkeitsfrage bei Marsilius von Inghen", ed. St. Wielgus, *Marsilius von Inghen. Werk und Wirkung*. Akten des Zweiten Internationalen Marsilius-von-Inghen-Kongresses, Lublin 1993, 119-164, especially 141-144. The relevant passages from Marsilius' question "Utrum in homine anima intellectiva distinguitur from anima sensitiva" have been edited in O. Pluta, "*Utrum intellectus utitur organo corporeo in intelligendo*. Eine verborgene Frage in den *De anima*-Quaestionen des Marsilius von Inghen", ed. M. Hoenen and P. Bakker, *Philosophie und Theologie des ausgehenden Mittelalters. Marsilius von Inghen und das Denken seiner Zeit*, Leiden/Boston/Köln 2000, 159-174.

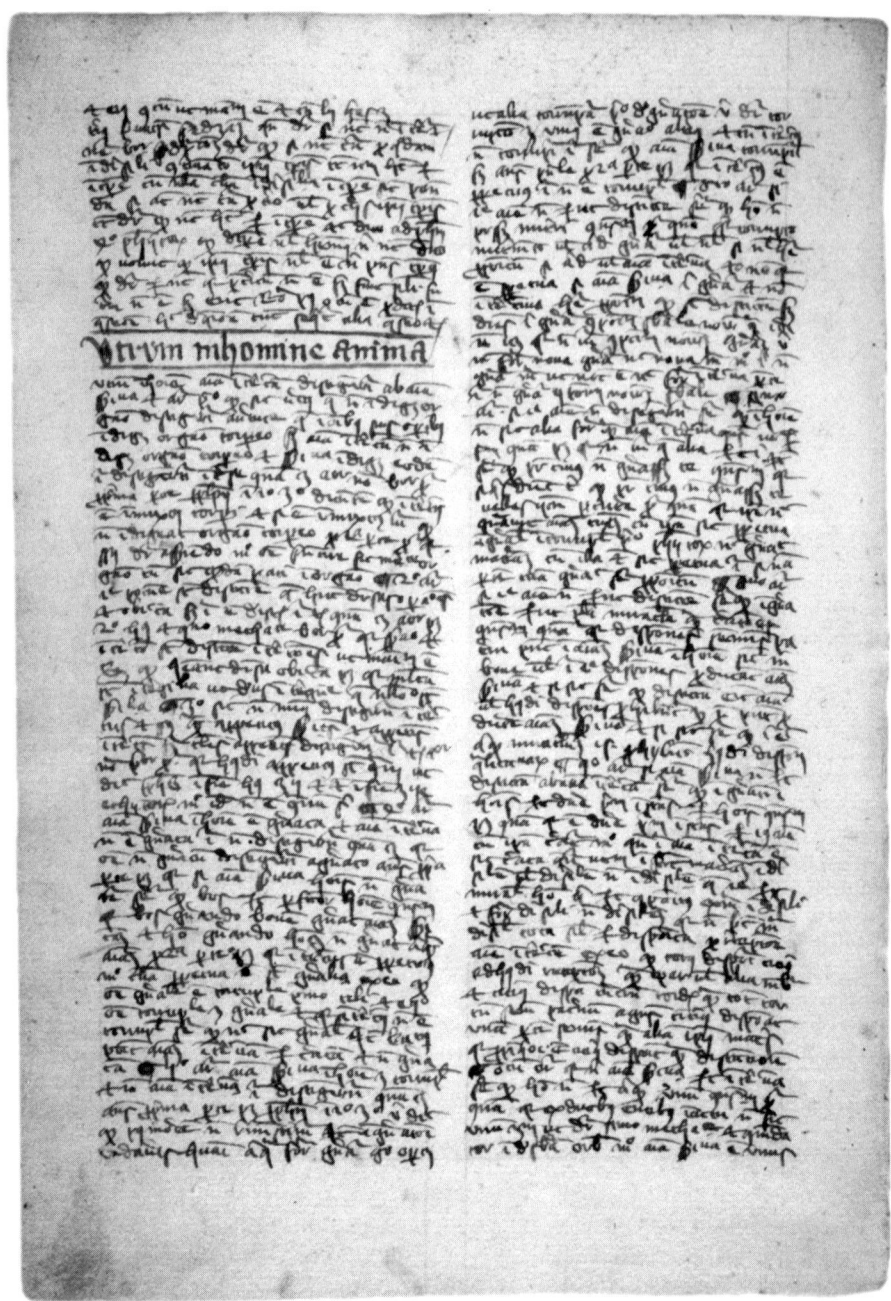

Fig. 1. Marsilius of Inghen, *Quaestiones in tres libros Aristotelis De anima*, lib. III, q. 10; Wien, Österreichische Nationalbibliothek, Cod. lat. 5437, f. 408v.

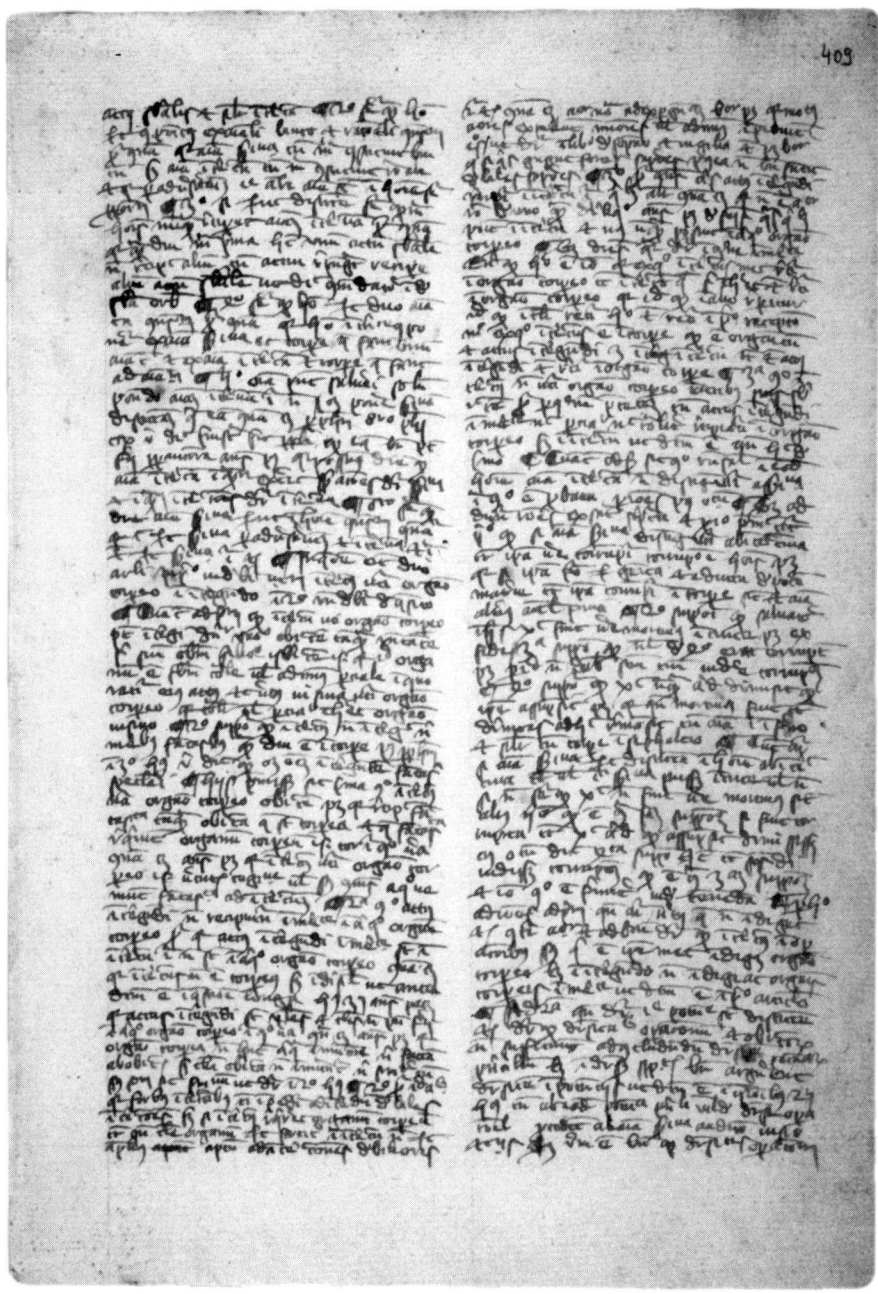

Fig. 2. Marsilius of Inghen, *Quaestiones in tres libros Aristotelis De anima*, lib. III, q. 10; Wien, Österreichische Nationalbibliothek, Cod. lat. 5437, f. 409r.

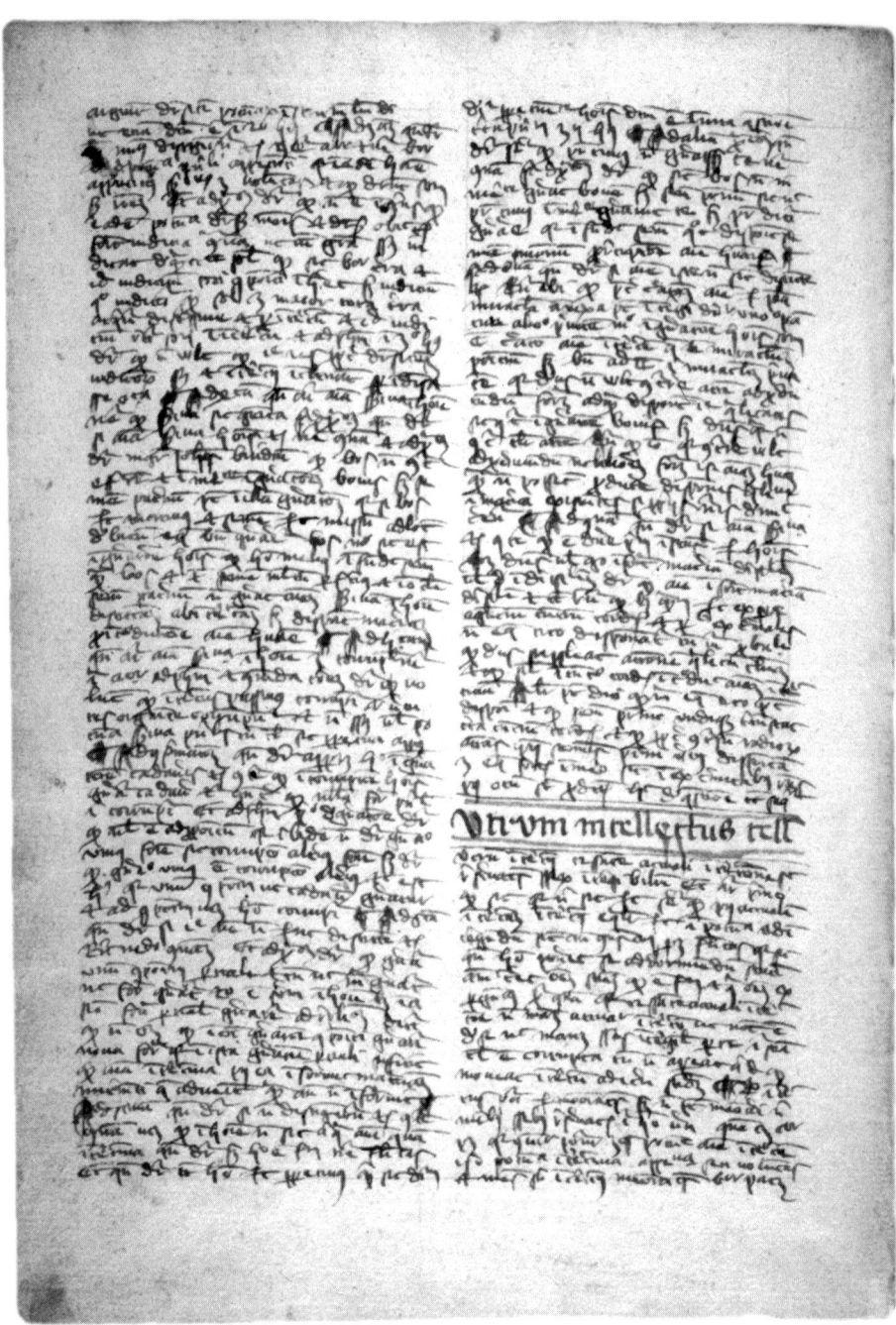

Fig. 3. Marsilius of Inghen, *Quaestiones in tres libros Aristotelis De anima*, lib. III, q. 10; Wien, Österreichische Nationalbibliothek, Cod. lat. 5437, f. 409v.

Our paper has thus once again confirmed the pioneering studies of Bruno Nardi and the more recent investigations of Antonino Poppi who both have always insisted on Pomponazzi's great debt to medieval sources.[49] However, despite the fact that Pomponazzi's solution of 1516 can already be found in Marsilius of Inghen, there are several elements in the *De immortalitate animae* which make Pomponazzi's position more elaborate than the views expressed in his early lectures or in the texts of his medieval precursors of the fourteenth and fifteenth centuries.[50]

So with respect to the theme of this conference I would like to conclude that we do not find an Aristotle in Pomponazzi that is completely new, instead we find a more elaborate view of Aristotle that builds upon medieval sources.

---

[49] Cf. e.g. with regard to Marsilius of Inghen: B. Nardi, *Studi su Pietro Pomponazzi*, Florence 1965, 272, 275; A. Poppi, *Introduzione all'aristotelismo padovano* (Saggi e testi, 10), Padova 1970, 25.

[50] Cf. Pine, *op. cit.*, 102-103.

Renaissance Readings of the *Corpus Aristotelicum* – not Among the Herbalists

by Peter Wagner

In the title I claim there were no readings of Aristotle in the Renaissance among the herbalists. This is of course, not true. Most of those learned people working with plants and their uses (botany as a science had not been invented yet) were philologists or medical doctors and could hardly have avoided the works of Aristotle in their studies. But they did not use him when it came to *res herbaria*. This is not surprising; we know of no work by Aristotle on botany, although he frequently referred to plants in works on other subjects.[1] It is my intention to demonstrate how, with one remarkable exception, Aristotle did not influence Renaissance herbalists, and also to offer an explanation why this was so.

Botany as a science had already fallen into disrepute among the Romans. Varro claimed in *de re rustica* that the works of Theophrastus were not useful to those who wanted to cultivate their fields;[2] and there the matter

---

[1] Aristotle does so in particular in his work on animals. The work *de plantis* often named among his minor works is not by him nor by Theophrastus as was sometimes assumed in the Middle Ages, but probably by Nicolaus Damascenus. Vide Ernst H. F. Meyer, *Nicolai Damasceni de plantis libri duo Aristoteli vulgo adscripti*, Lipsiae 1841 and Karen Meier Reeds, "Renaissance Humanism and Botany", *Annals of Science*, 33 (1976), 522.

[2] Varronis *de re rustica* Lib. 1. Ch. 5.1-2: "Sed quoniam agriculturae, quod esset initium & finis dixi, relinquitur quot partes ea disciplina habeat, ut sit videndum. Equidem innumerabiles mihi videntur, inquit Agrius, cum lego libros Theophrasti complures, qui inscribuntur, φυτῶν ἱστορίας & alteri φυτικῶν αἰτίων. Stolo, Isti, inquit, libri non tam idonei iis, qui agrum colere volunt, quam qui scholas philosophorum. neque eo, dico, quod non habeant & utilia, & communia quaedam, quapropter tu potius agriculturae partes nobis expone," *Scriptores rei rusticae veteres latini Cato, Varro, Columella, Palladius, quibus nunc accedit Vegetius de Mulo-Medicinae et Gargilii Martialis Fragmentum ...* curante Io. Matthia Gesnero, Lipsiae 1735, 151 ("But as I have stated the origin and the limits of the science, it remains to determine the number of its divisions." "Really," said Agrius, "it seems to me that they are endless, when I read the many books of Theophrastus, those which are entitled 'The History of Plants' and 'The Causes of Vegetation'". "His books," replied Stolo "are not so well adapted to those who wish to tend land as to those who wish to attend the schools of the philosophers; which is not to say that they do not contain matter which is both profitable and of general interest. So, then, do you rather explain to

remained until the Renaissance. Knowledge of plants and their uses was considered necessary for medical doctors and pharmacists (also for farmers, but it is not customary to mention them in learned contexts), and the books used and written by them were almost exclusively pharmaceutical handbooks dealing only with plants used in medicine. During the Middle Ages a few plants (approximately 30) were added in the books of simples to those named by Dioscorides, almost all having come to Europe from Northern Africa or Spain.

Economic progress in Italy in the early Renaissance was accompanied by an increasing interest in applied sciences (*artes sordidae*) such as mechanics, agriculture, medicine and surgery. The increased interest in personal observation in medicine, for example in dissections, affected related disciplines including pharmacy. As a consequence Dioscorides was studied more critically, and a series of editions and commentaries about him and Pliny followed. Most of them concentrated on textual problems, but the attempt was also made to identify plants named in the texts with those known to the editors. Ermolao Barbaro's *Castigationes Plinianae* (1492/93), Niccolò Leoniceno's *Plinii ac plurium aliorum ... errores* (1492) and the publication of Theodor Gaza's translation of Theophrastus (1483)[3]

---

us the divisions of the subject." Translation by William Davis Hooper, revised by Harrison Boyd Ash, Loeb Classical Library, Cambridge, Mass. 1934).

[3] Hermolai Barbari *Castigationes Plinianae*, Romæ 1492/93 is without a title; Nicolai Leoniceni *Plinii ac plurium aliorum auctorum qui de simplicibus medicaminibus scripserunt errores notati*, Ferrariae 1492; *Theophrasti de historia stirpium, et causis plantarum, Libri quindecim*, Theodoro Gaza interprete, Venetiis 1483.

The importance of e.g. Barbaro's work for the study of plants was recognized in the Renaissance. Leonhard Fuchs, who published the most popular herbal in the sixteenth century, wrote: "Inter eos autem qui strenue in hanc curam incubuerunt, mea quidem sententia primas tenet genere & eruditione clarus Hermolaus Barbarus, qui primus omnium, quod sciam, nostra ætate facinus longe pulcherrimum aggredi, eamque medicinæ partem neutique contemnendam, a tenebris in lucem reuocare ausus est. Nam initio suscepti illius laboris præstantissimum, atque multis iam seculis conprobatum medicæ materiæ scriptorem Dioscoridem Latio donauit. Quo feliciter peracto labore, Corollarium adiecit, quo nihil eruditius, nihil copiosius, nihil denique magis uarium post Plinium in latina lingua editum esse docti unanimi sententia fatentur. Quicquid enim a Theophrasto, Athenæo, Oribasio, Aëtio, Paulo, Polluce, Plinio aliisque cum Græcis tum Latinis eruditis admodum hominibus, quos nominare nunc nihil attinet, sparsim notatum est, hoc totum in Corollario suo, uno quasi fasce, complexus est Barbarus. Et quidem huius celeberrimi uiri studium eo magis a nobis prædicandum esse censeo, quod ipse primus quamvis professione medicus non esset, secure interim in utramuis aurem dormitantibus medicis nutanti tum brevique casuræ rei herbariæ auxiliares manus porrigere dignatus sit," see Leonhard Fuchs, *De*

initiated studies of plants in general. From these it became apparent that only a minority of the plants in Europe were actually named by the ancient authors,[4] not to mention the new ones pouring into Europe from the Americas and Asia as a consequence of the upsurge in foreign trade. Not only food plants and spices from abroad were investigated, but also plants brought back to adorn the luxurious new gardens laid out at the country seats of princes, nobles and merchants.

The interest in knowledge of plants led to the development of this research into a new science – botany, or as it was called then, *res herbaria*. The first step was the establishment in 1533 of a chair in botany for Francesco Buonafede at the University of Padua, the university of the state of Venice which dominated the trade in spices. The following year Luca Ghini was appointed to the University of Bologna as *lector simplicium*, and four years later he was made professor. New gardens containing all kinds of plants, not only simples, and thus named botanical gardens were

---

Historia stirpium commentarii insignes, maximis impensis et vigiliis elaborati, adiectis earundum vivis plusquam quingentis imaginibus, numquam antea ad naturæ imitationem artificiosius effectis & expressis, Basiliae 1542, p. 6 ("Among those who have vigorously applied their talents to this work, Ermolaus Barbaro, renowned by birth and erudition, is, in my opinion, the foremost, as he is the first of all in our time, as far as I know, who has ventured to set about this extremely noble task and bring from darkness into light this by no means unimportant part of medicine. At the start of this undertaking he gave Dioscorides to the Latin language, that most excellent author of *materia medica* who has been acknowledged for many centuries past. Having successfully finished this work, he added his *Corollary*; the learned unanimously recognize that nothing more erudite, nothing richer, nothing more manifold has been elaborated in the Latin language since Pliny. What was noted here and there by Theophrastus, Athenæus, Oribasius, Aëtius, Paulus, Pollux, Pliny and other very learned men Greek as well as Latin (there is no point in mentioning them here), all this Barbaro has embraced in his *Corollary* as in one bundle. I am of the opinion that the zeal of this famous man should be the more praised by us, since although he was not a professional physician, he was the first who thought fit to reach out helping hands to *res herbaria*, which at that time was staggering and about to fall, while the physicians were sleeping soundly on both ears"). This high opinion of the work of Barbaro is shared by Greene, who has written: "This was the most stupendous piece of textual criticism that ever one man accomplished or even dared to undertake ... the Pliny we now consult and read and understand, and therefore find instructive, is the Pliny that Ermolao Barbaro gave to the world," see Edward Lee Greene, *Landmarks of Botanical History*, edited by Frank N. Egerton with contributions by Robert P. McIntosh and Rogers McVaugh. Part 2, Stanford 1983, 559-60.

[4] It should be emphasized that the controversy between Leoniceno, Barbaro and Collenuccio over Pliny was probably decisive in demonstrating the necessity of personal observation when dealing with natural history even if the research was based on classical authors, see Reeds, 1976, 523-24.

founded at the Universities of Pisa and Padua in the 1540s (they still argue about which one was the first); Florence followed suit; and from Italy this new fashion spread over France and the Netherlands to the whole of Europe.[5]

The new professors, their students and colleagues had to confront the following problems:

1: Identification of the names in the classical works with plants they themselves observed.

2: Naming of European plants and of plants from other partly unknown continents, and research on their use in the economy (gardening and agriculture) and in medicine.

3: Organization of the plants and what was known about them in an efficient retrieval system.

The following innovations were available to the scientists:

1: Dried plants. It is not known exactly when botanists started to use plants dried under moderate pressure and glued on paper, but it is certain that Luca Ghini realized the value of this technique and built up a collection of such sheets, a *herbarium vivum*. Plants mounted on paper with information written on the sheet were easy to exchange with colleagues. The first instructions in this technique were published by Spigelius in 1606.[6]

2: Naturalistic drawings of plants. Such drawings are found in Italian herbaria of the fifteenth century; but when techniques of wood-engraving improved in the sixteenth century, those drawings made from living models, and not copied from earlier drawings, brought in their printed

---

[5] The foundation of university gardens was preceded by more or less private botanical gardens. Guiliano da Foligno laid out the first of these in the Giardini Vaticani in 1514. Teaching in simples started before the chairs were established; Leonardo Leggi began in Pavia in 1520, Ghini in Bologna in 1527, see Ambrosoli, Mauro, *The Wild and the Sown. Botany and Agriculture in Western Europe, 1350-1850*, Cambridge 1997, 100.

[6] Adriani Spigelii *Isagoges in rem herbariam Libri Duo ad illustrissimam quae Patavii est Germanicam nationem*, Patavii 1606. The instructions: "Hortos hyemales conficiendi ratio" lib. 1. cap. 58, 79-81.

form a hitherto unknown and much needed accuracy to the information about plants in printed books.

The importance of these innovations cannot be overestimated. The beautifully illustrated books of Otto Brunfels (*Herbarum vivae eicones*, Strasbourg 1530 with 135 drawings by Hans Weiditz) and Leonhard Fuchs (*De historia stirpium*, Tübingen 1542 with 511 drawings by Albrecht Mayer) established "a corpus of plant species which were identifiable with a considerable degree of certainty by any reasonably careful observer, no matter by what classical and vernacular names they were called by different authors, or in different countries. This group of plant portraits was not a general flora but at least it gave a fine basis on which a general flora could be founded at a time when the art of botanical description still had to be developed", as H.G. Morton phrases it in his *History of Botanical Science*.[7]

The reason why botanical illustration and the herbaria were of paramount importance were, first, that the descriptions by the ancient authors were in general insufficient for the identification or recognition of the plants described; and, second, that the same authors, except perhaps Theophrastus, did not provide a method and vocabulary of description which fulfilled the needs of Renaissance botanists.

As a modern botanist, one would suppose that Theophrastus was brought into prominence by the publication of Theodorus Gaza's translation in 1483; but that was not the case. Morton speculates that botanists were overwhelmed by the practical problems presented by the vast accession of new plants, native and exotic, with which they had to come to terms.[8]

Another reason could be that the plants discussed by Theophrastus grow in the eastern Mediterranean and Asia; and although a great many of them are also found in the western Mediterranean, this meant that his books were not particularly interesting to people who wanted to apply their knowledge.[9]

---

[7] A.G. Morton, *History of Botanical Science, an account of the development of botany from ancient times to the present day*, London 1981, 124.

[8] Morton 1981, 121-22.

[9] Euricius Cordus had warned herbalists against expecting to find the plants described by classical authors in his native Germany, see Euricii Cordi *Botanologicon*, Coloniae 1534, e.g. 40-41 and Greene, Part 1. 1983, 364-65. Rudolph Agricola read Pliny when in Italy, perhaps because it was easier to identify plants in the area where the author had lived, see

In a very interesting paper Karen Reeds presents another view.[10] Examining the regulations of several universities in southern Europe she explains that of the revived ancient botanists "only Galen and Dioscorides were widely used as textbooks at the medical schools. Pliny was at once too encyclopedic and too disorganized to lecture from effectively ... Theophrastus gave much more detailed and orderly information about plants; but his stress on the variety and causes of plant forms, patterns of growth and generation rather than on their medicinal virtues made his treatises unsuited to the professional needs of medical students. The flaws in Gaza's translation did not help either". To what extent Galen's *de simplicium medicamentorum facultatibus* was used to teach botany is difficult to determine:[11] "The lists of herbs in Book VI would have interested the botanically-minded physician, even though Galen practiced what he preached in the proemium to Book VI by giving no more than a vague phrase or two of description to the appearance of each plant".[12] Dioscorides' *de materia medica* became the most important textbook of botany in the sixteenth century, because he described the exterior of the plant as well as its habitat and uses. Teachers could of course supply information from the other classical works. A splendid example is Matthioli's *Commentarii in VI libros Pedacii Dioscoridis* 1554 based on Ruel's translation of Dioscorides,[13] but similar procedures were used for example by Brunfels

---

Karen Meier Reeds, *Botany in Medieval and Renaissance Universities*. New York & London 1991, 27. Reeds emphasizes that he was the first in a long line of Northern humanists who visited Italy to see the plants that Pliny had known.

[10] Reeds 1976, 519-42.

[11] It was however used, since the statutes of several medieval medical schools required lectures on it, see Reeds 1976, 526.

[12] Reeds 1976, 536.

[13] Ruel's Dioscorides was published in 1616; he also published a herbal, *De natura stirpium libri tres* Ioanne Ruellio authore, Parisiis 1536. Matthioli wrote in the preface that he preferred Ruel's interpretation, although two other excellent publications had been printed (by Ermolao Barbaro and Marcello Vergilio); he had chosen Ruel's version, not because he did not esteem the other two (on the contrary, they deserved the highest praise), but because his version was the one most commonly found in the hands of medical students. This argument seems to sustain the view of Reeds, that the book preferred is that which is most suitable as a textbook: "Cur Ioannis Ruellij Galli Medici eruditissimi interpretationem prætulerim, dignamque existimauerim, quæ præ cæteris in nostris commentarijs legatur, cum tamen duo alij uiri pariter & doctissimi Hermolaus Barbarus, & Marcellus Vergilius Florentinus, in idem studium nauiter incubuerint. Fateor ego ingenue, me Ruellij versionem sequutum esse, sed non propterea aliorum præclaros conatus contempsisse unquam; quin

and Fuchs.[14] Thus Theophrastus and Pliny found their way into the teaching of medical students as authors of plant lists providing information supplementary to that of Dioscorides.

The study of the plants themselves, in gardens or in the wild, was however considered indispensable. The corrections to Pliny in Barbaro's *Castigationes* and *Corollarium*[15] are unimaginable without a profound knowledge of plants. Barbaro described in a letter to a friend how he spent his evenings in a garden or by a river contemplating herbs and thinking about Dioscorides.[16] Leoniceno referred to his own observations and asked why we have our senses if not for use in recognition of the truth.[17] Collenucio also insisted on observations from nature. He claimed that it was not enough to read (classical) authors, look at plant pictures and peer into vocabularies; one ought also to "closely examine the plants themselves, note the distinctions between one plant and another ...".[18] Marcello Vergilio

---

potius utriusque studium semper admiratum: quippe quod uterque in eo maximam laudem promeruerit. Illud autem me magis mouit, ut Ruellium admiserim, quod eius conuersio omnibus facta sit uulgatior, ac frequentior in studiosorum manibus uersetur. Adde etiam, quod hæc communi omnium fere, medicorum præsertim iudicio præferatur. Cui nimirum nobis quoque libuit subscribere," Petri Andreae Matthioli Senensis medici, *Commentarii in sex libros Pedacii Dioscoridis Anazarbei de Medica materia ...* Venetiis 1565. Præfatio p. (2)

[14] Brunfels quoted under each plant name what the ancient authors had written about that particular plant, and added the commentaries of e.g. Barbaro and Marcello Vergilio. Fuchs followed the same procedure, but combined the separate quotations into one coherent text.

[15] Hermolai Barbari Patritii Veneti et Aquileiensis patriarchae *in Dioscoridem corollariorum libri quinque*, Venetiis 1516 more Veneto (=1517).

[16] Reeds 1976, 527. Epist. 45. E. Barbaro, *Epistolae, Orationes et Carmina*, a c. di V. Branca, Firenze 1943, vol. I, 61, "... contemplamur herbas et Dioscoridem cogitamus".

[17] "Cur enim nobis oculos et reliquorum sensuum opificia natura concessit, nisi ut ad prospiciendam investigandamque veritatem propriis possimus niti subsidiis?" ("Why has Nature granted us the eyes and other senses as means, unless to make it possible for us to discern and study the truth with our own resources?"). Nicolai Leoniceni Vicentini, philosophi et medici clarissimi *De Plinii et aliorum in medicina erroribus* lib. 2, cap. 8, in: *Opuscula: quorum catalogum versa pagina indicabit: Per D. Andream Leenium Medicum a multis, quibus scatebant, vitiis repurgata, atque annotatiunculis illustrata*, Basiliae 1532. Quoted from: Ernst H. F. Meyer, *Geschichte der Botanik. Studien. Vierter Band*, Königsberg 1857, 228.

[18] "Qui de herbis dicturus est, eum ego non tam librorum quam telluris, non tam litterarum quam agrorum studiosum esse oportere censeo, nec satis esse ad herbariam perdiscendam tradendamque herbarios scriptores legere, plantarum videre picturas, graeca vocabularia inspicere, magistri unius verbis addictum esse, sed rusticos montanosque homines interrogare oportet, herbas ipsas inspicere, vestigare differentias et, si fieri potest, periculum

Adriani, the translator of Dioscorides, referred to plants observed in a garden and suggested changes in the conception of cupuliferous *genera* which presuppose personal investigations.[19] Leoniceno's students, Giovanni Monardo and Antonius Musa Brasavola, continued their teacher's practice of looking at plants in nature. Brasavola also wrote a textbook for laymen (i.e. pharmacists), in which the teaching takes place during an excursion.[20] North of the Alps, Brunfels and Fuchs had plants drawn from nature; and another student of Leoniceno's, Euricius Cordus, recommended walking in the countryside, perhaps taking a book or two, and studying live, growing specimens of plants read about at home.[21] At the University of Montpellier in the 1530s Francois Rabelais promoted the study of plants; in his description of the education of Gargantua (1534) he stressed the importance of combining the reading of books with direct inspection of plants.[22] From 1550 teachers at Montpellier were obliged "to read to the students and to demonstrate the simples visually, from the feast

---

facere, experiri, rimari, quid unaquaeque in morbis possit etc." Quoted from: Meyer IV. 1857, 234 ("In my opinion, he who is to write about herbs, and hand the knowledge of them down, ought to study not only books but also the face of the earth, not letters alone, but also the open fields. For fitness to give instruction in botany it does not suffice that a man read authors, look at plant pictures, and peer into Greek vocabularies, and be accustomed to swear by the meaning of some particular word. He ought to ask questions of rustics and mountaineers, closely examine the plants themselves, note the distinctions between one plant and another; and if need be he should even incur danger in testing the properties of them and ascertaining their remedial values," translated in Greene, part 2, 1983, 551). Greene's translation is not accurate.

[19] Greene 1983, 575-77.

[20] Greene 1983, 589-93 and 664-84.

[21] Euricius Cordus *Botanologicon*, 26-27: "Quando itaque libet eamus, nulla in me mora erit, ego tamen, etiam si nulli adessetis, ultro pro consuetudine mea exiuissem, sumpto mecum uno et altero libello. Maxime enim ruri delector, ubi coram uiuas illas, de quibus domi legeram, herbas ad commendatas memoriae effigies confero, & contemplor, ipsasque tum nomenclaturas, tum etiam uires ab obuijs uetulis exploro, dehinc collatis ad earum historias omnibus maturo & quam sagace possum iudicio uel decerno uel opinor" ("So whenever it pleases you let us go forth. I will not keep you back; nevertheless I, just as if none of you were here, shall follow my usual practice of taking along a little book or two. I take the greatest delight in these sallyings into the country, where I can have before me fresh and growing those herbs which I have read about at home, and may compare them with the pictures of others which I carry in memory; also taking such note of their names and reputed virtues, as I may gather such from old women whom I meet upon the way. By the use of all these means I am better able to arrive at a sound conclusion, or at least a more probable opinion, about the identity of a thing," translation by Greene 1983, 366).

[22] Reeds 1991, 53-54.

of Easter to the feast of Saint Luke ... And to search for these simples in the city of Montpellier and its surroundings".[23] Jean Ruel, having published a Dioscorides translation in 1516,[24] issued *De natura stirpium* in 1536, in which he stated that he had been impelled by disagreements between ancient authors in describing the same plant to travel far and wide in order to examine the plants and get acquainted with them.[25] The outstanding field

---

[23] "... lire auxdits ecoliers, et montrer oculairement les simples, depuis la feste de Paques jusques a la feste de Saint Luc ... et pour chercher lesdits simples en ladite ville de Montpellier, et auxlieux circonvoisins ..." Reeds, 1991, 59. The order was given by the Royal circuit court at Béziers, probably at the instigation of Guilleaume Rondelet and Guilleaume Pellicier. Reeds assumes Rondelet had been inspired to this by Luca Ghini, whom he knew.

[24] Pedacij Dioscoridis Anazarbei *de medicinali materia libri quinque. De virulentis animalibus, et venenis cane rabioso, et eorum notis, ac remedijs libri quattuor*, Joanne Ruellio Suessionensi interprete, Parisiis 1516.

[25] "Siquidem & Theophrastus, & cunctis a Galeno prælatus Dioscorides in re herbaria, neque non apud nos Plinius, tam diuersi plerunque abeunt, ut in gratiam nulla orationis persuasione reuocari queant. Et, mehercle, nonnunquam in herbulæ cuiusdam facie repræsentanda, notas tam varie delineant, ut quiduis aliud potius, quam stirpem ipsam demonstrare videantur: aut certe eandem, multiplici prorsus effigie: quæ an talis usquam esse possit, plerique omnes dubitant. Qua re me tantorum impulit virorum dissidium, per vastas ire regionum multarum solitudines, inuia montium iuga peragrare, lacus inaccessos lustrare, abditas terræ fibras scrutari, hiantes vallium sequi specus, vel cum corpusculi huius periculo præcipitia nonnunquam tentare, ut inspectu etiam, nedum cognitione, res ipsas comprehenderem, de quibus eram scripturus. Nec minus laboriosa fuit euoluendis authoribus cura & sedulitas, præsertim Theophrasto: in quo notas stirpium, sparsim variis in locis, membratimque usque eo distractas licet intueri, ut nusquam gentium tota una stirps esse videri possit. Has tamen omneis colligere oportuit, & ut in unum coalescerent corpus, ad sese reuocare. Itaque frutices non paucos, vario & informi rerum commistu conflatos, resumtis undecunque licuit partibus repræsentaui; & velut coloribus redditis cuique, ut magis cognobiles essent, effeci," Ruellius 1536, dedic. p. A II-II ("For both Theophrastus and Dioscorides, whom Galen preferred in *res herbaria* to all the others, and also among us Pliny frequently disagree to such an extent that they cannot be reconciled by any words of persuasion; and, by Hercules, in describing a plant, they sometimes delineate its characteristics so differently that they seem to be exhibiting anything but the same plant, or the same but with a very different picture, so that almost everyone doubts if such a one can exist anywhere. Thus the disagreement of such great men has impelled me to traverse the empty deserts of many regions, to travel over impassable mountain ridges, to wander around inaccessible lakes, to explore the hidden entrails of the earth, to follow the gaping recesses of valleys, or sometimes to attempt precipices at great risk to my own body, in order to understand by observation, if not by knowledge, the things themselves about which I was going to write. No less painstaking was the care and sedulity with which I read the authors, Theophrastus in particular. In this author one can contemplate the characteristics of the plants scattered about here and there and torn limb from limb in such a way that it might seem impossible for a single complete plant to exist anywhere in the

botanist and observer, Hieronymus Tragus (Bock; 1498-1554), wrote excellent original descriptions of plants, although some of them were influenced by classical authors.[26] Matthioli insisted that nobody could confine himself to studying books; the student had to devote himself to frequent inspection of plants examining them in every detail at different times of the year, as he had learned from his tutor.[27]

By using this combination of the ancient authors, Dioscorides supported by Pliny and Theophrastus, and direct visual demonstration of plants,[28] most herbalists escaped the problem associated with descriptions and systematics.[29]

---

world. It has been necessary to collect all these characteristics and to bring them together in their proper places so as to unite them in one body. I have represented a large number of bushes, which had been fused together in a manifold and shapeless mixture of things, recovering their parts from wherever I could, and as if by restoring to each of them its own colours, I have succeeded in making them more recognizable").

[26] Greene reviews very carefully the descriptions of Tragus, see Greene, 1983, 307-27.

[27] Petri Andreae Matthioli Senensis medici *commentarii in sex libros Pedacii Dioscoridis Anazarbei de Medica materia* ... Venetiis 1565. Lib. primum Pedacii Dioscoridis Anazarbei, de medica materia. præfatio Dioscoridis. Commentarius Matthioli p. 3: "Veruntamen nemo in hac materia se peritum euadere confidat assidua tantum librorum lectione, etsi eos quidem grauissimi conscripserint auctores, nisi sæpius ad uisendas stirpes se contulerit, & quod a præceptore in herbarum agnitione diu exercitato, digiti demonstratione prius fuerit doctus, ac oculorum sensu, gustatuque, uarijs anni temporibus omnia hæc diligenter omni ex parte perpenda[n]t" ("Nobody should believe he can turn himself into an expert in this matter just by reading books, not even if they have been compiled by the most important authors, unless he devotes himself to the very frequent inspection of plants; and everything that he has previously been taught by an instructor with long experience in recognizing plants, by pointing out marks with the finger, by eyesight and sense of taste, all this he should carefully examine in every detail at various times of the year").

[28] Reeds 1976, 534-36.

[29] It should perhaps be noted that books about agriculture were influenced neither by the *corpus Aristotelicum* nor by Theophrastus. The most commonly read works in the early Renaissance, Palladius' *Opus agriculturae* and (later supplanting it) Pier de Crescenzi's *Liber cultus ruris*, were translated into Italian, French, German and (except Crescenzi) into English, and published in several editions. Ambrosoli has investigated the marginalia in these works in several libraries and found only one copy (Basle 1548) in which quotations from Theophrastus had been added (by an anonymous reader living in mid-sixteenth century, Ambrosoli 1997, 92). A German edition of 1490 and a Swiss of 1545 were supplemented with pictures of plants and animals drawn from nature (Ambrosoli 1997, 50). In husbandry the problem of identifying plants was thus solved in the same way as in medicine, that is, by means of illustrations. (Neither Palladius nor Crescenzi described the plants).

The first person to make a serious attempt at systematizing descriptions was the son of Euricius Cordus, Valerius Cordus (1515-44), whose works were published posthumously by Conrad Gessner in 1561 and 1563.[30] Cordus described approximately 500 plants, following a regular and morphologically consistent pattern beginning at the root and going upwards.[31] His limitations were ignorance of the functions of the floral parts and an insufficient terminology. His descriptions, far superior to those of his contemporaries, show that he was conversant with Theophrastus.

The problem with classification could not, however, be suppressed for ever. The number of known species increased from the 600 mentioned by Dioscorides and familiar in 1500 to 6000 named by Caspar Bauhinus in the *Pinax theatri botanici* of 1623. A retrieval system became a necessity. The questions then were: what characters should be chosen to distinguish one plant from another; and how should the plants be grouped?

A manuscript of Luca Ghini's, published in 1907,[32] shows that he worked on these problems.[33] From the correspondence of Conrad Gesner it appears that he considered the characteristics of floral parts, fruits and seeds to be of greater value than leaves for identification and discrimination.[34] Perhaps in recognition of the inadequate terminology (which

---

[30] Valerius Cordus was probably ignorant of Ruel's efforts to achieve greater precision in morphological description. In *De natura stirpium* Ruel had defined more exactly the form and figure of the vegetative parts and flowers of the plants and had expanded the vocabulary considerably (Ruellius 1536, 24-36). It is, however, significant for the conservatism of *res herbaria* that he did not change the descriptions of Dioscorides according to his own morphological system, but confined himself to improving them. The books by Valerius Cordus, posthumously published by Gesner were: *Historiae stirpium libri IIII* (with other works) in 1561 and *Stirpium descriptionis liber quintus* in 1563.

[31] This procedure is still used having been made sacrosanct by Linnaeus: "Descriptio ordinem nascendi sequatur ... Præstat naturam sequi a Radice ad Caulem, Petiolos, Folia, Pedunculos Flores," see Caroli Linnaei *Philosophia botanica in qua explicantur Fundamenta botanica cum definitionibus partium, exemplis terminorum, observationibus rariorum adjectis figuris aeneis*, Stockholmiæ 1751, § 328.

[32] Giovanni Batista de Toni, "I Placiti di Luca Ghini intorno a piante descritte nei commentarii al Dioscoride di P. A. Matthioli", *Memorie del Reale Isituto Veneto di Scienze, Lettere ed Arti*, 27 (1907) no. 8, 1 16: 17-42.

[33] Morton 1981, 156, note 40.

[34] Agnes Arber, *Herbals. Their origin and evolution. A chapter in the history of Botany 1470-1670*, Cambridge 1912, 138; Meyer 1857, 333-34 quotes from his letters e.g. "Ex his (sc. flore fructu radice) potius quam foliis stirpium naturae et cognationes apparent" ("From these (namely flower fruit and root) rather than from the leaves appear the natures and relationships of the plants").

he could not have avoided noticing as he worked on Cordus' manuscripts) he spent the last part of his life producing wonderful drawings of plants, depicting details from e.g. floral parts and fruits, later to be called analytical drawings, of a quality rivalled only 200 years later.[35] Euricius Cordus had emphasized that even good drawings could cause damage, if the wrong name was attached to them.[36] The eminent expositor Matthioli had also pointed out that even the best of drawings could not portray natural objects with perfect truthfulness or reveal the variation of a plant taxon.[37]

Andrea Cesalpino (1519-1603), a student of Luca Ghini, set himself the task of defining the problems, discussing the alternatives and suggesting a method and a system. After forty years of teaching botany and medicine at the University of Pisa he published his *De plantis libri XVI* in 1583. Of the sixteen books, the last fifteen contain descriptions of 1500 plants according to the method he had chosen. In the first book, upon which I

---

[35] The analytical drawings were intended as descriptions of characteristics; in one of the letters quoted by Meyer Gesner asks a friend for a drawing of a fruit "so that the location of the seeds in it may also be apparent. In this manner I am accustomed to add fruits and seeds to most of my paintings, in such a way that among so many plants each one may be distinguished more easily, and the pictures themselves may almost replace descriptions" ("ita ut seminum etiam situs in eo appareat. Sic enim soleo fructus ac semina plerisque picturis meis addere, ut in tanto stirpium numero singula facilius dignoscantur, et ipsae picturae descriptionum fere loco esse possint"), Meyer 1857, 333.

[36] Euricius Cordus 1534, 14: "Quo similius sua quæque facie pingitur, eo peius erratur, si non & uerum eidem nomen tribuitur" ("the closer the likeness with which each plant is depicted, the worse is the error if it is not also given its true name"). The harm done by incorrectly named figures is a continuing theme; Linnaeus refers to it thus in *Philos. bot.* 1741, § 332: "Pictor, Sculptor & Botanicus æque necessarii sunt ad figuram laudabilem. Si alter horum peccet, evadit figura vitiosa" ("Painter, engraver and botanist are equally necessary to produce a praiseworthy picture. If any one of them fails the result is a faulty figure").

[37] "At fieri quidem nequit, ut huiuscemodi stirpium uariationes ex libris, in quibus figuræ expressæ, atque etiam coloribus ornatæ habentur, omnes obseruari possint, quandoquidem plantæ ipsæ appictæ ex tot varijsque unam nobis duntaxat imaginem repræsentant. Huc etiam illud accedit, quod ea, quæ picturæ artificio fiunt, etsi ex optimi artificis penicillo emergant, nunquam tamen naturalium rerum lineamenta ad unguem referre, ac exprimere queunt, quanvis etiam naturam exactissime imitentur ..." Matthioli 1565, *Commentarii in Lib. primum Pedacii Dioscoridis Anazarbei de medica materia*. Præfatio Dioscoridis, commentarius Matthioli, p.4 ("It is impossible that all such variations of plants could be observed in books containing printed and even coloured figures, as the plants themselves, while drawn from so many and varied specimens, present only one figure to us. In addition to this the likenesses made by the skill of illustration, even if they come from the pen of the best artist, can never perfectly reproduce and express the features of natural objects, however exactly they may imitate nature").

will concentrate here, he discusses the nutrition, germination and growth of plants and their classification. Cesalpino was the first to do this since antiquity and was well versed in Aristotle and Theophrastus, as might be expected from one who had already discussed Aristotelian views in his *Quaestiones peripateticae*, published in 1571.

He first treats the nutrition of plants following the ideas of Aristotle and using homologies with animals, a procedure which Theophrastus had carefully avoided.[38] In his discussion of a possible circulation of food in the plant (as in animals) and its connection with internal heat he stresses the importance of the *cor medullae*, the junction of root and shoot in the embryo, because he considers it the centre of growth. Unlike Aristotle he looks for physical explanations for the imbibition of humor from the soil. He is also aware of the influence of external heat (climate) on the physiological processes in plants. Although his text is based on Aristotle, he does not mention him by name but refers instead to his own *Quaestiones*.[39] It is evident that the treatment of the classical text is controlled by personal observation and experiment.

In chapter IV Cesalpino describes plant organs as defined by Theophrastus and recognizes an orderly pattern of buds and leaves[40] as a characteristic of the plant. He also observes that buds always arise from leaf axils. He describes, as no one had since Theophrastus, seeds and embryos and their germination,[41] and, no doubt as a result of his interest in the *cor medullae*, is the first to recognize the importance of the position of the embryo in the seed.

His most important contribution was his attempt to establish a rational classification of plants. In the dedication to Duke Francesco de'Medici he claims to have done this on the basis of principles laid down by Theophras-

---

[38] *De plantis libri XVI* Andreae Caesalpini Aretini medici clarissimi doctissimique atque philosophi celeberrimi ac subtilissimi ad serenissimum Franciscum Medicem magnum Aetruriae Ducem, Florentiae 1583, 1-5. The quotations from the works of Aristotle in which he speaks of plants were collected and published in: Fr. Wimmer, *Phytologiae Aristotelicae fragmenta*, Vratislavia 1838.

[39] Caesalpinus 1583, 2.

[40] Caesalpinus 1583, 9.

[41] Caesalpinus 1583, 5-8 and 11-13.

tus.⁴² In fact he also relied on Aristotelian principles.⁴³ He intended to establish a classification based not on *accidentia*, for example pharmaceutical uses as in Dioscorides, but on natural order or relation.⁴⁴ "We look for those similarities and differences which make up the essential nature (*substantia*) of plants, not for those which are only accidental to them; for things perceived by the senses become comprehended primarily from their essential nature (*substantia*) and only secondarily from their

---

⁴² Caesalpinus 1583, (dedication p. 4).

⁴³ He does not mention Aristotle, but his discussion of nutrition and the homologizing with animals and his insistence on characteristics from the *cor medullae* all point to Aristotle rather than Theophrastus (who never mentions these views of Aristotle in *de historia* or *de causis plantarum*). He sometimes refers to his own *Quaestiones peripateticae*, e.g. p. 2 and p. 27.

⁴⁴ Caesalpinus 1583, dedic. p. (4 -5): "Cum igitur scientia omnis in similium collectione & dissimilium distinctione consistat, haec autem distributio est in genera & species veluti classes secundum differentias rei naturam indicantes, conatus sum id praestare in universa plantarum historia: ut si quid, pro ingenij mei tenuitate in huiusmodi studio profecerim, ad communem utilitatem proferam. Hanc vero tractandi rationem Theophrastus inter antiquos indicauit, sed in paucis est persecutus: Apud nostros autem Ruellius tentauit quidem, sed praeter ea, quae a Theophrasto excerpsit circa rationem communem, ulterius nequaquam est progressus. At Dioscorides tamquam Medicus solum communionem circa facultates Medicas accepit, quo ordine succos, lachrymas, radices, semina, & alias plantarum partes persecutus est. Aliis, quo facilius memoriae mandarentur, placuit eo ordine digerere, qui secundum nominis incipientes literas datus est: sed hic tamquam maxime fallax, & longissime a rei natura discedens a grauioribus huius scientiae authoribus reprobatus est. Qui autem secundum naturarum societatem assignatur, omnium facillimus reperitur, tutissimus, utilissimusque tum ad memoriam, tum ad facultates contemplandas ..." ("So, since all science consists in a collecting together of similar things and a distinction of dissimilar things, and since this is a division into *genera* and *species* as into classes which indicate the nature of a thing according to *differentiae*, I have attempted to carry out such a division in a complete history of plants so that if, with my modest abilities, I have made any progress in this kind of study, I may publish it for the general good. Among the ancients Theophrastus pointed to this method of treating the subject, but followed it only in a few instances. In our own time Ruellius has made the attempt, but apart from what he takes from Theophrastus concerning a general method, he has made no further progress. Dioscorides, however, being a physician, took account only of shared medicinal properties and according to their order he discussed saps, exudates, roots, seeds and other parts of plants. Others, to make it easier to commit (plants) to the memory, have preferred to arrange them in an order given by the initial letters of their names. But this order, being extremely misleading and so far removed from nature, has been rejected by eminent authors in this science. The order assigned according to natural relation is the easiest of all to find, the most complete, the most useful both for the memory and for considering the properties ...") and Lib. 1, Cap. XIII, p. 26.

accidents".⁴⁵ As Morton summarizes the matter, he "saw that while the characters of what he considered organs of growth and nutrition (root, stem, leaves) could be used to set up broad classes, the classes were arbitrary because they did not yield further useful or meaningful subclasses; whereas classes based on the characters of organs devoted to reproduction (by which he meant primarily the fructification) readily yielded further meaningful subclasses".⁴⁶ Consequently characteristics of reproductive organs (fruits, seeds) are used in the definitions of the higher classes, those of leaves, stems and roots in the definitions of the lower ones. The characters should be derived from the number, position and general aspect of the important parts.⁴⁷ These characters should be stable and independent of habitat, soil and climate. Having discussed this further, Cesalpino writes that he will use the stable characteristics of the reproductive organs, their number, position and aspect together with Theophrastus' division of plants into trees, shrubs, undershrubs and herbs. This he did, and in fact he succeeded in creating several groups (*genera* and families) still regarded as natural groups today. How strong his reliance on a practical approach was, is seen from the fact that although in theory he

---

⁴⁵ Caesalpinus 1583, 26: "Cum autem formarum similitudines et dissimilitudines quaeramus, ex quibus constat plantarum substantia, non autem eorum, quae accidunt ipsis: accidentia enim posterius innotescunt cognita substantia". The translation is by Morton 1981, 158, note 46.

⁴⁶ Morton 1981, 136.

⁴⁷ Caesalpinus 1583, 29: "Cum ad organorum constitutionem tria maxime faciant, scilicet, partium numerus, situs & figura, (magnitudo enim non uidetur speciem organi immutare, nisi simul figuram immutet: Solutio autem continui, aut unio ad numerum pertinent: durities, mollities, color & reliquae qualitates ad similares partes referuntur) natura secundum illorum differentias in fructibus condendis multis modis lusit, ex quibus uaria plantarum genera constituta sunt" ("As three things contribute especially to the constitution of organs, namely the number of parts, their position and form, (for size does not seem to change the appearance of an organ, unless the form changes at the same time: dissolution of what is continuous and union (of what is not united) appertain to the number: hardness, softness, colour and other qualities are referred to similar parts) nature has played in many ways in the construction of fructification according to the diversity of these (characteristics) from which the various *genera* of plants have been created"). The impact of this conclusion on the description of *genera* and *species* is seen in the relevant paragraph in Linnaeus 1751 § 327: "Descriptio ... partes depingat secundum Numerum, Figuram, Proportionem, Situm ... Notae characteristicae Descriptionis primariae semper observandae in omni parte plantæ, sunt a) Numerus, b) Figura, c) Proportio, d) Situs."

considered the *cor medullae* an important character, in practice he used it sparingly.[48]

He was not understood. His book had no illustrations, and as he created his own technical terms it was difficult to read and use in the recognition of plants. The Czech botanist Adam Zaluzansky quoted *de plantis*, but did not use the classification suggested there.[49] His great contemporaries Dodonaeus, Clusius, Dalechampius, and Lobelius published extensively and contributed to the advance of botany by describing and depicting new plants; but although Lobelius and Clusius arranged plants following non-pharmaceutical principles (Lobelius used to some extent the form of the leaf) they did not succeed in creating a useful system. However, as knowledge and the number of described plants increased they gained a better perception of natural affinities; this is seen from the fact that they grouped plants under a common generic name. Caspar Bauhinus did this from 1596 with great consistency, adding in a few words some easily recognizable characters for the sake of clearness.[50] In his monumental *Pinax theatri botanici* of 1623 he grouped all known names and descriptions into *genera* and *species*. He did not define his concept of these terms, although Columna in his *Ekphrasis* of 1616 had agreed with Cesalpino that *genera* should not be based on similarities of leaf form, "since the affinities of plants are indicated not by the leaf but by the characters of the flower, the receptacle and, especially, the seed".[51] But Bauhinus had perhaps expressed

---

[48] C.E.B. Bremekamp, "A re-examination of Cesalpino's classification", *Acta botanica Neerlandica*, 1 (1952), 582.

[49] He did however claim that botany was a science in its own right, not an appendix to medicine, see Morton 1981, 162, note 58.

[50] Casparus Bauhinus, ΦΥΤΟΠΙΝΑΞ seu enumeratio plantarum ab Herbariis nostro seculo descriptarum cum earum differentiis, Basiliae 1596, præfatio sig. 4v: "Plerisque nomen imposuimus, perspicuitatis gratia, cuius nomine communiter nota aliqua quæ a quolibet in planta observari potest, nomini addita" ("I have given a name to most of them for the sake of clearness, and for the same reason some characteristic, which can be observed by anyone in the plant, is generally added to the name"), quoted from Arber 1912, 140.

[51] Fabii Columnæ Lyncei *minus cognitarum rariorumque nostro coelo orientium stirpium* ΕΚΦΡΑΣΙΣ *qua non paucæ ab Antiquioribus Theophrasto, Dioscoride, Plinio, Galeno aliisque descriptæ, præter illas etiam in* Φυτοβασάνω *editas, disquiruntur ac declarantur* ... Romæ 1616 Pars altera, 62: "tam in hac, quam in aliis plantis, non enim ex foliis, sed ex flore, seminisque, conceptaculo, et ipso potius semine, plantarum affinitatem dijudicamus". The translation used is that of Arber 1912, 138-39. Gesner had made it clear in correspondence that a distinction should be drawn between *genera* and *species*, for example: "Existimandum est autem, nullas propemodum herbas esse, quae non genus aliquod

a common view in a letter to a friend when he wrote: "Cesalpino's book *De Plantis* has been much in my mind; I spent a long time reading it in order to use it for my classification. He is a learned man but very obscure; I had great difficulty in understanding him, and doubt whether he would be intelligible to beginners and students".[52] It was left to the botanists of the seventeenth century to raise description and classification to such a level that easily recognizable *genera* and species could be defined and a survey be made. In the process Aristotle was revived; Nehemiah Grew (1641-1712), in his anatomy, reintroduced Aristotle's principle of functional adaptation and applied it to the inner structure of plants.[53] The formidable Joannes Rajus (1623-1705) successfully continued Cesalpino's work on the natural divisions of the plant kingdom by means of observation, experiment and the careful study of Theophrastus, Cesalpino himself and all the other authors. When Pitton de Tournefort (1656-1708) established the *genus* as the basic unit of botanical classification[54] and Camerarius described the process of pollination,[55] the stage was set for the big clash in the eighteenth century between the Linnaean essential conception of the *genus* and the biological conception of the same advanced by Buffon, a dispute in which Aristotelian logic and biology played an essential role. But all this happened when the Renaissance was long past.

---

constituant in duas aut plures species dividendum" ("It should be considered that there are almost no plants which do not constitute some *genus* to be divided into two or more *species*"), quoted from Meyer 1857, 334. The letters had been published in 1577 and were quoted by Bauhinus in *Pinax*.

[52] Morton 1981, 162.

[53] Nehemiah Grew, *The Anatomy of Plants. With an Idea of a Philosophical History of Plants. And Several other Lectures. Read before the Royal Society*, London 1682.

[54] Joseph Pitton de Tournefort, *Elemens de botanique ou methode pour connoître les plantes,* Paris 1694, 13 sqq. Tournefort ascribed to Gesner the *genus*-concept (p. 17).

[55] R. J. Camerarius, *De sexu plantarum epistola*, Tübingen 1694.

Description, Division, Definition – Cæsalpinus and the study of plants as an independent discipline

by Kristian Jensen

In the sixteenth century the study of plants was pursued professionally in a wide range of different contexts, often related to one another, but each with an agenda set by the concerns of the discipline within which the study was exercised. However, there was no separate and independent discipline called botany and not even the word existed.[1] With two exceptions, I have not encountered the word botany or any of its derivatives in any sixteenth-century text. The two exceptions are the titles of Theodoricus Dorstenius's book *Botanicon*[2] and of Eurycius Cordus's *Botanologicon*.[3] These I believe do not represent examples of contemporary usage. Indeed, neither of the two authors use any word related to botany anywhere in their books, apart from the title-pages. The titles should be seen as part of the fashion, particularly prevalent in Germany in the mid-sixteenth century, for imaginative Greek names; this applied to books, as well as to people. A

---

[1] There is no word related to botany in Henri Estienne, *Thesaurus græcæ linguæ*, 4 vols, Paris: excudebat Henricus Stephanus, 1572. A few relevant words occur in the *Glossaria duo e situ vetustatis eruta*, Paris: excudebat Henricus Stephanus, 1573, col. 412, *inter alia* βοτανίζω, translated as "runco", to clear of weeds.

[2] *Botanicon, continens herbarum aliorumque simplicium quorum usus in medicinis est descriptiones et icones ad uiuum effigatas, ex præcipuis tam Græcis quam Latinis authoribus iam recens concinnatum. Additis etiam quæ neotericorum observationes et experientiæ uel comprobarunt denuo, uel nuper inuenerunt*, Frankfurt: Christianus Egenolphus, 1540.

[3] *Botanologicon*, Cologne: apud I. Gymnicum, 1534. Peter Dilg, *Das Botanologicon des Eurycius Cordus: Ein Beitrag zur botanischen Literatur des Humanismus*, Inauguraldissertation, Marburg an der Lahn 1969, 49, has suggested that the word *Botanologicon* is a humorous reference to the Greek verb for weeding, βοτανολογέω. This would have suited my argument, but unfortunately that meaning of the word is only attested in papyri and was apparently unknown in the sixteenth century. We have to accept that the title simply means "Dialogue on herbs". As for Dorstenius's work, it would be particularly hard to argue that it is a contribution to botany as a separate and independent discipline as we know it, for roughly a third of the book is taken up with a discussion of medical substances other than plants, such as earths, metals, stones etc.

roughly contemporary example is Conrad Gesner's *Mithridates*. The word *botanicus* begins to appear around 1600 — I have first come across it in a book from 1601 — but it seems not to have been much used even in the seventeenth century.[4] By the mid-eighteenth century the term botany was firmly established, well before the term biology, which W. Baron has established was first used in a publication in 1802.[5]

This is not to say that the study of plants did not develop dramatically during the sixteenth century. Charles Schmitt has said that in this area we have "one of the most important points of university scientific development of Renaissance Italy".[6] He and others have outlined this development in the most practical of terms, through the foundation of institutions. The first *horti medici* or *horti simplicium* were founded in Pisa and Padua around 1544,[7] and medical chairs dedicated to the study of simples were founded in Padua in 1533, in Bologna 1534, in Ferrara 1543, and in Pisa 1544.

While most plant studies were done by physicians, the economic importance of plants ensured that they were studied in the context of estate management. This occupation with plants by land owners is the subject of

---

[4] The first occurrence I have come across is "studiosos rei botanicæ" in the preface to Caspar Bauhinus, *Animaduersiones in historiam generalem plantarum Lugduni editam*, Frankfurt: excudebat Melchior Hartmann, 1601, p. 4. The first recorded occurrence in English is the word "botanique", quoted by Cotgrave as a French word in 1611; see *Oxford English Dictionary*, s.v. "botanic". It does not seem to have been naturalised as an English word until the mid-seventeenth century. Although the word botany and its relatives begin to emerge around 1600, they do not seem to have become very popular even in the seventeenth century. Among the titles of the Bodleian Library's 103,287 seventeenth-century books, I have found only two occurrences of "botan-" in the first two decades, both from 1619-20 and associated with the Bauhin brothers; three in the next two decades and ten in the decades from 1641 to 1660. More noticeable than the increased use of "botan-" is the decline in the occurrence of the word "simplex", as referring to medicinal simples.

[5] W. Baron, "Gedanken über den ursprünglichen Sinn der Ausdrücke Botanik, Zoologie und Biologie", *Medizingeschichte im Spectrum: Festschrift zum fünfundsechzigsten Geburtstag von Johannes Stendel*, ed. G. Rath and H. Schipperges (Sudhoffs Archiv, Beiheft 7), Wiesbaden 1966, 1-10.

[6] "Science in the Italian universities in the sixteenth and early seventeenth centuries", in *The Emergence of Science in Western Europe*, ed. M. P. Crossland, London 1975, 35-56, at p. 39; Schmitt does not discuss the use of words relating to "botan-".

[7] See, for instance, *Giardino dei semplici, I, Orto botanico a Pisa dal xvi and xx secolo*, ed. Fabio Barbieri et al., Pisa 1991.

Mauro Ambrosoli's fascinating book on plant studies and agriculture.[8] As in medicine, we find that a group of classical texts are central to the study of plants, but the canon is now different: Cato, Varro, Columella, and the *agrimensores* are the core texts.

Plants were also of professional interest to philosophers. In this group we should include Julius Caesar Scaliger's dialogue on the pseudo-Aristotelian *De plantis*, and his commentaries on Theophrastus's *De causis plantarum* and the *Historia plantarum*.[9] Conrad Gesner commends Scaliger's commentary on the pseudo-Aristotelian text in his work *De hortis Germaniae* from 1561.[10] Among philosophers with an interest in plants we must also include Hieronymus Cardanus: he saw his two large works *De subtilitate* and *De rerum uarietate*, each with a book devoted to plants,[11] as contributions to philosophy, and this was recognized by his contemporaries. In his preface to Valerius Cordus's commentary on Dioscorides, Conrad Gesner cited Cardanus as a "summus philosophus" in relation to plants.[12] Although much cited by sixteenth- and seventeenth-century authors on plants, Scaliger and Cardanus seem to have been ignored by modern historians of botany. Commentators on the pseudo-

---

[8] *Scienziati, contadini e proprietari: botanica e agricoltura nell'Europa occidentale 1350-1850*, Turin 1992. A sixteenth-century book discussing plants from this point of view is Charles Estienne's *Praedium rusticum*, Paris: Charles Estienne, 1554.

[9] *In libros duos qui inscribuntur De plantis Aristotele autore libri duo*, Paris: ex officina M. Vascosani, 1556; *Commentarii et animaduersiones in sex libros De causis plantarum Theophrasti*, [Geneva]: anchora Ioannis Crispini, 1566; *Animaduersiones in Historias Theophrasti*, Lyon: apud Ioannam Iacobi Iuntæ F., 1584. On Scaliger's works on plants see Kristian Jensen, *Rhetorical Philosophy and Philosophical Grammar: Julius Caesar Scaliger's Philosophy of Language*, Munich 1990, 38-45.

[10] Valerius Cordus, *Annotationes in Pedacii Dioscoridis Anazarbei De medica materia libros v. Eiusdem Historiæ stirpium libri iiii ... item Conradi Gesneri De hortis Germaniae liber recens*, Strasbourg: I. Rihelius, 1561, fol. 237r: "Aristotelis de stirpibus extant quidem libri duo, sed corruptissimi, ut nihil fere utilitatis inde rei hortensis studiosi homines referant: nonnihil uero e doctissimis Scaligeri in eos libros commentationibus."

[11] *De subtilitate libri xxi*, Nürnberg: apud I. Petreium, 1550; 3rd edn., Basel: ex officina Petreia, 1559, 8°; *De rerum uarietate libri xvii*, Basel: per Henricum Petri, 1557.

[12] Cordus 1561, fol. 237r: "Hieronymus Cardanus summus philosophus operis De uarietate rerum lib. vi cap. xxiii De plantarum cura inscripsit et c." See also Hieronymus Bock, *De stirpium maxime earum quæ in Germania nostra nascuntur usitatis nomenclaturis propriisque differentiis...commentariorum libri tres*, Strasbourg: excudebat Vuindelinus Rihelius, 1552, Conrad Gesner's preface, sig. c$_{iii}$r: "Hieronymus Cardanus medicus Mediolanensis libro octavo operis De subtilitate multa de plantis rara et egregia adfert, philosophice, medice et historice."

Aristotelian *Problemata* also dealt with plants, especially Antonius Musa Brasavola who discussed it in a plant related context.[13]

The study of medicine and the study of philosophy were closely related and there was much interaction between the two. Even when it was not stated explicitly philosophical considerations were never far from the surface of medical works. For example Leonhardus Fuchsius's work on plants from 1542 is beautifully illustrated.[14] This may seem a fairly neutral thing to do from a philosophical point of view; but before he published his illustrated *De historia stirpium* Fuchsius was already engaged in a polemic concerning the use of illustrations of plants. In 1530 he published a medical work correcting the errors, as he saw it, of contemporary physicians.[15] This work was attacked by Sebastian Montuus in 1533,[16] who stated that, unlike Dioscorides, Galen had not provided illustrations because pictures implied that one defined a *species* not *ex genere et differentia* but *ex genere et accidentibus*.[17] This material has been discussed by Kusokawa, who used it to show that Fuchsius's enterprise was one of a Galenic revival, but the debate has further implications. In his *Libri difficilium quæstionum* of 1540 it becomes clear that in a sense Fuchsius accepted Montuus's criticism. He distinguished between two types of *accidens*: some are *separabilia*, others *inseparabilia* and he argued, with a reference to Rodolphus Agricola, that definitions *ex genere et accidente inseparabili* were acceptable.[18] Montuus

---

[13] *Examen omnium simplicium medicamentorum quorum in officinis usus est. Addita sunt Aristotelis Problemata quæ ad stirpium genus et oleracea pertinent*, Lyon: sub scuto coloniensi, apud Ioannem et Franciscum Frellaeos, 1537.

[14] *De historia stirpium*, Basel: in officina Isingriniana, 1542.

[15] *Errata recentiorum medicorum*, Hagenau: in aedibus Iohannis Secerii, 1530.

[16] Sebastianus Montuus, *Annotatiunculæ in errata recentiorum medicorum per Leonhardum Fuchsium germanum collecta*, Lyon: B. Bouynyn, 1533.

[17] See Sachiko Kusokawa, "Leonhardt Fuchs on the importance of pictures", *Journal of the History of Ideas*, 58 (1997), 403-27. Kusokawa seems to elevate the concept of an accident to that of a Platonic idea by claiming that accidents of a plant can continue to exist after the plant has died; this may be due to a mistranslation of the word "præter" in a passage from Montuus, *Annotatiunculæ*, fol. 5r: "[definiuerunt] ex genere et accidentibus, quæ adesse abesseque possunt præter subiecti corruptionem constat". This prevents her from understanding fully what Fuchsius meant by *accidens*. Nor am I sure that Fuchsius is arguing from a specifically Galenic point of view, as suggested by Kusokawa; Montuus at least read Fuchsius as anti-Galenic.

[18] Leonhardus Fuchsius, *Libri iiii difficilium aliquot quæstionum et hodie passim controuersarum explicationes continentes magno studio aucti et recogniti*, Basel: in officina Roberti Winter, 1540, 92-5. Kusokawa ascribes Fuchsius's view to influence from

took the classical medical view that the essential *differentia* of a plant was its *vis*, that which made it medically effective, and he simply had no interest in plants without a medicinal function. Fuchsius agreed that the *vires* of plants are their essential differences, but he also wished to pay attention to the physical shapes which make it possible to distinguish one type of plant from another. His use of the distinction between *accidentia separabilia* and *inseparabilia* therefore was an attempt to introduce a set of concepts into plant description which would allow for a distinction between physical traits which are necessarily part of a *species* of plants and those which only belong to an individual plant. Though he refers to Agricola, Fuchsius here also depended on a reading of *De partibus animalium*, where the concept of essential accidents is elaborated, if finally rejected as a possible part of definitions.[19] In other words, Fuchsius was addressing the problem of how to mediate between plant description and plant definition as accepted in philosophical circles.

This was also a fundamental problem for Andreas Cæsalpinus.[20] Cæsalpinus was born in Arezzo in 1519, studied philosophy and medicine in Pisa where Simon Portius and Luca Ghini were among his teachers; he succeeded Ghini as professor of medicine and as director of the *hortus simplicium* in 1555. In 1592 he was made papal physician, and in 1603 he

---

Melanchthon, but in *Libri iiii difficilium aliquot quæstionum* Fuchsius names Agricola as a source for his view on accidents.

[19] *PA* 644b7.

[20] On Cæsalpinus in general see Ugo Viviani, *Vita ed opere di Andrea Cesalpino*, Arezzo 1922; idem, *Tre medici aretini*, Arezzo 1936, 5-72. *Césalpin, questions peripatiques*, with an introduction by M. Dorolle, Paris 1929; C. Bremekamp, "A re-examination of Cesalpino's classification", *Acta botanica neerlandica*, 1 (1953), 580-93; Karl Mägdefrau, *Geschichte der Botanik*, Stuttgart 1973, 37-8, and 41-3; idem, "Cesalpino, Andrea", in *Dictionary of Scientific Biography*, 18 vols, New York 1981, vol. XV, 80-81; Charles Lohr, *Latin Aristotle Commentaries II: Renaissance Authors*, Florence, 1988, 70; Charles Schmitt emphasized Cæsalpinus's importance, both within the University of Pisa and also in a wider context of European intellectual history in "The Studio Pisano in the European context of the sixteenth century", in *Firenze e la Toscana dei Medici nell' Europa del '500*, 3 vols, ed. Gian Carlo Garfagnini, Biblioteca di storia toscana moderna e contemporanea, Studi e documenti, 26; vol. I: *Strumenti e veicoli della cultura, relazioni politiche ed economiche*, Florence 1983, 19-36, at 29-31; on Cæsalpinus and the discovery of the circulation of the blood see e.g. Angelo Capecci, "Finalismo e meccanicismo nelle ricerche biologiche di Cesalpino e Harvey", *Aristotelismo veneto e scienza moderna: Atti del 25° anno accademico del Centro per la storia della tradizione aristotelica nel Veneto*, ed. Luigi Olivieri, 2 vols, Padua 1983, I 477-507.

died in Rome. The two works of his at the centre of my discussion are the *Peripateticæ quæstiones* of 1571[21] and his *De plantis* of 1583.[22]

Among historians of botany Cæsalpinus has been treated with mixed feelings; a baffled admiration is perhaps the best description of the prevailing attitude. He cannot be dismissed — he was after all called "primus systematicus" by Linnæus, who annotated his copy of Cæsalpinus with his own generic names throughout.[23] Most generous to him, perhaps, is A. G. Morton, who emphazises Cæsalpinus's important discoveries, but he notes that they were achieved despite an inappropriate Aristotelian framework.[24] The low opinion of Cæsalpinus among these botanical historians clearly reflects the poor opinion in which Renaissance Aristotelianism has previously been held. A reassesment of Cæsalpinus's Aristotelian study of plants does not seem premature.[25]

Perhaps surprisingly the most sympathetic detailed reading of Cæsalpinus's work on plants comes neither from a historian nor from a botanist, but from an anthropologist.[26] Scott Atran operates with a trinity of pre-Darwinian botanists, Aristotle, Cæsalpinus, and Linnæus. He does not regard Cæsalpinus's Aristotelianism as a deplorable drawback, but rather as the central feature of his thinking, which he presents in some ten pages of close readings of parts of Cæsalpinus's book on plants and of one section of his other major work, the *Peripateticæ quæstiones*. While he presents much of importance in Cæsalpinus's thinking on plants, Atran tends to

---

[21] *Peripateticarum quæstionum libri quinque*, Venice: apud Iuntas, 1571; later editions are Venice: apud Iuntas, 1593; the text also occurs in *Tractationum philosophicarum tomus unus*, [Geneva]: excudebat Eustachius Vignon, 1588; and in *Gazophylacium totius philosophiæ, sive Thesaurus selectiorum Aristotelicæ et Socraticæ philosophiæ quæstionum*, Cologne, 1646 (not seen); reprint of the 1571 edition Bruxelles: Culture et Civilisation, 1973.

[22] *De Plantis libri xvi*, Florence, apud Georgium Marescottum, 1583.

[23] See Agnes Arber, *Herbals: Their Origin and Evolution, A Chapter in the History of Botany* 3rd edn., Cambridge 1986, 143.

[24] *History of Botanical Science: An Account of the Development of Botany from Ancient Times to the Present Day*, London 1981, 128-41; also A. G. Morton, "Marginalia to Andrea Cesalpino's work in botany", Archives of Natural History, 10 (1981), 31-6.

[25] A good start has been made by Karen Meier Reeds, *Botany in Medieval and Renaissance Universities*, New York 1991, 19. She focuses on the universities of Montpellier and Basel, so it is appropriate that she devotes only one page to Cæsalpinus.

[26] Scott Atran, *Cognitive Foundations of Natural History: Towards an Anthropology of Science*, Cambridge 1990.

read his text as a direct response to Aristotle, unmediated by specific Renaissance philosophical concerns.

Atran begins by acknowledging his debt to Chomsky's notion that certain linguistic structures are part of the innate human make-up; implicitly he also draws on the new Darwinist wave,[27] where it is argued that our psychological make-up and hence our social behaviour is as determined as our bodies by evolutionary selection. Atran takes the determinism implicit in such studies further by arguing that not only is the capacity to classify innate, but that our common genetic heritage has provided us a with a shared specific way of classifying our world: common sense.[28] The greatest danger of his approach to classification is one of racism: if our categorisation of plants by pre-selected traits has been determined for us through evolution, the categorisation of people by pre-selected traits which are given special weight will also have to be seen as natural. However, for our present purpose it is important that, like the traditional historians of botany, Atran, with his ahistorical approach, ends up reading history as a determined march towards the pre-defined goal of modern science.[29] This enabled him to read Cæsalpinus as an unmediated response to Aristotle.

Atran found that Cæsalpinus owes his methodology more to the *Organon* than to other parts of the Aristotelian corpus.[30] The *Organon* was indeed close to the minds of well educated people of the sixteenth century, and certainly to Cæsalpinus. This is however particularly striking if seen with modern eyes: the fundamental concepts of the *Organon* are now so alien that similarities between Renaissance Aristotelian thinkers appear more obvious than the differences between them. However, Renaissance Aristotelians did not live in a consensual world; on the contrary, academic

---

[27] Perhaps best known from Richard Dawkin, *The Selfish Gene*, Oxford 1976.

[28] In rough outline, he finds similarities between the way pre-school age American children classify plants and the way they are classified by peoples who have traditionally attracted the attention of anthropologists, such as tribes of Indians and peoples on remote islands. Where tribal classification differs from that of American children, Atran finds that the former is a culturally determined one because, when more closely questioned, the tribesmen reveal a more fundamental system akin to the one proposed as general by Atran. The effect of interaction between the anthropologist and the peoples whom she studies is not considered by Atran. See e.g. Atran 1990, 44.

[29] For instance Atran 1990, 80: "...natural history after Cesalpino and Linnaeus gradually came to focus on determining species' genealogically-related affinities."

[30] Atran 1990, 142-3.

life was characterised by debate and often acrimonious controversy. We need to see Cæsalpinus in a light different from those who look for traits of the modern world, as part of a culture with aims and interests of its own. As we shall see Cæsalpinus's main concern with Aristotelian problems were not centred around the *Organon*.

Cæsalpinus considered that he approached the study of plants differently from Hermolaus Barbarus in his *Corollarium* of 1516. That is not surprising; after all Barbarus's observations were predominantly of a philological nature. It is more surprising that he found that the work of Johannes Ruellius[31] and of Antonius Musa Brasavola[32] were concerned with correlating knowledge of the ancients with current knowledge.[33] He also placed Mattioli and Anguillara[34] in that tradition, although he singled Anguillara out for having used "summum iudicium". The transmission of classical texts still caused problems,[35] but Cæsalpinus emphatically saw himself confronted with a different set of issues.

He had no doubt that there is a fixed number of *formæ* in nature, so that no new types of plant arise — assuming otherwise would have been a dangerous break with the account of divine creation. But while the number is fixed, the number known to students of plants had grown enormously. This was because during the sixteenth century the study of plants was increasingly no longer a local affair. The intensive correspondence of Ghini, Gesner, Dalecampius, Camerarius, Aldrovandi, Mattioli, and later Gaspard Bauhin, and their exchange of descriptions and of specimens, all contributed to an increment in the number of known plants. However, the most significant factor was information on plants from India and America. Cæsalpinus realized that, even if he tried, he could never describe all

---

[31] Johannes Ruellius, *De natura stirpium libri tres*, Paris: ex officina Simonis Colinæi, 1536.

[32] Brasavolus, *Examen*; cf. note 13 above.

[33] Cæsalpinus 1583, sig. a$_3$v: "Hanc uero tractandi rationem Theophrastus inter antiquos indicauit, sed in paucis est persecutus. Apud nostros autem Ruellius tentauit quidem, sed præter ea quæ a Theophrasto excerpsit circa rationem communem ulterius nequaquam est progressus."

[34] I have consulted Luigi Anguillara, *Semplici li quali in piu pareri a diversi nobili huomini scritti appaiono et nuouamente da G. Marinello mandati in luce*, Venice: appresso Vincenzo Valgrisi, 1561.

[35] Cæsalpinus 1583, sig. a$_2$v: "Obscura autem nam quæ apud antiquos comperta et ad posteriorum eruditionem literis mandata sunt, plerumque ob linguarum uarietatem nominis appellatione immutata, aut per multas transcribentium manus uitiatis uoluminibus, perplexa ualde et ambigua nobis relinquuntur."

existing plants.³⁶ This assessment was undoubtedly correct. While Dioscorides described some 500 plants, and medieval herbals far fewer, in 1623 Gaspard Bauhin listed over 6000 different plants in his *Pinax*, a tabulated index to all the works on plants known to him.

This overwhelming number of plants newly known to European scholars made Cæsalpinus set out his systematic project:

> What with such an immense number of plants, I feel the want of that which one normally aspires to in any other unstructured mass. For it is inevitable that all things will be thrown into unstable disorder, unless they are collected into ranks and divided into their proper classes, like an army in battle order. This is particularly relevant for the consideration of plants, for when our understanding is beset by an unstructured mass, the result is most often an ill-tempered debate over insoluble errors. For if the proper *genus* is not known, no description, however carefully propounded, can indicate an undisputed class; indeed most often it fails, for if the *genera* are jumbled together, everything else must of necessity be jumbled as well. All science depends on bringing similar things together and keeping dissimilar things distinct, that is, the division into *genera* and *species*, as it were into classes indicating the nature of the subject matter according to its *differentiæ*. That is what I have attempted to perform in my general account of plants, so that I can publish for the common good what little I have accomplished in this field of study.³⁷

Having set out his programme, Cæsalpinus had to establish the guiding principle for his classification. Mere description was clearly inadequate,

---

³⁶ Cæsalpinus 1583, sig. a₂v: "Nequaquam adhuc potui metam attingere, nam in dies, ut in prouerbio est, aliquid noui affert Aphrica, non quod natura nouas edat formas, aut nouas rerum pulchritudines effingat, sed quod ob numerum immensum nobis in dies nouæ ostendantur." Cæsalpinus drew on Garcia da Orta for knowledge of plants in India; his knowledge of South American plants came from Nicolás Bautista Monardes; see Cæsalpinus 1583, sig. a₃r-v.

³⁷ Cæsalpinus 1583, sig. a₃v: "In hac tamen immensa plantarum multitudine illud desiderari uideo, quod in alio quocumque agmine incomposito maxime expeti solet. Nisi enim in ordines redigantur et ueluti castrorum acies distribuantur in suas classes, tumultu et fluctuatione omnia perturbari necesse est. Id etiam tum [*ed. num*] maxime in plantarum examine contingere uidemus, cum enim inordinata multitudine obruatur intellectus, errores inextricabiles et morosæ altercationes utplurimum exoriuntur; ignorato enim proprio genere nulla descriptio quamuis accurate tradita certam <classem> demonstrat, sed plerumque fallit, nam confusis generibus omnia confundi necesse est. Cum igitur scientia omnis in similium collectione et dissimilium distinctione consistat, hæc autem distributio est in genera et species ueluti classes secundum differentias rei naturam indicantes, conatus sum id præstare in uniuersa plantarum historia, ut si quid pro ingenii mei tenuitate in huiusmodi studio profecerim ad communem utilitatem proferam."

given the great number of plants. He needed to find essential *differentiæ* of *species* of plants.

In a sense Cæsalpinus grappled with the same problem as had Leonhardus Fuchsius: how to establish philosophically acceptable *differentiæ* which take the physical appearance of the plant into consideration. But he approached his task completely differently from Fuchsius who produced an illustrated alphabetical and descriptive list. Cæsalpinus provided a system, and he explicitly rejected the option of using illustrations. While Fuchsius had still accepted the importance of medical *vires* as the essential *differentiæ* of plants, this was rejected by Cæsalpinus. Indeed he stated that he would not even mention the medicinal effects of plants.[38] He could not therefore follow Montuus's lead in rejecting illustrations as being inherently indicative only of accidents of plants. This ambiguous attitude to illustration explains why he had prepared illustrations and sent them to Francesco de' Medici, Grand Duke of Tuscany, although he felt that *differentiæ* are better expressed in words than in pictures.[39] His illustrations were, however, never published.[40]

Cæsalpinus's basic point of departure was the soul of plants, the vegetative soul. Here he already left Theophrastus and all sixteenth-century students of plants behind. The essence of the plant is its nutrition and its procreation. All the parts of the plant serve that essence; they therefore contribute to the final cause of the plant and are not accidental. In the first lines of his book he set out his view that the parts of the plant are the instruments of its soul: "The nature of plants has only been allotted that *genus* of soul whereby they can take nourishment, grow, and bring forth things similar to themselves, whereas they lack the power of feeling and of movement, which are the foundations of the nature of animals. Therefore

---

[38] Cæsalpinus 1583, p. 26: "Cum autem formarum similitudines et dissimilitudines quæramus ex quibus constat plantarum substantia non autem eorum quae accidunt ipsis; accidentia enim posterius innotescunt cognita substantia. Idcirco neque ex facultatibus medicatis neque ex alia utendi ratione, neque ex locis in quibus proueniant aut aliis huiusmodi genera eorum et species sunt constituendæ. Hæc enim omnia accidentia sunt."

[39] Cæsalpinus 1583, sig. a$_4$r: "Atque adeo certa ex hac breui descriptione paratur notitia, ut pictura certiorem efficere non possit: Non enim omnes differentias pictura exprimit, ut oratio."

[40] Cæsalpinus 1583, sig. b$_1$r, end of the letter of dedication.

it was appropriate that plants needed a much smaller apparatus of instruments than animals do."[41]

Because the final cause of the vegetative soul is reproduction, the seeds of plants become the basis for Cæsalpinus's scheme of division. This enabled him to distinguish between accidental and essential aspects of the physical appearance of the plant. It became possible to apply a simple practical test to discover if a particular physical feature is accidental or an essential *differentia*, a necessary part of the being of the plant in question, or instead an accidental feature, for instance caused by the plant growing in adverse or pampered conditions. If a plant comes true to seed you have a separate *species*; if it does not, then your parent plant merely exhibited some accidental features. By discarding the medical approach to plants and by focusing instead on the soul of plants and its instruments, it becomes possible to regard some aspects of the physical appearance of a plant as *differentiæ essentiales*, not as accidents.

But Cæsalpinus used other parts of the plant as bearers of *differentiæ*, in so far as they are instruments of the soul of the plant. This, however, presented a severe methodological problem: the problem of division and its relation to definition. Eckhard Keßler has recently suggested that in modern discussions of sixteenth-century Aristotelian method the focus on *regressus* has meant that scholars have overlooked the important role played by division, particularly after Petrus Ramus.[42]

I have not yet been able to find any indication that Cæsalpinus reacted to Ramus either negatively or positively, but there is no doubt that division, and more particularly a total rejection of bipartite division, was a central part of his method in the *De plantis*. The theoretical considerations behind the use of division are briefly outlined there, but they were discussed much more fully in his *Peripateticæ quæstiones* from 1571, twelve years before the publication of his *De plantis*. Particularly relevant is the chapter which is entitled: "A single *differentia*, even if it

---

[41] Cæsalpinus 1583, p. 1: "Cum natura plantarum illud solum genus animæ sortita sit quo alantur crescant et gignant sibi similia, careant autem ui sentiendi mouendique in quibus animalium natura consistit, iure optimo plantæ longe minori instrumentorum apparatu indiguerunt quam animalia." The discussion of the functions of the parts relative to procreation occurs mainly on pp. 6-7.

[42] Eckhard Kessler, "Method in the Aristotelian tradition: taking a second look", in *Method and Order in Renaissance Philosophy of Nature*, ed. Daniel A. Di Liscia, Eckhard Kessler, and Charlotte Methuen, Aldershot 1997, 113-42.

were an *ultima differentia*, is not enough to constitute that which is to be explained".[43] The two texts which he uses most intensively are the *Metaphysics*, text 43 of book seven, or in more modern terms *Metaph.* Z 12, and book 1 of the *De partibus animalium*. The first fundamental problem is one of reconciling the two texts. The more detailed of the two is the one in the *De partibus animalium*. There Aristotle rejects the Platonic bipartite division;[44] for instance, animals divided into footed or not footed, the footed animal divided into two-footed or four-footed, the two-footed animal divided into the cloven-footed and the not cloven-footed; the cloven-footed into two-toed and many-toed. The final point of such a division would lay claim to being an *ultima differentia*, the one *differentia* which constitutes the essence of the being in question. This is unacceptable because it will often constrain one to pick out a *differentia* from accidental features, such as being many-toed, which is an accidental feature of man.

If you take the *differentia* of having multi-cloven feet, it includes in itself the *differentia* of having feet. Within this system, therefore, only the *ultima differentia* would be an integral part of the definition of the thing in question. All *differentiæ* which are at a higher point in the division would be redundant, and the definition would become tautological, in so far as a *genus* with a *differentia* constitutes the definition of a *species*.[45] This implies that there is the same number of *species* as there are *ultimæ differentiæ* in this system, and that is manifestly not the case. Cæsalpinus suggests that the Porphyrian tree is responsible for this type of division having found a place in the Peripatetic tradition, despite what he sees as Aristotle's clear-cut rejection of it.[46] Except for the frank remarks about Porphyrius this does not appear to modern scholars an exceptional interpretation of the

---

[43] Cæsalpinus 1571, Liber 1, quæstio 6, fols 14r-18r: "Vnicam differentiam etiam si ultima fuerit, non sufficere ad ipsum quid est explicandum."

[44] Especially Plato, *Sophist*. 212c.

[45] On this see, for instance, Alexander of Hales, *In duodecim Aristotelis Metaphysicæ libros dilucidissima expositio*, ed. Propertius Resta de Talleacotio, Venice: apud Simonem Galignanum de Karera, 1572, book 7, text 43, fol. 228r.

[46] Cæsalpinus 1571, fol. 14v: "Omnia autem hæc contingunt ex modo definiendi per diuisionem bipartitam, quem modum etiam Porphyrius exempli gratia tradidit in constitutione arboris substantiæ, unde forte orta est occasio errandi in peripatetica doctrina."

De partibus animalium, but it was vehemently attacked by Nicolaus Taurellus in his polemic against Cæsalpinus.[47]

Much more remarkable is his approach to the passage in the *Metaphysics*. In effect he contextualized it and said that it had been misunderstood; it has been thought that Aristotle put forward his own view, whereas Cæsalpinus suggested that Aristotle showed what absurd results would arise from following the defective Platonic bipartite division.[48] A little later Cæsalpinus elaborated on this and said that the reason why Aristotle did not make it clear that he was showing the absurdity of the Platonic division is to be found in his aim with this passage: that of showing the necessity of unity in that which constitutes a definition. The purpose of this passage was therefore not primarily one of rejecting the Platonic bipartite division but one of showing the need for unity in any type of definition. Nevertheless, he sustained that Aristotle here did not conclude "tanquam uerum ex ueris", but "tanquam absurdum ex prauo definiendi modo".[49]

Cæsalpinus finally concluded that there is no *ultima differentia* for most phenomena. The *differentiæ* used for a definition must be arrived at by independent multiple divisions of the *genus*: "From this we can conclude that no definition can be based on a single *differentia*; on the contrary, the *genus* must always be included, which sometimes signifies *actus* and sometimes *materia*. Additionally, in the definition of an *ultima species* we must assume several *ultimæ differentiæ* in its essence which are derived from different sets of oppositions; one of these does not include another

---

[47] *Alpes cæsæ, hoc est Andreæ Cæsalpini... monstrosa et superba dogmata, discussa et excussa*, Frankfurt am Main: apud M. Zachariam, 1597, pp. 78-91.

[48] Cæsalpinus 1571, fol. 14r: "Afferunt quoque in hanc sententiam Aristotelis testimonium 7. Metaph. text. 43 [Metaph. Z 12] ubi in definitionibus secundum diuisionem datis, si non superflua futura sit, crebro iisdem repetitis neque diuisio secundum accidens fiat, inquit: Manifestum est quod ultima differentia rei substantia erit et diffinitio. Putauerunt enim illud Aristotelem concludere tanquam uerum ex ueris, non tanquam absurdum ex prauo definiendi modo secundum diuisionem, ut Plato faciebat. Res autem tota explicatur 1. de Part. an. cap. 2 & 3."

[49] Cæsalpinus 1571, fol. 15r: "Non uidetur autem Aristoteles 7. Metaph. text. 43 inferre tanquam absurdum ultimam differentiam esse rei definitionem, quoniam non erat eius intentio in illo loco methodum illam redarguere, cum alibi abunde fecisset. Sed uolebat ostendere quomodo ea quæ in definitione ponuntur, unum quid sunt. Ostenditurque hoc primum in definitionibus secundum diuisionem traditis, unum esse, quia una tantum differentia ultima definitio est, si rite fiat. Quoniam autem hoc non contingebat in aliis definitionibus idcirco alia ratione oportuit ostendere unitatem partium definitionis, quod post multas dubitationes tandem ostendit 8. Metaph. tex. 15 & 16."

differentia, but they are one, with one as *materia* another as *actus*; that is the way in which they constitute a unity...From this is obvious that it is totally unaristotelian to seek an *ultima differentia* to equate with each species".[50]

Cæsalpinus observed that his notion of definition relying on several *ultimæ differentiæ* derived from separate divisions could be challenged by using *Physics* book 1, text 50, and *Metaphysics* 7 text 49, where it is said that a unity cannot be formed from *contraria*. He responded that Aristotle in those passages referred only to *genera simplicia*, such as for instance geometric shapes, not to *substantiæ compositæ*.[51]

Cæsalpinus is quite close to a modern reading of the passage, such as that of Andrea Falcon who says that "in *Metaph*. Z 12 Aristotle is concerned with the unity of definition and appeals to division because this method can help him to solve this particular definitional puzzle".[52] However, I have not found a similar interpretation of this passage of the *Metaphysics* in any of the commentaries which were commonly read in the sixteenth century. Indeed Matthias Aquarius in his *Dilucidationes* of 1584, essentially a commentary on Thomas Aquinas, found that Aristotle in *Metaphysics* book 7 text 43 concluded that a *differentia inferior* included *formaliter* the *differentiæ superiores*. Aquarius, in other words, took at face value the type of division which Aristotle discussed.[53]

While one can see that the passage from the *Metaphysics* can be open to different interpretations, it may seem difficult for a modern reader to avoid Cæsalpinus's conclusion that Aristotle in the *De partibus animalium* came

---

[50] Cæsalpinus 1571, fol. 18r: "Ex his igitur patet nullam definitionem dari posse per unicam differentiam, sed ubique necessarium esse genus, quod alicubi actum, alicubi materiam significat. Præterea in ultimarum specierum definitione in substantiis propter multiplicem compositionem plures ultimas differentias assumendas esse ex diuersis contrarietatibus, quarum una alteram non includat, sed solum una sit, ut materia, altera ut actus: sic enim unum fiunt ... Ex quibus manifestum est quam illi recedant a sententia Aristotelis qui in omnibus quærunt ultimam quandam differentiam cum specie æqualem."

[51] Cæsalpinus 1571, fol. 15r-v: "Quod autem dixit Aristoteles in omni genere uno unam esse contrarietatem, per unum genus significat simplex."

[52] Andrea Falcon, "Aristotle's theory of division", in *Aristotle and After*, ed. Richard Sorabji (Bulletin of the Institute of Classical Studies, Supplement 68), London 1997, 127-41.

[53] Matthias Aquarius, *Dilucidationes in xii libros primæ philosophiæ Aristotelis*, Rome: ex typographia Bartholomæi Bonfadini et Titi Diani, 1584, 407-9: "An differentia diuisiua generis inferioris includat formaliter superiores"; the answer on p. 409 is "Ultima conclusio est affirmatiua respondens quæstio principalis. Differentia inferior claudat in se superiorem formaliter, seu differentia superior clauditur in inferiori."

down on the side of definition from *differentiæ* obtained from several separate divisions. However, it was not quite that obvious in the sixteenth century. In Augustinus Niphus's commentary on the *De partibus animalium* some clear limitations are laid down as to how far this criticism of the bipartite division is allowed to go. Niphus referred to Boethius, who approved of the bipartite division, and he confined the relevance of Aristotle's view to division within the natural world, because Aristotle had learnt about it from practical common people, such as hunters and fishermen.[54] To Niphus, therefore, Aristotle's criticism of Plato is relevant within this practical world, but does not apply to logic and metaphysics.

Niphus is well known for being Platonizing, but others took a position very similar to his. In his commentary on the *De partibus animalium* published in Venice in 1574, three years after Cæsalpinus's *Peripateticæ quæstiones*, Daniel Furlan seems close to Niphus's view. Furlan was reluctant to concede that Aristotle in the *Metaphysics* 7 text 43 completely rejected the notion of bipartite division, although he did admit that Aristotle kept its use within narrow confines. He also sustained that there was no contradiction between the *Metaphysics* and the *De partibus animalium*, because, in complete contrast to Cæsalpinus, he understood Aristotle to have talked about essential *differentiæ* in the former work and about accidental *differentiæ* in the latter.[55]

---

[54] Augustinus Niphus, *Expositiones in omnes Aristotelis libros. De historia animalium lib. ix. De partibus animalium et earum causis. lib. iiii. Ac De generatione animalium lib. v*, Venice: apud Hieronymum Scotum, 1546, p. 19: "Boethius quidem locutus est de diuisione secundum sui naturam, atque quo ad rationem logicam et metaphysicam rationem, et uerum dicit quoniam cum diuisio omnis sit per opposita et oppositio non cadit nisi inter duo, recte dixit diuisionem debere fieri per duo aut per ea quæ reduci posssunt ad duo. Sed quia Plato locutus est de diuisione animalium, ut facit ad scientiam naturalem de eis, et non ad logicam uel metaphysicam, recte Aristoteles eum refutauit, cum diuisio quæ fit per duo transcendat rationem physicam ac uulgarem, per quam animalia uult exponere. Accepit enim Aristoteles scientiam de animalibus non a metaphysicis uel logicis, sed a uulgaribus, quia uel a piscatoribus uel a uenatoribus uel a pastoribus uel ab iis qui mundum et syluas et loca ferina peragrarunt, qui non metaphysici uel logici fuerunt."

[55] Daniel Furlan, *In libros Aristotelis De partibus animalium commentarius primus*, Venice: apud Ioan. Baptistam Somaschum, 1574, especially pp. 260-1: "In septimo Metaphysicorum libro quæstionem arduam de rei quæ definienda suscipitur natura, discutit Aristoteles... Quibus uerbis aperte demonstrat in definitione extremam differentiam esse, quæ rei essentia est; superiores autem esse superuacaneas quæ sententia nostræ huic non aduersatur, in qua statuit unam extremam satis non esse, sed plures alias afferendas, et ipsas extremas. Aduersaretur autem alioquin, si dixisset species ab una differentia extrema tantum constitui. Sed quoniam hoc etiam sentit Aristoteles, et eo in loco tacite intelligit, non est dicendum

Thus Niphus and Furlan agreed that Aristotle's criticism of bipartite division is limited and that the *differentiæ* used in natural history are accidental, not essential. This is clearly distinct from the approach of Cæsalpinus. His project was to be able to treat the natural world as a proper object for study at a strictly scientific level, and for this he needed to establish essential differences in the material world.

Among modern students of Aristotle, it is a point of dispute whether his system of division allows classification; D. M. Balme thinks that it does not.[56] More recently, Andrea Falcon has argued that it is true that Aristotle did not himself use his system of division for classification, but exclusively for definition; on the other hand, he finds that there is nothing in Aristotle's approach which precludes classification.[57]

Cæsalpinus clearly concluded that a division performed simultaneously from many *differentiæ* will lead to a form of classification while, for instance, Niphus evidently thought that classification was not the purpose of division. Discussing Aristotle's rejection of the Platonic bipartite division, he observed that he did not see it as a problem if division has the effect that one animal through different *differentiæ* ends up being placed in two or more separate *genera*.[58]

To my knowledge Jacob Schegius (1511-87) is the sixteenth-century author who comes closest to Cæsalpinus in accepting the universal validity of Aristotle's criticism of bipartite division. In his commentary on the *Topica*, he makes a digression and comments at length on our passage from the *De partibus animalium*, and reads it firmly as a rejection of bipartite division as a method of obtaining *differentiæ* for one's definitions.[59]

---

quæstionem illam definire Platonicorum sequentem placita. Nam cum in iis libris sit, qui omnium sunt exquisitissimi, absurdum est eam præsertim quæstionem quæ ad essentiam et quid est pertinet, in qua potissimum primus philosophus est occupatus, ita soluere. Sed hoc in loco de accidentariis et extremis differentiis loqui, in Metaphysica autem de forma et essentia, quam una tantum differentia significat."

[56] D. M. Balme, "Aristotle's use of differentiae in zoology", in *Articles on Aristotle*, ed. J. Barnes et al.. vol 1, London 1975, 183-93.

[57] Falcon 1997, note 52 above.

[58] Niphus 1546, p. 16: "Sed non uidetur absurdum genus unum per differentias diuersas reponi in diuersis generibus ut ranam, quæ ponitur in genere terrestrium cum quiescat in terra et in genere aquatilium cum cibum accipiat in aqua."

[59] *Perfecta et absoluta definiendi ars, ab Aristotele tractata ex exposita sexto Topicorum, qui est de definitione et septimo qui est de eodem et alio libris*, Tübingen, apud uiduam Ulrici Morhardi, 1556, pp. 112-20, on Topica Book 6, text 35.

Eckhard Keßler[60] has suggested that Schegius might be an interesting place to begin looking for an Aristotelian interest in division; and indeed this has proved to be right; it is also obvious that Schegius's remarks are directed against Ramus. While I have not yet found any striking similarities between Cæsalpinus's discussion of the relevant passage from the *De partibus animalium* and Schegius's, a connection cannot be excluded.

Cæsalpinus's use of division for classification rather than solely for definition is connected with the practical situation which he wanted to address. With the influx of plants from the Indies, plant *species* no longer constituted a finite number which could, at least in theory, be individually defined. Cæsalpinus's system of classification aimed also at being comprehensive of plants not yet discovered. This is where classification, and not merely definition, through division by *genera* and non-ultimate *differentiæ* comes into its own. When confronted by a previously undescribed plant, one would be able to place it within the system and at least give it a generic name, even if one did not know its *species*.[61] The predictive value of a classification system is, in fact, a central criterion in modern considerations on plant taxonomy.[62]

It is in the natural world that Cæsalpinus finds the proof of his view that division has to be performed simultaneously from many *differentiæ*. If one were to define by only one *ultima differentia*, all plants would belong to one *species*, all animals which can move would belong to one: the lion and the dog would belong to one *species*: for there is only one vegetative soul and only one sensitive soul. By rejecting the notion of an *ultima differentia* and by steering completely clear of bipartite division, Cæsalpinus could create his classification of plants, but this principle would not have been sufficient for him to create a scientific and systematic approach to plant classification and description. We have seen how his account of the physical parts of plants as instruments of the soul enabled him to regard them as essential *differentiæ*, not as *accidentia*, whether *separabilia* or *inseparabilia*, thus providing a solution which had ramifications far beyond the description of plants. This willingness to regard the physical reality as

---

[60] Kessler 1997, cf. note 42 above, p. 138.

[61] Cæsalpinus 1583, sig. a₄r: "Ad memoriam autem pollet quoniam in compendio sub generibus ordinatis clauditur pene immensus plantarum numerus, adeo ut et quæ antea numquam uisæ sunt, unicuique liceat in suam classem redigere, et, si innominata sit, nomine sui generis appellare."

[62] See e.g. C. Jeffrey, *An Introduction to Plant Taxonomy*, 2nd edn., Cambridge 1982, 44-5.

part of the legitimate realm of study for the philosopher is characteristic for his thought.

As long ago as 1860, in his disputation on the salient points in Cæsalpinus's philosophy, Carl Johan Sundström focused on Cæsalpinus's view that *materia* as a *subjectum* is *corpus quatenus corpus*.[63] Although he does not refer to Sundström, Carlo Colombero has more recently taken a similar view of *materia* in Cæsalpinus's philosophy.[64] Both Sundström and Colombero based their descriptions of Cæsalpinus's thought on question 7 of book four of the *Peripateticæ questiones* entitled: "Materiam primam corpus esse quatenus corpus". There Cæsalpinus argued against the notion that *materia* is potentiality, stating that this would lead to the view that in *composita* there would not be both *materia* and *forma*, but only *forma*, because *potentia* becomes actuality, rather than being compounded with it.[65] Cæsalpinus maintains that *materia* is a *subjectum*, not composed of act

---

[63] Carl Johan Sundström, *Framställning af hufvudpunkterna i Andreae Cesalpini Filosofi. Akademisk Afhandling som, med tillstånd af Vidtberömda Filosofiska Fakulteten i Upsala för Filosofiska Gradens erhållanda kommer att offentligen försvaras ... 19 Maj 1860*, Uppsala 1860, 12: "Betragtar man åter materiens actus, så är hon något absolut och en substans i sitt slag, derföre snarare subjekt än materia, ehuru fullkomligare eller ofullkomligare, alltefter som hon är närmare eller mera aflägsen från ändamålet. Hvad är nu detta enkla, som utgör det i all vexling permanenta, eller hvad är, närmare bestämd, den första materien såsom subjekt? Cæsalpinus svarar, att hon är kroppen i allmänhet, kroppen, försåvidt han är kropp, utan någon bestämd qualitet, endast bestämd genom utsträckningen i rummets tre dimensioner." (Again, if one looks at the *actus* of the *materia*, then *materia* is something absolute and in its way a *substantia*, and is therefore rather subject than *materia*, although more or less perfectly so according to how far the *materia* is from its final goal. Now, what is this one thing which constitutes permanency in all change, or more exactly what is the first *materia* seen as subject? Cæsalpinus answers that it is body in general, body in so far as it is body, without any specific actuality, only determined by its of extension in the three dimensions of space").

[64] In his article "Il pensiero filosofico di A. Cesalpino", *Rivista critica di storia della filosofia*, 32 (1977), 269-84, especially at pp. 282-4 where he paraphrases sections of Cesalpino's *Quæstio* 7,4; Colombero sees Cæsalpinus's view as a development of an opinion discussed but rejected by Simon Portius in his *De rerum naturalium principiis... Libri duo quibus plurimæ eæque haud contemnendæ quæstiones naturales explicantur*, Naples: excudebat Matthias Cancer, 1553. Colombero also hints at some interesting comparisons between Cæsalpinus's and Bernardinus Telesius's view of *materia*.

[65] Cæsalpinus 1571, fol. 84v: "Nullum igitur alium actum materiæ primæ esse putauerunt quam ipsam potentiam ... Sed et hæc sententia patitur difficultates ... Præterea materia pars est compositi, ut æs æneæ statuæ (3. Phys. 66) At potentia in actum transit non componitur cum actu ut uisus in speciem quæ uidetur et intellectus in id quod intelligitur. Non ergo duæ essent naturæ in compositis, materia scilicet et forma, sed forma tantum, ut iis contingit quæ sine materia sunt."

and potentiality, but having being *ex actu* in so far as it is viewed as a *subjectum*, and as *potentia* in so far as it viewed as receiving the *forma*, which is the cause for its existence.⁶⁶ Having discussed various possibilities, Cæsalpinus concludes that *corpus* is *substantia materialis* with actual existence and knowable to the senses.⁶⁷

Sundström noted that Cæsalpinus's interpretation of *materia* is far removed from that which he, as a nineteenth-century philosopher, read as Aristotle's view; but he also pointed out, with Heinrich Ritter, that Cæsalpinus's notion of *materia* was the beginning of Descartes's account of the general qualities of corporeal substances.⁶⁸ It remains to be fully explored if there is a historical link forward to the seventeenth century, to Cartesianism, or the scientific revolution, but it is evident that along with the rejection of bipartite division Cæsalpinus's view of *materia* is fundamental for his insistence on regarding the physical manifestations of nature as an integral part of the philosophical domain; it is equally clear that this was a consistent part of his philosophy and that ultimately this enabled him to classify plants according to physical features, seen as essential *differentiæ*.

The practical effect of his approach is explained in book 1, chapter 13 of the *De plantis*.⁶⁹ Here Cæsalpinus briefly reassumed his arguments now with plants firmly in mind. If you define by *ultima differentia* and believe that only the *forma* of the plant's soul can be the basis for discovering its *ultima differentia*, then you would end up by having to think of all plants

---

⁶⁶ Cæsalpinus 1571, fol. 85r: "Nos igitur dicimus primam materiam ultimum esse subiectum in quod resoluuntur transmutabilia quatenus transmutabilia sunt; neque componi amplius ex actu et potentia; esset enim generabilis; esse autem partim actu partim potentia; actu quidem quatenus subiectum quoddam est; potentia autem quatenus respicit perfectiones ad quas ordinatum est; earum enim gratia est, non per se ipsum. Cum igitur consideratur potentia, informis et inaffecta est ... Cum autem consideratur eius actus, absolutum quiddam est et substantia sui generis, ideo subiectum potius quam materia."

⁶⁷ Cæsalpinus 1571, fol. 87r: "Dicimus igitur corpus ut corpus esse substantiam materialem et actu existentem et sensui notam."

⁶⁸ Sundström 1860, 12: "Ritter anmärker, at i Cæsalpini och de följande Peripatetikernas lära om denna materiens allmänna natur ligga fröen til Cartesi lära om utsträckningen såsom den allmänna egenskapen hos den kroppsliga substansen"; "Ritter notes that Cæsalpinus and later Aristotelians in their doctrine of the general nature of *materia* provide the seed for Descartes's doctrine of the extent as well as the general quality of bodily substance"; Sundström refers to "H. Ritter, *Geschichte der Philosophie* Theil 9, p. 654ff. l.c. sid. 66."

⁶⁹ Cæsalpinus 1583, pp. 26-8.

as belonging to the same *species*.⁷⁰ The first function of the vegetative soul is nutrition; roots, shoots, and stems are instruments of the soul in this respect and can form the basis of division according to their firmness and their number. The second function is reproduction, and the chief instrument of the vegetative soul is here the fruit and its seeds. They are the basis for establishing the *genera* of plants.⁷¹ The number of seeds, their position, and their form are the most important elements in Cæsalpinus's scheme of division;⁷² and having established them as essential *differentiæ* of the vegetative soul he can begin a scientific division of plants into *genera* and *species*.

Cæsalpinus's reassessment of the role of the natural world within the philosophy of nature had clear consequences for the position of the study of plants, and ultimately of other areas of study in relation to other academic disciplines, in particular medicine. His book on plants contains frequent critical remarks about the attitude of *medici*; for instance he rejected Dioscorides's order of dealing with plants on the ground that it was suitable for a physician but not for a philosopher.⁷³ He was engaged in an attempt to establish the study of plants as a scientific study; and he saw that in doing so he had to make it distinct from medicine. The possible practical uses of the findings of a discipline is accidental to it and do not determine its scientific structure.⁷⁴ It is not by chance that for Cæsalpinus in this context the central text of the Aristotelian corpus was the *De partibus animalium*, and neither Theophrastus's nor the pseudo-Aristotelian works on plants, for in the *De partibus animalium* Aristotle discussed the causality of the parts of animals, and was therefore engaged

---

⁷⁰ Cæsalpinus 1583, p. 27: "Alii differentias secundum formam ex anima tantum colligi oportere putantes, coguntur fateri omnes plantas unius speciei esse, cum unicam animæ partem, quæ uegetatiua appellatur, sortitæ [*ed.* sorbitæ] sint omnes. At ostensum illud quoque est, differentias formam constituentes etiam ex materia, quæ illius gratia data est, colligi oportere; si igitur in plantis indifferentes essent partes ad operationes secundum illam animæ partem præstandas, una esset omnium plantarum species."

⁷¹ Cæsalpinus 1583, p. 28: "Et merito ex modo fructificandi multa emerserunt plantarum genera: in nullis enim aliis partibus tantam organorum multitudinem et distinctionem natura molita est."

⁷² Cæsalpinus 1583, p. 29: "Cum ad organorum constitutionem tria maxime faciant, scilicet partium numerus, situs, et figura ... natura secundum illorum differentias in fructibus condendis multis modis lusit, ex quibus uaria plantarum genera constituta sunt."

⁷³ Cæsalpinus 1583, sig. a₄r.

⁷⁴ Cæsalpinus 1583, p. 26, cf. note 38 above.

with universally valid observations, not with their application to particular instances.

In 1592 the Bohemian writer Adam Zaluzansky took this topic up again. He argued that while tradition demanded that the study of plants — he calls it *herbaria* — was dealt with as part of medicine, the law of method demanded that it should become a separate discipline, for no discipline should be confused with its practical use.[75] The incipient separation of plant studies as an independent and scientific discipline thus seems to be firmly placed in the Aristotelian world of the sixteenth-century.

This philosophical view of medicine as unscientific, and the proposal of ways of finding a scientific way of studying subjects which had hitherto been medical *Hilfswissenschaften* is in many ways parallel to Zabarella's view of a *scientia naturalis*, as it has been explained by Heikki Mikkeli.[76]

Two Paduan students of anatomy followed paths similar to the one which Cæsalpinus had indicated for the study of plants, that of establishing a philosophically sound anatomical science distinct from any practical medical use to which it might be put. This has been discussed by Mikkeli with regard to the Paduan physician Hieronymus Capivacceus whose treatise *De methodo anatomica* first appeared in 1593;[77] while Andrew Cunningham has written about the "Aristotle project" of Hieronymus Fabricius de Aquapendente.[78] We find that Cæsalpinus's approach to a

---

[75] I have consulted not the first edition of 1592, but rather *Methodi herbariæ libri tres*, Frankfurt am Main: e collegio Paltheniano, 1604; sig. B₁r: "Herbariæ nomine uulgo comprehenditur permista et confusa quædam plantarum ac medendi doctrina. Quare nequid instituto deesse uideatur de utraque ea arte separatim dicendum est. Medicinam enim herbariæ connectere consuetudo coegit, separatim uero utramque tradere methodi lex exigit. Omnium enim artium doctrina ab uso suo disiungenda et separanda est."

[76] Heikki Mikkeli, "The foundation of an autonomous natural philosophy: Zabarella on the classification of arts and sciences", in *Method and Order in Renaissance Philosophy of Nature*, ed. Daniel A. Di Liscia, Eckhard Kessler, and Charlotte Methuen, Aldershot 1997, 211-28, esp. 221-2; Heikki Mikkeli, *An Aristotelian Response to Renaissance Humanism: Jacopo Zabarella on the Nature of Arts and Sciences*, Helsinki 1992, 165.

[77] Mikkeli 1992, 156-7.

[78] Andrew Cunningham, "Fabricius and the Aristotle project in anatomical teaching and research at Padua", in *The Medical Renaissance of the Sixteenth Century*, ed A. Wear, R. K. French, and I. M. Lonie, Cambridge 1985, 195-222; see also Andrew Cunningham, *The Anatomical Renaissance: The Resurrection of the Anatomical Projects of the Ancients*, Aldershot 1997 and Nicholas Jardine, "Keeping order in the School of Padua", in *Method and Order in Renaissance Philosophy of Nature*, ed. Daniel A. Di Liscia, Eckhard Kessler, and Charlotte Methuen, Aldershot 1997, 183-209, at 205.

scientific discipline of plant studies was thus in the forefront of a much broader move towards redefining the relationship between medicine and the natural sciences. Like anatomy, the study of plants had hitherto been considered practical and unscientific occupations, subordinate to medicine. Along lines later to be explored in anatomical studies by Capivacceus and Fabricius, Cæsalpinus established an approach to the study of plants which could ensure a basis for a new philosophical acceptance of the study of the natural world.

Caspar Bartholin

by Sten Ebbesen

1 Introduction
Caspar Bartholin was a Danish Aristotelian of the early seventeenth century. In this article I will try to assess how far he was from his medieval scholastic predecessors, or, in other words: are the notions of "renaissance" and "modernity" useful concepts in an attempt to understand his work.

2 Vita[1]
Anyone who ever took an interest in the learned Denmark of the seventeenth century knows the Bartholins. They were a dynasty of professors, and being a member of the dynasty was an important qualification for achieving a professorship at the University of Copenhagen. Lack of that qualification was among the reasons why the greatest Danish scientist of the century, Nicholas Steno, did not obtain a chair in his home country. The founder of the dynasty was one Caspar Bartholin, who lived from 1585 till 1629. Little Caspar received a good training in Latin and, it is claimed, also in Greek, before being matriculated at the university of Copenhagen in 1603.

In 1604 Caspar went abroad with a modest grant from the chapter of Lund. It probably played a role that his father was a pastor in Malmø, which belonged to the diocese of Lund. He only returned seven years later after studies in several seats of learning in the Empire, the Netherlands, and in Italy. During his first year abroad he came to Wittenberg and became a pupil of Jacobus Martini (1570-1649). To supplement his meagre travel grant he soon began to teach various philosophical subjects, and he continued to do so for several years both in Wittenberg and in other places to which his travels took him. In 1610 he became a doctor of medicine in Basle and the following year he returned to Denmark, became professor of

---

[1] Brief biography with ample information about editions of C. Bartholin's philosophical works in Ch. Lohr, *Latin Aristotle Commentaries II: Renaissance Authors*, Firenze 1988, 34-35. More extensive biography in *Dansk Biografisk Leksikon*, 3rd ed., Copenhagen 1979, 1: 470-472. For bibliography, see also W. Risse 1998.

Latin, married the daughter of a professor of medicine, and was soon himself promoted to the more lucrative post of professor of medicine. In 1624 he switched to a chair in theology. On his death in 1629 he left five sons, three of whom were to become professors at his own university.

3 Opera

In his early youth when he earned his keep by teaching philosophy, Bartholin produced brief manuals of logic and metaphysics which were published in Strassburg and Basle in 1608. Later followed similar compendia of physics and ethics. The book on physics (1625) seems to have obtained only one printing,[2] but the others were frequently reprinted. One occasion for reprints was a royal order of 1619 that Bartholin produce school books of philosophy – i.e. his books were given a preferential treatment in the Danish educational system. But Royal Danish favour does not suffice to explain the many printings. In the first half of the seventeenth century the market for Bartholin's books seems to have comprised large parts of protestant Europe.

I shall concentrate on the logical works, but first a word about the compendium of metaphysics, the *Enchiridion Metaphysicum* from 1608.[3] Before the actual beginning of the work, Bartholin dresses a list of "the names of those who by their writings have illuminated the *Metaphysics* and have reached our hands."[4]

The occurrence of a number of post-medieval names, such as Timpler,[5] is unsurprising. But notice that both Averroes and several well-known scholastic thinkers also turn up: Alexander of Hales,[6] Albert the Great, Thomas Aquinas, Giles of Rome, John Duns Scotus, Antonius Andreæ,

---

[2] *Enchiridion physicum.* Books of his with such titles as *Physicae generalis præcepta, Physicae specialis præcepta* (several editions each) and *Systema physicum* (1628) may be suspected of being at least partly identical with the *Enchiridion,* but I have not checked on this. Bibliography in Risse 1998, vol. 6.

[3] I have used the edition from Strassburg 1625.

[4] On a page before p. 1: "Nomina eorum qui Metaphysicam scriptis illustrarunt, & ad manus nostras pervenerunt."

[5] Clemens Timpler's *Metaphysicae systema methodicum* was printed 1604, 1606, 1607 and 1608 (Risse 1998, 3: 30-32).

[6] Alexander of Hales wrote no commentary on the *Metaphysics,* but that of Alexander of Alexandria (1270-1314) soon became attributed to him and was printed under his name in Venice 1572. See Ch. Lohr, "Medieval Latin Aristotle Commentaries", *Traditio,* 23 (1967), 354; Risse 1998, 3: 23.

Walter Burley,[7] Paul of Venice.[8] Moreover, two of the post-medieval figures mentioned were thinkers steeped in scholastic learning, Nifo and Suarez.

Three Greeks are included in the list: Alexander of Aphrodisias,[9] Philoponus[10] and Michael Psellus. There is nothing un-medieval about using Greek Aristotle commentaries, only in the case of the *Metaphysics* no relevant work was available before the sixteenth century. It remains to be investigated whether these Greeks had any significant effect on the contents of Bartholin's work, and if so, whether their influence contributed to distancing it from the medieval tradition.

I doubt that Bartholin had really read all the authors he names, though he claims that they had reached his hands. For instance, it is a little suspicious that he calls John Philoponus "Philoponeus", and his mention of Psellus is very suspicious. No *Metaphysics* commentary is attested, and the most frequently printed work of his in the sixteenth century seems to have been *De daemonibus*.[11] Anyhow, the clear message of Bartholin's list of authors is one of continuity: Greeks, Latins and Arabs from all ages have done serious work on metaphysics.

Now to logic. The publishing history of Bartholin's logical works is a little complicated, but basically they are two. One is called *The Doorkeepers* or *Dooropeners (Janitores) of Logic*. It consists of one treatise on the nature of logic and another on Porphyry's five universals. The other work is an *Enchiridion Logicæ* which already in Bartholin's own time

---

[7] Ch. Lohr, "Medieval Latin Aristotle Commentaries", *Traditio*, 24 (1968), 179 lists no printed edition of Burley's commentary on the *Metaphysics*, but has the entry "G. Burlaeus, *Metaphysicales quaestiones et defensiones Thomae Aquinatis* (Venezia 1494) (GW V 681: not authentic)".

[8] Ch. Lohr, "Medieval Latin Aristotle Commentaries", *Traditio* 28 (1972), 318 knows no edition of Paul of Venice's *Metaphysics* commentary, nor does Risse 1998. The work meant could be Paul's *Metaphysicarum disputationum summa*, printed in Paris 1521 (Risse 1998, 3: 12).

[9] Risse 1998, vol. 3 mentions 1527, 1536, 1544, 1551, and 1561 editions of the Latin translation of Alexander's *Metaphysics* commentary.

[10] Actually Pseudo-Philoponus. For this work, see S. Ebbesen, *Commentators and Commentaries on Aristotle's Sophistici Elenchi. A Study of Post-Aristotelian Ancient and Medieval Writings on Fallacies* (Corpus Latinum Commentariorum in Aristotelem Graecorum VII.1-3), Leiden 1981, 3: 86-87. A Latin translation by F. Patrizzi appeared in 1583.

[11] Risse 1998, vol. 1.

appeared in several versions. It incorporates most of the material from the *Doorkeepeers* and contains new chapters on matters not treated there.¹²

4 Sources

I have done no independent research on the sources used by Bartholin, so I will have to trust Wilhelm Risse who in 1964 passed a devastating judgement on my compatriot:¹³

> Martinis Schüler Bartholinus schrieb dann in seinen äusserst bescheidenen, aber viel gelesenen Lehrbüchern lediglich aus besseren Werken ab. Er behauptet zwar, durch eklektische Blütenlese die Logik zu bereichern. Tatsächlich verkümmern bei ihm aber alle Probleme zu einem dürftigen Vokabular. Zugleich verschwimmen die Lehrunterschiede der Schulen, und gegensätzliche Lehrstücke gelten als miteinander verträglich.

Immediately before this section on Bartholin, Risse has a longer one on the logic of Cornelius Martini (1568-1621), and comparison of his report on Martini with the contents of Bartholin's works leaves no doubt about the dependence. Cornelius Martini had been the teacher of the Jacobus Martini (no relative) under whom Bartholin studied, so there is little doubt where Bartholin got his ideas about whom to imitate.¹⁴ Cornelius Martini was a professed anti-Ramist, and Bartholin also became one. This fact should weigh heavily in his favour. Ramism was a major threat to real logic. It is usually thought to have died out in Denmark shortly after 1600, but as late as 1640 a Danish-trained bishop introduced the use of Ramus' *Dialectica* in the cathedral school of Skálholt in Iceland (then under the Danish crown). Bartholin deserves credit for having assisted in exorcizing the evil

---

¹² *Janitores Logici Bini*. First edition, s.l., 1607. I have seen the editions from Copenhagen 1622 and Strassburg 1624. No apparent differences. I have used the Copenhagen edition.

Enchiridion Logicæ, first edition Strassburg 1608. I have used the (perhaps slightly revised) edition entitled *Logica Maior*, Copenhagen 1625; for this work I shall use the abbreviation *LM*.

Logicæ Peripateticæ Præcepta. First edition, s.l., 1609. I have seen the Strassburg 1629 edition. Apparently the work is just an abbreviation of the *Enchiridion*.

¹³ W. Risse, *Die Logik der Neuzeit*, Stuttgart/Bad-Cannstatt 1964, 458.

¹⁴ The extracts from Jacobus Martini's logic printed in Risse 1964, 1: 501ff. show several points of agreement with Bartholin, so it seems possible that the latter depended only indirectely on Cornelius Martini.

spirit of Peter Ramus, even though he was not totally successful at first – the Icelandic Ramist had been his personal pupil![15]

5 A Schoolman's View

I am now about to present you with the results of a reading of Bartholin's logic,[16] but first I have to switch persona and become a medieval scholar. He will be the speaker in the rest of section 5.

*

The ways of the Lord are inscrutable, and I am a manifest proof of this. My name is master Steno of Dacia. After studying a couple of years at Oxford I went to Paris and became a master of arts there in 1350. I next taught at the university of Paris for some years before returning to Denmark where I died here in Copenhagen in 1375.[17] I was, however, resuscitated in the present year 1625 after the incarnation of the Lord with the specific purpose that I read and comment on Dr Bartholin's logic. And in particular I am under the obligation to report whether or to which degree I feel it is a work from a different culture than my own. I have done my reading and I am now about to present my comments. I am aware that two hundred and fifty years have passed since my death but I know nothing about what has happened in the meantime except for a few facts that I could glean from Dr Bartholin's remarks, supplemented with a few pieces of information that I have obtained from my host, Dr Fincke,[18] in whose house I am now living. Dr – or as they say nowadays: Professor – Fincke teaches medicine; he happens to be the father-in-law of Dr Bartholin, and his own son also has a chair in the university of Copenhagen. Imagine: they have married university staff these days! Fincke is a nice man, though philosophically somewhat naive. About myself I may mention that I am quite well read in treatises on logic and Aristotle commentaries, both from my own century,

---

[15] See G. Hardarson, "Latin philosophy in 17th century Iceland", in M. Skafte Jensen, ed., *A History of Nordic Neo-Latin Literature*, Odense 1995, 302-308.
[16] The following is based on Bartholin's *Logica Maior [LM]*, supplemented with the *Janitores*.
[17] Master Steno's career is not a typical one. Few Danes went to Oxford; until the mid-fourteenth century many went to Paris, but afterwards they preferred the universities of the Empire.
[18] For the lives of Thomas Fincke (1561-1656) and his son Jacob (1592-1663), see *Dansk Biografisk Leksikon*, 3rd ed., Copenhagen 1980, 4: 398-399.

the fourteenth since God became man, and from the preceding two centuries. Needless to say, I know the Philosopher very well.[19]

Let me comment first on Dr Bartholin's Latin style. It is generally OK, though slightly affected, especially his vocabulary is somewhat funny. Why does he say *accidentarius* instead of *accidentalis*? Well, you can call things whatever you please – *voces sunt ad placitum* – but reasonable men follow Aristotle's advice in *Topics* II[20] and stick to common usage whenever possible. Does Dr Bartholin also say 'incidentary' instead of 'incidental'? Also, why on earth does he insist on saying *categoriæ* instead of *prædicamenta*? Of course, everybody knows that *kathegoria* is Greek for *prædicamentum*, but what's the purpose of dropping a good Latin word that has been used for centuries in favour of a Greek one? I just don't get the idea. He also writes a lot of words in Greek characters which, I admit, I cannot quite read. I wonder whether he can, or whether this is just pretence. He annoys me somewhat by being strangely lax in his terminology, using *synonymum* and *univocum* indiscriminately, even forming a syllogism in which one and the same term is now designated by means of the word 'synonymum', now by the means of 'univocum'. I have heard from Dr Fincke that such un-logical use of rhetorical devices was a characteristic of a certain Petrus Ramus from the sixteenth century, whom Dr Bartholin otherwise has the good sense to reject and combat. According to Dr Bartholin, the followers of Mr Ramus had the cheek to define logic as the art of speaking well: *ars bene disserendi*.[21] It seems that in spite of Dr Bartholin's rejection of this preposterous view of logic, he has not quite escaped being infected with the venom of rhetoric. Anyhow, he is not a hopeless case, I think. A little course in the importance of logical rigidity might make him all right.

I shall speak of the over-all structure of the work in a moment, but let me say a word about the manner of presentation. The work is divided into small sections, each starting with a concisely formulated theorem of logic

---

[19] Steno's ability to survey the history of his discipline for more than a hundred years is most unusual for a medieval schoolman.

[20] Cf. Aristotle, *Topics* 2.1.109a27-33, 2.2.110a12-22.

[21] *Janitores* I.vii.13 (172): "illam" *sc.* definitionem "Rameorum, quâ Logica definitur ars benè disserendi". The Ramists were inspired by Cicero's rendition, in *De oratore* 2.38.157, of a Stoic definition. Actually, some medievals accepted related formulations (without the 'bene'), but then their idea of how one ought to "disserere" was very different from Pierre de la Ramée's.

followed by a lengthier comment and explication of the theorem. Dr Bartholin shows bad form by repeatedly polemicizing against named opponents,[22] he ought to know that if you need to refute somebody's thesis you do not mention his name, you just call him 'some people' – *quidam* or *aliqui*. In my day some theologians had taken up this disgusting habit of ridiculing other masters, but I had hoped it would not spread to logic.[23] Anyhow, in the main, the format of Dr Bartholin's book is of a well-known type. I may remind you that John Buridan used the same way of presentation in his handbook of logic: first a chunk of the concise text of his own modification of Peter of Spain's *Summule Logicales*, then an exposition with discussion of important points.[24]

Now to the over-all structure. I have no difficulty in understanding the structure of Dr Bartholin's Logic. He simply follows the order of the *Organon*, moving from Porphyry' *Isagoge* to the *Sophistical Refutations* via *Categories, Perihermeneias, Prior* and *Posterior Analytics,* and *Topics*. Dr Bartholin disguises this slightly by means of a division into two parts: A "common" part about the form of syllogism, and a "proper" part about the matter of syllogism. I do not remember having seen another handbook of logic that claimed to have this bipartite structure,[25] though Dr Fincke claims that it derives from Averroes.[26] But at least it is no news that via the

---

[22] E.g., *LM* 5v: "In fumum ergo abit Kechermanni exceptiuncula."

[23] W. Courtenay, *Schools and Scholars,* Princeton 1987, 254-5 notes that naming of both predecessors and contemporaries spreads in English *Sentences* commentaries in the fourteenth century.

[24] John Buridan († ca. 1360) taught the arts at Paris from the 1320s till his death. His philosophical œuvre was to be tremendously influential in Central and Northern Europe. The date of his *Summulae* is a matter of dispute – dates from the 1320s to the 50s have been proposed. Under the general editorship of the present writer, the first printed edition is being published these years at Ingenium Publishers, Nijmegen, as vol. 10 of the series *Artistarium*, and with the title "Johannes Buridanus, *Summulae*". So far part 10-2 (*De praedicabilibus*, ed. L.M. de Rijk 1995) and 10-3 (*In Praedicamenta*, ed. E.P. Bos 1994), have appeared. Further fascicles are expected in 1999. The introductions in each fascicle contain extensive bibliographies.

[25] *Janitores* I, viii: "Commodissimè a Neotericis dividitur Logica in partem communem et propriam. Illa syllogismi formam, hæc materiam explicat." Almost identical formulation in *LM* 13r. *Neoterici* are the schoolmen; cf. Dominicus Soto, *Summulae,* Salamanca 1554 (rp. Hildesheim 1980), 1rA: "Primum autem, atque adeo individuum elementum quod ad rem pertinet, Dialecticæ est, quam grammatici dictionem, nos verò (ut neotericorum usui hoc nomen demus) dicamus terminum."

[26] Cf. *Commentarii Collegii Conimbricensis e Societate Jesu In universam dialecticam Aristotelis Stagiritæ,* Cologne 1607 (rp. Hildesheim 1976), col. 67: "Auerroes in præfatione

theories of terms and propositions you reach the doctrine of syllogistic form in the *Prior Analytics*, whereas the demonstrative, dialectical and sophistical syllogisms differ in matter because they have different sorts of premisses – necessary, probable or apparently probable as the case may be.[27] Furthermore, Dr Bartholin's division of the *Organon* into two parts yields almost the same result as the good old division into *Ars Vetus* and *Ars Nova*, as he is fully aware. He even explains why one part is called old and another one new; he thinks this is an old-fashioned way of saying first and subsequent, and in this respect he agrees with the great John Buridan, though he shows no awareness of the fact.[28] Finally, while stressing the

---

ad 1. Poster. distribuit Logicam in universalem, & particularem: universalem videtur appellare eam partem, in qua disserendi formæ nullius materiæ habitu respectu, absolutè proponuntur: quæ ideo communis censetur, quia ad omnem materiam est indifferens, & indeterminata, omnibusque accommodari potest. Hæc libris Prædicamentorum, Perihermenias, & de Priore resolutione ab Aristotele comprehenditur, & explanatur. Particularem vocat eam partem, quæ docet, quo pacto disserendi formulæ variis materiis, necessariis, probabilibus, & improbabilibus, seu falsis applicentur. Hanc partem complexus est Aristoteles duobus libris de Posteriore resolutione, octo de Topicis, & duobus de Sophismatis." Cf. Averroes, *Commentarii Magni in Analytica Posteriora*, in *Aristotelis Opera* I.2, Venice 1562 (rp. Frankfurt am Main 1962), f. 2v. This work of Averroes' was not available to the medievals. Bartholin seems to have inherited the distinction from Jacobus Martini; see W. Risse 1964, 1: 502.

[27] See, e.g., L.M. de Rijk, ed., *Anonymi auctoris franciscani Logica "Ad rudium"*, Nijmegen 1981, 93: "Argumenta servantia formam sillogisticam, cuiusmodi sunt sillogismi, sunt in duplici differentia. Quidam enim non concernunt materiam sed tantum formam, cuiusmodi est sillogismus simpliciter, idest non contractus ad certam et determinatam materiam sed solum ad certam et determinatam formam, de quo tractat Philosophus in Libro Priorum. Quidam autem sillogismi concernunt non solum formam, ymo etiam materiam. Et tales sunt in triplici differentia. Aliqui enim concernunt materiam necessariam; et isti vocantur sillogismi demonstrativi. Aliqui concernunt materiam probabilem; et isti vocantur sillogismi dialectici. Aliqui concernunt materiam apparentem; et isti vocantur sillogismi sophistici." This text dates from ca. 1335.

[28] *Janitores* I.viii.2: "Nam majores nostri quod prius erat solebant vetus vocare, quod posterius novum." Similarly *LM* 13v. Cf. Iohannes Buridanus, *Expositio Isagoges Porphyrii*, in: R. Tatarzynski, "Jan Buridan. Kommentarz do *Isagogi* Porfirisza", *Przeglad Tomistycny* 2 (1986), 111-195, at p. 123: "Quare autem haec dicitur Vetus Ars et illa Nova? Potest dici rationabiliter, quod materia rei praecedit tempore rem quae fit ex ea, et illud quod praecedit tempore dicitur antiquius. Modo termini et enuntiationes, de quibus agitur in libris *Praedicamentorum* et *Peri Hermeneias*, sunt partes materiales ex quibus fiunt argumentationes. Ideo possunt dici Veteres in respectu totalis argumentationis et ob hoc pars logicae tractans de eis vocata est Logica Vetus." In reality, the names are due to the fact that one part of the *Organon* became known to the Latins later than another. Notice that in the Middle Ages the *Prior Analytics* belonged to *Ars Nova*.

essential completeness of Aristotle's logic, Dr Bartholin – quite in accordance with a tradition established, I think, a century before my times – recognizes that not only Porphyry but also Gilbert the Porretan and Boethius made some useful additions to Aristotle's work.[29]

Oh, by the way, I notice that he also presents a division according to the mental activities involved: first there is the apprehension of simple objects *(simplicium comprehensio)*, that is concept-formation; next comes composition and separation of concepts, i.e. the formation of affirmative and negative propositions; and finally there is reasoning on the basis of such propositions. This corresponds to a division of the *Organon* into *Categories, Peri hermeneias* and the books on syllogistic, and it is one I know well from thirteenth-century works.[30] Dr Bartholin rejects the traditional divisions into prescriptive and applied logic and into inventive and judicative logic,[31] but at least in the former case his rejection is more verbal than real, for he does not deny that in one respect logic may be prescriptive and in another applied; it seems that all he wants to deny is that certain chunks of the *Organon* are prescriptive and others applied logic. In-

---

[29] *LM* 11r-v, after mentioning Archytas and other predecessors of Aristotle's: "Recentiores addiderunt nonnulla: Porphyrius doctrinam Universalium: Porretanus postpraedicamenta uberiùs explicata, Boëtius multa de definitione, divisione, et Syllogismis hypotheticis. Primus autem Aristoteles, magnum illud mundi miraculum, perfectam conscripsit logicam; et ab aliis confuse inventa collegit, explicavit, perfecit. Ramus invidiâ nescio quâ inflatus hanc laudem Aristoteli detrahere nititur." Cf. *Janitores* I.vii.2 (148). For a medieval presentation of the *Organon* and the auxiliary works, see, e.g., Radulphus Brito (1290s), *Prooemium in Quaestiones super logicam veterem,* in: S. Ebbesen & J. Pinborg, "Gennadios and Western Scholasticism. Radulphus Brito's *Ars Vetus* in Greek Translation", *Classica et Mediaevalia*, 33 (1981-82), 263-319, at p. 289 and pp. 301-305.

[30] *Janitores* I.viii.3: "Simplicium apprehensioni respondet Tractatus Categoriarum, Compositioni et divisioni liber de interpr. Ratiocinationi ex compositis et divisis uterque Analyticorum de syllogismo in genere." *LM* 94v, at the beginning of the section corresponding to *Perihermeneias*: "Hactenus instrumenta primæ operationis mentis: nunc secunda, quomodo nimirum res simpliciter apprehensæ coniungi vel invicem negari debeant." Cf., e.g.,Thomas Aquinas, *Expositio Analyticorum Posteriorum*, Prooemium; Simon of Faversham, *Quaestiones super Libro Elenchorum*, ed. S. Ebbesen, Th. Izbicki, J. Longeway, F. del Punta, E. Stump (Studies and Texts 60), Toronto 1984, at *QV* 1, p. 28: 103-111.

[31] *LM* 15r, *Janitores* I.ix. In *Janitores* Bartholin concludes: "Ideò autem spernenda" – sc. the distinction – "quia Logica docens et utens una eademque ars est, licet diverso respectu sit docens et utens." Bartholin uses the medieval terms *docens/utens* (cf. S. Ebbesen, "Logica docens/utens", *Historisches Wörterbuch der Philosophie* 5 (1980), 353-355, Basel). But he replaces the medieval pair *inventiva/iudicativa* with *inventrix/iudicatrix* in the distinction derived from Cicero, *Topics* II.6: "Omnis ratio diligens disserendi duas habet partis, unam inveniendi, alteram iudicandi."

terestingly, I notice that he ascribes the division to the blessed Thomas and to Scotus, and even refers to precise places in their works. Elsewhere he quotes Albert and Giles of Rome. So, at least some of the great thinkers of the thirteenth century continue to enjoy their well-deserved fame.[32] I miss, however, the names of some of the great logicians of my own century – where is Ockham, or Buridan? Can they really have fallen into oblivion? Perhaps he does not want to mention Ockham because he died excommunicate and impenitent.[33] But Buridan was never tainted with even a suspicion of heresy. Some traits of Dr Bartholin's works remind me of those two giants, and more generally of my own century. He strongly argues that logic is about concepts, mental entities that is, and not about extramental things or about linguistic entities. Vocal words are secondary to mental terms and we could have a logic without vocal words. He also stresses that logic is a mental disposition, a *habitus intellectualis*.[34] The word 'logic' is derived from the Greek *logos*, but it should be noted that *logos* is ambiguous as to mental and vocal *logos*. It is mental *logos* that is relevant for logic, he says.[35] That is reminiscent of Ockham and Buridan, but Dr

---

[32] The logical works attest to the same view of a continuous history of philosophy that we saw in the handbook of metaphysics (section 2, above). *Janitores* I.ii.11 (30) mentions Scotus and the Scotists, Thomas and the Thomists, Boethius, Albert, Fonseca, Toletus, Casus, Giles of Rome, Tartaretus, Javellus, and others. In I.ii.16 (80) we are referred to Boethius, Albert, Avicenna, Alfarabi, Alexander, Philoponus, Simplicius and Ammonius.

[33] See G. Gál, "William of Ockham Died Impenitent in April 1347", *Franciscan Studies*, 42 (1982), 90-95.

[34] *LM* 1r: "Logica est habitus intellectualis organicus a philosophis ex habitu philosophiae genitus, 2ᵃ noemata ex primis efficiens, ut sint instrumenta discernendi verum a falso." According to Risse 1964, 1: 502 "habitus intellectualis organicus" was Zabarella's definition of logic, and was also used by J. Martini. Bartholin's "secunda noemata ex primis effficiens" and similar formulations are rephrasings of the medieval "Logica est de secundis intentionibus adiunctis primis", an oft-repeated quotation of Avicenna. At *LM* 19r-v Bartholin treats *noema, notio, species, conceptus, imago* and *intentio* as synonyms and tries to explain what first and second intentions are. Ockham had expressed himself as follows in *Expositionis ad libros artis logicae prooemium*, ed. E. Moody, in Guillelmi de Ockham Opera philosophica II, St. Bonaventure 1978, 7: "ista scientia, saltem principaliter, tradit notitiam conceptuum vel intentionum per animam fabricatarum [...] Et hinc est quod ista scientia dicitur rationalis."

[35] *LM* 1v. *Janitores* I.i.1: "Logica autem ratiocinandi, non sermocinandi ars est. Duplex est enim λόγος: ενδιαθετος, ad quem Logica (potest enim intus quis secum ratiocinari &c.) & προφορικὸς, ad quem Grammatica et Rhetorica." For a thirteenth-century statement of the same distinction, see, e.g., Simon of Faversham, *op. cit.*, QN 1.21-23, p. 104 (w. footnote): "Logica enim est de actu rationis. Unde et logica dicitur rationalis scientia, logica enim non dicitur a "logos" quod est sermo, sed a "logos" quod est ratio – "logos" enim est

Bartholin lacks all the resolute consistency with which they followed up on the claim that both terms, propositions and the art of logic are mental entities. He shows some determination when he wants to read *ratio* instead of *oratio* in the definition of a syllogism: According to him a syllogism is primarily a thought or reasoning, not an utterance.[36] True enough, but I think he goes too far here, for the 'utterance' should, of course, be understood as a piece of mental language. Anyhow, the affinity to Ockham and Buridan totally disappears and he sounds much more like someone from the late thirteenth century when he says that in Aristotle's *Categories* "things are not considered insofar as they are – for to look at them that way is the metaphysician's job – but in logic they are considered insofar as they are predicated".[37] If he really means that, he must take concepts and extramental things to be fundamentally identical. Actually, he must accept the notion of a common nature which can have two modes of being, such that *qua* existing it is extramental and *qua* object of thought it is a concept. That was a common view in the late thirteenth century, and it could also be found in my own, but it certainly was not the view of Ockham or Buridan.

A minor point in Dr Bartholin's table of contents intrigued me when I first saw it. He called the first section of his first part "On categoremes and categories" as if 'categoreme' were another word for 'predicable' or 'universal', and when I got to the relevant point in the text it turned out that this is indeed what he thinks.[38] Doesn't he know that a categoreme is a word that signifies constituents of reality as opposed to such function-words as 'every' 'begins' and the other syncategoremes? Actually, he seems to have no concept of syncategoremes. Strange!

---

aequivocum apud Graecos." For the role of mental language in Ockham, see Cl. Panaccio, "La philosophie du language de Guillaume d'Occam", in: S. Ebbesen, ed., *Sprachtheorien in Spätantike und Mittelalter* (Geschichte der Sprachtheorie 3), Tübingen 1995, 184-206.

[36] *LM* 126v-127r: "Syllogismus est ratio, in quâ [...] Alii in definitione explicant λόγον per Orationem. At sciendum 1. veritatem priùs esse in ratione. 2. syllogismum esse rationis potiùs instrumentum. 3. eumque sæpe fieri à tacente."

[37] *Janitores* I.viii.6 (185): "Dicendum ergò res in Categoriis à logico considerari non quatenus sunt (quod Metaphysici est) sed quatenus prædicantur."

[38] The section title is *De categorematis et categoriis*. The equation of categoremes and predicables occurs in *LM* 17v: "Quare autem Categorematum seu Prædicabilium Tractatus Categoriis loco præponi debeat, secùs quàm nonnulli factitant, in fine capitis primi dicemus." For the medieval notions of categoremes and syncategoremes, see N. Kretzmann, "Syncategoremata, exponibilia, sophismata" in: N. Kretzmann, A. Kenny & J. Pinborg (eds.), *The Cambridge History of Later Medieval Philosophy*, Cambridge 1982, 211-245.

Another minor point that has intrigued me is his inclusion, in the section on demonstration, of a treatment of method, definition and division. Now, already the great Buridan included definition and division when he decided to add a treatise on demonstration to the topics treated by Peter of Spain in the *Summule*,³⁹ but it took me some time to figure out what Dr Bartholin means by *method* here. It turns out that in a strict sense, method for him is simply demonstrative proof, but in wider sense it comprises the ordering of the parts of a science or art. He refers to a great debate between someone called Zabarella and a Mr Piccolomineus (barbaric names! Why can't they be called something decent like Francis or James?), the former holding that what is better known to us should come first, the latter being in favour of the natural order. Dr Bartholin tries to get the best of two worlds by first voting for nature, then saying that the limitations of human understanding may make the other order necessary.⁴⁰ Big deal! In my century and the one before it this was not the sort of thing we would discuss at length in handbooks of logic, but of course the subject would be touched on in proems to Aristotle commentaries and when commenting on the passages in *Physics I* and *Posterior Analytics I* where Aristotle distinguishes between what is prior to nature and what is prior to us.

I have no time for a detailed review of the main body of Dr Bartholin's book, his summaries, that is, of the doctrine of the *Organon*. Suffice it to say that I have found no radically new ways of looking upon things, in fact just about everything sounds very familiar, not so much because it reminds me of my own contemporaries but because it reminds me of the logic books of some three to four generations before me. You find old rules like "An analogical term used alone stands for its best-known significate",⁴¹ and you find an understanding of whole subdisciplines of logic that is very much like what was standard a hundred years before my time. Let me exemplify:

---

³⁹ Treatise 8 of Buridan's *Summulae*, is *De definitionibus, divisionibus et demonstrationibus*; it has no counterpart in Peter of Spain. An edition by L.M. de Rijk is to appear soon (cf. note 24).

⁴⁰ The long chapter (Pars Propria, I. viii) *De methodo et ordine* is found in *LM* 194r-205r.

⁴¹ *LM* 46r: "Regula de analogia: Analogum per se positum stat pro suo significato famosiori". The rule was a thirteenth-century creation; cf. the quotations in Ebbesen 1981, 3: 257-8.

The doctrine of Aristotle's *Topics* is interpreted in the light of Boethius' doctrine in his *On Topical Differences*,[42] and – most interestingly – Dr Bartholin not only employs Boethius' distinction between a topical difference, which is the name of some set of correlative terms, say "opposites" or "cause and effect", and on the other hand a topical maxim, say "if an effect is posited, its cause must also be posited" – not only that, but he also sees the thirteen fallacies of the *Sophistical Refutations* as so many topics, their names – equivocation, amphiboly etc. – being topical differences, while the maxims are such propositions as "Where there is the same word or sentence, there is the same sense and signification".[43] This is an interpretation of the fallacies that I know only from thirteenth-century sources. Fun to see that it has had a come-back. Not surprisingly, Dr Bartholin uses Alexander of Aphrodisias' distinction between materially and formally false arguments in his interpretation of the very first sentence of the *Sophistical Refutations*. That is what people had been doing for at least two hundred years when I lived. What does surprise me, however, is his total neglect of Alexander's classification of fallacies in speech as resting on an actual, potential or imaginary ambiguity. In that respect he is quite different from the men of the thirteenth century, but maybe this shows the end effect of a development that started when the Venerable Inceptor began to ridicule the classification about 1320.[44]

---

[42] For the medieval habit of reading Aristotle's *Topics* with Boethian spectacles, see N.J. Green-Pedersen, *The Tradition of the Topics in the Middle Ages*, München 1984.

[43] *LM* 246r: "Medius autem terminus sophisticus, est qui apparenter quæstionem probat contra ignorantem rerum et verborum significationes. Eruitur etiam ex certis notis, titulis, locis Sophisticis. Sicut enim in loco Dialectico duo sunt: Maxima et differentia maximæ, quæ est ipsa loci appellatio: Ita hoc loco differentiæ maximarum sunt ipsæ 13 appellationes seu loci sophistarum; ex quibus explicitè contentas maximas colligere possumus. ut: si in æquivocatione et amphibolia dicat Sophista: Ubi est eadem dictio vel oratio, ibi idem sensus et significatio etc. Quod tamen falsum; ideoque ut plurimum supprimitur a Sophistâ." For the medieval interpretation of the Aristotelian fallacies as *loci*, see S. Ebbesen, "The Way Fallacies were Treated in Scholastic Logic", *Cahiers de l' Institut du Moyen-Age Grec et Latin*, 55 (1987), 107-134, at pp. 117-119. There is no sign of the medieval interpretation in Toletus or Conimbricences, *opp. citt.*

[44] For the distinctions between material and formal errors, and between actual, potential and imaginary ambiguity, see Ebbesen 1987. For Ockham's attitude to the last-mentioned distinction, see S. Ebbesen, "[Review of] Guillelmi de Ockham *Expositio super libros Elenchorum*, ed. F. del Punta", *Vivarium*, 20 (1982), 142-153, at p. 144.

Dr Bartholin uses traditional examples of ambiguity, such as "Whoever lives forever is", though by some silly slip of the pen he has made it into "whoever lives forever immortal is".[45] Only quite occasionally do I find something I have never or rarely seen before. In the fallacy of accent, for instance, he has the traditional sort of word-boundary ambiguity illustrated by 'quies' (one or two words? – *quies* "quiet", *qui es* "[you] who are"); ambiguity as to aspiration: *ara/hara* ("altar, swineshed"); and quantity: *péndere/pendêre* ("hang" transitively or intransitively).[46] But then he has one that he calls *in gestu orationis*, where the point is that it makes a difference whether you pronounce a sentence in a way that indicates assent or one that indicates irony or that it is a question. It makes a difference whether the teacher says matter-of-factly "This pupil is very clever" or sneers "This pupil is veeery cleeever".[47] That is an interesting observation, and one that I think I have only seen mentioned under the fallacy of accent once before, namely in John Buridan's *Summulae*. I am pretty sure it does

---

[45] *LM* 247r: "Quicquid vivit semper, immortale est; Leo vivit, ergo Semper immortalis est." Cf. Peter of Spain, *Tractatus*, called afterwards *Summule logicales*, ed. L.M. de Rijk, Assen, 1972, § 7.61, pp. 118-119 on 'quicquid vivit semper est'.

[46] *LM* 247v. Bartholin lists six types of fallacy of accent, viz.: *1. In compositione vocis* (example: *quies*), 2. *In spiritu* (*ara/hara*), 3. *In litera* (*equus/æquus*), 4. *In quantitate* (*populus, pendere*), 5. *In gestu orationis* (for example, see below), 6. *In tono* etc.. The examples *quies, (h)ara, populus* and *pendere* all occur in Peter of Spain's and (Ps.-)Thomas Aquinas' treatment of the fallacy of accent. See Peter of Spain, *op. cit.*, §§ 7.79-80; Thomas Aquinas, *De fallaciis*, in: *Opera omnia iusssu Leonis XIII P.M. edita, tom. 43*, Roma 1976, ch. IX, 409-410. In the Middle Ages, when ancient *equus* and *æquus* were both spelled *equus*, this example was used to illustrate equivocation. See, e.g., the text in S. Ebbesen, "Texts on Equivocation. Part II", *Cahiers de l'Institut du Moyen Age Grec et Latin* 68 (1998), 99-307, at p. 228. Bartholin's conservative choice of examples contrasts with that of the Coimbra commentators who do not use a single of the medieval standard examples of the fallacy of accent (two of their examples, *(h)omine* and *res(#)publica,* were not quite unknown in the Middle Ages, but were not standard ones). See *Comm. Collegii Conimbricensis*, cols. 757-758.

[47] *LM* 247r: "In gestu orationis vel diversitate pronunciationis ironicâ vel assentoriâ vel interrogativâ. Ut: Qui dicit te doctum esse, laudat te; Præceptor dicit te doctum esse (scilicet) Ergo."

not occur in any of the standard authors from the century before mine,[48] and, if you do not mind, I am a bit of a specialist on fallacies.

I notice that Dr Bartholin knows the traditional objection to sophistics as a special branch of study, namely that what is straight judges both itself and what is crooked *(rectum est iudex sui et obliqui)*, as the Philosopher says, so that the books on good syllogisms ought to suffice.[49] He also knows the objection to studying sophistics that it teaches us to cheat rather than to seek out the truth, and he continues to use Alexander of Aphrodisias' defence of the study of such nasty things, viz. that Aristotle does not teach us fallacies in order that we may cheat other people but in order that we may avoid being cheated and may be able to refute sophists. For unless you know the knot you cannot untie it. And just at doctors must learn about both medicines and poisons, so we must learn about both good and bad argumentation.[50] In my own days Alexander's commentary on the

---

[48] Thus neither in Peter of Spain's nor in Ps.-Thomas' treatises on fallacies, and neither in Albert the Great's nor in Giles of Rome's commentary on the *Elenchi*. A rudimentary form of the distinction between declarative and interrogative intonation may be found in Albert's analysis of the Virgilian "Heu quianam tanti cinxerunt aethera nimbi" (*Expositio Sophisticorum Elenchorum*, 1.2.10, in: *Opera omnia*, ed. A. Borgnet, Paris 1890, vol. 2, 552B). John Buridan, in his *Summulae* VII (I use an unpublished edition by H. Hubien), after an interesting analysis of the declarative/interrogative case, adds: "Ad istum etiam modum pertinent diversitates vocum prout eas aliter proferimus praecipientes, aliter rogantes, aliter irati, aliter ironizantes, et sic de multis aliis modis." He offers no example. John Dorp (about 1400) exemplifies with a master ironically saying "Oh, what a faithful servant you are!" (*Perutile compendium totius logice Joannis Buridani cum preclarissima Solertissimi Viri Joannis dorp expositione*, Venice 1499 (rp. Frankfurt/M. 1965). We are closer to Bartholin's formulation in Franciscus Toletus, *Introductio in universam Aristotelis Logicam*, in: *id.*, *Opera omnia Philosophica*, Cologne 1615, 88B (rp. Hildesheim 1985; first edition Rome 1561): "Prouenit etiam tertiò hæc fallacia, quando cum pronunciatione mutatur gestus, quod fit in Ironiis, mutatur enim sensus per ironicam pronunciationem" (follows an example different from Bartholin's). An even closer match with Bartholin is found in *Commentarii Collegii Conimbricensis ...*, col. 758: "Quintum" sc. genus fallaciae accentus "denique nascitur ex diversitate pronuntiationis, ironicæ, aut seriæ: interrogatoriæ, et assertoriæ. Unde hæc sophismata fabricantur. Qui dicit te egregiè respondisse, laudat te, sed præceptor cum reprehendit, ait te egregie respondisse, igitur cum te reprehendit laudat te. Item [...] Deceptio primi sophismatis, oritur ex sensu ironico pro serio." In manuscript form, the Coimbra logic had existed at least since the 1570s.

[49] *Janitores* I.viii.8: "Quòd cognito recto non opus sit præscribi de obliquo, cùm rectum sit judex sui et obliqui." Cf., e.g., Aegidius Romanus, *Expositio supra libros Elenchorum*, ed. Augustinus de Meschiatis de Bugella, Venezia 1500, f. 4rB. The argument was already used by Robert Kilwardby (ca. 1240) in his unpublished commentary on the *Elenchi*.

[50] *Janitores* I.viii.8 (196 ff.); *LM* 243v.

Sophistical Refutations was impossible to lay hands on, I only knew it through quotations in older authors. When I read Dr Bartholin's (unacknowledged) loans from Alexander I got curious whether the book had been rediscovered in the meantime, and I asked Dr Fincke about it. It turned out that he owned a copy, but it was a new translation, done about 1540,[51] and Dr Fincke was most surprised to learn that there had been an earlier one. He thought we people of days of old were totally ignorant of the work. I am not sure, but a belief in their own superiority over men of the past may be characteristic of this age. At one point Dr Bartholin lists the five aims that Aristotle says sophists strive to obtain. He then adds, "Of course, in this more civilized and well-educated age of ours most of these things may be easily warded off, but in days of old the sophists aimed at ...".[52] In my days we used to think that there had been some progress since the time of Aristotle, but we did not speak in such a disparaging way of the past.

Well, it is time I arrive at the conclusion.

I have had some minor difficulties with Dr Bartholin's language. He sometimes uses the words in slightly different senses from what I am accustomed to. Then he has this funny habit of throwing in things in Greek characters, but usually he explains them in Latin. Sometimes, though, I have had to depend on the good services of Dr Fincke to understand the Greek. Generally speaking, however, Latin has shown its continuing ability to resist change, so the differences between Dr Bartholin's Latin and mine are insignificant. His technical terms are almost all of them ones I am familiar with, and this does not only apply to the terms that come straight

---

[51] Fincke's ownership of the book is my free imagination. Remarkably, the formulations used by Bartholin are no closer to Dorotheus' translation than to James of Venice's, as known from medieval quotations (the work itself is no longer extant). They may be paraphrases of the medieval quotations rather than derived from a reading of the text itself. For Dorotheus' translation and its medieval predecessor, see Alexandri Aphrodisiensis *In VIII Libros Topicorum Aristotelis Commentatio*, Pseudo-Alexandri *Annotationes In Librum Elenchorum Aristotelis*. Übersetzt von Guillelmus Dorotheus. Neudruck der 1. Ausgabe Venedig 1541 mit einer Einleitung von Sten Ebbesen (Commentaria in Aristotelem Graeca, Versiones latinae temporis resuscitatarum litterarum 6), Stuttgart-Bad Cannstatt 1996. The fragments of the medieval translation were collected in vol. 2 of Ebbesen 1981. The *Elenchi*-commentary thought both by the medievals and by Bartholin's contemporaries to be by Alexander of Aphrodisias was, in actual fact, the work of Michael of Ephesus (12th c.).

[52] *LM* 245v "Quamquam autem sæculo hoc nostro emunctiori et eruditiori pleraque hæc facillimè caveantur: tamen sophistarum olim scopus erat ...".

out of Aristotle. The structure of the work has caused me no serious difficulties. As for the contents, there are, of course, lots of things about which I disagree with Dr Bartholin, but he very rarely presents a view I have not heard about before. The strangest thing about his logic is not what is there. It is what is not there. There is not a word about supposition, i.e. what terms stand for in particular contexts, and consequently nothing about ampliation and restriction of supposition.[53] OK, Aristotle does not really treat the subject, and if Dr Bartholin only intends his survey of logic as an epitome of the contents of Aristotle's books this is all right in a way. But apparently he thinks he has covered all of logic.[54] How can he think he has done that?

Also, he spends surprisingly little space on consequences: a general definition of a consequence, a division of consequences into material and formal, but, as anyone knows, a coherent syllogistic requires a coherent theory of consequences in general.[55] Or don't people know nowadays? Now, as I think I have mentioned, Dr Bartholin's handbook of logic is closer related to products of the time of my grandfather than to those of my age and he never mentions the great discoveries of my century, so this may be part of the reason why the consequences almost are not there. This part of logic did not really begin to blossom till about 1,300 years after the Word became flesh. But supposition theory was well developed before then, and so were many other parts of logic ignored by Dr Bartholin.

Dr Fincke tells me that many people nowadays think they have much better translations of Aristotle than we had in my time, and that therefore their interpretation of his works is very different and much superior to ours. I can only say that if Dr Bartholin is representative of the present generation, next to nothing has changed in the way people read the *Organon* except that they seem to have forgotten certain parts of logic not explicitly developed by the Philosopher. Their logic is an impoverished one compared to that of my day, but what is left is much like things I knew.

---

[53] For an introduction to the notions of supposition, restriction and ampliation, see P. Spade, "The Semantics of Terms", in: N. Kretzmann & al., *Cambridge History of Later Medieval Philosophy*, 188-196.

[54] See note 29, above.

[55] *LM* 128r-v. For an introduction to late medieval theories of *consequentiae*, see I. Boh, "Consequences", in: Kretzmann & al., *Cambdige History of Later Medieval Philosophy*, 300-314. For their rise after 1300, see N.J. Green-Pedersen 1984, 265ff.

6. Epilogue

I will now divest myself of my medieval persona. The conclusion ought to be clear. The case of Caspar Bartholin suggests that the sixteenth-century revolt against scholastic logic had managed to kill most of the important un-Aristotelian medieval sub-disciplines of logic and most of the remarkable achievements of the fourteenth century. When Aristotle himself was also nearly thrown out, the Wittenberg school and sensible men everywhere thought this was too much. Without reviving the specifically medieval disciplines they reverted to an interpretation of the *Organon* that was fundamentally medieval and anchored in the thirteenth century, while they did not develop new un-Aristotelian or un-medieval branches of logic. The contribution of the sixteenth century had been almost purely negative. As far as logic is concerned, the so-called Renaissance was neither a rebirth of ancient theories nor the beginning of modernity. No ancient theory – whether Aristotelian or Stoic – was re-born, and a genuinely new logic only developed in the nineteenth-twentieth centuries. Genuinely new interpretations of Aristotle's logic had to wait all the time till the twentieth century, when the new un-Aristotelian logic had become widely accepted. A good contemporary theory is the best background for asking intelligent questions of the Stagirite's text.

JOANNES COTTUNIOS DI VERRIA E IL NEOARISTOTELISMO PADOVANO

di Antonis Fyrigos

1. Non credo di violare la tematica e i termini cronologici stabiliti dal programma di questo incontro sul "Nuovo Aristotele" proponendo la "lettura" dei testi aristotelici prospettata da Joannes Cottunios di Verria (1574-1657)[1] nella sua prima opera filosofica intitolata *De triplici statu animæ rationalis* (Bologna, 1628).[2] Pubblicata due anni dopo la morte di Francesco Bacone, quest'opera offre una lucida messa a punto della disputa concernente l'interpretazione "genuina" della dottrina aristotelica del νοῦς (e della problematica ad essa inerente circa la possibilità, o meno, di una dimostrazione razionale dell'immortalità dell'anima umana), che a partire dalla pubblicazione del Lib. I del *De Anima* di Alessandro di Afrodisia ad opera di Girolamo Donato (1495), impegnò i filosofi dei due più importanti centri dell'aristotelismo, Padova e Bologna, e vide l'alessandrismo urtare contro l'averroismo ed il tomismo. Ora, se si vuol tener conto del fatto che, nel passare in rassegna un gran numero di commenti alle opere aristoteliche (accanto a quelli di Alessandro di Afrodisia, di Calcidio e di Giovanni Filopono vanno qui presi in esame anche quelli di Averroè, di S. Tommaso, ma anche di Bessarione e di Giorgio Gemisto Pletone e di tanti altri ancora), e nel mettere a confronto molte traduzioni latine delle stesse allo scopo di valutarle dal punto di vista stilistico e contenutistico, Cottunios

---

[1] Cf. Z. N. Tsirpanlis, *Οἱ Μακεδόνες σπουδαστὲς τοῦ Ἑλληνικοῦ Κολλεγίου Ρώμης καὶ ἡ δράση τους στὴν Ἑλλάδα καὶ στὴν Ἰταλία (16ος αἰ. - 1650)*, (Μακεδονικὴ Βιβλιοθήκη, Δημοσιεύματα τῆς Ἑταιρείας Μακεδονικῶν Σπουδῶν, 35), Thessaloniki 1971, 72-83: 125-159; idem, *Τὸ Ἑλληνικὸ Κολλέγιο τῆς Ρώμης καὶ οἱ μαθητές του (1576-1700). Συμβολὴ στὴ μελέτη τῆς μορφωτικῆς πολιτικῆς τοῦ Βατικανοῦ* (Ἀνάλεκτα Βλατάδων 32), Thessaloniki 1980, 397-399.

[2] Il titolo completo dell'opera si può leggere in E. Legrand, *Bibliographie hellénique ou Description raisonée des ouvrages publiés par des Grecs au XVIIe siècle*, vol. I, Paris 1894, 263-364. Il libro conoscerà anche una seconda edizione nel 1645 (cf. E. Legrand, *ibid.*, vol. II, Paris 1894, 24-25). Per gli esemplari di questo libro oggi esistenti in varie Biblioteche, v. Th. Papadopoulos, *Ἑλληνικὴ Βιβλιογραφία (1466 ci. - 1800). Τόμος πρῶτος. Ἀλφαβητικὴ καὶ χρονολογικὴ ἀνακατάταξις*, Atene 1984, nn. 3215-3216 (D'ora in poi, nel rinviare a questo lavoro di Cottunios, useremo la seguente abbreviazione: J. Cott., *De tr. st.*).

offre traduzioni e interpretazioni alternative, presentandosi così a sua volta come originale "traduttore" e "commentatore" di diverse opere di Aristotele, soffermarsi su questo personaggio misconosciuto proponendone la "lettura delle letture" dei testi aristotelici risulta più che giustificato.

2. Il *De triplici statu animæ rationalis* – un volume in folio, di pp. xiv + 356 + xxxvi – si divide in dieci *Disputationes*, ciascuna delle quali si suddivide in varie *Sectiones*. In esse l'autore, dopo aver definito la quiddità dell'anima razionale (*Disput.* I), esamina la sua origine (*Disput.* II), il modo della sua produzione (*Disput.* III) nonché quello della sua unione con il corpo (*Disput.* IV), per poi affrontare la tematica centrale dell'intero trattato, vale a dire l'immortalità dell'anima razionale (*Disputationes* V-VII). Dopo una esauriente disamina concernente l'intelletto possibile (*Disput.* VIII) e l'intelletto agente (*Disput.* IX), l'autore conclude la sua trattazione esponendo lo *status* dell'anima razionale conseguentemente alla sua separazione dal corpo (*Disput.* X).

La teoria sostenuta da Cottunios in questa sua opera si può riassumere come segue. L'anima razionale non è una particella della natura divina né un *excerptum* di essa; non è armonia né crasi né un *accidens* nell'universo; non è materia né corpo né un composto di materia e forma.[3] Piuttosto, sulla base delle definizioni che leggiamo nel Lib. II del *De anima* di Aristotele, essa viene definita come *entelechia*, vale a dire come *actus primus substantialis*.[4]

Opponendosi all'emanatismo e al traducianismo,[5] Cottunios sostiene, trovando in ciò concorde anche Aristotele, che l'anima razionale viene infusa nel corpo "dal di fuori" (*deforis accedere*).[6] Ciò ovviamente non significa che l'anima preesiste al corpo: nel respingere questa tesi platonica (e qui certo non poteva mancare un'esauriente confutazione della dottrina

---

[3] Cf. J. Cott., *De tr. st.*, *Disput.* I, *Sectiones* I-IV e VII (cf. pp. 1a – 10b).
[4] Cf. Aristot., *De anima*, Lib. II, 1, 412 a 25-26 e *ibid.*, 2, 414 a 12-13. Di queste definizioni Cottunios presenta una serrata analisi in *De tr. st.*, *Disput.* I, *Sectio* VI (pp. 12b – 18b).
[5] Cf. J. Cott., *De tr. st.*, *Disput.* II, *Sectiones* I-II e V (pp. 22a – 27a e 34b – 38b rispettivamente).
[6] Cf. J. Cott., *De tr. st.*, *Disput.* II, *Sectio* IV (cf. pp. 31a -34a). La provenienza "dal di fuori" dell'anima razionale viene dimostrata sulla base dei seguenti passi aristotelici: *De generat. anim.*, Lib. II, c. 3 (736 b 27 ss.); *De anima*, Lib. I, c. 4 (405 b 19) e *Metaph.* Λ, 3 (1070 a 24-29).

origeniana),[7] Cottunios risulta condividere la dottrina dell'animazione ritardata, sostenuta dalla scolastica occidentale, sostenendo che, rispetto a Platone, lo Stagirita presenta una teoria più consona con la dottrina cristiana, dal momento che anche secondo lui l'anima, *actione superioris agentis*, viene creata in quel preciso istante del tempo in cui il corpo, una volta acquisiti gli organi addicenti alla prole umana, diviene distinto e perfetto:[8] peraltro, l'anima razionale viene creata *non ab aliqua intelligentia*, ma da Dio.[9]

Nel confutare la *sententia* di Averroè secondo cui vi è un'unica anima assistente per tutti gli uomini,[10] Cottunios sostiene che, secondo lo Stagirita, *animas intellectrices ad numerum hominum dispertitas esse, veluti veras eorum formas*;[11] dello stesso parere è anche Platone, anche se il filosofo di Atene, allontanandosi dalla verità, considerò le anime razionali solo come "assistenti" dei corpi e "moventi" i corpi.[12]

L'immortalità dell'anima razionale, di cui Cottunios è strenuo difensore e nei confronti della quale ci soffermeremo più avanti, viene da lui dimostrata *ex auctoritatibus Aristotelis*;[13] *ex fundamentis et rationibus Aristotelis*[14] e, infine, *ex morali et prisca Philosophia*.[15]

Molto spazio dedica Cottunios alle tematiche concernenti l'intelletto possibile e l'intelletto agente.[16] Nel respingere le relative teorie di Alessandro di Afrodisia e di Averroè (l'intelletto possibile – precisa Cottunios – non è *preparatio* o *aptitudo animæ* né immaginazione né, considerato in sé, può identificarsi con la sostanza stessa dell'anima),[17] il Nostro sostiene che l'intelletto possibile è una *facultas* dell'anima e una *forma accidentaria*, che sgorga dall'anima stessa e da questa differisce:[18] in quanto tale, l'intellet-

---

[7] Cf. J. Cott., *De tr. st.*, *Disput*. III, *Sectio* IX (pp. 68a – 70b).
[8] Cf. J. Cott., *De tr. st.*, *Disput*. III, *Sectio* III (pp 50a – 53b).
[9] Cf. J. Cott., *De tr. st.*, *Disput*. III, *Sectio* VI (pp. 58a – 60b).
[10] Cf. J. Cott., *De tr. st.*, *Disput*. IV, *Sectio* II (pp. 76a – 82a).
[11] Cf. J. Cott., *De tr. st.*, *Disput*. IV, *Sectio* III (pp. 82a – 85b).
[12] Cf. J. Cott., *De tr. st.*, *Disput*. IV, *Sectio* IV (pp. 85b – 88b).
[13] Cf. J. Cott., *De tr. st.*, *Disput*. V, *Sectiones* I-X (pp. 97a – 149b).
[14] Cf. J. Cott., *De tr. st.*, *Disput*. VI, *Sectiones* I-X (pp. 150a – 206b).
[15] Cf. J. Cott., *De tr. st.*, *Disput*. VII, *Sectiones* I-XIII (pp. 207a – 266b).
[16] Cf. J. Cott., *De tr. st.*, *Disput*. VIII, *Sectiones* I-VIII e *Disput*. IX, *Sectiones* I-XII (pp. 267a – 294b e 295a – 342b rispettivamente).
[17] Cf. J. Cott., *De tr. st.*, *Disput*. VIII, *Sectiones* I-IV (pp. 267a – 280a).
[18] Cf. J. Cott., *De tr. st.*, *Disput*. VIII, *Sectio* V (pp. 280a – 284b).

to possibile è immateriale, immortale, *impermixtus* e separabile dal corpo. Quanto all'intelletto agente, esso non può identficarsi con Dio, né con una qualche intelligenza inferiore a Dio;[19] né alcuno dei filosofi greci (né Teofrasto né Temistio né Simplicio) ha mai sostenuto che l'intelletto possibile o quello agente, di cui parla Aristotele, si possa in qualche modo intendere con un *quid* estrinseco all'anima razionale o una sostanza separata; né si può dire che l'intelletto agente è *habitus primorum principiorum* o che può identificarsi con l'intelletto possibile nel momento in cui intende in atto (*prout actu intelligit*):[20] piuttosto, anche l'intelletto agente è vera facoltà dell'anima razionale, è radice e fonte dell'intelletto possibile ed è incorruttibile e immortale.[21]

Una volta separate dal corpo, le anime o volano verso il cielo, se virtuose, o precipitano verso l'inferno, se appesantite da azioni immorali.[22] In tal modo, esse si inseriscono in un "luogo" proprio dei corpi e delle sostanze immateriali create, il cosiddetto *locus definitivus*, che si contraddistingue dal *locus circumscriptivus*, conveniente ai corpi e alle sostanze corporee in quanto, mentre quest'ultimo luogo presuppone *ut totum locatum toti loco, et pars locati parti loco respondeat*, il primo invece presuppone *quod res aliqua ex modo existendi ita alicubi sit, ut ei repugnet simul alibi esse*.[23] In questo loro *status*, ogni anima separata ha conoscenza di sé *non per aliquam speciem* ma per se stessa e, avendo coscienza di sé, conosce di essere stata creata e, quindi, conosce Colui da cui dipende la sua esistenza; parallelamente, le anime razionali hanno conoscenza anche degli Angeli e, *multo magis*, delle altre anime separate.[24]

Infine, i tre *loca* o *receptacula* dell'inferno in cui migrano le anime in peccato sono: l'*infernus inferior* (o *ignis æternus, ignis inextinguibilis, gehena ignis, locus ignis et sulphuris*); il *purgatorium* (ove le anime pie, dopo un determinato tempo di espiazione, guadagnano il Paradiso) e, infine, il luogo che i Padri chiamano *limbum* o *sinum Abrahæ*, ove si collocano le

---

[19] Cf. J. Cott., *De tr. st.*, *Disput*. IX, *Sectiones* I-VI (pp. 295a – 315a).
[20] Cf. J. Cott., *De tr. st.*, *Disput*. IX, *Setiones* VII-VIII (pp. 315b – 327b).
[21] Cf. J. Cott., *De tr. st.*, *Disput*. IX, *Sectiones* IX-XII (pp. 327b – 342b).
[22] Cf. J. Cott., *De tr. st.*, *Disput*. X, *Sectio* I (p. 344a).
[23] Cf. J. Cott., *De tr. st.*, *Disput*. X, *Sectio* II (p. 344b).
[24] Cf. J. Cott., *De tr. st.*, *Disput*. X, *Sectio* V (pp. 350a – 353a).

anime di coloro che hanno vissuto piamente prima della venuta del Cristo o di coloro che non sono cristiani.[25]

3. Ad una rapida lettura del *De triplici statu animæ rationalis* è facile arguire che il *Leitmotiv* dell'argomentare di Cottunios è costituito dalla sua non infondata constatazione secondo cui, malgrado la loro convinzione, i ψυχόθνητοι καὶ φιλοσώματοι[26] suoi *Antagonisti* non interpretano in maniera genuina il pensiero dello Stagirita giacché essi o "leggono" Aristotele senza un'adeguata conoscenza della lingua greca (come nel caso di Averroè)[27] o sviluppano teorie basandosi su traduzioni erronee dei testi aristotelici (come appunto nella maggior parte degli alessandristi).[28] Se quindi la sua condizione di greco conterraneo di Aristotele costituisce per Cottunios un vanto,[29] la conoscenza della lingua greca e la sensibilità della medesima da lui possedute vengono prospettate come garanzia delle traduzioni e interpretazioni, che dei testi aristotelici egli proporrà in questo suo trattato.[30]

L'esame di Cottunios concerne sia singoli termini filosofici dei testi aristotelici sia passi piuttosto estesi degli stessi. Così, ad es., egli mette in rilievo che in talune traduzioni latine delle opere aristoteliche non si tiene dovutamente conto della sostanziale differenza che passa tra i verbi νοεῖν (*intelligere*) e ξυνίειν (*comprehendere*), dal momento che entrambi vengono resi con *intelligere*,[31] o tra i verbi δοκεῖ (*videtur*), φαίνεται (*apparet*) e ἔοικεν (verbo, quest'ultimo, precisa Cottunios, che ha un'accezione affermativa piuttosto che dubitativa), i quali, invece, vengono di solito resi con un univoco *videtur*.[32] Riferendosi all'espressione aristotelica τύπῳ διωρίσθω (che leggiamo in *De anima*, Lib. II, c. 1 [413 a 9-10]), nel mettere in risalto l'improbabile traduzione della stessa con *pingui Minerva* proposta da

---

[25] Cf. J. Cott., *De tr. st.*, *Disput.* X, *Sectio* VI (pp. 353a – 354b).
[26] Cf. ad es. J. Cott., *De tr. st.*, *Disput.* V, *Sectio* I (p. 102b: ψυχόθνητοι καὶ φιλοσώματοι) e *ibid.*, *Disput.* VI, *Sectio* I (p. 150a: ψυχόθνητοι).
[27] Cf. ad es. J. Cott., *De tr. st.*, *Disput.* IV, *Sectio* III (p. 85a).
[28] Cf. J. Cott., *De tr. st.*, p. x iniziale non numerata e *ibid.*, *Disput.* V, *Sectio* X (p. 143 b).
[29] Cf. J. Cott., *De tr. st.*, p. x iniziale non numerata: "Mihi uerò patria est præclara illa ciuitas Veria, seu Beræa, quæ uix mille passus Libanoua distat" (= "Mia patria è la gloriosa città di Verria, o Berea, che dista appena mille passi da Libanova [= denominazione moderna di Stagira, la patria di Aristotele]").
[30] Cf. J. Cott., *De tr. st.*, pp. x-xi iniziali non numerate.
[31] Cf. J. Cott., *De tr. st.*, *Disput.* V, *Sectio* II (p. 104b).
[32] Cf. J. Cott., *De tr st.*, *Disput.* V, *Sectio* III (p. 111a).

Ioachino Perionio,³³ e nel segnalare che in un codice latino il termine τύπῳ viene erroneamente reso con *figura*,³⁴ Cottunios fa rilevare che, in questa espressione come pure in altre analoghe (τύπῳ λέγειν, τύπῳ λαμβάνειν, τύπῳ ἀποδεικνύειν ecc.), il termine τύπῳ va tradotto con *summatim* o *simpliciter*.³⁵ Né poteva certo mancare un giudizio severo nei confronti della bizzarra resa del termine *entelechia* con *perfectihabia*, proposta da Ermolao Barbaro,³⁶ nonché nei confronti di alcune altre traduzioni discutibili, che leggiamo in Francesco de' Vieri (detto "secondo"),³⁷ in Agostino Nifo³⁸ e in altri.

Che sia sufficiente l'errata traduzione di un solo termine greco per condurre verso interpretazioni inattendibili e fuorvianti dei testi aristotelici lo si può constatare, rileva Cottunios, da una serie di casi. L'affermazione ad es. di S. Tommaso secondo cui Anassagora avrebbe considerato l'intelletto come il principio dell'intero agire umano da cui ogni cosa trae movimento³⁹ si fonda sostanzialmente sull'impropria traduzione dell'e-

---

³³ Si veda infatti *Aristotelis de animo libri tres*, Ioachimo Perionio (...) interprete. *Eiusdem Perionij in eosdem libros observationes* (...), Parisiis, Apud Thomam Richardum (...), 1549, f. 17v. La stessa traduzione leggiamo anche nella riedizione dell'opera del 1552 (cf. *Aristotelis De animo Libri III*, Ioachimo Perionio interprete: per Nicolaum Grouchium correcti et emendati. Lutetiae, Ex officina Michaelis Vascosani (...) 1552, p. 32).

³⁴ E' ovviamente arduo identificare qui, come pure negli altri casi, i codd. cui Cottunios ha impostato il suo lavoro; e ciò ha ostacolato una doverosa verifica delle riserve da lui espresse nei confronti delle traduzioni latine e, quindi, della validità oggettiva del suo giudizio critico. Ad ogni modo, il termine τύπῳ viene tradotto con *figura* presso molti traduttori; cf. ad es. *Commentaria Simplicii* (...) *in tres libros De anima Aristotelis, de græca lingua in Latinam nuperrimè translata*. Evangelista Lungo Asulano interprete (...), Venetiis, Apud Hieronymum Scotum, 1564, f. 16v. In *Simplicii Commentarii in Libros De Anima Aristotelis*, quos Ioannes Faseolus Patavinus ex græcis latinos fecit (...), Venetiis Apud Octavianum Scotum, 1543, f. xlii il τύπῳ viene tradotto con *Adumbrate*.

³⁵ Cf. J. Cott., *De tr. st.*, *Disput*. V, Sectio II (p. 103a).

³⁶ Cf. J. Cott., *De tr. st.*, *Disput*., V, Sectio IX (pp. 135b – 136a).

³⁷ Cf. J. Cott., *De tr. st.*, *Disput*. V, Sectio I (p. 100b).

³⁸ Cf. J. Cott., *De tr. st.*, *Disput*. V, Sectio IV (pp. 112b – 113a).

³⁹ Cf. J. Cott., *De tr. st.*, *Disput*. VI, Sectio II (p. 157a-b). Il testo di S. Tommaso riportato da Cottunios ("Et hoc est, inquit S. Thomas, quod dicit Aristoteles, Anaxagoram potuisse intellectum, ut imperet, ut suo nimirum imperio omnia moueat; ita ut quasi dicat Aristoteles per comparationem, sicut Anaxagoras posuit intellectum esse immixtum, ad hoc, ut imperet, ita oportet nos ponere intellectum esse immixtum, ad hoc, ut cognoscat") corrisponde con quanto dice S. Tommaso in *Sentencia Libri De Anima*, III, 1 (cf. S. Thomae de Aquino, *Opera omnia iussu Leonis XIII P. M. edita*. Tomus XLV, 1. *Sentencia Libri De Anima*, cura et studio Fratrum Praedicatorum, Roma-Paris 1984, 203.98-130). Si

spressione ἵνα κρατῇ <scil. ὁ νοῦς>, che leggiamo in *De anima*, Lib. III, c. 4 (429 a 19-20), con *ut imperet* o con *ut dominetur*,[40] mentre in questo caso il verbo ha il significato di *teneo*, vale a dire *capio, apprehendo*.[41] Un altro caso è costituito dal passo *De anima*, Lib. I, c. 4 (408 b 24-25), ove Aristotele sostiene che "τὸ νοεῖν ... μαραίνεται qualora un organo si corrompe": tenendo conto che la giusta traduzione del verbo μαραίνεται non è *corrumpitur*, come si legge nei codd. consultati da Cottunios, ma *languescit*, allora è possibile dedurre agevolmente che, anche in questo testo, il Filosofo si mostra chiaramente sostenitore dell'immortalità dell'anima, specie se si tiene conto che, subito dopo, egli aggiunge: "in se stesso, <scil. τὸ νοεῖν> è impassibile".[42] In maniera analoga si può parlare anche nei confronti di *De anima* Lib. I, c. 1 (403 a 4-11) ove, nel formulare il dubbio: o l'intelligenza è una specie di fantasma, o almeno non si esercita senza il concorso della fantasia, Aristotele pone sul tappeto la difficile questione della separabilità o meno dell'anima dal corpo. Nel precisare che in questo testo lo Stagirita fa una netta distinzione tra le varie affezioni e operazioni che l'anima subisce ed opera congiuntamente con il corpo (com'è ad es. la collera, il coraggio, il desiderio ecc.), e quelle che paiono proprie dell'anima (com'è l'intelligere, τὸ νοεῖν), Cottunios contesta l'interpretazione "mai sentita prima" che ne propose Pietro Pomponazzi, secondo cui nella mente di Aristotele in nessun modo l'intelletto umano ha un'operazione del tutto indipendente dal corpo, da cui riceve i caratteri dell'individualità,[43] mettendo in rilievo che essa è inattendibile soprattutto

veda anche: Eiusd., *De unitate intellectus contra Averroistas*, c. I (cf. S. Thomae de Aquino, *Opera omnia*, cit., t. XLIII, Roma 1976, 295.367-374).

[40] La traduzione dell'espressione ἵνα κρατῇ con *ut imperet* si legge nelle opere di S. Tommaso (cf. nota precedente) e in molti altri traduttori o commentatori di Aristotele (cf. ad es.Thomae de Vio (...), *In libros Aristotelis De anima commentaria* (...), Bononiae, Apud Sebastianum Bonomium, 1617, p. 185; *Commentarii Simplicii* (...) *in tres libros De anima Aristotelis*, tradotti da Evangelista Lungo Asulano (...) (cit. sopra, nota 34), f. 59. In *De tr. st.*, *Disput*. VI, *Sectio* II (p. 157a), Cottunios riproduce il testo di un'altra traduzione (di cui non segnala la paternità) ove l'ἵνα κρατῇ viene reso con *ut dominetur*.

[41] Cf. J. Cott., *De tr. st.*, *Disput*. VI, *Sectio* II (p. 158a, ove Cottunios afferma: "Anaxagoras posuit intellectum nostrum impermixtum a corpore ἵνα κρατῇ, ut teneat [dicimus uerò communi consuetudine, teneo, idest, intelligo], capiat, et apprehendat").

[42] Cf. J. Cott., *De tr. st.*, *Disput*. V, *Sectio* I (p. 101b). Il testo aristotelico in questione viene ampiamente discusso da Cottunios in *Disput*., V, *Sectio* X (pp. 142b – 144b).

[43] Cf. J. Cott., *De tr. st.*, *Disput*. V, *Sectio* I (p. 99b) e *Disput*. V, *Sectio* II (p. 103a-b). Si veda P. Pomponazzi, *De immortalitate animae*, a cura di G. Gentile (Opuscoli filosofici. Testi e documenti inediti e rari 1), Messina – Roma 1925, specialm. pp. 16, 18, 20-21, 32-33 e 48.

per ragioni di carattere filologico: la formula verbale οὐκ ἐνδέχοιτο, infatti, piuttosto che con *non contingit* va tradotta *non contingerit*; quanto poi alla formula οὐκ ἂν εἴη, questa va resa con *non esset* piuttosto che *non erit*: quest'ultima traduzione, precisa il filologo greco, sarebbe appropriata se nel testo greco avessimo οὐκ ἔσται ο οὐκ ἔσεται. La corretta traduzione dal punto di vista filologico del testo aristotelico permette a Cottunios di concludere che la separabilità e, quindi, l'immortalità dell'anima, è fuori discussione.

Che Aristotele abbia sostenuto l'immortalità dell'anima individuale si desume, secondo Cottunios, anche da una corretta analisi dal punto di vista filologico di *Metaph.*, Λ, 3 (1070 a 24-29), ove, dopo aver sostenuto che "le cause motrici sono cause che preesistono ai loro effetti, mentre le cause formali coesistono con i loro effetti (la figura della sfera di bronzo esiste insieme con la sfera di bronzo)", lo Stagirita si propone di esaminare "se la forma esista anche dopo la dissoluzione del composto".[44] Cottunios fa notare, innanzi tutto, che l'espressione οἷον εἰ, molto frequente nelle opere aristoteliche, va intesa come un solo lemma, οἰονεί, che nell'attico ha il significato di *sicut, ut, videlicet:* essa quindi non esprime qualcosa in maniera dubitativa, ma assolutamente affermativa.[45] Quanto poi al testo che segue (Φανερὸν ... τὰς ἰδέας), egli osserva che l'espressione διά γε ταῦτα (la quale *siue latinus interpres, seu typographus, turpiter offendit*), essendo *notio causalis*, non va tradotta *quod præter hæc* bensì *ac propter hæc*. Ora, soggiunge il Nostro, affinché non si deducesse erroneamente, in seguito all'affermazione aristotelica secondo cui dopo la dissoluzione del corpo

---

Per una migliore comprensione di quanto viene detto presento la traduzione latina esaminata da Cottunios (corrispondente in linee generali con quella che si può leggere nel *De immortalitate animae* del Pomponazzi), mettendo tra parentesi quadre le correzioni da Cottunios stesso proposte: "Si autem [*Si uerò* Cott.] est et hoc imaginatio [*phantasia* Cott.] quædam, aut non sine imaginatione [*phantasia* Cott.], *non* contingat utique [*non contingeret utique* Cott.] hoc sine corpore esse; si igitur est aliqua animæ operatio, aut passionum propria, continget utique ipsam separari; si uerò nulla est propria ipsius, non utique erit [*non utique esset* Cott.] separabilis".

[44] Cf. J. Cott., *De tr. st.*, *Disput.* V, *Sectio* VII (pp. 122a – 124a). Anche qui presento la traduzione latina esaminata da Cottunios, mettendo tra parentesi quadre le correzioni da lui apportate: "Si autem aliquid posterius permanet, considerandum est. In quibusdam enim nihil prohibet, ueluti si [*ueluti si: sicut* Cott.] anima tale sit [*tale est anima* Cott.], non omnis, sed intellectus, omnem namque fortassis impossibile est. Manifestum itaque est, quod præter hæc [*quod præter hæc: ac propter hæc* Cott.] non oportet ideas esse: homo namque hominem generat, singularis aliquem".

[45] E a questo proposito Cottunios rinvia al *Thesaurus linguae graecae*.

nulla impedisce che permanga *aliquam animam, nempè intellectum*, che ciò che rimane è una sorta di idea platonica, il Filosofo ha la premura di soggiungere subito dopo: *homo enim hominem generat, singularis aliquem*; il che vuol significare che, mentre l'idea è *forma communis multis*, ciò invece che egli considera permanere dopo la corruzione del corpo *est aliquid ac singulare;* in tal modo Cottunios prende anche le dovute distanze dalle obiezioni mosse contro il Pomponazzi da Agostino Nifo, sostenendo che, in questo testo aristotelico, non viene ammessa la realtà delle idee, anche se *post mortem* qualcosa comunque permane.

Un altro caso ancora, che può testimoniare come talune deduzioni concernenti il pensiero aristotelico siano inattendibili per via dell'interpretazione filologicamente scorretta di taluni testi è costituito dall'analisi del *De anima*, Lib. III, 5 (430 a 11-26), il capitolo più problematico e discusso dell'intero trattato,[46] ove lo Stagirita, sviluppando quanto accennato in *ibid.*, Lib. I, c. 1, tratta dell'intelletto in potenza e dell'intelletto produttivo. Nel presentare la *translatio* latina, che si può leggere in molti codici latini, *maximè ab Argyropylo latinitate donatis*,[47] Cottunios vi apporta cinque correzioni di carattere filologico. Innanzi tutto, egli fa notare che nella traduzione latina risulta assente la parola greca ὥσπερ, *sicut*, la quale invece è presente in tutti i codici greci: *Apud me* – dice molto significativamente Cottunios – *sunt tres, et quidem uetusti, in quibus omnibus lego* Ἐπεὶ δ' ὥσπερ.[48] In secondo luogo, dell'espressione greca immediata-

---

[46] Cf. J. Cott., *De tr. st.*, *Disput.* IX, Sectio V (p. 107a).

[47] Cf. J. Cott., *De tr. st.*, *Disput.* IX, Sectio V (pp. 306b – 309b). Presento qui di seguito la traduzione esaminata da Cottunios, segnalando tra parentesi quadre le correzioni da lui apportate: "Quoniam autem [post *autem, sicut* add. Cott.] in omni natura est aliquid, hoc quidem materia unicuique generi, id autem est, quod [quod: *quia* vel *quòd*, sc.apposito apice, ne pronomen intelligatur, Cott.] potentia omnia illa, alterum autem causa et factiuum, quod [quod: om. Cott.] faciendo omnia [*èo quia facit omnia* Cott.] quod ars ad materiam passa est [*ut ars ad materiam accidit* vel *ut arti respectu materiæ*, vel *sic, sicut ars cum materia facit* vel *ut ars cum materia facit* Cott.], necesse est et in anima has existere differentias. Et est quidam talis intellectus [*Et est hic quidem talis intellectus* Cott.], quia omnia fit: [quia omnia fit: clarius *èo quia omnia fit*, vel *hic uero, quia omnia facit* Cott.] quidam uerò, qui omnia facit, ut habitus quidam; quale est lumen."

[48] Dicasi per inciso, che l'ὥσπερ viene accolto nelle edizioni di G. Biehl (Bibliotheca Scriptorum Graecorum et Romanorum Teubneriana), Lipsiae 1884, e di A. Jannone (Societé d'Edition Les Belles Lettres), Paris 1966. Nell'edizione di W. D. Ross (Scriptorum Classicorum Bibliotheca Oxoniensis), Oxonii 1959, l'ὥσπερ viene incluso entro parentesi quadra: consultando l'apparato critico, si apprende che l'ὥσπερ viene omesso nella *Themistii paraphrasis*.

mente seguente (τοῦτο δὲ ὅτι – ἐκεῖνα), la parola ὅτι [ὃ molti codd.] viene erroneamente resa con *quod*, dal momento che essa ha qui il significato di *quia, quoniam, quòd*. Ma anche nei confronti dell'espressione τῷ ποιεῖν πάντα, che nella traduzione latina presa qui in esame viene resa con *quod faciendo omnia*, la parola *quod*, avverte Cottunios, è da eliminare, giacché il senso più corretto dell'espressione aristotelica è *faciendo omnia*, o ancora *eò quia facit omnia*. Quanto poi alla traduzione dell'espressione οἷον ἡ τέχνη, essa, piuttosto che con *quod ars ad materiam*, si deve rendere con *sicut ars, vel ut ars*. Infine viene preso in considerazione il verbo πέπονθεν che, sempre nella *translatio* da lui riportata, viene erroneamente reso con *ad materiam passa est*. Che cosa mai può patire l'arte? – (si) chiede Cottunios! Il πέπονθεν (da πάσχω), puntualizza il filologo greco, non significa solo *pati* ma, tra l'altro, anche *accidere alicui*. Sgomberato il campo da ogni equivoco di carattere propriamente filologico e stabilita la più retta traduzione del testo aristotelico qui menzionato, Cottunios propone di questo testo aristotelico l'interpretazione seguente: "Come in ogni natura c'è qualcosa che costituisce la materia e (...) qualcos'altro che è causa e fattivo (...), così pure nei confronti dell'anima intellettiva, che è natura, è necessario che si verifichi questa differenza, vale a dire che ve ne sia un principio materiale e un principio agente".[49]

La questione dell'ὥσπερ di *De anima*, III, c. 5 (430 a 10) testé menzionata – che concerne più propriamente la critica testuale dei testi aristotelici – induce ad affrontare un altro aspetto dell'analisi cottuniana atto a rilevare che, non di rado, gli errori e le imperfezioni delle traduzioni latine sono a loro volta riconducibili al ricorso, da parte di molti traduttori e commentatori latini, a dei testimoni non autorevoli della tradizione manoscritta. Un esempio significativo in tal senso è costituito dall'analisi filologico-filosofica della seconda parte del *De anima*, Lib. III, 5 [430 a 17-19]).[50] Basandosi su questo testo, alcuni commentatori di Aristotele, tra cui Tommaso de Vio, detto Gaetano o Caietano (e contro il quale Cottunios indirizza prevalentemente il suo discorso),[51] hanno dedotto che qui lo

---

[49] Cf. J. Cott., *De tr., st., Disput.* IX, *Sectio* V (p. 309a).
[50] Cf. J. Cott., *De tr. st., Disput.* V, *Sectio* V (pp. 113b – 120a); vedi anche *ibid., Disput.* IX, *Sectio* X (pp. 332a – 337a).
[51] Cf. J. Cott., *De tr. st., Disput.* V, *Sectio* V (p. 113b-114a, ove Cottunios richiama propriamente il *Commento* del Caietano) e *ibid., Disput.* IX, *Sectio* X (pp. 332a, ove Cottunios è più vago: "Circa quem textum sunt qui uelint etc"). Cf. Thomae de Vio (...), *In libros Aristotelis De anima commentaria* (...), cit., pp. 206 e 214-215.

Stagirita, lungi dal sostenere la separabilità esistenziale e, quindi, l'immortalità dell'intelletto possibile,[52] vuole piuttosto esprimere, accanto alle tre *conditiones* comuni all'intelletto agente e all'intelletto possibile (separabilità, immistione e impassibilità) anche una quarta, propria dell'intelletto agente: e cioè che è *substantia actio existens*.[53] Già di per sé di difficile interpretazione, questo testo aristotelico risulta ancor più problematico per via della *obscura et inuoluta traslatio* latina. Nel presentare quindi varie traduzioni latine di esso,[54] il Nostro mette in rilievo la difficoltà che presenta la traduzione dell'espressione τῇ οὐσίᾳ ὢν ἐνεργείᾳ, nei confronti della quale le traduzioni latine presentano sostanziali differenze: dopo aver precisato che, ad una attenta lettura del testo, l'espressione τῇ οὐσίᾳ non si riferisce all'intelletto agente ma, più propriamente, all'anima in quanto tale, e dopo aver messo in rilievo che come ben sanno *græcanicæ, seu diuinæ potius linguæ, periti*, il participio ὢν ha anche il significato di *cum sit, seu quia est*, Cottunios sottolinea che i codd. greci non danno ἐνέργεια, ma ἐνεργείᾳ (in dativo): termine che va tradotto con *actu*. Conseguentemente, egli propone di questo passo aristotelico la seguente traduzione (che si avvicina a quella di Argyropoulos e della *traslatio Philoponi*): *Et hic intellectus separabilis est et immixtus et impassibilis, substantia cum sit actu* (ovvero *quia substantia, seu substantialiter est actu*, o ancora, *quia est actus ipsi substantiæ*). Tale traduzione permette al Nostro di offrire la seguente interpretazione, certamente più consona col testo analizzato e col pensiero

---

[52] Cf. J. Cott., *De tr. st.*, *Disput.* V, *Sectio* V (pp. 113b – 114b).

[53] Cf. J. Cott., *De tr.. st.*, *Disput.* V, *Sectio* V (pp. 114b ss.); e *Disput.* IX, *Sectio* X (pp. 332a ss.).

[54] Cf. J. Cott., *De tr. st.*, *Disput.* V, *Sectio* V (p. 115a): "Errandi uerò causa ipsi (scil. Caietani) fuit, an uaria, eaque obscura satis et inuoluta latina præfatæ sententiæ (scil. Arist., *De anima*, Lib. III, 5 [430 a 17-18]) translatio, an praua eius intelligentia. Textus est: καὶ οὗτος ὁ νοῦς χωριστὸς καὶ ἀμιγὴς καὶ ἀπαθής, τῇ οὐσίᾳ ὢν ἐνεργείᾳ. Communis translatio, quam etiam sequitur Auerroes, habet: *Et hic intellectus separabilis est et immixtus et impassibilis, substantia actio existens*. In antiqua uerò translatione, quam etiam habet S. Thomas et amplectitur Caietanus, iacet: *Substantia actu ens*. Alia, quam habet Augustinus Nyphus: *Et hic intellectus separabilis et impermixtus et impassibilis secundum substantiam est, qui est actu*. Alia, quæ continetur in commentarijs Simplicij, è græcis latinitati donatis à Ioanne Faseolo: *Et is intellectus separabilis et immixtus et impassibilis sua ex substantia existens actus*. Argyropolus transtulit: *Et is intellectus separabilis est et non mixtus, passioneque uacat, cum sit substantia actus*. Conuersio Philoponi habet: *Et hic intellectus separabilis est et immixtus et affectione uacuus, cum substantia sit actus*. Alij denique alio uertere modo, quorum translationes nec referre nec impugnare, tametsi facillimum foret, in præsentia opus."

di Aristotele: "ciò che è in atto è più nobile di ciò che è in potenza; l'intelletto agente è, nei confronti dell'intelletto passivo, come ciò che è in atto rispetto a ciò che è in potenza; *ergo*: l'intelletto agente è più nobile dell'intelletto paziente; e poiché l'intelletto possibile è separato, impassibile e immisto, a maggior ragione lo sarà l'intelletto agente".[55]

4. Le considerazioni immediatamente precedenti hanno privilegiato l'esame filologico di Cottunios volto ad evidenziare la cattiva "lettura" (nel senso più stretto del termine), da parte degli Averroisti ed Alessandristi, dei testi aristotelici e, quindi, sottolineare l'inattendibilità delle loro interpretazioni aristoteliche, che gli stessi reputavano "genuine". Sulla base di questi esempi, qui proposti per ovvi motivi con estrema sintesi e linearità, è possibile affermare che, nel suo insieme, il lavoro di Cottunios, che comunque non è privo di considerazioni di carattere prettamente filosofico, comprende complessivamente cinque tappe: a) individuazione del testo originale greco di Aristotele, che i suoi *Antagonisti* proponevano per suffragare le loro tesi, ed analisi strettamente filologica dello stesso; b) confronto delle traduzioni latine a lui note del testo aristotelico individuato, segnalazione degli errori in esse riscontrati e, possibilmente, individuazione della traduzione più corretta (o meno difettosa) dal punto di vista filologico; c) presentazione di una sua nuova traduzione latina; d) interpretazione filosofica del testo aristotelico da lui stesso analizzato e tradotto; e, infine, e) corroborazione della traduzione e interpretazione da lui prospettate col rinvio ad altri passi aristotelici. Tutto ciò ci permette di

---

[55] Cf. J. Cott., *De tr. st.*, *Disput.* V, *Sectio* III (p. 110a), *Disput.* V, *Sectio* V (pp. 115a e 116a) e *Disput.* IX, *Sectio* X (p. 332b). E' bene qui sottolineare che, benché la totalità quasi dei mss. greci dia a questo punto la lezione ἐνεργείᾳ (in dativo), lezione che si legge tra l'altro anche in Temistio, Filopono, Sophonias (sec. XIII-XIV) e in altri commentatori di Aristotele, la lezione invece ἐνέργεια (in nominativo), contro cui si oppone Cottunios, risale a Simplicio, da cui fu accolta da taluni commentatori latini e, dopo le edizioni moderne di A. Torstrik e H. Bonitz (sec. XIX), dalla maggior parte delle edizioni critiche moderne (G. Biehl, *Aristotelis De Anima*, ed. II, O. Apelt, Lipsiae 1911; A. Jannone, *Aristote, De l'Âme*, Paris 1980; W. D. Ross, *Aristotelis De anima*, Oxonii 1959 ecc.). Ma, come è stato giustamente osservato, tale lezione "textum <Aristotelis> non tantum non reddit clariorem verum potius multo obscuriorem, cum in naturalem fluxum argumentationis Aristotelicae ideam introducat, quae cum eo non bene cohaeret": cf. P. Siwek, *Aristotelis De Anima, Libri tres graecae et latinae* (Pont. Univ. Gregoriana, Textus et Documenta, Series Philosophica, 8), Romae 1933, vol. III, p. 325 (nota 399). Vedi anche Eiusd., *Le 'De anima' d'Aristote dans les manuscrits grecs* (Studi e Testi 241), Città del Vaticano 1965, p. 18, nota 1 della p. 17.

affermare che, malgrado non abbia presentato dei testi aristotelici una traduzione latina vera e propria, tuttavia Cottunios, oltre che filologo accorto e buon conoscitore di Aristotele e delle molteplici tematiche dell'aristotelismo del suo tempo, si può considerare a sua volta "traduttore" e "commentatore" sobrio e rigoroso dei testi aristotelici non senza interesse e originalità.

Maggiormente propenso verso la filosofia aristotelica, più consona a suo dire ai dogmi cristiani, che verso quella platonica (malgrado i Padri della Chiesa abbiano in un primo momento preferito questa alla prima), Cottunios non sembra condividere senza numerosi *distinguo* la teoria della sostanziale concordia dottrinale tra Aristotele e Platone. Parallelamente, egli si discosta senza esitazione alcuna dal naturalismo di Alessandro di Afrodisia che, col sostenere la mortalità dell'anima, aveva stravolto radicalmente il pensiero del Filosofo, si oppone alle soluzioni platonizzanti di Agostino Nifo, critica l'interpretazione aristotelico-alessandristica del de Vio, polemizza contro l'integralismo alessandrista di Pietro Pomponazzi (che primo, dopo Alessandro, *accerrimè pugnavit pro animorum mortalitate*), prende le distanze dalle posizioni immanentistiche di Simone Porzio e da quelle alessandriste di Jacopo Zabarella, mentre, nei confronti dell'eclettismo del suo maestro Cesare Cremonini, Cottunios preferisce mantenere un silenzio, forse ossequioso. Passando all'altro versante egli, nel confutare Avicenna, Avicebron e, con maggior asprezza ed ironia, Averroè (nel ricordare con una certa insistenza che l' *Arabs* ignorava la lingua greca, Cottunios sostiene, tra l'altro, che la *Unitas intellectus ab eo inducta est monstrum in Philosophia*[56]), mostra di condividere sostanzialmente la *aurea doctrina*[57] del Dottor Angelico, che viene citata quasi in ogni pagina del suo libro e che, tranne qualche rara eccezione,[58] viene da lui ampiamente condivisa, mentre, di fronte a preoccupazioni teologiche, egli si affida ossequiosamente all'insegnamento della Chiesa di Roma e all'autorità del Pontefice romano.[59] Sicché Cottunios, greco di nascita, trovandosi nel bel mezzo della vivace disputa tra aristotelisti, diciamo, 'eterodossi' (averroisti

---

[56] Cf. J. Cott., *De tr. st.*, *Disput*. VIII, Sectio V (p. 280a: v. anche p. xi finale non numerata); vedi anche *supra*, nota 27.

[57] Cf. J. Cott., *De tr. st.*, *Disput*. III, Sectio IV (p. 57b); si veda anche *ibid.*, *Disput*. II, Sectio II (p. 25b), ove la dottrina di S. Tommaso viene definita *sincerè peripatetica*.

[58] Cf. ad es. J. Cott., *De tr. st.*, *Disput*. V, Sectio V (p. 115b); si veda anche quanto da noi detto sopra, nei confronti dell'espressione ἵνα κρατῇ.

[59] Si veda ad es. J. Cott., *De tr. st.*, *Disput*. IV, Sectio V (p. 96b).

e alessandristi) e aristotelisti 'ortodossi' (tomisti), si schierò senza esitazione alcuna nelle file di questi ultimi, al punto da potersi annoverare tra gli esponenti più convinti e convincenti della Seconda Scolastica.

Ciò che comunque sorprende nell'opera di Cottunios non è tanto la sua ferma aderenza alle posizioni dottrinali della Chiesa cattolica, quanto la conoscenza piuttosto marginale della filosofia greca cristiana del primo millennio: benché infatti i nomi di Gregorio di Nissa, di Gregorio Nazianzeno, dello Pseudo-Dionigi Areopagita e di alcuni altri pensatori greci vengano non di rado da lui menzionati in questa sua opera, si ha tuttavia l'impressione che la sua non sia una conoscenza esauriente e diretta di questi autori, ma limitata e indiretta, derivante da quanto se ne può ricavare dalla lettura delle opere dell'Aquinate e degli altri tomisti; conseguentemente, egli non sfrutta talune acquisizioni filosofico-teologiche della filosofia cristiana greca del primo millennio, che avrebbero potuto dare al suo trattato un maggior interesse ed una più spiccata originalità. Così, ad esempio, trattando della creazione dell'anima da parte di Dio, egli non fa alcuna menzione della (reale?) distinzione in Dio tra *ousia* ed *operazioni* o *potenze* di Dio e, quindi, non specifica che già in Clemente Alessandrino, che si può considerare il fondatore delle teorie del creazionismo e dell'animazione immediata, a creare l'anima dell'uomo non è la *sostanza* di Dio ma una *potenza* della sostanza di Dio o, ancora, un "angelo";[60] e trattando della problematica concernente lo *status* dell'anima dopo la morte, egli ignora l'acquisizione filosofica presente in maniera più o meno esplicita in vari esponenti della filosofia greca cristiana che, nel considerare l'uomo *naturaliter* (per natura) un *synolon* inscindibile di corpo-e-anima, prevede che anche *post mortem* l'anima non si separi totalmente dal corpo, ma continui a rimanere presso gli elementi materiali in cui si era inserita all'inizio.[61]

Benché le notizie concernenti gli anni della sua giovinezza e della sua prima formazione siano piuttosto scarse, è ragionevole dedurre che Cottunios nacque nell'ortodossia. Peraltro, formatosi in Occidente (sappiamo infatti che egli, proveniente da Tubinga, all'età di 33 anni raggiunge Roma),

---

[60] Per l'intera questione si veda L. Rizzerio, "Le problème des parties de l'âme et de l'animation chez Clement d'Alexandrie", *Nouvelle Revue Théologique*, 111 (1989), 389-416.

[61] Si veda ad es. Gregorii Nysseni, *De anima et Resurrectione Dialogus, qui inscribitur Macrinia*, PG 46, 44 A 8 – 48 C 3 e *ibid.*, 72 C 5 – 80 A 12. Analoghe affermazioni si possono riscontrare negli scritti di Massimo il Confessore e Giovanni Damasceno.

Cottunios, anche per via della sua permanenza piuttosto lunga nel Collegio atanasiano in Roma (1605-1613) ove avrà senz'altro avuto modo di conoscere la scolastica e la teologia cattolica, ne è rimasto talmente influenzato, da decidere di allontanarsi ben presto dalle posizioni teologiche greche e di abbracciare il cattolicesimo. Sicché egli, non solo perché scrive in latino, si mostra per mentalità mille miglia lontano dal mondo greco, anche se, nella realtà dei fatti, in cuor suo si sente greco.[62] Il suo contributo nell'ambito filosofico, proprio perché indubbiamente inquadrato nel contesto della Seconda Scolastica, trovasi in stridente contrasto col positivismo "rivoluzionario", come è stato definito, del suo contemporaneo, l'ateniese Teofilo Coridalide (1560-1646),[63] anche questi aristotelico, discepolo del Cremonini e allievo del Collegio greco.

5. Dopo il *De triplici statu animæ rationalis*, Cottunios pubblicherà sempre a Bologna le *Lectiones* di filosofia da lui tenute nella *Celeberrima Bononiensis Academia* dal titolo *In primum Aristotelis librum de Meteoris* (Bononiae 1631).[64] Ma sarà il periodo successivo, quello padovano (1632-1657), che risulterà più importante per l'attività editoriale del Nostro. A quest'ultima fase della sua vita, infatti, risalgono un *Manuale scholasticum de uitiis et peccatis* (1635),[65] tre *Orationes academicæ*,[66] i *Commentarii lucidissimi in octo libros Aristotelis De physico auditu* (1648),[67] la *Expositio uniuersæ logices* (1651)[68] e i suoi *Commentarii in quattor libros Aristotelis*

---

[62] E' significativa a questo proposito la sua decisione di fondare a Padova una scuola per giovani greci, il cosiddetto Collegio Cottuniano (1653), ove si formeranno generazioni intere di giovani greci: Cf. Z. Tsirpanlis, *Οἱ Μακεδόνες σπουδαστές*, cit., pp. 145-146 (dove trovasi ulteriore bibliografia).

[63] Cf. Cl. Tsourkas, *Les débuts de l'enseignement philosophique et de la libre pensée dans les Balkans. La vie et l'oeuvre de Théophile Corydalée (1570-1646)* (Ἑταιρεία Μακεδονικῶν Σπουδῶν. Ἵδρυμα Μελετῶν Χερσονήσου τοῦ Αἵμου 95), Thessaloniki 1967, specialm. pp. 197-210. Si veda però il parere opposto di L. Benakis, espresso nella recensione del libro di Tsourkas in *Ἑλληνικά*, 23 (1970), 399-404.

[64] Cf. E. Legrand, *op. cit.*, I, p. 299; Th. Papadopoulos, *op. cit.*, n. 3220. Allo stesso periodo risale anche un opuscolo dal titolo *De conficiendo epigrammate liber unus*: cf. E. Legrand, *op. cit.*, I, p. 307; Th. Papadopoulos, *op. cit.*, n. 3214.

[65] Cf. E. Legrand, *op. cit.*, I, pp. 330-331; Th. Papadopoulos, *op. cit.*, n. 3221.

[66] I loro titoli sono: *De formis Rerumpublicarum*, *De vera nobilitate* e *Oratoria liminaris*: cf. E. Legrand, *op. cit.*, I, pp. 396-398; Th. Papadopoulos, *op. cit.*, nn. 3222-3224.

[67] Cf. E. Legrand, *op. cit.*, V, p. 62-63; Th. Papadopoulos, *op. cit.*, n. 3211.

[68] Cf. E. Legrand, *op. cit.*, II, p. 50; Th. Papadopoulos, *op. cit.*, n. 3217 (il libro dal titolo *Compendiosa logica in usum scholarium* [Patavii 1669], che viene descritto dal Papa-

de cœlo (1657).⁶⁹ All'inizio del 1657 (anno della sua morte), Cottunios pubblicherà i *Commentarii lucidissimi in tres Aristotelis libros de Anima*,⁷⁰ con i quali egli suggellerà la sua attività di "traduttore" e "interprete" di testi aristotelici.

Trascurato in Grecia perché scrive in latino,⁷¹ e ignorato in Occidente verosimilmente perché "greco", Cottunios è rimasto ingiustamente misconosciuto – se non proprio sconosciuto. Questo breve intervento, il primo, che io sappia, in cui il pensiero filosofico di Cottunios viene studiato direttamente sulle sue opere (anche se, in questa sede, limitatamente ad una sola di esse e, quindi, suscettibile per forza di cose di rettifiche e di ampliamenti),⁷² nel presentare questo personaggio, indubbiamente non di primissimo piano, all'attenzione degli specialisti dell'aristotelismo, vorrebbe prospettare una giusta collocazione del "Cottunios greco" nel contesto dell'aristotelismo occidentale, e del "Cottunios latino" nel panorama delle lettere greche.

---

dopoulos in *ibid.*, vol. II, n. *422, forse è riedizione della *Expositio universae logices* o, meglio, un riassunto della stessa). Nel 1653 Cottunios pubblica anche gli *Epigrammi graeci*: cf. E. Legrand, *op. cit.*, II, pp. 57-58; Th. Papadopoulos, *op. cit.*, n. 3218; Z. Tsirpanlis, *Οἱ Μακεδόνες σπουδαστές*, cit., pp. 138-145.

⁶⁹ Cf. E. Legrand, *op. cit.*, V, p. 71; Th. Papadopoulos, *op. cit.*, n. 3210.

⁷⁰ Cf. E. Legrand, *op. cit.*, II, p. 96; Th. Papadopoulos, *op. cit.*, n. 3212.

⁷¹ Cf. K. Th. Dimaràs, *Ἱστορία τῆς Νεοελληνικῆς Λογοτεχνίας. Ἀπὸ τὶς πρῶτες ρίζες ὥς τὴν ἐποχή μας*, Atene 1968⁴, ove a p. 92 l'autore afferma: "Cottunios [...] appartiene alle lettere occidentali, perché ha scritto i suoi libri in latino". Non sono infondati i *distinguo* che a questa affermazione del Dimaràs formula Z. Tsirpanlis in *Οἱ Μακεδόνες σπουδαστές*, cit., p. 132.

⁷² Ad eccezione di talune indicazioni piuttosto generiche concernenti la vita e le opere di Cottunios (come ad es. B. Knös in *L'histoire de la Littérature néo-grecque. La période jusqu'en 1821*, Göteborg – Uppsala 1962, 347-348) la totalità degli studiosi, nel riferirsi al pensiero filosofico di Cottunios, sono soliti a ripetere il giudizio espresso da Nicola Comneno Papadopoli, *Historia Gymnasii Patavini* (...), t. I, Venetiis 1726, Apud Sebastianum Coleti, pp. 368-69, secondo cui Cottunios avrebbe confutato la teoria del suo maestro Cesare Cremonini.

POLITICAL ARISTOTELIANISM IN THE SEVENTEENTH CENTURY

by Bo Lindberg

This paper differs from the others of this volume in at least two respects: it is chronologically late in dealing with the seventeenth century, and it concerns the end of Aristotelianism rather than its triumph and flourishing. In consequence, Aristotelianism will appear in a more traditional perspective than is suggested in the title of the symposium and the name of the network organizing it, where Aristotle is seen as a contributor to the origins of modernity. The focus is on how and with what success ancient political doctrine could be adapted to early modern realities, and Aristotelianism will in the end appear as unmodern, at least in the eyes of the seventeenth century.

Political Aristotelianism is of course a vast and diffuse phenomenon that appears in various versions in different countries. What I say here will pertain to the Lutheran universities of northern Europe. My sources are texts from Swedish universities – which were very much like those of northern Germany – and some texts by German Aristotelians.

Elementary Aristotelianism
What was political Aristotelianism in the seventeenth century? Aristotelianism had been embedded in the scholarly heritage of Europe since the middle ages. During the sixteenth century, there was a renewal of Aristotelianism in all fields of knowledge, partly stimulated by better knowledge of the Aristotelian texts in the Greek original, partly by new needs. The "neo-Aristotelianism" of the late sixteenth century appeared as a subtle interest in scientific method (Zabarella) as well as a refined instrument in the intensified discussion of theological matters that followed the Reformation. The so-called controverse theology practised by Catholics, Lutherans and Protestants alike had as one of its presuppositions the revival of Aristotelianism. Not least in Lutheran Germany around 1600 Aristotelianism reconstructed positions which had been temporarily weakened by the influence of Ramism.

The pattern for political Aristotelianism is similar. Aristotelian ethics and politics had pervaded scholarly discussion of moral philosophy since the middle ages. In Germany it had been incorporated in Melanchthon's influential doctrine, which was adapted to Lutheran needs. With neo-Aristotelianism the study of Aristotle's *Politics* increased, and the work established itself firmly at the universities as the foundation of political discourse. Aristotle provided the elementary concepts, terms and topics according to which social and political phenomena were discussed in lectures, disputations, orations and dissertations. Most political treatises followed the Aristotelian series of human associations from the simplest between husband and wife to the state with its citizens. The same goes for the distinction between *civitas* and the *respublica* with its different forms of government, monarchy, aristocracy, democracy, mixed government etc. Other topics of this common political wisdom were the ideas that man is a social being and that good government aims at the good of the whole state, not only of those who govern; yet another topic was the question why states change and how this can be prevented.

This elementary Aristotelianism was communicated in compendia of the *Politics* of Aristotle – rarely by reading Aristotle himself. In such compendia and commentaries, the student found a rather "pure" Aristotle, shortened and distorted here and there, and certainly not the original Aristotle in his Greek context, but nevertheless what we could call Aristotelian political doctrine.

This is not to say that students were taught to be adherents of Aristotle in political affairs. Political Aristotelianism was elementary, it provided tools but no clear-cut norms for the distribution of power or political action. In actual teaching, the Aristotelian material was mixed and overlaid with elements from other political theorists. Normally, the political course at the universities was an eclectic concoction of doctrines aiming not at theoretical coherence and consequentiality but at the legitimizing of the existing order.

This eclecticism can be illustrated with some examples from the University of Uppsala. According to the constitutions of 1626, the Professor of Ethics and Politics was expected to lecture on Johannes Althusius *or* Theophilus Golius, a German commentator on Aristotle, and to illuminate the precepts with examples from the Bible, Herodotus,

Thucydides, Livy and others.¹ In 1625 the professor of Uppsala University Jonas Magni presented a series of dissertations in which Aristotelian concepts, definitions and propositions taken from the German Henning Arnisaeus and the Englishman John Case, both of them Aristotelians, were combined with arguments from Justus Lipsius, Jean Bodin, and Johannes Althusius. The result was a doctrine that supported limited monarchy and the tempered royal government which prevailed in Sweden during the reign of Gustavus Adolphus.²

Thus, on the pedagogical level of university teaching, elementary Aristotelianism was the substrate of various contemporary or quite recent theorists. It also coexisted and could be merged with other sources of political argument like the Bible, natural law and political humanism in the tradition of Lipsius. It is telling that Johannes Schefferus, a German immigrant from Strassburg who was Professor of Eloquence and Politics in Uppsala from 1648 to 1679, wrote during his career not only a compendium of Aristotle but a commentary on the first book of Livy and an introduction to natural law as well.³

Elementary Aristotelianism was thus a common language⁴, shared by almost everybody who wrote about politics. Above the pedagogical level of elementary Aristotelianism there was, however, a more pronounced and conscious political Aristotelianism represented by more advanced theorists than the authors of compendia. Such Aristotelians were John Case in Oxford (died 1599) – whom we leave aside here, since he did not belong to the Lutheran sphere⁵ – and Henning Arnisaeus and Hermann Conring in Germany. Arnisaeus and Conring had much in common. They were both professors in Helmstedt, Arnisaeus from 1613 to 1620 and Conring from

---

[1] C. Annerstedt, *Upsala universitets historia* bihang 1, Uppsala 1877, 278.

[2] Jonas Magni, *Philosophiae civilis pars posterior seu specialis aliquot comprehensa disputationibus*, Upsaliae s.a.

[3] Johannes Schefferus, *Breviarium politicorum Aristotelis*, Holmiae 1684; *Regnum Romanum vel in T. Livii Patavini librum primum excercitationes politicae* VII, Upsaliae 1665; „Sciagraphia juris naturae" (manuscript in several copies, University Library of Uppsala).

[4] The term „language" is nowadays often used by historians of political theory of the Skinnerian-Pocockian school to describe political ideas in context. Vide R.A. Pocock, *Politics, language, and time, Essays on political thought and history*, London 1972. As a rule, they refer to political languages that have more political significance than the language I have in mind here, which is rather a technical and ideologically neutral language.

[5] On his philosophy and political thought, vide C. B. Schmitt, *John Case and Aristotelianism in Renaissance England*, Montreal 1983.

1632 to his death in 1681. Neither of them was a specialist in politics, as indeed were none of the political theorists of the early modern era. Both were prominent medical scientists and physicians. Arnisaeus left Helmstedt in 1620 for Copenhagen to become physician to the Danish king. Conring likewise had a short stay at Queen Christina's court in Stockholm around 1650. He enjoyed great fame as a polyhistor; he was one of the last to embrace the whole field of knowledge including such new areas as the history of German law, where he broke new ground with fundamental research.

In politics, Arnisaeus was the author of two books of a general character, the *Doctrina politica in genuinam methodum, quae est Aristotelis, deducta* (1605) and *De republica seu reflectionis politicae libri duo* (1615). In addition to these, he wrote treatises on more specialized political issues, and a number of academic dissertations.[6] Conring's political production was more philosophical and detached from practical politics. His most important work was *De civili prudentia liber unus* (1662), which is an introduction to political science and deals more with the state of the discipline of politics than with politics itself. His political works further included academic dissertations and an edition of Aristotle's *Politics* in the original language with a parallel Latin translation.[7]

What were the distinguishing Aristotelian features in the more pronounced Aristotelianism of Arnisaeus and Conring ?

One important thing about the political Aristotelianism of these scholars was its independence of theology. To the jurists and officials of the princely states in protestant Germany, Aristotelian politics made possible a secular analysis of political issues that was compatible with Luther's separation of the spiritual and secular spheres; in practice it legitimized princely control of ecclesiastical affairs.[8] Arnisaeus gave this secularization of politics a theoretical foundation. He denounced the doctrine of the *analogia entis* by which Thomistic philosophy had maintained a bridge between the

---

[6] The political doctrine of Arnisaeus has been thoroughly analysed by H. Dreitzel, *Protestantischer Aristotelismus und absoluter Staat. Die „Politica" des Henning Arnisaeus (ca. 1575-1636)*, Wiesbaden 1970. On Conring, see D. Willoweit, „Herman Conring", in *Staatsdenker im 17. und 18. Jahrhundert*, hrsg. von M. Stolleis, 2. Aufl., Frankfurt am Main 1987.

[7] Conring's political writings are collected in *Hermanni Conringii ... Opera omnia, tomus III continens varia scripta politica*, ed. J.G. Goebel, Brunswigiae 1730, photographic reprint Göttingen 1970.

[8] P. Petersen, *Geschichte der aristotelischen Philosophie im protestantischen Deutschland*, Leipzig 1921; R. Tuck, *Philosophy and government 1572-1651*, Cambridge 1993, 124 sq.

knowledge of the observable world and the knowledge of a transcendent God; metaphysics could not say anything about the essence of God.[9] In this way, the prerequisites for a secularized political doctrine were created. Conring followed up this emancipation from the scholastic frame of political theory and seems to have had no problems with the theologians.

This secularization meant a return to Aristotelian politics in the sense that Aristotle himself had not been a Christian and had had no religious aims in his political doctrine. It was also to some extent a resuscitation of the "Averroist tradition" within Aristotelianism, although with less antagonism towards the scholastic use of Aristotle than had often been felt by other Averroist philosophers.

Another, more specifically Aristotelian feature concerns method. Arnisaeus, in his *Doctrina politica in genuinam methodum, quae est Aristotelis, reducta,* deals quite a lot with method, as the title indicates. He is eager to show that politics is a practical science in the Aristotelian sense. Accordingly it should be studied by resolutive or analytical method. You should start from the aim and the whole and then identify the matter in and with the help of which the aim is realised. That is, the state is the aim and form, and the minor associations and the citizens are the matter. It is difficult to see that this methodological question could have been of any political or ideological significance. Rather it is a purely academic issue. In arguing for his methodology, Arnisaeus criticizes John Case, who has allegedly misunderstood Aristotle.[10] This indicates that methodology was an issue within the Aristotelian camp rather than something that brought Aristotelianism into conflict with other traditions.

A third distinguishing Aristotelian feature, and one of more ideological significance, is the "naturalness of society", i.e. the presumption that man is by nature a social being and that the fundamental social relations between men are ordained by nature. This means that the subordination of human beings to each other is equally natural: women under men, children under their parents, slaves and servants under their masters, and citizens under their superiors. It is natural and rational for man to live in unequal relations. The state with its order, its laws and its subordination of man to man is both natural and good.

---

[9] Dreitzel *op. cit.* 53-86.

[10] Arnisaeus, *Doctrina politica in genuinam methodum, quae est Aristotelis, reducta,* Leipzig 1623, 24 (first edition in 1605).

This Aristotelian concept of the state was opposed to all ideas of a fundamentally different condition of equality and absence of law preceding the state. Varieties of such an idea were the Christian concept of paradise and the theory of the state of nature within the doctrine of natural law. According to the Aristotelian view, as represented for instance by Aquinas and shared by seventeenth century Aristotelians, the state would have been introduced in the state of innocence, had that persisted. Not even the angels could exist without some sort of hierarchical order.[11] This interpretation of the idea of natural social relations became a support for those who wanted to preclude egalitarian interpretations of the state of nature and the contract theory implicated in it; if inequality was ordained by nature, one could dismiss all ideas of an original equality which either persisted or in some way ought to be restored. Here, the Aristotelian argument of the naturalness of society definitely had a conservative ideological function.[12]

As mentioned above, the German Aristotelians distanced themselves from the scholastic Aristotelian tradition with regard to the relation of politics to theology. But on the ideologically crucial issue of social hierarchy they seem to have stayed within the scholastic framework and used the same argument that had become a conservative cornerstone in the Thomistic tradition of scholasticism.

A fourth Aristotelian trait is the concept of the citizen. If the naturalness of society was an idea with conservative implications, the concept of the *civis* was one with a more radical potential. In *Politics* 1275b, Aristotle says that the citizen is defined first and foremost by his participating in the courts and in government. This was the point of departure for the Aristotelians' discussion of citizenship. It is an awkward definition, however, considering the political order they wanted to defend and legitimize. Aristotle's definition of the citizen is one of the points in his doctrine where the republican and democratic implications are most apparent. The notion of the citizen taking part in government and court justice is not easily compatible with the absolutist princely state which the Aristotelian scholars of Lutheran Europe had before their eyes. Not that Aristotle himself was fully democratic in his concept of citizenship, which

---

[11] On Arnisaeus and these ideas, see Dreitzel, *op. cit.* 178 sq.

[12] Examples are the German political humanists Johannes Boeclerus and Johannes Schefferus and the theologian Valentin Alberti; see B. Lindberg, *Naturrätten i Uppsala 1655-1720*, Uppsala 1976, 41 sq.; 62 sqq., 143 sq.

excluded not only slaves, women, metics and other temporary residents but also craftsmen. But even if citizenship was restricted to a minority of the members of a state, the concept had republican connotations and smacked if not of democracy at least of aristocracy, which could be problematic enough to a government with absolutist aspirations.

So the German Aristotelians were eager to point out that citizenship was restricted and that one was more or less of a citizen depending on one's degree of participation in state affairs. Arnisaeus advanced the sophisticated argument that everybody who originally joined a *civitas* was a citizen, but as soon as the *civitas* got a form of government and became a *res publica*, the citizens withdrew from full citizenship, to a greater or lesser degree depending on whether the *res publica* was a monarchy, an aristocracy or a democracy.[13] In assuming the original equality of the citizens, Arnisaeus' theory resembles the idea of the state of nature that was more or less articulated in the tradition of natural law. Whether he had that idea in mind or not is difficult to decide. Conring points out that one is a citizen in proportion to one's participation in the state. He does not apply this definition to contemporary Germany, but mentions the nobility of Poland and the patricians in Venice as social categories who can be called citizens.[14]

But above all the Aristotelians modified the republican and civic implications of their master's political heritage by adding to it Jean Bodin's doctrine of sovereignty. Bodin's doctrine that the *summa potestas* of the state does not know any superior was shared by almost every political theorist around 1600, and certainly by all the German Aristotelians. The doctrine of sovereignty was essential to the concept of the early modern state. With it went the definition of the citizen as "liber homo alterius potestati subjectus", which focussed on the citizen's subjection and left

---

[13] Arnisaeus, *op. cit.* 104.

[14] Conring, „Dissertatio de cive et civitate"(1653) §8, in: *Opera omnia*, tomus III, 724. Among Conring's dissertations there are texts where the political order of the ancient *polis* is described in Aristotelian terms with a strong civic flavour. In „Dissertatio de optima republica" (1652, in *Opera omnia* tomus III, 823-39) the government of the middle class is described in Aristotelian terms and „Dissertatio de democratia" (1643; in *Opera omnia* tomus III 788-97) gives a fairly neutral description of this form of government. But both texts are academic and historical in character and do not refer to contemporary issues. It is noteworthy, however, that Conring had dissertations discussed on topics which might have been interpreted in a libertarian way or provoked libertarian thought. – On Arnisaeus' and Conring's concepts of citizenship, vide M. Riedel, art. „Bürger" in *Geschichtliche Grundbegriffe* Bd. 1, 1972, 678 sqq.

little room for his participating in courts and government. In consequence of this, they used the word *subditus* (subject) parallel to *civis*, and laid much more stress on it than on the ancient notion of the citizen.[15] Arnisaeus increased the absolutist flavour of his doctrine by following Augustine, Luther, Lipsius and others who described the state as an *ordo imperandi et parendi*, an order of governing and obedience. This did not prevent him, or Conring for that matter, from criticizing Bodin's definitions of both the citizen and the state. But this was academic polemic on minutiae; the important thing is that both Arnisaeus and Conring accepted Bodin, and adhered to his doctrine of the state.[16]

Political Aristotelianism in seventeenth century Germany was thus Aristotelian only in a restricted sense. The social and civistic, to some extent democratic, potential of Aristotle's *Politics* was suppressed; instead Aristotelian method and concepts became the support of praxis and ideology that were very different from what is normally associated with Aristotle. This is not to say that Aristotle was used in an absurd way. After all, he too considered monarchy to be the best form of government.

But the absolutist interpretation of Aristotle was by no means the only one. Aristotle was protean and could deliver arguments in favour of different political ends. For instance, the desirable political order that was described in Aristotelian terms by John Case in England was very close to the English political situation during the reign of Elizabeth. Case could accept a more liberal interpretation of the Aristotelian citizen, since there was a parliament in England, the members of which participated in government under royal leadership.[17] And if we turn to Sweden in the first decades of the seventeenth century, we find a political situation where the word *civis* may have had some flavour of aristocratic citizenship. Royal power was limited by so called "fundamental laws" and the role of ephors as checks on royal power was discussed in academic dissertations.[18] The form of government was described as tempered and as a *monarchia mixta*. This was not done with reference to Aristotle, however; it was rather the

---

[15] Arnisaeus on „summa potestas" and „jura majestatis" in *Doctrina politica* 209-222, on „subditi" ibid. 230-265; on „cives" ibid. 104-119.

[16] Dreitzel *op. cit.* 144. Arnisaeus criticizes Bodin in *Doctrina politica* 103, 119 sq. Conring on Bodin in „Dissertatio de cive et civitate", *Opera omnia* tomus III, 724 sq.

[17] R. Tuck, *op. cit.* 148 sqq.

[18] N. Runeby, *Monarchia mixta: maktfördelningsdebatt i Sverige under den tidigare stormaktstiden*. Stockholm 1962, 154-208.

doctrine of Johannes Althusius that had this libertarian influence, perhaps together with that of John Case. But the presence of Aristotelian concepts of citizenship, participation and civil liberty in the everyday language of politics that was described earlier may have stimulated aristocratic self-confidence.[19] On the House of Nobility in Stockholm, there is an inscription saying: "Fortitudo civium est regni fundamentum". It is very likely that "civium" here, if translated into Swedish, would have referred to the nobility, whose position was strong when the inscription was made. The fact that the word *regnum* is also included in the inscription indicates that aristocratic republicanism should be no threat to the monarchy.

The end of political Aristotelianism
During the decades around 1700, political Aristotelianism slowly disappeared from the universities in Lutheran Europe. There still appeared compendia of the *Politics*, and in some places Aristotle remained basic political reading well into the 18th century. But the vital element in the teaching of ethics and politics was no longer Aristotelianism but natural law. Natural law, in the version of Samuel Pufendorf, replaced Aristotelian moral philosophy, i.e. ethics and politics. The *De officio hominis et civis* of Pufendorf, published in 1673, described the duties of man as human being and citizen, the duties of a human being corresponding to Aristotelian ethics and the duties of the citizen to Aristotelian politics.

That political Aristotelianism faded away is no surprise, considering the general decline of Aristotelian philosophy in the late seventeenth century. In natural philosophy, Cartesianism – the philosophy of Descartes – was the great challenge to Aristotelian dominance, and hard struggles were fought between the old and the new philosophy at various universities in the Netherlands, Germany and Scandinavia.[20] In many respects, natural law was a counterpart to Cartesianism in the field of law and moral philosophy. Natural law was part of the new mechanistic world picture, where the

---

[19] G. Barudio speaks of the aristocratic and Aristotelian ethos of Swedish political culture during the time of chancellor Axel Oxenstierna (*Absolutismus – Zerstörung der 'libertären Verfassung'. Studien zur karolinischen Eingewalt in Schweden zwischen 1680 und 1693*, Wiesbaden 1976). But there is little textual evidence for the specifically Aristotelian character of this ethos.

[20] R. Lindborg, *Descartes i Uppsala. Striderna om "nya filosofien" 1663-1689*, Uppsala 1965; A. Tering, *Descartes und der Eingang seiner Ideen in die schwedischen Ostseeprovinzen Estland und Livland im 17. und frühen 18. Jahrhundert*, Tartu 1996.

world was explained in terms of matter moving according to the laws of nature. On the other hand, political Aristotelianism was rooted in the same organicist, teleological and hierarchic ontology as Aristotelian physics and metaphysics.[21] The crucial assumption that unequal and subordinate relations are immediately ordained by nature was the effect of this hierarchic and teleological metaphysics and the expression of the common foundations of Aristotelian theoretical and moral philosophy.

It is tempting to interpret the decline of political Aristotelianism in this context of a shift of world view. This would imply that Aristotelian politics had a deeper significance than the merely terminological and technical one identified above. Political Aristotelianism could be regarded as an underlying paradigm for political discourse in the early seventeenth century. The doctrine of the naturalness of society and the derivative idea of natural inequality could be described as the essential element in political Aristotelianism regarded as an intellectual rather than a terminological phenomenon.

This interpretation is probably true to some extent. But it is difficult to verify it empirically. The affinity between natural law and Cartesianism on the one hand and philosophical and political Aristotelianism on the other does not seem to have attracted much notice in the seventeenth century.[22] The quarrels between Aristotelians and Cartesians about physics and metaphysics had no close parallels in the field of politics between the adherents of Aristotelian politics and natural law. It is true that Pufendorf had a serious dispute with Lutheran theologians, but it was about the role of divine revelation in natural law, not about Aristotelian issues. It seems that the specifically Aristotelian elements in political theory were overlaid by so many various doctrines that they did not provoke criticism for ideological or philosophical reasons. I may be wrong in this, since my overview of university conditions in Germany is limited, but I think it is correct to say that the difference between Aristotelianism and natural law was not experienced and articulated in the way we would expect, considering our established views of their philosophical incompatibility.

---

[21] On Pufendorf's metaphysical world picture, see H. Denzer, *Moralphilosophie und Naturrecht bei Samuel Pufendorf*, München 1972.

[22] For the Swedish case, see Lindberg, *op. cit.* 114-125.

The historical argument

Instead, criticism of Aristotelian politics was formulated on the pedagogic level and in historical terms. By emphasizing the specifically ancient roots of Aristotle's doctrine, it could be argued that Aristotelian moral philosophy was no longer relevant to the description of contemporary society and politics. This argument presupposed a consciousness of the differences between antiquity and contemporary Europe. Such historical consciousness of the gap between the ancients and the moderns began to grow in the sixteenth century. In the field of law, a decisive step had been taken as early as 1567, when François Hotman pointed out that "Roman law is the most useless of all studies to a modern Frenchman", since the society of both the Roman republic and the Empire was different from that of France.[23] This insight subsequently caused the emergence of the so called "mos gallicus" in jurisprudence, which was a blow to the authority of the *Corpus Juris Civilis*.

On German soil, this historical consciousness manifested itself later and was no obstacle to the rise of neo-Aristotelian political science around 1600. This is not to say, however, that prominent Aristotelians like Arnisaeus and Conring ignored the differences between antiquity and their own time. They reflected on their adaptation of Aristotle to modern conditions and were aware that Aristotle did not cover all phenomena of the modern world.

Arnisaeus admitted that Aristotle could not say anything about the feudal system ("fiduciariis regibus et principibus" and "feudis"), and that he had very little to say on sovereignty.[24] Conring pointed out various Aristotelian assumptions which were no longer valid in contemporary political doctrine. The idea that man is a *zoon politikon*, a political animal, must be modified, since human life does not presuppose that a man lives in a state. Man endeavours to live together with others, and to that extent Aristotle was right, but the state is not a necessary requirement for a decent human life. A consequence of this is Conring's remark that ethics and politics are not connected in reality in the same way as in Aristotle. Ethics deals with another sort of happiness than politics; only incidentally is human happiness dependent on the state.[25] Both these modifications of

---

[23] Quoted from P. Burke, *The Renaissance Sense of the Past*, London 1969, 34.

[24] Arnisaeus, *op. cit.* 13.

[25] *De civili prudentia liber unus* (1662) cap. VI, in *Opera omnia* tomus III, 307, 310 sq.

Aristotelian doctrine indicate that the *polis* and the community of citizens as Aristotle saw them are irrelevant in Conring's society, not only because the state is different but also because Christian religion requires another relation between ethics and politics than the Greek *polis*.

Further, Conring, in talking about the place of politics among other disciplines, points out that politics is no longer regarded as identical with rhetoric, as it was in antiquity.[26] This is an observation of historical fact. It is not very sophisticated, but it clearly illustrates the degree to which Hermann Conring was aware of the cleft that separated the politics of the seventeenth century from that of ancient Greece. This perception of historical difference, however, did not cause Conring to question the relevance of "Aristoteles noster", as he calls him.

I do not know who first raised the argument in Germany that Aristotelian politics was outmoded. But one good candidate is Samuel Pufendorf, who made his career in Germany and Sweden during the 1660s, 70s, and 80s.

In the university library of Lund in southern Sweden there is a fragment of a manuscript entitled *De politica graecanica*. Its few lines seem to be the introduction to or presentation of a treatise on the "Greek doctrine of politics". The author announces what can be called a historical contextualizing of classical politics and ethics. Plato and Aristotle, he says, had in mind a state quite different from ours when they shaped their doctrines. Their doctrine is not universal and cannot be adapted to each and every state. Therefore, their texts should not be recommended to students. The author also promises to show that the virtues described by Aristotle in his ethics are adapted to the Greek state and hence should not be taught in states which differ from that of the Greeks.[27]

---

[26] *Op. cit.* cap. IV, 297.

[27] The manuscript is slightly damaged but fully understandable:
„Tractatus DE POLITICA GRAECANICA.
/.../ ostenditur, quale civitatis genus prae/.../ *habuerint* Plato atque Aristoteles, ad quod /.../ dogmata retulerint. Unde manifestum erit /*eos veheme*/nter errare qui libros Platonis de Legibus aut Aristotelis libros Politicorum pro universali quapiam politica venditant, quaeque ad quodvis civitatis genus adplicari possit ac debeat; simulque prave istam politicam Graecanicam in disparis generis civitatibus juventuti commendari.
Appendicis loco demonstrabitur, Aristotelem in Ethicis subinde ad civitatis Graecanicae indolem respexisse, virtutesque ab ipso designatas nihil aliud esse, quam officia civis in tali republ., qualem ipse sibi tanquam optimam et perfectissimam fingebat. Adeoque Aristotelis Ethicam inutiliter doceri in tali republ. quae a civitate Graecanica diversae est indolis."

Various circumstances indicate that Pufendorf is the author of the fragment and that it was written around 1674. Pufendorf mentions the project on the *De politica graecanica* – which was never completed – on later occasions.[28] One of them is a letter in German to Christian Thomasius in 1688, where Pufendorf is more explicit in contextualizing the ethics of Aristotle, and indeed ancient politics and ethics as a whole.

He first points out that, according to Plato, politics is prior to ethics. This is the same observation that we found in Conring. To both him and Pufendorf, ethics is independent of state and politics; in Pufendorf's doctrine this manifests itself in the title of his book *De officio hominis et civis*, where the duties of man, irrespective of his living in a state or not, are deduced from human nature and argued to be more fundamental than those of the citizen.

Next, Pufendorf contextualizes the virtues listed in Aristotle's Nichomachean Ethics by deducing them from the democratic Greek state. Fortitude, he holds, is a virtue because the task of the most prominent citizens is to defend the state – oddly enough Pufendorf here refers to the far from democratic guardians in Plato's republic. Temperance became a virtue in order to prevent the citizens who took part in common meals (here he probably refers to the "prytaneis" in Athens) from consuming public resources by unlimited hunger and thirst. The virtues of liberality and magnificence are explained by the habit among the rich of sponsoring games, warships and other things. Magnanimity and modesty were virtues in order to make the citizens check and modify their civil ambition and their quest for honours and glory. Justice was a necessary virtue since the citizens were obliged to serve as judges in court. The rest of the virtues Pufendorf explains by reference to the national character of the Greeks (a genio Graecae nationis): they were irascible, liked to converse and to mock.[29]

(University Library of Lund, Handlingar under Gustaf Otto Stenbocks kansleriat 2).

[28] It is mentioned in the preface of the second edition of *De jure naturae et gentium* and in a letter to Justus Schomer in 1690, published by D. Döring, *Pufendorf-Studien. Beiträge zur Biographie Samuel von Pufendorfs und zu seiner Entwicklung als Historiker und theologischer Schriftsteller*, Berlin 1992, 188. Also, the handwriting is apparently that of Pufendorf. Pufendorf was professor „juris naturae et gentium" at the university of Lund from its foundation in 1668 until 1676.

[29] Pufendorf to Thomasius, June 19 1688, in K.Varrentrap, „Briefe von Samuel Pufendorf I", *Historische Zeitschrift*, 70 (1893), 30 sqq.

One may question the reasonableness of the explanations, but there is no doubt that Pufendorf uses an argument of historical contextualization. Interestingly, he describes the Greek state in general as democratic. In fact, the democratic character of the Greek state is the decisive difference that makes Aristotle and ancient politics as a whole unsuitable in the seventeenth century.[30]

Conclusion
The evidence produced here indicates that political Aristotelianism declined not primarily because its terminology became obsolete – some of it survives to the present day. Nor did it vanish because of its alliance with and involvement in Aristotelian physics and metaphysics. Instead, it disappeared because it reflected a political order that no longer existed.

It is noteworthy that in the manuscript from the early 1670s Pufendorf's argument against Aristotle is formally pedagogical: students should not read Aristotelian textbooks any more. Pufendorf may even have had a petty motive for his opinion: to replace the textbooks on Aristotle's politics and ethics with his own *De officio hominis et civis*. Still, it is clear that his opinion was based on more principled reasons too, for example in his letter to Thomasius. Disputes on pedagogic issues often reveal deeper theoretical tensions, and that was certainly the case with Pufendorf's contextualization of Aristotle.

Pufendorf did not say that Aristotelianism had become *unmodern*. The idea of progress implied in that word is absent in his texts; nor did he express any value judgements on whether it was good or bad that Aristotle had become obsolete.

But we – who know what was to come – can say that Pufendorf found Aristotelianism unmodern because it was too democratic. Today, democracy is hailed everywhere. So what was considered unmodern in the seventeenth century has become high fashion in our time.

And Aristotle is definitely – and always will be – more modern than Samuel Pufendorf.

---

[30] Cf. Pufendorf's *De jure naturae et gentium* VII:2:20, where he rejects citizenship as defined by Aristotle as relevant to democracies only („ad democratias duntaxat quadrat").

INDEX
(of names and passages in Aristotle's works)

Acciaiuoli, Donato 28, 32, 35, 36, 37, 38, 39, 40, 41, 42
Achillini, Alessandro 90
Acindynus, Gregorius 66
Agricola, Rudolph 109, 110, 117, 171, 188, 189
Albert of Saxony 81
Albert the Great 34, 150, 154, 208, 216, 220
Alberti, Leon Battista 44, 47, 48, 50, 53
Alberti, Valentin 246
Albertus Magnus 70
Albinus 139
Alcinous 139
Aldrovandi, Ulisse 192
Alexander of Alexandria 208
Alexander of Aphrodisias 84, 86, 87, 88, 90, 91, 93, 94, 95, 97, 100, 136, 139, 147, 148, 149, 150, 151, 153, 154, 155, 156, 157, 158, 159, 209, 216, 219, 221, 222, 225, 227, 237
Alexander of Hales 142, 208
Alfarabi 72, 139, 216
Alfonso the Wise 140
Alfonso X of Castile 13
Althusius, Johannes 242, 243, 249
Ambrosius Flandinus 157
Ambrosoli, Mauro 176, 187
Ammonius 142, 216
Anaxagoras 230
Andrea di Piero da Milano 32
Andreasi, Osanna 129
Andreæ, Antonius 208
Andronicus Rhodius 79, 138, 140, 144, 145
Apellicon Teius 144, 145
Apollo 135
Apostolis, Michael 63
Aquarius, Matthias 198
Aquinas, Thomas, *See* Thomas Aquinas
Argyropoulos, Isaac 64

Argyropoulos, John 27, 31, 33, 36, 61, 62, 63, 64, 65, 67, 68, 69, 70, 71, 72, 73, 74, 75, 76, 77, 90, 110, 112, 235
Aristoteles of Mytilene, 147
Aristoteles 10, 11, 12, 15, 16, 17, 18, 20, 21, 25, 27, 28, 29, 31, 36, 37, 38, 39, 41, 42, 43, 44, 45, 49, 51, 54, 55, 61, 62, 63, 64, 65, 70, 71, 79, 80, 82, 84, 88, 91, 103, 106, 110, 119, 120, 121, 122, 126, 132, 133, 134, 135, 136, 137, 138, 139, 140, 141, 142, 143, 144, 145, 147, 151, 152, 153, 156, 158, 159, 165, 167, 179, 180, 183, 190, 191, 196, 197, 198, 199, 200, 203, 205, 209, 211, 212, 215, 218, 221, 222, 223, 224, 225, 226, 228, 229, 231, 232, 234, 236, 237, 241, 242, 243, 245, 246, 248, 249, 251, 252, 253, 254
APo. 111, 143, 213, 218
APr. 111, 114, 143, 213, 214
Ars Nova 214
Ars Vetus 214
Cael. 70, 79
Cat. 143, 213, 215, 217
de An. 22, 29, 45, 47, 79, 87, 90, 144, 147, 148, 152, 153, 226, 229, 231, 233, 234, 235
EE 29
EN 10, 11, 14, 15, 16, 18, 20, 22, 27, 28, 29, 31, 32, 34, 35, 36, 38, 39, 40, 41, 42, 106, 111, 112, 135, 253, 254
GA 226
GC 79, 86, 87, 88, 90, 91, 95, 98, 100
HA 70
IA 70
Int. 143, 213, 215
MA 70
Mem. 44, 54
Metaph. 80, 106, 196, 197, 198, 199, 208, 209, 226, 232
Mete. 79, 88
MM 29

255

Oec. 135
Organon 191, 192, 213, 214, 215, 218, 223, 224
PA 70, 189, 196, 197, 198, 199, 200, 201, 204
Parva Naturalia 45, 79
Ph. 45, 47, 49, 79, 86, 87, 88, 89, 90, 91, 93, 94, 100, 110, 112, 115, 122, 198, 218
Pol. 10, 15, 16, 17, 20, 135, 136, 242, 244, 246, 248, 249, 254
SE 213, 219, 220, 221, 222
Sens. 44, 45, 47, 48, 114
Spir. 45
Top. 111, 200, 212, 213, 219
Arnisaeus, Henning 243, 244, 245, 247, 248, 251
Athenagoras 136
Atran, Scott 190, 191
Augustinus 133, 139, 141, 248
Aureolo, Pietro 136
Austin, John L. 12
Averroës 10, 20, 22, 71, 72, 87, 97, 137, 139, 140, 144, 147, 149, 151, 153, 154, 156, 208, 213, 225, 227, 229, 237
Avicebron 237
Avicenna 70, 72, 76, 81, 139, 151, 216, 237
Bacon, Francis 100, 106, 126, 225
Baconthorp, John 136
Bagolino, Girolamo 150
Balme, David M. 200
Barbaro, Ermolao 112, 142, 143, 168, 169, 172, 173, 192, 230
Baron, W. 186
Bartholin, Caspar 207, 208, 209, 210, 211, 212, 213, 214, 215, 216, 217, 218, 219, 220, 221, 222, 223
Bartolomeo de Spina 157
Barudio, Günter 249
Bauhin, Caspar 177, 182, 186, 192, 193
Becchi, Guglielmo 33, 36
Bekker, Immanuel 79
Bertrando del Poggetto 21
Bessarion 61, 62, 63, 64, 65, 66, 67, 68, 69, 70, 71, 73, 74, 75, 76, 77, 140, 225
Bianchi, Luca 31, 36

Blasius de Parma 48
Blum, Paul Richard 90
Boccaccio, Giovanni 19, 21
Boccadiferro, Ludovico 122
Bochner, Salomon 43, 44, 45, 52
Bock, Hieronymus, *See* Tragus, Hieronymus
Bodin, Jean 243, 247, 248
Böckler, Johann H. 246
Boëthius 66, 76, 120, 139, 199, 215, 216, 219
Bonifacius VIII 18, 19
Bonitz, Hermann 236
Brasavola, Antonius Musa 174, 188, 192
Brito, Radulphus, *See* Radulphus Brito
Brocardo, Antonio 157
Brunelleschi, Filippo 43, 53, 58
Brunetto Latini 12, 13, 14, 15, 17, 18, 19, 20, 25
Brunfels, Otto 171, 173, 174
Bruni, Leonardo 11, 14, 27, 31, 36, 137, 139
Buccaferrea, Ludovico, *See* Boccadiferro, Ludovico
Buffon, Georges Louis Le Clerc 183
Buonafede, Francesco 169
Buridan, John 148, 151, 152, 153, 154, 155, 156, 157, 159, 160, 213, 214, 216, 217, 218, 220
Burley, Walter 58, 115, 209
Caietano, *See* Tommaso de Vio
Calcondila, Demetrio 33
Camerarius, Rudolf Jakob 183, 192
Campanella, Tommaso 99
Canini, Angelo 150
Capella, Martianus, *See* Martianus Capella
Capivaccio, Girolamo 205, 206
Caracalla 147
Cardano, Girolamo 95, 96, 97, 187
Carmody, Francis J. 15
Casali, Giovanni Vincenzo 58
Case, John 11, 27, 243, 245, 248, 249
Casus 216
Caterina da Racconigi 129
Cato Major 187

Cerroni, Umberto 25
Cesalpino, Andrea 178, 179, 181, 182, 183, 189, 190, 191, 192, 193, 194, 195, 196, 197, 198, 199, 200, 201, 202, 203, 204, 205, 206
Chalcidius 225
Champier, Symphorien 106
Charlemagne 140
Chomsky, Noam 191
Christina, Queen of Sweden 244
Chrysostomus Javelli, *See* Javelli, Chrysostomus
Cicero 14, 17, 29, 38, 110, 120, 125, 131, 139, 212, 215
Clagett, Marshall 54
Clement of Alexandria 238
Clement V 19
Clichtove, Josse 118, 119, 120, 121, 125, 126
Clusius, Karl 182
Coimbra commentators 219, 220, 221
Collenuccio, Pandolfo 169, 173
Colombero, Carlo 202
Columella 187
Columna, Fabius 182
Conring, Hermann 243, 244, 245, 247, 248, 251, 252, 253
Constantine the Great 24
Contarini, Gasparo 157
Cordus, Euricius 171, 174, 177, 178, 185
Cordus, Valerius 177, 178, 187
Coridalide, Teofilo 239
Cotgrave, Randle 186
Cottunios, Joannes 225, 226, 227, 229, 230, 231, 232, 233, 234, 235, 236, 237, 238, 239, 240
Cranz, F. Edward 88
Cremonini, Cesare 237, 239, 240
Crescas, Hasdai 137, 140, 145
Crescenzi, Pier de 176
Cripps, Henry 152
Cunningham, Andrew 205
Curtius, Ernst R. 10
Cusanus, Nicolaus 140, 144
Dalechamp, Jacques 182, 192

Dante Alighieri, 12, 13, 18, 19, 20, 21, 22, 23, 24, 25
Descartes, René 203, 249
Devlin, Keith 45
Diogenes Laertius 72, 142
Dioscorides 168, 172, 173, 174, 175, 176, 177, 180, 187, 188, 193, 204
Dodoens, Rembert 182
Domenico de Clivaxo 48
Donato Acciaiuoli, *See* Acciaiuoli, Donato
Donato, Girolamo 28, 87, 151, 158, 225
Dorotheus, Guillermus 222
Dorp, John 220
Dorsten, Theodor 185
Duns Scotus, John 37, 140, 208, 216
Edward I 25
Elizabeth, Queen 248
Epictetus 139
Este, Ercole d' 109
Euclides 48, 49, 50, 51, 52, 53, 55, 120
Eugene IV 140
Eustratius 38
Fabricius de Aquapendente, Hieronymus 205, 206
Falcon, Andrea 198, 200
Ficino, Marsilio 113, 114, 137, 139, 140
Filippo Brunelleschi, *See* Brunelleschi, Filippo
Fincke, Thomas 211, 212, 213, 221, 222, 223
Fonseca, Pedro da 216
Fracastoro, Girolamo 95
Francesca, Piero della, *See* Piero della Francesca
Francesco Cattaneo Diacceto, *See* Diacceto, Francesco Cattaneo
Franciscus Zenobii de Diacceto, *See* Zenobii de Diacceto, Franciscus
Frederick II of Hohenstaufen 14
Fuchs, Leonhard 168, 171, 173, 174, 188, 189, 194
Furlan, Daniel 199, 200
Gaetano, *See* Tommaso de Vio
Galeazzo Maria Sforza, *See* Sforza, Galeazzo Maria

Galenus 73, 94, 95, 117, 121, 136, 139, 172, 188
Garcia da Orta 193
Garin, Eugenio 11, 27
Gaspary, A. 61
Gaza, Theodore 61, 62, 64, 65, 68, 69, 70, 71, 72, 73, 74, 75, 76, 77, 144, 168, 171, 172
Gemistus Pletho, George, *See* Pletho, George Gemistus
George of Trebizond 63, 65, 113, 141
George Scholarius, 66, 76
Gerard of Cremona, 149
Gesner, Conrad 177, 178, 182, 183, 186, 187, 192
Ghini, Luca 169, 170, 175, 177, 178, 189, 192
Giannozzo Manetti *See* Manetti, Giannozzo
Gilbert the Porretan 215
Giles of Rome 208, 216, 220
Giovanni da Viterbo 14, 15, 17
Golius, Theophilus 242
Greene, Edward Lee 169
Gregor of Nazianz 238
Gregor of Nissa 238
Grew, Nehemiah 183
Grosseteste, Robert *See* Robert Grosseteste
Guarino, Battista 109, 110
Guiliano da Foligno 170
Guillelmus Alvernus *See* William of Auvergne
Gundisalvo, Domingo 149
Gustav Adolph of Sweden, 243
Hankins, James 11, 27
Henry VII of Luxemburg 19, 20
Hermias 139
Herodotus 242
Hervé de Nédellec 136
Hesse of Krakow, Benedikt 157
Heytesbury, William 58
Hierocles 139
Hieronymus 133
Hippocrates 94, 95, 116, 120, 121
Hobbes, Thomas 89
Hotman, François 251
Hugh of Saint Victor 107, 108, 113, 114, 122, 142
Ishāq ibn Hunain 151
Jacobus Stapulensis, *See* Lefèvre d'Étaples, Jacques
Jamblichus 139
James of Venice 222
Javelli, Chrysostomus 82, 83, 216
Johannes Damascenus 238
Johannes Grammaticus 158
John Argyropoulos, *See* Argyropoulos, John
John Pecham, *See* Pecham, John
John XXII 19, 21
Julius II 134
Juno 135
Jupiter 135
Kepler, Johannes 51
Keßler, Eckhard 126, 195, 201
Kilwardby, Robert, *See* Robert Kilwardby
Kraye, Jill 29, 31, 35, 41
Kristeller, Paul Oskar 11
Kusokawa, Sachiko 188
Lambin, Denys 32
Landino, Cristoforo 109
Latini, Brunetto, *See* Brunetto Latini
Lawrence of Lindores 157
Lefèvre d'Étaples, Jacques 32, 38, 40, 126, 127
Leggi, Leonardo 170
Leijenhorst, Kees 89
Leo X 141
Leonardo Bruni, *See* Bruni, Leonardo
Leonardo da Vinci 11, 27, 31, 123
Leoniceno, Niccolò 117, 168, 169, 173, 174
Linné, Carl von, 177, 190
Lipsius, Justus 243, 248
Livius 243
Lobelius, Mathias 182
Lohr, Charles 83
Lokert, George 153
Louis of Bavaria 19, 21
Louis XII 134

Luther, Martin 244, 248
Magni, Jonas 243
Maier, Anneliese 80, 81
Maimonide, Moses 140
Mair, John 153
Manardi, Giovanni 117
Manfredi 14
Marsilius of Inghen 81, 157, 161, 165
Martianus Capella 111
Martini, Cornelius 210
Martini, Jacobus 207, 210, 213, 216
Matthioli, Pietro Andrea 172, 176, 178, 192
Maximilian I 134
Maximus Confessor 238
Mayer, Albrecht 171
Medici, Cosimo I de' 28
Medici, Francesco de' 179, 194
Melanchthon, Philipp 188, 242
Michael of Ephesus 222
Mikkeli, Heikki 205
Moerbeke, William of, See William of Moerbeke
Mohler, Ludwig 61, 62, 70, 77
Monardes, Nicolás Bautista 193
Monardo, Giovanni 174
Montuus, Sebastian 188, 189, 194
Moreaux, P. 148, 149
Morton, A. G. 171, 181, 190
Moses 134
Muret, Marco Antonio 40
Murmellius, Johannes 122
Musuro, Marco 158
Nardi, Bruno 19, 165
Nicholas of Amsterdam 157
Nicholas V 140
Nicolas Oresme, See Oresme, Nicolas
Nicolaus Damascenus 167
Niphus, Augustinus 157, 199, 200, 209, 230, 233, 237
Nizolio, Mario 106
Numenius 139
Ockham, William of, See William of Ockham
Oresme, Nicolas 49, 50, 54, 55, 58
Ovitt, George 107

Oxenstierna, Axel 249
Pade, Marianne 67
Palladius 176
Pannartz, Arnold 62
Panofsky, Erwin 44
Papadopoli, Nicola Comneno 240
Patrizi, Francesco 99, 130, 131, 137
Paul of Venice 67, 209
Pecham, John 48, 51
Pelacani of Parma, Biagio 157
Pellicier, Guilleaume 175
Perionio, Ioachino 230
Perotti, Niccolò 67, 68, 69, 77
Peter of Spain 213, 218, 220
Petrarca, Francesco 38, 110, 130, 137, 139, 140
Philip the Beautiful 25
Philoponus, John 135, 139, 140, 145, 209, 216, 225, 236
Piccolomini, Francesco 218
Pico della Mirandola, Federico 134
Pico della Mirandola, Giovan Francesco 129, 130, 131, 132, 133, 134, 135, 136, 137, 138, 139, 140, 141, 142, 143, 144, 145
Pico della Mirandola, Giovanni 133, 141
Pico della Mirandola, Ludovico 134
Pier Vettori, See Vettori, Pier
Piero della Francesca 47, 48, 53, 55
Pierre de la Ramée, See Ramus, Petrus
Pietro della Corvara 21
Pitton de Tournefort, Joseph 183
Plato 37, 39, 61, 62, 63, 64, 65, 71, 72, 82, 131, 133, 134, 139, 140, 199, 227, 237, 252, 253
Pletho, George Gemistus 61, 63, 137, 139, 140, 225
Plinius Secundus, Caius 125, 142, 168, 169, 171, 172, 173, 176
Plotinus 66, 139
Poliziano, Angelo 32, 33, 39, 41, 110, 111, 112, 113, 114, 116, 121, 125, 126, 127
Pomponazzi, Pietro 83, 84, 85, 86, 87, 88, 90, 95, 97, 148, 154, 157, 158, 159, 160, 161, 165, 231, 233, 237
Poppi, Antonino 165

259

Porphyrius 65, 66, 69, 70, 71, 75, 76, 145, 196, 209, 213, 215
Portius, Simon 90, 91, 92, 93, 94, 95, 97, 189, 202, 237
Priscianus 120
Proclus 139
Psellus, Michael 209
Pseudo-Aristoteles
    De plantis, 167, 187
    Pr., 188
Pseudo-Dionysius Areopagita 238
Pseudo-Philoponus 209
Ptolemaeus 51, 53, 120
Ptolemaeus Philadelphus 143
Pufendorf, Samuel 249, 250, 252, 253, 254
Pyrrhon 139
Pythagoras 120, 134
Quintilianus 142
Rabelais, François 174
Rackham, H. 11
Radulphus Brito 66
Rajus, Joannes 183
Ramus, Petrus 130, 131, 195, 201, 210, 211, 212
Raphael Donati de Franceschis, *See* Donati de Franceschis, Raphael
Razes 70
Reeds, Karen Meier 171, 172, 175
Reisch, Gregor 103, 106, 108, 114
Renan, Ernest 100
Rinuccini, Alamanno 35
Risse, Wilhelm 210, 216
Ritter, Heinrich 203
Robert d'Anjou 19
Robert Grosseteste 10
Robert Kilwardby 108, 114, 115, 221
Rondelet, Guilleaume 175
Rotondò, Antonio 31
Rovere, Francesco della 63
Ruel, Jean 172, 175, 177, 192
Scaliger, Julius Caesar 187
Scheffer, Johann 243, 246
Schegius, Jacob 200, 201
Schmitt, Charles B. 11, 130, 186
Scholarius, George, *See* George Scholarius

Schomer, Justus 253
Seneca 139
Senese, Oliviero 33
Septimius Severus 147
Sextus Empiricus 129, 139
Sforza, Galeazzo Maria 64
Siger of Brabant 154
Silvester I 24
Simplicius 112, 139, 140, 142, 143, 145, 216, 228, 236
Sixtus IV 63
Skinner, Quentin 12
Sophocles 66
Sophonias 236
Spigel, Adriano 170
Stapulensis, Jacobus, *See* Lefèvre d'Étaples, Jacques
Steno of Dacia 211, 212
Steno, Nicholas 207
Strozzi, Ciriaco 33, 34
Suárez, Francisco 209
Sulla 139, 144
Sundström, Carl Johan 202, 203
Sweynheym, Konrad 62
Swineshead, Richard 58
Tartaretus 216
Taurellus, Nicolaus 197
Telesio, Bernardino 95, 97, 98, 99, 100, 202
Tempier, Étienne 11
Themistius 136, 142, 143, 228, 236
Theocritus of Chio 132
Theodore Gaza, *See* Gaza, Theodore
Theon 48
Theophilus graecus, *See* Theophilus Protospatarius
Theophilus Protospatarius 116
Theophrastus 138, 140, 142, 144, 145, 167, 168, 171, 172, 173, 176, 177, 179, 180, 181, 183, 187, 194, 204, 228
Thomas Aquinas 10, 15, 20, 31, 34, 66, 76, 114, 142, 150, 198, 208, 216, 220, 225, 230, 231, 237, 238, 246
Thomasius, Christian 253, 254
Thucydides 243

Tignosi, Niccolò 28, 35, 36, 37, 38, 39, 40, 41, 42
Timpler, Clemens 208
Toletus, Franciscus 216, 219, 220
Tommaso de Vio 234, 237
Tragus, Hieronymus 176
Trapezuntius, George, *See* George of Trebizond
Tyrannio 144, 145
Valla, Giorgio 121
Valla, Lorenzo 24, 66, 121, 130, 131, 133, 137, 139
Varchi, Benedetto 123, 124
Varro, Marcus Terentius 167, 187
Vasoli, Cesare 10, 33
Venetus, Paulus, *See* Paul of Venice
Venturini, Simone 33
Vergilio Adriani, Marcello 172, 173, 174
Vernia, Nicoletto 115, 116
Vettori, Pier 28, 29, 31, 32, 33, 34, 35, 37, 39, 40, 41
Vieri, Francesco de' 230
Villani, Giovanni 14
Vinay, Gustavo 19, 21
Visconti, Giangaleazzo 14
Vives, Juan Luis 123, 124, 125
Weiditz, Hans 171
Weisheipl, James A. 109
Wieland, Georg 34
William of Auvergne 150
William of Moerbeke 10, 15
William of Ockham 216, 217
William of Paris 150
Witelo 48, 50, 54
Witte, Karl 19
Wittgenstein, Ludwig 12
Zabarella, Jacopo 118, 205, 216, 218, 237, 241
Zaluzansky, Adam 182, 205
Zimara, Marcantonio 116
Zupko, John A. 156